The Peace of Illusions

The Peace of Illusions

American Grand Strategy
from 1940 to the Present

CHRISTOPHER LAYNE

Cornell University Press

A volume in the series *Cornell Studies in Security Affairs,*
edited by Robert J. Art, Robert Jervis, and Stephen M. Walt

First published 2006 by Cornell University Press
First printing, Cornell Paperbacks, 2007

Printed in the United States of America

Library of Congress Cataloging-in-Publication Data

Layne, Christopher.
  The peace of illusions : American grand strategy from 1940 to the present
/ Christopher Layne.
    p. cm. — (Cornell studies in security affairs)
  Includes bibliographical references and index.
  ISBN 978-0-8014-3713-7 (cloth : alk. paper)
  ISBN 978-0-8014-7411-8 (pbk. : alk. paper)
  1. United States—Foreign relations—20th century.   2. United States—Foreign
relations—2001–   3. United States—Foreign relations—Philosophy.   4. Hegemony—
United States—History—20th century.   5. National security—United States—History—
20th century.   I. Title.   II. Series.
  JZ1480.L38 2006
  327.73009'045—dc22   2005032191

Cornell University Press strives to use environmentally responsible
suppliers and materials to the fullest extent possible in the publishing
of its books. Such materials include vegetable-based, low-VOC inks
and acid-free papers that are recycled, totally chlorine-free, or partly
composed of nonwood fibers. For further information, visit our website
at www.cornellpress.cornell.edu.

Cloth printing   10 9 8 7 6 5 4 3 2 1
Paperback printing   10 9 8 7 6 5 4 3 2

For Gabriela

—whose love fills my life with joy and makes all things possible

Contents

Acknowledgments

Long before the argument presented in this book crystallized, the intellectual seeds were planted, and nurtured, by my association with three friends and sometime collaborators: Ted Galen Carpenter, Ben Schwarz, and Alan Tonelson. Before it was fashionable, individually and in coauthored articles, we were raising issues that are now an accepted part of the debate about American grand strategy: the perils (for the United States and the world) of American hegemony, and the inevitable transformation from unipolarity to multipolarity; the need for the United States to adopt a "free hand" grand strategy (which we variously described as offshore balancing or strategic independence); the fraying of the transatlantic relationship, manifested by NATO; the need to adopt a restrained grand strategy that balances ends and means; and the role of economic expansion—the Open Door—as a factor driving American grand strategy both before and after the cold war. Ted, Ben, Alan, and I took a lot of heat for making such arguments back in the 1980s and early 1990s. Even in the intellectual world, being in the first wave of an assault is a lot more dangerous than being in the follow-up echelon. It is gratifying to see that with the passage of time others not only have acknowledged that the arguments we developed are an important—and legitimate—part of the debate, but also, in some cases, that they have embraced those arguments (not infrequently without acknowledging their provenance).

Writing a book is a lonely struggle, and yet the input of colleagues and friends is a vital part of the process. Others see the flaws in logic and problems with evidence to which the author is oblivious. Others may contribute fresh insights that clarify and advance an author's thinking. I have benefited immeasurably from assistance of this kind. First, I am deeply indebted to John Mearsheimer and Robert Art, who reviewed this book for Cornell University Press. They read the manuscript carefully, made trenchant comments, and challenged me to make revisions to improve the quality of my argument. As colleagues, reviewers, and—most of all—as friends they set a high bar while simultaneously providing encouragement. I don't know whether I cleared the bar, but I do know that this book is incomparably better than it would have been otherwise.

I am similarly grateful to friends and colleagues who read and commented on drafts of the manuscript in its entirety: Ted Carpenter (Cato Institute), Roger Kanet (University of Miami), Keir Lieber (Notre Dame), Chris Preble (Coalition for a Realistic Foreign Policy), Ben Schwarz (*The Atlantic*), and John A. Thompson (St. Catherine's College, Cambridge).

In addition, I benefited enormously from the help I received with respect to specific chapters. My friend and Bush School of Government and Public Service colleague Mike Desch was supremely helpful in critiquing the final drafts of chapters 7–10. Jerry Taylor (Cato Institute) gave me a crash course in the economics of the international oil industry (though I am not certain that he would give me a passing grade). Finally, when it comes to academic collegiality, Eugene Gholz and Daryl Press were instrumental in improving the sections of chapter 8 concerning the roles of economic openness and oil in U.S. grand strategy. They graciously allowed me to read the draft of their forthcoming paper on the role of Persian Gulf oil in U.S. strategy.

Finally, Brad Thayer (Missouri State) deserves special mention. He and I are veterans of the academic equivalent of Passchendaele. Since we first became friends more than a decade ago, Brad has heard—no doubt ad nauseam—my various conceptualizations, and reformulations, of this book. He has been a great sounding board, and his friendship has sustained my morale.

Outside of the profession, three of my dearest long-time friends, Howard and Marcia Daniels, and Bill Lasarow, were always there for me. They supported me in times of professional struggle and were a willing (I think!) audience whenever I needed to vent while writing the book. Also, Howard read the penultimate draft of the manuscript in its entirety and offered excellent suggestions for improvement.

In the course of writing this book, I received financial support from the Earhart Foundation, the Smith Richardson Foundation, and a Research and Writing Grant from the John D. and Catherine T. MacArthur Foundation. This support not only facilitated completion of the book but enabled me to remain alive professionally. Without this support, I would have been forced back into the soulless and intellectually arid practice of law.

When it comes to writing a book, an author's family plays a critical role—and pays a price. My parents, William and Naomi Layne, have always been there for me. I am glad they no longer have to ask, "Is it finished yet?" My in-laws, Stella and Grigore Marin, were visiting us during the six months when I completed the revisions to the manuscript and provided emotional support (and Stella kept me going by cooking delicious central European comfort food). My daughter and my son, Ashleigh and Decebal, were wonderfully supportive. And they put up with all those times when I was present physically but lost in thought.

The person who contributed most importantly to this book is my wife, Gabriela. A brilliant scholar and accomplished author in her own right, she understands the process of writing and all the emotional stresses—and frustrations—that go with it. She read the draft chapters of this book and provided me with unsparing critiques that helped me to improve it. In every way, this book is as much hers as it is mine. Without her, there would have been no book.

The Peace of Illusions

Introduction

This book is about U.S. grand strategy since the early 1940s and, perforce, about America's role in the world. More precisely, it is about U.S. *hegemony*. I address five central questions concerning U.S. grand strategy. The first two of these questions are primarily historical. From 1940 to 1991 did the United States follow an offshore balancing grand strategy, or did it instead pursue a strategy of hegemony beyond the Western Hemisphere? And why did it pursue that strategy? The remaining questions are about U.S. grand strategy from 1991 to the present. First, what is America's current grand strategy, and is that strategy the same as, or different from, the grand strategy of 1940–1991? Second, is it a wise grand strategy? Third, if not, what is the best alternative to the current grand strategy? These are not "academic" questions. Rather they are—as the advertisement for a popular television crime drama series puts it—"ripped from today's headlines."

This book is not a chronicle of the grand strategy of the Bush II administration or of the two administrations that preceded it. Nevertheless, the real world events that have shaped U.S. grand strategy since the Bush II administration took office—9/11, the war on terror, the March 2003 invasion and subsequent occupation of Iraq, and mounting tensions with Iran and North Korea caused by those two states' nuclear ambitions—cast a long shadow. One of my objectives in this book is to put these events into historical perspective and to show that they are part of a larger pattern that extends back to the early 1940s. Here, I take issue with those who have argued that the Bush II administration's approach to U.S. grand strategy—its determination to maintain overwhelming U.S. geopolitical dominance and its muscular idealism—breaks sharply with the principles and assumptions that guided earlier U.S. policymakers.[1] Nothing could be farther from the truth. Take the administration's resolve to use America's preponderant power to ensure that other states cannot entertain the "hope of surpassing, *or equaling*, the power of the United States."[2] Here the administration simply reaffirmed the policy adopted by its two immediate predecessors.

The Bush II administration's decision to invade Iraq and overthrow Sad-

1

dam Hussein is another example of continuity in U.S. grand strategy since 1989. As we now know, that decision had nothing to do with 9/11, the war on terror, or Iraq's nonexistent weapons of mass destruction. Rather it was a war of hegemony intended to establish U.S. military and ideological dominance in the Persian Gulf and the Middle East. Iraq was not the first, but merely the latest, U.S. war of hegemony since the cold war's end. Since the cold war waned in the late 1980s the United States has been involved in a series of such military interventions.

Few raised their eyebrows about Panama (1989) or Haiti (1994, 2004). After all, the United States has a track record of wielding a big stick to maintain stability in its own backyard. But the two wars with Iraq (1991, 2003), the U.S. military interventions in the Balkans (Bosnia in 1995, Kosovo in 1999), and the invasion of Afghanistan (2001) do stand out. The first war with Iraq was fought to exert U.S. geopolitical primacy in the Gulf. The Balkan interventions aimed to "strengthen Washington's control of NATO, the major institution for maintaining U.S. influence in European affairs" and to "project American power into the East Mediterranean region where it could link up with a growing U.S. military presence in the Middle East."[3] Afghanistan allowed the United States to do more than go after al Qaeda and the Taliban. The United States shored up its strategic position in the Middle East while simultaneously extending its reach into Central Asia and, in the process, challenging Russia's influence in Moscow's own backyard.

Had the cold war not ended it is doubtful that the United States would have fought these wars. Why did the cold war's end lead to a new wave of U.S. expansion? That's easy. After the Soviet collapse, the United States stood head and shoulders above the rest of the world, militarily and economically. The United States, moreover, was imbued with an expansive conception of its world role and its interests. By removing the only real check on U.S. power, the Soviet Union's demise presented the United States with the opportunity to use its capabilities to exert more control over—to "shape"—the international political system and simultaneously to increase its power. When the risks of doing so appear low—and the potential rewards appear high—states with lots of power usually succumb to the temptation to use it. In the years since the cold war the United States has extended its strategic reach because it has had the motive, means, and opportunity to do so.

It is often said, with respect to U.S. grand strategy, that the al Qaeda attacks on New York and Washington, D.C., "changed everything." But they didn't. After 9/11—as before—geopolitical dominance has been the ambition of the United States. If anything, 9/11 gave the Bush II administration's "hegemonists" a convenient—indeed, almost providential—rationale for implementing policies they would have wanted to pursue in any event, including "regime change" in Iraq (and possibly Iran); the projection of U.S. power into the Middle East and Central Asia; a massive five-year defense buildup, which, when completed, will result in U.S. military outlays exceeding the combined defense budgets of the rest of the world's states; and a nuclear strategy that aims at attaining meaningful nuclear superiority over peer competitors and simultaneously ensuring that regional powers cannot develop the capacity to deter U.S. military intervention abroad. In short, the Bush II administration has sought security by expanding U.S. power and pursuing hegemony.[4] In this respect it has stayed on—not left—the grand strategic path followed by the United States since the early 1940s.

What Is America's Grand Strategy?

The fundamental argument I make in this book is simple. The story of American grand strategy over the past six decades is one of expansion, and that strategy's logic inexorably has driven the United States to attempt to establish its hegemony in the world's three most important regions outside North America itself: Western Europe, East Asia, and the Persian Gulf. That is, the United States has aimed for "extraregional" hegemony. If the United States today is, indeed, an extraregional, or "global," hegemon, it is not, as Barry Posen suggests, an "accidental" one.[5] Unlike Britain, the United States did not become an extraregional hegemon in a fit of absentmindedness.

The U.S. rise to global dominance has been enabled by extraordinary geopolitical fortune, but Washington deliberately has strived for that hegemony since the early 1940s. Washington's ambitions were not driven by the cold war but transcended it. The cold war was superimposed on an existing hegemonic grand strategy that the United States would have pursued—or attempted to pursue—even if there had been no rivalry with the Soviet Union. Indeed, the foundations of postwar U.S. grand strategy were in place well *before* the cold war commenced or even was anticipated by officials in Washington.

My argument that extraregional hegemony is the goal of U.S. grand strategy directly challenges John Mearsheimer's thesis in his important book, *The Tragedy of Great Power Politics*.[6] Mearsheimer claims that the United States is a "regional hegemon"—dominant *only* in its own backyard, the Western Hemisphere—and that in Europe and East Asia the United States acts as an "offshore balancer." Up to a point, of course, Mearsheimer is correct: the United States certainly is hegemonic in its own backyard. However, U.S. expansion did not stop at the water's edge. Rather, as Mary Ann Heiss observes, "as the twentieth century dawned" the United States was "ready to use its new position [as regional hegemon] as a springboard for expanding its influence and interests to other areas. It was ready, in other words, to transform its hemispheric hegemony into a global one."[7]

Hegemony is an important concept in the study of international politics, but it is hard to define. Nevertheless, by drawing on the definitions used both by realist scholars and international political economists, we can get a good handle on what hegemony means. First—and fundamentally—hegemony is about raw, hard *power.* Militarily, a hegemon's capabilities are such that "no other state has the wherewithal to put up a serious fight against it."[8] Economically, a hegemon occupies a position of "economic supremacy" in the international system and enjoys a "preponderance of material resources."[9] Economic dominance is important not only because wealth is the foundation of military power but also because it is a source of hegemonic power in its own right and a key factor driving hegemonic expansion. Second, hegemony is about the dominant power's *ambitions*—the purposes for which it uses its power. A hegemon acts self-interestedly to create a stable international order that will safeguard its security and its economic and ideological interests.[10] Third, hegemony is about *polarity.* Because of its overwhelming advantages in relative military and economic power, a hegemon is the only great power in the international system, which is, therefore, by definition unipolar.[11] Fourth, hegemony is about *will.* Not only must a hegemon possess overwhelming power, it must purposefully exercise that power to impose order on the international system.[12] When it comes to grand strategy, hegemons practice the adage "If you've got it, flaunt it."

Fundamentally, hegemony is about *structural change,* because "if one state achieves hegemony, the system ceases to be anarchic and becomes hierarchic."[13] Of course, as Robert Gilpin has noted, "no state has ever completely controlled an international system," and thus hegemony is a relative, not an absolute, concept.[14] When a great power attains hegemony, as, for example, the United States did in Western Europe after World War II, it means that the system is more hierarchic—and less anarchic—than it would be in the absence of hegemonic power. Implicit in Gilpin's observation that hegemony is a relative concept is a subtle, but important, point: although the United States is an extraregional hegemon, it is not what students of international politics once called a "universal empire." The United States is not omnipotent.

Although the United States is the most powerful international actor since imperial Rome, there clearly are limits to its ability to shape international outcomes. The United States has been unable to suppress the insurgency in Iraq (just as it did not prevail in the Vietnam War) and unable to compel either North Korea or Iran to halt their nuclear weapons programs. Does this mean that America's hegemonic power is illusory? Does this mean the United States is not an extraregional or global hegemon after all? Clearly not—at least not if we understand what power is and is not. As Kenneth Waltz has pointed out, power does not mean the ability to get one's way all the time.[15] Material resources never translate fully into desired outcomes (a point military strategists acknowledge when they observe that "the enemy has a vote" in determining the degree to which one's own strategic goals will be realized). Rather, a state is powerful if it gets its way more of the time than others do. Precisely because the United States is an extraregional hegemon, a marked asymmetry of influence favors it. In international politics, the United States does not get all that it wants all the time. But it gets most of what it wants an awful lot of the time, and it affects other states far more than other states affect it.

Combined, these elements warrant my claim that since the early 1940s the United States has sought—and to a great extent attained—extraregional hegemony. During the past six decades and more the United States has enjoyed military and economic dominance. Since the 1940s, the United States assiduously has pursued a unipolar distribution of power in the international system. And, in the three regions that matter the most to it, it has maintained a permanent military presence to prevent the emergence of new poles of power and to maintain the kind of regional peace and stability deemed essential to upholding a U.S.-dominated international order. Although America's grand strategic ambitions may not always be realized (or realized fully), in shaping international political outcomes the United States today still has far more influence than other states.

Is Hegemony a Wise Grand Strategy?

Great powers have two basic grand strategic options: they can pursue geopolitical dominance, or they can seek to maintain a roughly equal distribution of power among the great powers. My argument is that by following a hegemonic grand strategy, the United States will provoke a geopolitical backlash. I realize that this may seem like an oddly contrarian argument for two reasons. First, today U.S. hegemony is a fact of international political life, and it will be for some time to come. The United States is, as Robert Art puts it in his important recent study of U.S. grand strategy, "the most powerful global actor the world has ever seen."[16] America's position is unprecedented, because the United States is the only great power in the history of the modern international state system to have attained hegemony in its own region *and* to have attained hegemony extraregionally.

Second, if hard power counts in international politics—and it counts for an awful lot—why shouldn't the United States, as offensive realism prescribes, seek to amass overwhelming power? Can the United States, to paraphrase the Duchess of Windsor, ever be too rich, too powerful, or too well armed? For most of those who think about U.S. grand strategy, the answer is "no." Ever since the Soviet Union's demise, the ascendant view among students of American grand strategy is that hegemony advances U.S. interests and that the United States can maintain its preeminence far into the future.[17] Indeed, it has been suggested that the only meaningful debate about U.S. grand strategy today is which variant of hegemony the United States should pursue.

Students of American grand strategy have advanced creative arguments to support the view that the United States is an exception to the historical rule and that it will not suffer the fate that has befallen other great powers that have sought hegemony. Some realists argue that the present unipolar distribution of capabilities in favor of the United States is so overwhelming as to be insurmountable.[18] Invoking "balance of threat" theory, other realists claim that the United States can squelch any inclinations others may have to balance against it by following accommodative policies that will allay their fears of U.S. dominance.[19] According to liberals, the United States can be a successful hegemon because it is a "benevolent" hegemon.[20] Finally, liberals and balance-of-threat realists alike argue that other states will acquiesce in U.S. hegemony if that predominance is exercised multilaterally through international institutions. By voluntarily accepting restraints on its exercise of power, it is claimed, the United States reassures others that they need not fear U.S. power.[21]

As I will show, these various arguments that hegemony will prove to be a winning grand strategy for the United States are not persuasive. One of history's few incontestable lessons is that the pursuit of hegemony invariably is self-defeating, because it provokes counter-balancing efforts by other states and leads to what Paul Kennedy famously called "imperial overstretch." The United States enjoys no privileged immunity from the fate of hegemons.

This book, in part, is policy prescriptive. Although the question of which grand strategy the United States should pursue is one of policy, it has an important theoretical dimension.[22] Indeed, the very concept of grand strategy involves a relationship between theory and policy, because grand strategy is a state's theory about how it best can create security for itself.[23] In making grand strategy, policymakers build on their assumptions about "how the world works"—their models (even if only implicit models) of international politics. Grand strategy is, as Stephen Walt puts it, a set of cause-and-effect hypotheses postulating which policies are most likely to produce the strategic outcomes that policymakers desire. The success of a state's grand strategy depends, therefore, "on whether the hypotheses [policymakers] embrace are correct."[24] To weigh and assess America's grand strategic alternatives judiciously, it is necessary to understand the causal logic of the competing theories that underlie them.

By laying out the reasons why the United States should follow an offshore balancing strategy instead of sticking with its current pursuit of extraregional hegemony, I aim to contribute to the real-world debate about U.S. grand strategy. In making the case for offshore balancing, I reject Barry Posen's claim that, in 9/11's wake, the debate about U.S. grand strategy "has narrowed to a dispute between primacy and selective engagement, between a nationalist, unilateralist version of hegemony, and a liberal, multilateral version of hegemony."[25] Because there are no significant differences between primacy and selective engagement, Posen's claim is tantamount to saying there no longer is an ongoing debate about U.S. grand strategy. Offshore balancing is, I believe, the only viable grand-strategic alternative to hegemony.

When great powers chose between (or among) alternative grand strategies, the important question is which is likely to yield the most security. In the history of the modern international system, some great powers have had little choice but to seek security by trying for hegemony, but the United States has not been one of them. In fact, far from bolstering its security, its hegemonic grand strategy renders the United States less secure. First, over time—and I concede that "how long" is an important question—new great powers will emerge (or old ones, like Russia, will revive), and balance against U.S. dominance. Second, U.S. hegemony fuels terrorism against the United States by groups such as al Qaeda. In this respect, 9/11 itself is a reminder that U.S. predominance has spawned new, "asymmetric" responses to U.S. preeminence. Third, until new poles of power emerge to offset U.S. military preponderance, the United States will succumb to the "hegemon's temptation"—employing its formidable military capabilities promiscuously and becoming entangled in conflicts that it could avoid. Finally, over time, a hegemonic grand strategy will lead to the enervation of U.S. power (imperial overstretch). The United States can escape these consequences by adopting an offshore balancing grand strategy.

In making the case for offshore balancing, I am also taking dead aim at the central assumption that has undergirded American grand strategy since at least 1940. That strategy has been based on what one might call *strategic internationalism:* the belief that to be secure, the United States must exert the full panoply of its power—military, economic, and ideological—on the international system in order to shape its external environment. Here, 9/11 and the Iraq quagmire constitute a grand strategic crossroads for the United States that should force policymakers—and *citizens*—to question whether strategic internationalism delivers as advertised or rather that it makes the United States more *in*secure. As those with some knowledge of the great foreign policy debates in U.S. history will recognize, this is not a new question, though it has been largely dormant since Pearl Harbor. Recent events, however, lend urgency to revisiting it.

Why Is the United States Following the Wrong Strategy?

If bad fates ultimately befall hegemons, and if the United States could escape these consequences by following an offshore balancing grand strategy, why has the United States pursued extraregional hegemony? This crucial question has both historical and theoretical dimensions. To answer it, I must explain America's grand strategic behavior since the early 1940s. This complex and challenging task shapes the organization of this book and the methods I use to support my argument.

My approach in this book is rooted firmly in neoclassical realism.[26] Neoclassical realists, as well as diplomatic historians, believe that grand strategies result from the interaction of systemic factors—especially the distribution of power in the international system—and domestic dynamics. This is certainly true of the United States. As Thomas G. Paterson says, it is the *interplay* of structural and unit-level variables that explains U.S. grand strategic behavior. The international system conditions U.S. grand strategy, he observes, but does not control it. "For that control," Paterson observes, "we look inward at a number of factors: economic, strategic, political, ideological, cultural, and social."[27] To explain America's foreign policy since the early 1940s, I propose a theory of American grand strategy that I call "extraregional hegemony theory."

America's pursuit of extraregional hegemony results, I believe, from the causal linkages between the distribution of power in the international system and intervening domestic variables. In explaining U.S. grand strategy, structural realism is a helpful "first cut," because it allows us to gauge how strategy is affected by America's place in the international system.[28] Following World War II, the United States possessed overwhelming material capabilities relative to all other states in the international system (including the Soviet Union). The regional hegemony of the United States in the Western Hemisphere provided a secure geopolitical platform from which it could seek extraregional hegemony. Moreover, World War II caused an important shift in the distribution of power between the United States and Western Europe. As a result, the United States had both the means and the opportunity to impose its hegemony over postwar Western Europe. Similar factors—overwhelming U.S. material capabilities plus the Soviet Union's demise—created the opportunity for another round of hegemonic expansion after 1989. Simply stated, structural factors in 1945 and 1989 gave the United States both the opportunity and the means to expand beyond the Western Hemisphere. However, structural factors do not tell us *why* the United States *chose* to do so. To find the motive for America's hegemonic expansion we must look at domestic factors.

I believe that the "Open Door" explains America's drive for extraregional hegemony.[29] The Open Door school of U.S. diplomatic history holds that beginning in the late nineteenth century the United States has pursued an expansionist—indeed, hegemonic or even imperial—policy, first in the Western Hemisphere and then in East Asia, Europe, and the Persian Gulf. The Open Door holds the answer to an important puzzle: Why didn't U.S. grand strategy change when the cold war ended? Why did U.S. forces stay "over there" instead of "coming home?" The Open Door incorporates both economic expansion and ideological expansion and links them to U.S. national security. Open Door economic expansion created new interests that had to be defended by projecting U.S. military power abroad, shaped policymakers' perceptions of how those interests were threatened, and led to a new conception of America's security requirements by transforming the goal of U.S. grand strategy from national defense to national security. "National security," Melvyn P. Leffler observes, "meant more than defending territory."

Rather, it meant "defending the nation's core values, its organizing ideology, and its free political and economic institutions."[30] The Open Door is as much about ideology as it is about economic expansion and the distribution of power in the international system. Indeed, these factors are linked inextricably, because U.S. strategists believed that the nation's core values could be safe only in an international system underwritten by hegemonic U.S. power and open both to U.S. economic penetration and to the penetration of American ideology. This is what William Appleman Williams called an "Open Door world." Because of the Open Door, U.S. policymakers defined threats not only in terms of the distribution of power in the international system but also ideologically in terms of threats to America's "core values."

Again, the Open Door helps to illuminate the wellsprings of America's grand strategic behavior. It is a realist grand strategy, however, it is also—to borrow Robert Art's phrase—a "*realpolitik* plus" grand strategy.[31] The Open Door world described by Williams is a world shaped by liberal—Wilsonian—ideas. The Open Door reminds us, therefore, that although the liberal approach to international relations theory doesn't carry much weight as a *theory* of international politics, it packs a huge and pernicious punch in *policy* debates about American grand strategy. U.S. foreign policy elites subscribe to its key contentions about America's stake in an economically and politically "open" international order.

Now it's easy to say, as some realists do, that the Wilsonian vision of an Open Door world is simply window dressing invoked by U.S. policymakers as a smoke screen to mask the fundamentally realpolitik nature of U.S. grand strategy. However, the role of Wilsonian ideology in U.S. grand strategy cannot be dismissed so cavalierly—it is far too deeply entrenched in America's political culture and foreign policy tradition for that. In fact, the subtle interplay between Wilsonianism and realism has been the hallmark of U.S. grand strategy.[32] U.S. grand strategy defines U.S. national interests in terms of power, economic openness, *and* the promotion of U.S. ideals—which is why it has been described by others as "liberal realism," "national security liberalism," or (as Charles Krauthammer puts it) "democratic realism."[33] From the standpoint of realist theory these terms are oxymorons. But oxymoronic or not, these descriptions tell us something important about how policymakers think about U.S. grand strategy: although, as realists know, the liberal approach to international relations theory is wrongheaded, when they incorporate Wilsonianism into grand strategy, U.S. policymakers are—or, more accurately, *believe* they are—being hardheaded, not woolly headed.

In grand strategy terms American liberalism is muscular—*offensive*—not "idealistic." It postulates cause-and-effect linkages about how the United States can gain security. The spread of democracy and of economic openness are embedded in U.S. grand strategic thought because policymakers believe an Open Door world fosters U.S. power, influence, and security. Wilsonianism holds out the promise of peace for the United States. As I demonstrate, however, this is a peace of illusions. Far from creating peace and enhancing U.S. security, the pursuit of an Open Door world is the motor that drives America's quest for extraregional hegemony. Wilsonian ideology is a potent generator of U.S. overexpansion and of unnecessary military entanglements abroad. Wilsonianism makes the United States less, not more, secure.

The Need for a Neoclassical Explanation

Structural realist theories would not predict America's pursuit of extraregional hegemony during the past six decades. Structural realism's main insight—that great power behavior is driven by the imperative of attaining security in the highly competitive realm of international politics—has, at best, only limited applicability to the United States. The United States is a sui generis case of great power grand strategy, because, since the early twentieth century, the United States has been far more secure than any great power in modern history. From an *objective* standpoint the American homeland essentially has been unthreatened, so security imperatives cannot explain U.S. expansion or the U.S. pursuit of extraregional hegemony. Yet, paradoxically, U.S. policymakers have perceived the international environment as highly threatening. Consequently, they have believed that establishing extraregional hegemony is the only way to ensure America's security. The big question, of course, is why they have believed this.

To answer this question "we must move beyond the relatively spare world of neorealist theory and incorporate unit-level factors as well."[34] In the U.S. case, precisely because the competitive pressures of the international system press the United States only weakly, domestic factors play a much greater role in explaining U.S. grand strategy than they do in explaining other great powers' grand strategies.[35] The inability of structural realist theories to account for U.S. grand strategic behavior invites the formulation of a theory of grand strategy to fill the explanatory vacuum.

I realize that extraregional hegemony theory might be criticized as "non-parsimonious" by some purist international relations scholars. The fact that extraregional hegemony theory attributes U.S. grand strategy to the *interaction* of three variables—the distribution of power in the international political system, U.S. economic expansion, and ideology—does not mean, however, that it is a "grab bag" of theories, or variables, or a "laundry list" explanation of U.S. grand strategy.[36] I claim that three things have mattered *and* that causally they were—and still are—inextricably interrelated. Far from being mutually exclusive explanations of American grand strategy, the distribution of power in the international system, economic expansion, and ideology are interconnected. I show how these variables are linked causally—that is what historical explanation is all about. Solid historical explanation is the best way to test international relations theories.[37]

Neoclassical realists understand that the real world is complex, not simple. Hence, the neoclassical school blends structural realist theory with historical explanation. Indeed, as Gideon Rose comments, neoclassical realism stresses "detailed historical analysis."[38] Recognizing that even the simplest explanations of a particular state's grand strategy are complex, neoclassical realists sacrifice "rigor" for richness.[39] Rather than make a fetish of parsimony, they understand that case studies of a particular great power's grand strategy need to pay attention to "historical context and particularity."[40] Historians are no less interested than political scientists in testing propositions analytically and identifying chains of causation that connect explanatory variables.[41] Leading diplomatic historians—John Lewis Gaddis and Melvyn Leffler are notable examples—use international relations theory in their own work. At the same time, they remind us that there is no escape from complexity. Indeed, as Leffler observes, complexity is beneficial, because "we multiply the interplay of variables, arouse controversy about their relative importance, and vastly augment the realm for creativity."[42] This is the intellectual spirit that informs this book.

METHODOLOGICAL APPROACH

My aim is to lay out extraregional hegemony theory and see how well it measures up in explaining America's behavior during the last sixty-some years. Extraregional hegemony theory builds on both offensive and defensive realist theories to construct a theory of U.S. grand strategy. Then, using "process tracing," I test extraregional hegemony theory with a detailed case study, focusing primarily on Western Europe, of America's grand strategy from the early 1940s to the present. Process tracing enables us "to evaluate the separate causal links that connect explanatory variables with the predicted outcomes" and to see whether policymakers "speak, write, and otherwise behave in a manner consistent with the theory's predictions."[43] To determine whether U.S. policymakers have acted as extraregional hegemony theory predicts, I rely heavily on primary sources. For the period from 1945 to the early 1970s, I have used archival materials extensively. For the post-1989 period, I have looked at official publications and statements of key policymakers.

Ideally, to establish the *global* scope of America's hegemonic ambitions, I would like to have included a detailed examination of U.S. grand strategy with respect to East Asia and the Persian Gulf. Although I do make some reference to the role of those two regions in U.S. grand strategy, the limitations of space and time prevent a detailed discussion. Nevertheless, I believe the focus on Western Europe makes sense for several reasons. First, after World War II, for the United States, Western Europe was the most important region of the world economically and strategically.[44] Moreover, America's post-1945 European commitment illustrates the interplay between Open Door imperatives and American military commitments. Specifically, America's European grand strategy shows how the Open Door required the exercise of U.S. hegemony to maintain peace within postwar Western Europe. Second, because of its latent power and historical role in international politics, Western Europe was the most likely region to give birth to new poles of power capable of contesting Washington's postwar preponderance in the non-Soviet world. Consequently, to prevent the rise of new poles of power in Europe, the United States was motivated to exercise hegemony there.

My argument about U.S. grand strategy toward Western Europe has a larger message: that the preservation of U.S. geopolitical dominance and Open Door imperatives (and the two are connected intimately) have been the key factors shaping U.S. grand strategy since the early 1940s. If I am correct that extraregional hegemony theory explains America's European grand strategy, it should also explain U.S. strategy toward other areas—such as East Asia and the Middle East—where it has similar interests. Finally, the Western European case has important theoretical implications in its own right. Many are familiar with Mearsheimer's argument that the United States is not—and cannot be—an extraregional hegemon. Consequently, even a single example of U.S. hegemony outside the Western Hemisphere would raise important questions about offensive realist theory—at least with respect to its ability to explain America's grand strategic behavior.

PLAN OF THE BOOK

I will first show that U.S. grand strategy presents a puzzle, because neither defensive nor offensive realism predicts that the United States would seek extraregional hegemony. To solve this puzzle, I explain why the United States has sought hegemony outside the Western Hemisphere. To test this extraregional hegemony theory, chapters 2 through 5 detail U.S. grand strategy. Chapter 2 shows how the foundations of America's extraregional hegemony grand strategy were laid as World War II still was being fought, and describes how U.S. ambitions were shaped by the interaction of structural factors, the economic Open Door, and the political Open Door. In particular, I show that, before World War II ended, the United States aimed at establishing itself as the sole great power in the postwar international system. Chapter 3 describes U.S. grand strategy toward the Soviet Union in the early cold war years, and, building on the argument in chapter 2, shows that the United States aspired to eliminate the Soviet Union as a great power rival, and thereby bring about a unipolar distribution of power in the international system. In chapter 4, I trace the Open Door foundations of America's postwar Western European grand strategy and show that the logic of that grand strategy would have caused the United States to impose its hegemony over Western Europe even if there had been no Soviet threat.

In chapter 5, I demonstrate that during the cold war, rather than welcome the emergence of an independent pole of power in Western Europe to which—had it been acting as an offshore balancer—it could have "passed the buck" of containing the Soviet Union, the United States acted decisively to prevent the emergence of such a Western European power center. I also answer two critical questions about America's post-1989 grand strategy. First, given the common understanding that America's post–World War II military commitment to Europe (and East Asia) was driven by the need to contain the Soviet Union, when the Soviet Union collapsed, why didn't the United States "come home" from Europe (and East Asia) militarily? Second, if the United States really is an offshore balancer, instead of welcoming the European Union's efforts to create an independent military capability, why has the United States strongly opposed them?

In chapters 6–8, the focus shifts to current and future U.S. grand strategy. Chapter 6 shows that with respect to grand strategy, the sources of U.S. conduct are found now—just as they were after World War II—in the concept of an Open Door world, which has been rechristened the "virtuous circle" by U.S. policymakers. In Chapter 7 I show why America's hegemonic grand strategy is not sustainable beyond another decade or two and explain how it makes the United States less, not more, secure. Finally, in chapter 8, I make the case that offshore balancing is a better future grand strategy for the United States than a grand strategy of extraregional hegemony.

* * *

Grand strategy—what Edward Meade Earle called "the highest type of strategy"—is the most crucial task of statecraft.[45] As Geoffrey Parker observes, grand strategy "encompasses the decisions of a state about its overall security—the threats it perceives, the way in which it confronts them, and the steps it takes to match ends and means."[46] Distilled to its essence, grand strategy is about determining a state's vital interests—those important enough to fight over—and its role in the world. From that determination springs a state's alliances, overseas military commitments, conception of its stake in the prevailing international order, and the size and structure of its armed forces. "The crux of grand strategy lies," Paul Kennedy observes, "in *policy*, that is, in the capacity of the nation's leaders to bring together all of the elements, both military and non-military, for the preservation and enhancement of the nation's long-term (that is, in wartime *and* peacetime) best interests."[47] Of course, while well-conceived grand strategies maximize a great power's "best interests," flawed grand strategies have the opposite effect. In making grand strategy, therefore, it is important that policymakers "get it right."

Today, U.S. policymakers are *not* getting it right. I hope that this book will stimulate a more searching debate about America's future grand strategic options than heretofore has occurred. The real choice facing Americans is whether the United States should remain wedded to the pursuit of extraregional hegemony or whether it should adopt an offshore balancing grand strategy. For better or worse, the grand strategy the United States chooses to pursue has real-life consequences for Americans—a lesson of 9/11 and Iraq that seemingly has yet to sink in. That is why the debate about American grand strategy is important.

CHAPTER ONE

Theory, History, and U.S. Grand Strategy

Does the United States need to pursue hegemony to gain security (offensive realism), or should it be an offshore balancer (defensive realism)? Both approaches lead to a paradoxical conclusion: neither predicts that the United States should seek extraregional hegemony. The United States *should* be an offshore balancer, but the empirical record demonstrates that it *is not*. Because it is not structurally determined, the U.S. pursuit of extraregional hegemony since the early 1940s is a puzzle that needs to be explained. In this chapter I lay out in detail extraregional hegemony theory, a theory of U.S. grand strategy that explains why the United States has striven for extraregional hegemony during the last six decades. In chapters 2–5, I test extraregional hegemony theory's explanatory power with a case study of U.S. grand strategy since 1940.

Offensive versus Defensive Realism: Hegemony or Balance of Power?

Realism is the most important school of thought in the study of international politics.[1] "Realism," David L. Anderson observes, "is not beyond criticism, but since the time of the Greek historians it has provided a behavioral paradigm of rational cost-benefit calculations of the national interest in an essentially anarchical international environment."[2] Realists subscribe to several "hardcore" assumptions about the nature of international politics: the international system is state-centric; it is "anarchic"; and it is a "self-help" system.[3] For realists, international politics is an ongoing struggle among states for power and security. By power, realists mean that great powers strive to gain *relative* power advantages over their rivals.[4] Realists also recognize that the great powers' competition for security causes the (misnamed) "security dilemma," which really should be called the "insecurity condition."[5] Because the world is a competitive, potentially dangerous place, realists believe that the most basic goal of great powers is to gain security, and thus ensure their survival.[6] While they agree about realism's core assumptions, however, offensive and defensive realists disagree sharply about several important questions, the most crucial of which is whether seeking hegemony is a wise grand strategy for great powers.[7]

DEFENSIVE REALISM

The distribution of power in the international system can be unipolar (a single, hegemonic great power), bipolar (two great powers), or multipolar (three or more great powers).[8] Because they believe that a more or less equal diffusion of power among two or more great powers is more conducive to peace and stability than the concentration of power in the hands of a single power, defensive realists argue that states should not seek to maximize their power but only to maximize their security.[9] Great powers should avoid expansionist, and hegemony-seeking, grand strategies. As Stephen Van Evera claims, great powers are not constrained to be hegemony seekers, because the "structure of power is benign" in international politics and therefore "provides more disincentives than incentives for aggression."[10]

Defensive realists believe that security usually is plentiful in the international system, because the security dilemma is modulated by certain "structural modifiers," especially the "offense/defense balance" of great power military capabilities (which, in turn, is a function of geography and military technology).[11] Defensive realists assert that the advantage usually favors the defense, which means that great powers should be pretty confident that others won't attack them.[12] When defense has the upper hand, great powers are very secure, and thus they can forego expansion and offensive military postures and focus on mutually beneficial cooperation.[13] Defensive realists argue that great power expansion is doubly misguided: not only is there no systemic imperative for great powers to expand but such behavior is self-defeating. Defensive realists claim that great powers that adopt power-maximizing grand strategies end up being less, not more, secure.[14]

For defensive realists, there are two main reasons that power-maximizing strategies cause *in*security for the great powers that adopt them. First, because costs mount over time, and even "successful" expansion inexorably leads to strategic overstretch. The pursuit of security through expansion weakens the domestic economic base on which great powers' security ultimately rests.[15] Second, the ironclad rule in international politics is that instead of aligning with a would-be hegemon ("bandwagoning"), other great powers join forces to defeat it ("balancing") by building up their own military capabilities and/or entering into counterhegemonic alliances. As Barry Posen states, not only does balance-of-power theory suggest that "expanding hegemons will be opposed and stopped" but there is *"ample historical evidence that this is the case."*[16] However, the historical record raises an important conundrum: If structural imperatives only rarely cause great powers to pursue

16

expansion, and if power-maximizing behavior is self-defeating, why have successive great powers made bids for hegemony?

For defensive realists, the answer is found at the domestic level. Great powers that pursue expansionist grand strategies are "bad" or "greedy" states—those that, because of various domestic "deformations," want more than security.[17] According to defensive realists, because these domestic pathologies take root and flourish in nonliberal states, the antidotes to great power expansionism are economic interdependence and democracy. Thus in their diagnosis of, and prescription for, "irrational" state behavior, many defensive realists are closet liberals.[18]

OFFENSIVE REALISM

Unlike defensive realists, offensive realists believe that security in the international political system is scarce.[19] Consequently, offensive realists believe that to gain security, great powers are impelled to pursue expansionist, offensive strategies that aim at maximizing their power and influence at their rivals' expense.[20] Unlike defensive realists, who claim that expansionist grand strategies cause the security dilemma, offensive realists believe that such strategies are a logical consequence of the insecurity condition.[21]

The most important statement of offensive realism is John Mearsheimer's *The Tragedy of Great Power Politics,* which argues that expansion and power maximization are the only strategies that allow great powers to gain security. As Mearsheimer puts it, "States quickly understand that the best way to ensure their survival is to be the most powerful state in the system."[22] Even great powers that would prefer to be "security maximizers" are constrained to adopt power-maximizing grand strategies.[23] Indeed, I would argue, the distinction drawn by defensive realists between security-maximizing and power-maximizing strategies is a distinction without a difference. Because a state's power is the foundation of its security, the two are connected inextricably. Offensive realists and defensive realists alike agree that attaining security is the goal of the great powers' grand strategies, which means that the real difference between them is not about whether great powers are "power maximizers" or "security maximizers" but about *how much power* a state needs to be secure.

Unlike defensive realism, which holds that great powers should seek only the minimum amount of power needed to ensure their survival, offensive realists maintain that great powers can never settle for having "just enough" power, because it is impossible to know just how much power is sufficient to guarantee their security. For Mearsheimerian offensive realists, therefore, "the pursuit of power stops only when hegemony is achieved," because for great powers "the best way to ensure their security is to achieve hegemony now, thus eliminating any possibility of a challenge by another great power."[24] There are two key reasons why seeking hegemony is the most

Table 1 Realist Theories: Implications for Theory of American Grand Strategy

Realist Theory	Prediction for U.S. Hegemony	Implications for Theory of American Grand Strategy
Defensive Realism	No U.S. hegemony because hegemony is self-defeating	—Unit-level factors explain U.S. pursuit of hegemony
First wave of Offensive Realism (Zakaria, Gilpin, Labs)	U.S. expansion (Possibly hegemonic): 1. increasing relative power/material capabilities 2. opportunities for advantageous expansion	—Look at distribution of power to 1. determine if U.S. relative power/material capabilities are rising 2. if opportunities for advantageous expansion are created —look at domestic factors to determine how U.S. security is defined; how U.S. interest is defined; how threat is defined
Second wave of Offensive Realism/Offshore Balancing Theory* (Mearsheimer Version)	No extraregional U.S. hegemony: 1. stopping power of water 2. strategic advantages of offshore balancing	—Stopping power of water is absolute barrier to global hegemony
Extraregional Hegemony Theory*	Extraregional U.S. hegemony if: 1. stopping power of water can be overcome 2. distribution of power presents favorable opportunities for expansion	—Look at distribution of power and O/D balance to see if stopping power of water can be overcome —Look at unit level factors to explain why U.S. foregos advantages of offshore balancing

Note: *Theory of American Grand Strategy
O/D = Offense/Defense Balance

promising route for great powers to gain security. First, a hegemon's overwhelming power dissuades others from challenging it.[25] Second, hegemony is the best response to uncertainty both about others' intentions and about present and future distributions of power in the international system.[26]

Mearsheimer defines a hegemon as "a state that is so powerful that it dominates all the other states in the system. In essence, a hegemon is the only great power in the system."[27] At this point, however, Mearsheimer introduces an important qualification. Although the logic of offensive realism suggests that great powers will seek global hegemony, there are insuperable obstacles to attaining it.[28] In fact, he says, "there never has been a global hegemon, and there is not likely to be one anytime soon."[29] The reason is geography—specifically what Mearsheimer pithily calls the "stopping power of water."[30] In the argot of military strategists, the problem is one of power projection: the farther a state goes from home, the less of a wallop its military punch packs. Water, Mearsheimer says, prevents great powers from transporting the amount of military power needed to establish dominance over distant regions.

Because global hegemony is out of reach, the best a great power can hope for, Mearsheimer contends, is to become a hegemon in its *own region*.[31] When he describes a hegemon as a state powerful enough to dominate all the others in the "system," the system to which he refers is regional—not the international system as a whole. Once a great power becomes a regional hegemon, he says, it has "achieved the pinnacle of power."[32] At that point, further expansion is impossible and it becomes a status quo, security-maximizing power. In other words, its grand strategy ceases to be an offensive realist one and becomes instead a defensive realist strategy.

Defensive and Offensive Realism and a Theory of Grand Strategy

Defensive realism's core tenet is that hegemonic grand strategies are self-defeating. Defensive realists believe that only very rarely are there structural constraints, or incentives, that push great powers to become hegemony seekers. In contrast to defensive realism, Mearsheimer's version of offensive realism holds that structural constraints impel great powers to seek security by striving to attain *regional* hegemony. At the same time, his theory holds that the stopping power of water precludes regional hegemons from gaining global hegemony. Applied specifically to the U.S. case, defensive and Mearsheimerian offensive realism both predict (albeit for different reasons) that the United States will not pursue extraregional hegemony.

Although they are structural theories, offensive and defensive realism can be used to construct theories of grand strategy—theories that predict the behavior of specific states rather than systemic outcomes. As such, they can be used to construct a theory of *U.S.* grand strategy, and to answer important questions about U.S. strategic behavior: Does the United States need to gain extraregional hegemony to be secure? Is extraregional hegemony likely to prove a winning grand strategy for the United States? Offensive and defensive realism provide similar answers, which underscores a larger point. Although scholars have a vested interest in "product differentiation," as theories of grand strategy there are important points of convergence between offensive and defensive realism.

Insecurity may be a problem for great powers, but all great powers are *not* equally insecure. A few great powers in modern history, in fact, have enjoyed a high degree of security. Because they explain systemic outcomes, structural

Table 2 Continental Great Powers versus Offshore Great Powers

	Relative Security/Insecurity	Causes of Relative Security/Insecurity	Indicated Grand Strategy
Land Powers	Very vulnerable	Geographic proximity to rival land powers	Hegemony: gain security by eliminating rivals and becoming the only great poiwer
Offshore balancers	Relatively invulnerable	Geographic distance from rival powers plus military capabilities	Offshore balancing: take advantage of multipolarity to "buck-pass" to others task of stopping rising hegemon

theories tend to overlook the fact that the individual strategic circumstances of great powers can vary widely. However, when used as theories of specific states' grand strategies, defensive realism and offensive realism do a good job of capturing this variance. Geographic proximity to rival powers and military capabilities are the key determinants of great power security or insecurity.[33]

Grand strategy is like real estate: location matters. It makes a huge difference whether a great power is a continental or an insular power. Continental great powers sharing the same neighborhood with powerful rivals face intense systemic pressures and have the strongest incentives to seek security by eliminating their rivals; that is, by gaining hegemony. As Mearsheimer says, "The most dangerous states in the international system are continental powers with large armies."[34] In a closely packed continent filled with rivals armed to the teeth, Europe's great powers lived in continual apprehension about their security, because geography was not a barrier to invasion. Each of Europe's great powers confronted the ongoing danger that it could be invaded—even conquered—by the others.[35] With respect to continental great powers, Mearsheimer provides a powerful, and convincing, explanation of why those states were compelled to seek security through hegemony and lands a knockout punch on defensive realism. There is no need to invoke "domestic deformations" to account for the European great powers' hegemony-seeking grand strategies. They had no real choice. Only by obtaining the "mastery of Europe" could they hope to be secure.

On the other hand, in grand strategy terms, offshore great powers live in a very different world from their continental counterparts. For them, distance—combined with formidable military capabilities—shifts the offense/defense balance in their favor. The "stopping power of water" is an essentially defensive realist concept. Unlike the continental great powers, offshore ("insular") great powers like England (in its great power heyday) and, even more, the United States, enjoy a high degree of relative security.

Because they are protected by hard-to-traverse moats, it is difficult for continental great powers to attack them.[36] Precisely because geography renders them relatively invulnerable, offshore great powers do not need to become hegemons in order to be secure.

Although it doesn't need to gain extraregional hegemony to be secure, an offshore power may have the opportunity to do so. Is this a wise, or winning, grand strategy? The conventional wisdom is that defensive realists say "no" and offensive realists say "yes" (or "maybe"), but the two theories converge on this issue more than has been recognized. Defensive realists believe that hegemons are always defeated in the end by the counterbalancing actions of other great powers. And, indeed, the pages of modern international history are littered with the wreckage of failed bids for hegemony: the Habsburg empire under Charles V, Spain under Philip II, France under Louis XIV and Napoleon, and Germany under Hitler. To this list, some would add Germany under Wilhelm II and post-Victorian England.

Offensive realists pretty much concede that defensive realism is right on this point. For example, writing in 1991, Mearsheimer acknowledged that "hegemony is only rarely achieved."[37] Would-be hegemons lose for the very reasons given by defensive realists: "because threatened states have strong incentives to join together to thwart an aspiring hegemon, and because the costs of expansion generally outrun the benefits before domination is achieved, causing extension to become overextension."[38] In *Tragedy of Great Power Politics,* Mearsheimer's position shifted somewhat. He acknowledges that all of the European great powers that tried to attain (regional) hegemony failed to do so because they were defeated by the counterbalancing efforts of others.[39] Nevertheless, he says, it is not invariably is foolish to try for (regional) hegemony: "although it is difficult to achieve," the "pursuit of regional hegemony is not a quixotic ambition."[40]

Why is Mearsheimer now more bullish on pursuit of regional hegemony than he was in 1991? First, a would-be hegemon always can hope that "collective action" problems will enable it to win before a counterhegemonic alliance can form to stop it. Second, contrary to what defensive realists assert, there are many examples in which offensive military strategies have worked, and conquest has paid off, for great powers. This claim, though true—and important—falsely conflates successful offensive strategies and beneficial territorial conquest with the attainment of hegemony. Moreover, the examples Mearsheimer invokes all have an "other than that Mrs. Lincoln . . ." quality.[41] The most important reason that seeking regional hegemony is not "windmill tilting" according to Mearsheimer is that there is one example would-be hegemons can point to as "proof" that regional hegemony can be attained: the United States. However, the relevance of the American example for other would-be regional hegemons is doubtful.[42]

Why did the United States succeed in gaining hegemony in the Western Hemisphere, when all of the European great powers that tried to do so failed to gain hegemony on the Continent? This is a grand strategic no-brainer. The distribution of power in Europe differed markedly from that in the Western Hemisphere. Bids for European hegemony failed, because the distribution of power in Europe was multipolar: other great powers could—and did—coalesce to muster sufficient countervailing power to defeat aspiring hegemons. The United States, on the other hand, succeeded in attaining regional hegemony because when its expansion gathered steam in the late nineteenth and early twentieth centuries, it was expanding into a power vacuum. No great powers—either regional or extraregional—were capable of opposing—much less stopping—U.S. hegemonic expansion in the Western Hemisphere.[43] The U.S. case is sui generis and thus is not a model for would-be regional hegemons in Eurasia.

The United States's pursuit of regional hegemony was a smart strategy because it was essentially unopposed. The pay-offs in security and economic gain were high, and the costs were negligible. For the European great powers, however, although the potential rewards of continental hegemony were attractive, the chances of reaping them were low. Even so, the attempt to gain mastery in Europe was not necessarily foolish. The core claims of offensive and defensive realism do not inherently conflict. Mearsheimer's formulation of offensive realism tells us something very important: great powers that live in very dangerous neighborhoods—like the European great powers—face almost irresistible structural pressures to break out of the omnipresent insecurity condition and try to gain security by attaining hegemony. Defensive realism, on the other hand, reminds us that when confronted by a rising hegemon, other great powers have equally powerful incentives to defeat it. It is this clash of competing strategic imperatives that invests international politics with its tragic quality. However, not all great powers need be swept up in this tragedy.

Ultimately, on one point at least, defensive realism is correct: up until now, the pursuit of hegemony has been self-defeating. The clear implication is that the United States should not seek extraregional hegemony, because it is likely to be opposed by Eurasian great powers and to run into the kind of geopolitical resistance it did not encounter in the Western Hemisphere. Defensive realism poses an important question about U.S. grand strategy: Why should an offshore great power that already is extraordinarily secure follow an expansionist grand strategy and risk having the fate of hegemons befall it? Since emerging as a great power in the late nineteenth century, the United States has not faced the same intense systemic constraints that weighed on the European great powers. As an insular great power the United States is in a uniquely advantageous position. Because of geography and military capabilities, it has enjoyed—and even after 9/11 still does (or could)—something very close to absolute security. Even if, as a general proposition, security in the international system often is scarce, for the United States it has been abundant.

Table 3 Offshore Balancer Threat Matrix

Continental Balance of Power	Offense/Defense Balance	Threat
Robust multipolarity	SPOW: high confidence OSP capabilities: robust	Very low
Failing multipolarity	SPOW: low confidence OSP capabilities: weak	Very high
Regional hegemon	SPOW: low confidence OSP capabilities: weak	Extreme
Regional hegemon	SPOW: high confidence OSP capabilities: robust	Low
Failing multipolarity	SPOW: high confidence OSP capabilities: robust	Low

Note: SPOW = stopping power of water
OSP = offshore great power

Is the United States an Offshore Balancer?

Both offensive and defensive realism predict that the United States *should* be an offshore balancer, which raises the empirical question: Does the grand strategy of the United States since the early 1940s conform to this prediction? Whether the United States is an extraregional hegemon or an offshore balancer is a crucial predictor of future U.S. grand strategic behavior and its likely consequences. First, as an extraregional hegemon, the United States will be the target of counterhegemonic balancing by other states. On the other hand, "offshore balancers do not provoke balancing coalitions against themselves."[44] Second, as an extraregional hegemon, the United States will maintain a significant forward military presence in Europe, East Asia, and the Persian Gulf because it has—or more correctly, perceives it has—a vital stake in maintaining stability in those regions. As an offshore balancer, however, the United States will retract its military power from Europe, East Asia, and the Gulf in the relatively near future, and will only return to Eurasia if the threat of a rising regional hegemon reemerges.

Most of the leading students of U.S. grand strategy today believe that the United States is an extraregional hegemon—if not, indeed, a global one. However, John Mearsheimer notably has argued that the United States has been an offshore balancer ever since it emerged as a great power. Indeed, in *Tragedy of Great Power Politics,* in addition to his structural theory of offensive realism, Mearsheimer also proposes a *defensive* realist theory of U.S. grand strategy, which purports to explain why the United States is an offshore bal-

Table 4 Offshore Balancing Theory: Empirical Problems

Empirical Yardstick	Expected U.S. Policy	Empirical Problems
Polarity	Encourage multipolarity	U.S. strategy aims at extraregional hegemony/unipolarity
Strategy	Buck-passing	U.S. opposes emergence of independent poles of power in Eurasia to which it could buck-pass
Reason for U.S. military engagement in Eurasia	Counterhegemonic only	U.S. military forces not retracted from Europe after dissipation of hegemonic threat —Soviet threat to Europe vanished by early 1960s —Western Europe capable of balancing Soviet Union by early 1960s —U.S. keeps NATO intact after collapse of Soviet Union (1989–91)
U.S. as regional pacifier in Eurasia	No	—U.S. interests in regional stability drive U.S. commitment to Western Europe ("America: Europe's pacifier") —U.S. establishes hegemony in Western Europe to pacify it

ancer.[45] Mearsheimer's theory makes explicit predictions about what grand strategy the United States will follow and provides clear metrics to determine whether America's grand strategic behavior conforms to those predictions.

Mearsheimer says that, having attained regional hegemony, the United States is a status quo power and that, because of the stopping power of water, it cannot seek extraregional ("global") hegemony.[46] To maintain this position as the sole regional hegemon in the international system, the United States acts as an offshore balancer with respect to Europe and East Asia to ensure that no peer competitor (regional hegemon) emerges there.[47] As an offshore balancer, America's preferred strategy is buck-passing.[48] If a rising hegemon appears in Europe or East Asia, the United States prefers to let the great powers in the area do the strategic heavy-lifting of balancing against it. America's offshore balancing grand strategy is *counterhegemonic*—it intervenes militarily in Eurasia *only* if a potential hegemon cannot be contained successfully by the regional balance of power.[49] Once the hegemonic threat has been checked and the regional balance of power has been restored, American military power is retracted from Europe and East Asia.[50] As an offshore balancer, the United States does not act as a peacetime regional stabilizer by keeping its troops in Europe or East Asia. As Mearsheimer puts it, U.S. troops are sent to Eurasia "to prevent the rise of peer competitors, not to maintain peace."[51]

Is the United States in fact pursuing an offshore balancing grand strategy? Four key empirical tests can be distilled from Mearsheimer's explanation of U.S. grand strategic behavior. First, what are the United States's grand strategic aims? Do U.S. policymakers aim to attain extraregional hegemony, and, if so, are U.S. policies consistent with this declared aim? Second, do U.S. grand strategists favor multipolarity? If the United States indeed is, and has been, an offshore balancer, we should see evidence that in the post–World War II and post–cold war periods U.S. policymakers have favored a multipolar international system. Because it is a "buck-passing" strategy, offshore balancing is viable *only* in a multipolar international system. Offshore balancing is a lot like football: if you want to pass the buck (or ball) there has to be someone to catch it. Third, is U.S. military engagement in Europe and East Asia counter-hegemonic only? Finally, does the United States act during peacetime as a regional stabilizer in Europe and East Asia?

HEGEMONY AS A GOAL OF U.S. GRAND STRATEGY

Since the cold war, U.S. policymakers repeatedly have stated their global hegemonic ambitions. The first notable example was the Pentagon's *Defense Planning Guidance* (*DPG*) for fiscal years 1994–1999, the initial draft of which was leaked to the *New York Times* in March 1992.[52] The *DPG* stated that the objective of U.S. grand strategy would be to maintain U.S. hegemony by preventing the emergence of new great power rivals in Europe and East Asia. Although it toned down the rhetoric about unipolarity, the Clinton administration embraced the hegemonic grand strategy outlined in the *DPG* and declared that the United States was "the world's preeminent power" and the "only superpower on earth."[53] President Clinton said the United States was not simply the sole great power in international politics but "truly the world's indispensable nation."[54] The *1997 Quadrennial Defense Review,* prepared by the Pentagon during the Clinton administration, stated that U.S. grand strategy aimed to "sustain American global leadership" by reducing the chances that new great, or regional, powers could emerge to challenge the United States.[55] In its *2002 National Security Strategy* and *2001 Quadrennial Defense Review,* the Bush II administration made it plain that it is even more strongly committed to maintaining American global hegemony than were the Bush I and Clinton administrations.

Declaratory policy, of course, is one thing. America's actual grand strategic behavior is something else. However, as the case study in chapters 2–5 shows, the United States consistently has sought to expand its power and attain a position of hegemony in the international system—not only after 1989 but from the early 1940s and throughout the cold war as well.[56]

MULTIPOLARITY AND U.S. GRAND STRATEGY

Far from welcoming multipolarity—as it should do as an offshore balancer—the United States abhors it. In June 2003, in the immediate aftermath of the U.S. invasion of Iraq, National Security Adviser Condoleeza Rice found it "troubling" that "some have spoken admiringly—even nostalgically—of 'multipolarity,' as if it were a good thing, to be desired for its own sake."[57] Rice's hostility is broadly shared by U.S. strategists, because they believe that multipolar systems are unstable and war prone. As the revised draft of the Bush I administration's *DPG* stated, "It is not in our interest . . . to return to earlier periods in which multiple military powers balanced one against another in what passed for security structures, while regional, or even global peace hung in the balance."[58] This distrust of multipolarity was reaffirmed in the *2002 National Security Strategy*, which declared that the United States is "attentive to the possible renewal of old patterns of great power competition."[59] The antidotes to multipolar instability are U.S. hegemony and military dominance. As Zalmay Khalilzad, a senior official in the Bush I and Bush II administrations, puts it, "U.S. leadership [i.e., continued American hegemony] would be more conducive to global stability than a bipolar or a multipolar balance of power system."[60]

This hostility to multipolarity is not simply rhetorical. During the early 1960s, the United States intervened decisively to prevent the emergence of an independent pole of power in Western Europe. And, more recently, the United States has opposed the efforts of the European Union (EU) to create an independent military capability. These are not the responses of an offshore balancer, which should welcome the emergence of new power centers to which it could devolve the responsibility for maintaining the regional balance of power in Europe.

IS U.S. MILITARY INVOLVEMENT IN EURASIA COUNTERHEGEMONIC ONLY?

If the United States only intervenes counterhegemonically in Europe, why, a decade and a half after the end of the cold war, are U.S. troops still there (and in East Asia)? After all, the Soviet Union's collapse removed the very hegemonic threat that U.S. forces ostensibly were there to counter. Mearsheimer's answer is that institutional inertia explains the continuing post–cold war presence of U.S. forces in Europe and East Asia. Just give it a little time, he says, and those troops will come home. However, it is not just the last fifteen years since the cold war's end that poses a problem for this argument, because the Soviet "threat" ceased to be a convincing rationale for the U.S. military presence in Europe long before the Soviet Union collapsed. Writing in 1990, Fred Charles Ikle—a senior Pentagon official in the Reagan administration and a defense intellectual of impeccably hawkish credentials—suggested that the Soviet threat to Western Europe had vanished by the mid-1950s.[61] Moreover, by the early 1960s, Western Europe had recovered from World War II's ravages and possessed sufficient latent hard power capabilities to counter the Soviet Union unaided by the United States. In other words, counterhegemony no longer required a U.S. military presence on the Continent. At any point during the 1960s, 1970s, or 1980s U.S. troops could have come home from Europe, which is what should have happened if the United States was acting as an offshore balancer.

AMERICA'S HEGEMONIC ROLE AS
PEACETIME REGIONAL STABILIZER

Contrary to assertions that the United States commits its military power to Europe (and East Asia) only for counterhegemonic purposes, one of American grand strategy's bedrock assumptions is that the United States must provide "reassurance" and security to its Eurasian allies by acting as the "stabilizer" or "pacifier" in Europe and East Asia, and in the key areas of the periphery (especially the Persian Gulf). The U.S. military interventions in Bosnia and Kosovo, for example, illustrate America's ongoing peacetime role as "Europe's pacifier." American grand strategy is predicated on the belief that if the United States abdicated its role as regional stabilizer, Europe and East Asia would sink back into the bad old days of multipolar power politics, and the ensuing regional instability would jeopardize important U.S. economic interests.

To keep U.S. allies in Europe and East Asia from going their own way geopolitically, the United States must act as regional stabilizer. Should it abandon this pacifying role, it is believed, the entire fabric of America's hegemonic strategy would unravel. As the 1997 *Quadrennial Defense Review* somewhat delicately put it, if the credibility of the U.S. commitment to maintaining regional stability is questioned, that "in turn could cause allies and friends to adopt more divergent defense policies and postures, thereby weakening the web of alliances and coalitions on which we rely to protect our interests abroad."[62] The importance of the United States's regional stabilizer role was emphasized by Defense Secretary William J. Perry to rebut the notion that America's military presence, and alliances, in Europe and East Asia "are relics of the Cold War." Perry rejected as seductive, but dangerous, the argument "that we should pull back our forces . . . and allow normal balance-of-power politics to fill the security vacuum." If the United States did this, he claimed, historical animosities would reemerge and arms races would be triggered, causing instability and "dramatically increasing the risk of regional conflict."[63] America's interest in maintaining regional peace and stability is linked crucially to U.S. economic interests. As Defense Secretary William Cohen observed, "instability . . . destroys lives *and markets*."[64] On the other hand, the United States's alliances and security commitments "underpin the political stability on which the prosperity of civilized nations is built."[65]

There is nothing new about America's role as a peacetime regional stabilizer or the marriage of Washington's concerns about the geopolitical and economic consequences of regional instability. Even if there had been no Soviet threat, after World War II the United States would have become militarily committed on the Continent because its interests required it to assume the role of regional stabilizer. Ironically, even Mearsheimer seemingly acknowledges that America's post-1945 role in Western Europe and East Asia really was that of a hegemon and regional stabilizer, not that of an offshore balancer. "The United States," he observes, "maintained troops in West Germany and Japan during the Cold War, and although it surely was a benevolent occupier, it did not allow either of its allies to build the required military might to become a great power."[66] It's hard to imagine a better description of American hegemony, and the concomitant U.S. preference for unipolarity. Moreover, as Mearsheimer revealingly admits, the U.S. military presence in Europe "made it almost impossible for France and Germany to fight with each other and thus has eliminated the main cause of fear between them. *In essence, hierarchy replaces anarchy in areas controlled by U.S. forces.*"[67] This really gives away the game on the issue of whether the U.S. has sought extraregional hegemony. The replacement of anarchy by hierarchy is Mearsheimer's own definition of hegemony.[68] To be sure, he does state that after World War II "American forces were in Europe to contain the Soviet Union, not to maintain peace" and that Western Europe's postwar "long peace" was a happy byproduct of Washington's containment strategy.[69] However, as will become evident, this is a doubtful assertion.

Extraregional Hegemony Theory Explains U.S. Grand Strategy

As Kenneth Waltz observes, the most important attribute of a good theory is its "ability to explain."[70] Extraregional hegemony theory is my explanation of America's grand strategic behavior since the early 1940s. It is a neoclassical realist theory of U.S. grand strategy that incorporates systemic and domestic variables. Systemic factors constitute the permissive conditions for U.S. expansion. Domestic factors—Open Door economic and ideological expansion—explain the motives underlying American grand strategy, *why* the United States has behaved as it has.

In contrast to offensive realism, extraregional hegemony theory holds that far from being structurally determined, the U.S. decision to pursue extraregional hegemony in Europe following World War II was a matter of choice. That is, the U.S. pursuit of extraregional hegemony fundamentally was determined by domestic factors. However, for the United States to follow this strategy successfully, three systemic preconditions had to be met. First, the United States needed to enjoy a significant relative power advantage over the other major states in the international system. Second, because rising powers usually expand into regions where they won't encounter strong opposition, the distribution of power between the United States and Western Europe had to tilt decisively in America's favor.[71] Both conditions existed when World War II ended, and they facilitated the United States's grand strategy of extraregional hegemony. The third precondition was U.S. regional hegemony in the Western Hemisphere.

Before a great power reasonably can aspire to global hegemony, it first must gain dominance over its own region. The history of the European state system from 1500 to 1945—the successive failed attempts by great powers to establish "mastery in Europe"—largely was about gaining regional hegemony and then using it as a launching pad to bid for global hegemony. The European powers failed to attain extraregional hegemony because they were unable to first establish preponderance on the Continent. The United States, on the other hand, is the only great power successfully to have gained regional dominance, the prerequisite for extraregional hegemony. Indeed, *only* an insular great power like the United States can attain extraregional hegemony. In the race for global hegemony, continental powers are big-time long shots. With their hands full dealing with each other, continental powers are in no position to acquire the power projection capabilities needed to challenge a distant regional hegemon successfully and establish extraregional hegemony. To survive the competition in their own neighborhood, Europe's continental powers needed big armies. However, even the wealthiest and most powerful continental states have lacked the means to be dominant on land (to bid for hegemony in their own region) while simultaneously being dominant at sea (to challenge for hegemony in distant regions).[72] Precisely because it never has had to worry about rivals in its own region, once the United States emerged as a great power and established its primacy in the Western Hemisphere, it has been free to concentrate its resources and ambitions on seeking extraregional hegemony.

THE OPEN DOOR AND AMERICAN EXPANSION

When World War II ended, the United States enjoyed an almost unfettered range of grand strategic choices. To explain why the United States adopted a postwar grand strategy of extraregional hegemony we must look at domestic factors. The "Open Door" interpretation of U.S. diplomatic history best explains how policymakers conceived of U.S. interests and what threats they perceived there to be to those interests. Open Door imperatives tipped the scale of grand strategic choice against offshore balancing and in favor of extraregional hegemony.

The Open Door school—most closely identified with William Appleman Williams and his students—is one of the three main schools of diplomatic history that seek to explain America's postwar external policies.[73] The Open Door school's interpretation of U.S. grand strategy emphasizes "the continuity of a conscious, aggressive, expansionist, and self-interested America."[74] David Healy has captured the synthesis between the Open Door and American capabilities: "In modern history, those nations which were capable of extending their power or influence beyond their own borders have normally sought a way to do so. Those who control power also harbor goals and aspirations, and it is not strange that they should use the one to serve the other."[75] At the end of World War II, the United States was enormously powerful, and its international aspirations were expansive. The United States sought "to expand its political and territorial control" and "to create an international political environment and rules of the system" that would allow it to attain its "political, economic, and ideological interests."[76] The Open Door tells us that economic and ideological concerns drove America's hegemonic expansion after World War II. Although its critics often claim otherwise, it is not an economically deterministic interpretation of U.S. grand strategy but an explanatory tool that is useful precisely because it weaves into a single seamless interpretative tapestry the threads of hegemony, security, expansion, economic dominance, and ideology. It is a far more subtle and penetrating interpretation of U.S. grand strategy than its critics acknowledge.[77]

The Open Door school's "revisionism" was controversial intellectually and politically, becoming entangled with bitter debates about Vietnam, the cold war's origins, and America's ambitions in international politics.[78] Those debates never really ended, and their echoes reverberate in the debates about America's post–cold war and post-9/11 grand strategy. It is time to take a fresh look at the Open Door interpretation of U.S. grand strategy, because, as Michael Hogan observed, it "constitutes perhaps the most creative contribution to our field in the last century and the only contribution to frame a grand, master narrative for American diplomatic history."[79] The Open Door is especially useful because its interpretation of U.S. grand strategic behavior *during* the cold war tells us a lot about America's *post*–cold war grand strategy, and, consequently, allows us to understand why 1989–91 was not a grand strategic watershed for the United States.

THE OPEN DOOR AND AMERICAN CORE VALUES

As Williams put it, the goal of U.S. grand strategy has been to create an "Open Door world"—an international system, or "world order," made up of states that are open and subscribe to the United States's liberal values and institutions and that are open to U.S. economic penetration. An Open Door world rests, therefore, on two pillars: the economic Open Door (maintaining an open international economic system) and the political Open Door (spreading democracy and liberalism abroad).[80] These pillars are linked by the *perception* that "closure" abroad threatens the survival of American core

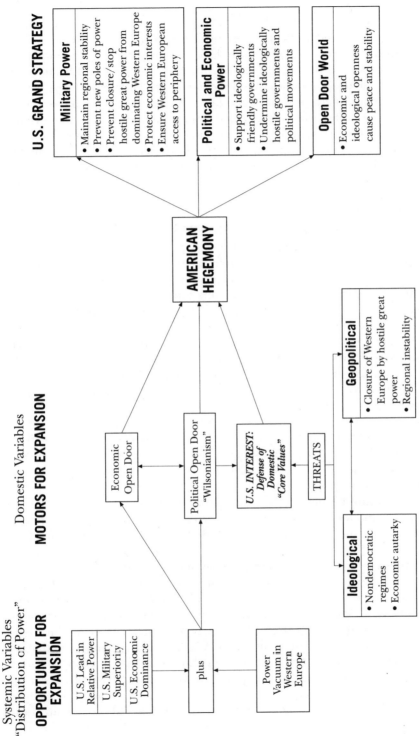

Figure 1. Extraregional Hegemony Theory: Explaining Post–World War II U.S. Hegemony in Europe

values—what policymakers call "the American way of life"—at home.[81] These threats are measured, in the first instance, by whether the international environment favors openness or closure. U.S. policymakers fear that important regions of the world—especially in Europe and East Asia—will be closed to the United States economically and ideologically, "cut[ting] off the oxygen without which American society, and liberal institutions generally, would asphyxiate."[82] In other words, U.S. grand strategy is based on the Open Door–derived assumption that political and economic liberalism cannot flourish at home unless they are safe abroad. This deeply rooted belief was reiterated by President George W. Bush in his second inaugural address, when he declared, "The survival of liberty in our land increasingly depends on the success of liberty in other lands."

Williams, Walter LaFeber, and other leading Open Door historians have demonstrated that from at least the 1880s U.S. economic expansionism has been based on two linked factors. First, U.S. policymakers have believed that prosperity is the key to domestic political stability and have *perceived* that America's prosperity depends on access to overseas markets, investment opportunities, and raw materials.[83] Economic expansion thus is the prerequisite for avoiding political and social unrest at home.[84] Second, the Open Door's flip side is apprehension about the consequences of "closure"—fear of what would happen to American core values if the United States were denied economic access to key overseas regions. U.S. policymakers believe that the United States would have to adopt a regimented, state-planned economy, including government-imposed restrictions on imports, exports, and capital flows.

The Open Door has always been more than simply an explanation of the role of economic factors in the U.S. grand strategy. Ideology, or what Williams called the "American system," is at the heart of the Open Door.[85] America's domestic economic and political system can be safeguarded only in a world that is sympathetic ideologically to the United States.[86] Specifically, if ideologically hostile states—Nazi Germany, imperial Japan, the Soviet Union—dominated Eurasia, the United States would have to transform itself economically and politically to defend itself. As Ross A. Kennedy observes, the fear that in an ideologically closed world the United States would be hard-pressed "to avoid becoming an authoritarian, militarized state constantly on the verge of war" was articulated by Woodrow Wilson.[87] The danger posed by powerful, ideological states in Eurasia is not the threat of invasion but that "some sort of militaristic tyranny might develop at home as America tried to protect itself from overseas enemies."[88] That is, it would have to become a "garrison state" with a large standing military and a war economy to support it. The United States also would have to adopt "a cynical diplomacy steeped in the cynical pragmatics of power."[89] Finally, if *ideologically* hostile great powers dominated Eurasia and closed it to the United States, it would be left alone in a totalitarian world, and its democratic form of government would be at risk.[90] As Frank Ninkovich observes, while the United States doubtless could survive as an independent great power in such a world, U.S. policymakers have feared it could do so only by redefining itself: "America's self-conception as a nation, its political and economic culture, and the American creed, all these would have to change."[91]

The Open Door blurs the line demarcating domestic politics from foreign policy, because the security of America's core values is seen as being tied not only to the distribution of power in the international system but, even more, to economic expansion abroad and to the outside world's openness to America's liberal ideology. Indeed, the Open Door prescribes that American economic power should be used precisely for the purpose of restructuring the international political system along lines that are congenial with America's ideology.[92] American imperialism has been what Williams calls "the imperialism of idealism," as well as the imperialism of free trade. The Open Door thus married two dominant themes in U.S. history, "a heritage of expansionism and a conviction of mission."[93] Economic expansion has gone hand in hand with the extension globally of American political ideology.[94]

THE ECONOMIC OPEN DOOR AS A GENERATOR OF U.S. STRATEGIC COMMITMENTS ABROAD

The recurring theme of Open Door historians is that of U.S. expansionism, or America's search for opportunity.[95] After fulfilling its manifest destiny by expanding across the North American continent, in the late nineteenth century, with its rising relative economic power pushing it rapidly toward great power status, the United States began to expand abroad. At first, U.S. expansionism was primarily economic. The United States did not seek direct control of territories overseas (except of Hawaii, the Philippines, and Puerto Rico—the latter two acquired as a result of the Spanish-American War). Rather, Open Door expansion was similar to the "informal imperialism" (or "imperialism of free trade") of nineteenth-century Britain.[96] However, the nature of U.S. Open Door expansion began to change once the United States attained great power status. Although the impetus for the United States's Open Door expansion has been economic, it has crucial geopolitical implications. The Open Door always has been a strategy that has aimed to use "America's preponderant economic strength" to extend "American economic and political power throughout the world"—that is, to expand U.S. economic and political influence.[97] Open Door economic interests became the catalyst for expanding America's strategic reach and its ideological ambitions.

U.S. policymakers believe that Open Door U.S. economic expansion requires an international political system conducive to trade and investment and that war and instability are bad for business. Consequently, the United States has sought to create an international political environment that is hos-

33

pitable to openness.[98] To preserve this needed geopolitical stability, the United States has taken on the role of hegemonic stabilizer in regions where it has important economic interests. By the same token, for the Open Door to remain open, other countries need to be stable internally, so that trade will not be disrupted and U.S. foreign direct investments will not be jeopardized by political upheaval or expropriation.[99] The United States has a vested interest in having other countries be run by the "right" kind of governments, that is, those that eschew mercantilistic or autarkic economic policies and embrace the nation's incorporation, or integration, into an open—American-dominated—international economy.[100] As Williams observed, the Open Door disposed Washington to regard as a danger any state that adopted policies "that challenged or limited" American economic expansion.[101]

Starting with its interventions in the Caribbean and Latin America in the 1890s, the United States cracked down hard on revolutionary, nationalist governments that threatened to close their countries to U.S. economic penetration. This set a pattern for U.S. grand strategy. The antidotes to closure are economic development and democratization abroad. And, if that has not worked, as a last resort the Open Door has mandated U.S. intervention (covert or military) to remove or block the coming to power of regimes whose policies are or would be inimical to openness, and to prop up friendly regimes. The Open Door dictated U.S. hostility toward Russia following the 1917 Bolshevik Revolution and to Germany and Japan during the 1930s.[102] U.S. opposition to the Soviet Union, Germany, and Japan also was rooted in the fear that their economic nationalism would close areas under their control to U.S. economic *and* ideological penetration.

THE OPEN DOOR AS A CAUSE
OF PEACE AND STABILITY

The economic Open Door embodies the grand strategic commitment of the United States to an open international economic system. Economic openness is a vital U.S. interest because it is regarded as the keystone both of its economic well-being and domestic political stability. Just as important, however, it has a crucial security dimension, because—drawing on the supposed "lessons of the 1930s"—U.S. policymakers believe that international economic openness is essential to peace and stability in the international political system (or, conversely, that closure and economic nationalism cause war). The economic Open Door promises to deliver three huge benefits for the United States: prosperity, political tranquility at home, *and* peace abroad. In this respect, the economic Open Door tracks with commercial liberalism—a set of propositions developed by liberal international relations scholars about how economic openness purportedly causes peace (and also contributes to the spread of democracy).[103]

The economic Open Door and commercial liberalism make the same three central claims about the grand strategic effects of international economic openness. First, by guaranteeing all states equal access to overseas markets and raw materials, economic openness removes an important cause of international competition and war, because instead of fighting to gain access to markets and resources, states can get rich by trading.[104] Second, because an open international economy helps them become wealthy, states will avoid wars, which disrupt mutually beneficial, wealth-creating, trade. In other words, because they are "interdependent" in an open international economy, states are shooting themselves in the foot economically if they fight one another. Third, the economic Open Door contributes to U.S. security by bringing prosperity to other countries, and thereby bolstering their domestic political stability. At the same time, international economic openness prevents other states from adopting autarkic policies that would close their markets to the United States, and thereby jeopardize U.S. prosperity.

By helping to defuse the causes of war and revolution, the Open Door is supposed to generate the very international order and stability it requires.[105] In Williams's words, "Defined as a goal because of its vital importance for the continued success of the domestic economic system, it was also considered a means to build the empire of peace and prosperity that would secure the world for continued expansion in the years to come."[106] Here, the economic and political Open Doors fuse seamlessly: economic openness fosters political liberalization and democratization abroad. There is a virtuous circle between the economic and political Open Doors, because each reinforces the other. The spread of democracy is perceived as a key U.S. interest because it purportedly reinforces peace, stability, and openness in the international system, and thereby enhances U.S. security. The political Open Door is the manifestation of Woodrow Wilson's liberal approach to international politics, which has bequeathed to the United States a twofold grand strategic legacy. First is the belief that states' domestic political systems determine whether their external policies are peaceful or warlike, that is, that "defects in states cause wars among them."[107] Second is the corollary proposition that the United States can be secure only in a world constituted of states whose domestic political systems mirror that of the United States and that "defects" in other states can be remedied by using U.S. power to transform non-democracies into democracies.[108]

THE OPEN DOOR AND U.S. HEGEMONY

Ultimately, as Williams intimated, the logic of the Open Door—the policy of "virtuous omnipotence" that encompassed U.S. goals and aspirations—led to American hegemony.[109] Indeed, America's Open Door economic, political, and ideological aims could not be realized without U.S. hegemony. Williams argued that the U.S. vision of a postwar international order—conceived by U.S. policymakers during World War II—was based on the assumption of U.S. hegemony (with Britain as a supporting junior partner).[110] Nevertheless, Williams did not explore fully the phenomenon of hegemony, a task left to other Open Door diplomatic historians and to political scientists who have articulated hegemonic stability theory.[111] As they have pointed out, following World War II there are two basic reasons why pursuit of America's Open Door objectives caused the United States to adopt a hegemonic grand strategy.

First, the United States's post-1945 economic and financial dominance meant that it had the wherewithal to create and maintain an open international economic system, and its Open Door economic interests—which are opposed to closure, mercantilism, and policies of national economic self-sufficiency (autarky)—compelled it to do so. Second, after World War II, the United States possessed overwhelming military power, which it wielded to maintain order and stability in the international political system. In its hegemomic role, U.S. hard power forms the bedrock of an open economic system, because it deters other powers from pursuing strategies of closure and protects the international economic system from "external antagonists, internal rebellions, and internecine differences."[112] That is, as a hegemon, the United States took on the role of geopolitical stabilizer (or "umpire" and "cop").[113] In this role, the United States is required to use its military power to stabilize—or pacify—regions that are deemed economically vital. By creating new U.S. interests abroad that had to be defended, the economic Open Door pulled U.S. military power along in its wake. The overseas extension of U.S. economic interests was the catalyst for the extension abroad of U.S. military power.

Distinguishing Extraregional Hegemony Theory from Offensive Realism

At first extraregional hegemony theory may seem like an offensive realist explanation of U.S. grand strategy. Both are theories of hegemonic expansion. Mearsheimer's theory of offensive realism is an elegant explanation of why (some) great powers have powerful incentives to seek (regional) hegemony. Extraregional hegemony theory uses the Open Door to explain why the United States has sought to gain hegemony over regions outside the Western Hemisphere. Mearsheimer's theory holds that great powers act offensively to maximize their power—to gain security—by achieving dominance. Extraregional hegemony theory similarly holds that the United States has acted offensively by striving for extraregional hegemony and to establish itself as the sole great power in the international political system. However, unlike Mearsheimerian offensive realism—which holds that the pursuit of (regional) hegemony by continental Eurasian great powers is a structurally determined phenomenon—extraregional hegemony theory holds that America's pursuit of hegemony in regions outside the Western Hemisphere is primarily driven by Open Door—domestic—considerations and is *not* structurally determined. That is, the Open Door, not objective security considerations, explains why the United States has pursued extraregional hegemony.

Extraregional hegemony theory has some resemblance to a pre-Mearsheimer version of offensive realism, which I call first-wave offensive realism.[114] First-wave offensive realism posits that great powers expand rationally (that is, when the benefits of expansion outweigh the costs) and opportunistically against weaker opponents.[115] Its core claim is that as great powers gain in relative power, they define their interests more expansively, and the perception of threats to their interests similarly expands.[116] Capabilities determine intentions—great powers expand because they have the hard power capabilities to do so.[117] First-wave offensive realism contains an important kernel of truth: great powers harbor external ambitions, which expand as they become more powerful. More to the point, as their relative power increases, great powers develop the hard power capabilities to pursue their ambitions. The marriage of power and ambition is crucial: it's one thing for a state to have external aspirations, it is something else entirely to have the power to realize them. Here the Open Door interpretation converges with American expansion. Since becoming a great power, the United States has used its material capabilities to pursue an Open Door world in which its extraordinarily broad set of economic and ideological aspirations can be realized.

On the other hand, first-wave offensive realism says nothing about the origin or content of a specific great power's external ambitions. Moreover, while predicting that rising great powers expand, it fails to predict whether expansion will be minimal (taking a more active role in international diplomacy), maximal (pursuit of hegemony), or something in-between (building up its military, acquiring overseas bases).[118] The theory is silent about the motives and assumptions of a great power's grand strategy. Applied to U.S. grand strategy, first-wave offensive realism does not shed light on the purposes for which U.S. power has been—and is—used. In contrast, by incorporating domestic variables—the economic Open Door and the political Open Door—to explain U.S. grand strategy, extraregional hegemony theory explains why the United States has sought extraregional hegemony.

* * *

From 1890 until World War II, the United States implemented the Open Door in the Caribbean and Latin America. In this respect America's Open Door grand strategy was like a play that the producers open in Hartford to make sure it is ready for Broadway. Before World War II, the United States "played Hartford" as a regional hegemon. By the time World War II ended it had its hegemonic act down pat and was ready to open on the big stage—in this case, by asserting its hegemony extraregionally in Western Europe. As I demonstrate in my case study in chapters 2–4 the goals the United States set for itself on the Continent following World War II, and the strategy it employed to attain them, show that the Open Door's causal logic inexorably led the United States to establish its hegemony in Europe. As I also show, America's Open Door ambitions—the very backbone of its grand strategy—transcended the cold war, which explains why the United States has remained in Europe following the Soviet Union's collapse and why it continues to act as the Continent's hegemonic stabilizer.

CHAPTER TWO

World War II and the Foundations of American Global Hegemony

The foundations of post-1945 grand strategy of the United States were laid during World War II. Two points emerge clearly. First, the wartime evolution of U.S. postwar grand strategy is in conformity with extraregional hegemony theory's predictions. Second, the key aims of America's *postwar* grand strategy were outlined even as World War II was being fought, well *before* the cold war's onset. During World War II, U.S. policymakers realized that their nation's enormous relative power gains created an unparalleled opportunity to mold the postwar international system, leading to an ambitious conception of America's postwar strategic, economic, and ideological interests. Well before World War II ended, Washington had concluded that U.S. postwar "global" hegemony was the prerequisite for attaining these postwar objectives.

The Interwar Roots of American Global Hegemony

At the end of World War I, the United States was the world's leading economic power and *potentially* the dominant military power. Nevertheless, the conventional wisdom—based on the fact that the United States didn't join the League of Nations and played a limited role in international security affairs—is that during the interwar years the United States followed an "isolationist" foreign policy. Diplomatic historians have shown, however, that during the 1920s the U.S. stance toward Europe was anything but isolationist.[1]

Although the United States did not seek extraregional hegemony on the Continent following World War I, it nevertheless exercised what Frank Costigliola has described as an "awkward dominion" in Europe.[2] The goals of Washington's post–World War I European grand strategy foreshadowed its post–World War II Continental objectives.[3] Believing that America's prosperity was linked to its trade with Europe, Washington wanted to foster an integrated, interdependent European economy. Consequently, because U.S. interests required a politically and economically stable Europe, Washington was the prime mover behind the Dawes and Young plans, which addressed

39

the troublesome issue of German reparations. During the 1920s Washington promoted Germany's economic reconstruction and its political reintegration into Europe. Of course, the United States failed to achieve its post-1919 grand strategic goals through the exercise of awkward dominion.

Why didn't the United States seek extraregional hegemony in Europe after the end of World War I, instead of waiting until 1945? After all, America's relative power had increased dramatically as a result of the war. U.S. policymakers clearly harbored hegemonic inclinations, and they believed that U.S. interests had become extensive enough to be affected by conflict almost anywhere in the world.[4] Moreover, Washington's Open Door economic and ideological interests in Europe were the same in 1919 as they were in 1945. And, given its economic and financial power following World War I, the United States might have been expected to assume the mantle of hegemony in the international economic system, as hegemonic stability theory predicts it should have done. Yet, although the U.S. flexed its muscles occasionally in interwar diplomacy and economic affairs, it remained mostly content with its role as regional hegemon in the Western Hemisphere.

The 1920s and 1930s were a transitional period in which the United States was positioning itself to grasp the mantle of global hegemony that it would seize when World War II ended.[5] Although most of the pieces were in place for the U.S. pursuit of extraregional hegemony, a very important one was not. During the interwar years, there were no structural incentives that might have jolted the United States out of its posture of strategic detachment toward Europe, causing it to seek extraregional hegemony on the Continent. Specifically, after World War I, Europe was still multipolar. Despite the effects of the war, Britain and France, and even Germany and the Soviet Union, remained great powers. This affected U.S. grand strategy in two related ways. First, until the mid-1930s, there was no danger Europe would be closed to the United States either economically or ideologically, because no hostile great power threatened to dominate the Continent. Second, because there were multiple poles of power on the Continent, during the interwar years Europe did not present the United States with an opportunity for advantageous, low-risk expansion. Had the United States sought to expand into Europe during the interwar period, it would have been resisted.[6]

When World War II ended, conditions were far more conducive to U.S. expansion. Because of what Hajo Holborn called "the political collapse of Europe," after World War II Western Europe, in effect, was zero polar.[7] It was a power vacuum into which the United States could expand. Moreover, in 1945 the "stopping power of water" was not an impediment to U.S. hegemony on the Continent. The United States successfully projected massive power across the Atlantic and conquered Western Europe in 1944–45. To be sure, it was a fortuitous coincidence of circumstances that enabled the United States to overcome the stopping power of water.[8] But what the great, pioneering baseball executive Branch Rickey said about the national pastime is just as true for great powers in the realm of grand strategy: it's always better to be lucky than to be good. When World War II ended, the United States already was in Western Europe militarily in a big way. Together, America's overwhelming postwar military and economic power, and the distribution of power between the United States and Western Europe in 1945, afforded the United States the *means* and *opportunity* to engage in hegemonic expansion on the Continent. The Open Door provided a powerful *motive* for it to remain there.

America's Preponderance of Power after World War II

Because it was the only great power to record absolute and relative gains in its wealth and power, the United States emerged from World War II in a position of unprecedented economic ascendance.[9] The United States also emerged from the war predominant militarily. Notwithstanding its purportedly vaunted land power, the Soviet Union was in no position to challenge the United States, because in relative power the United States was "vastly superior" to the Soviet Union.[10] Because of its huge edge in strategic airpower and naval power, only the United States had the capability to project massive military power over great distances. And until 1949 the United States retained a monopoly on nuclear weapons (and a meaningful nuclear superiority well into the early 1960s). Finally, as a result of wartime operations, America's military reach had expanded. Far from being stopped, the United States projected formidable land and naval power across the water into Western Europe (and East Asia).

Even as World War II was ongoing, U.S. policymakers understood that the war's end would find the United States in an overwhelmingly powerful position in international politics. Geopolitical changes caused by the war—especially the acceleration of Britain's decline and the "political collapse" of Europe—would present the United States with favorable opportunities for expansion.[11] Unsurprisingly, even before World War II ended, U.S. policymakers had begun to redefine America's security interests as global in scope, rather than merely regional. This was underscored in President Franklin D. Roosevelt's October 1944 telegrams to British Prime Minister Winston Churchill and Soviet leader Joseph Stalin, which declared that "there is in this global war literally no question, either military or political, in which the United States is not interested."[12] During his 1945 mission to Moscow, presidential envoy Harry Hopkins reiterated to Stalin that America was a *global* power and, thus, legitimately was concerned with events in Soviet-occupied Poland (a country where, before World War II, the United States had no discernible strategic interests), because "the interests of the United States were world wide and not confined to North and South America and the Pacific Ocean."[13] U.S. military planners held a similar view of America's postwar role. As Army Chief of Staff George C. Marshall stated: "It no longer appears practical to continue what we once conceived as hemispheric defense as a satisfactory basis for our security. We are now concerned with the *peace of the entire world*."[14]

Following World War II, U.S. policymakers seized the opportunity—afforded by vastly enhanced U.S. relative power and material capabilities—to control the international system by acting hegemonically and building a postwar order that would advance the political, economic, and ideological interests of the United States. Indeed, this process was under way *before* the U.S. entry into the war as an active belligerent. On New Year's Day 1940, Secretary of State Cordell Hull stated that when peace was restored, the United States would, in its "own best interest," use its "moral and material influence in the direction of creating a stable and enduring world order" so that international politics did not again "assume such a character as to make of them a breeding ground of economic conflict, social insecurity, and, again war."[15]

U.S. postwar planning began in December 1939, when Hull appointed a departmental committee to study the problems of postwar peace and reconstruction.[16] The committee's charge was "to survey the basic principles which should underlie a desirable world order to be evolved after the termination of present hostilities and with primary reference to the best interests of the United States."[17] The United States took the lead in building the foundations of the postwar international order, because of its power—and because policymakers believed it was to America's advantage to do so.[18] Washington's planning for the postwar international system culminated at the 1944 Dumbarton Oaks and Bretton Woods conferences, which laid the groundwork, respectively, for a postwar collective security organization (the United Nations) and the postwar international system of multilateral trade.[19]

The postwar international economic system was the fulcrum of U.S. grand strategy. The Bretton Woods accords reflected the U.S. postwar commitment "to maintain a world economic order based on free trade and currency convertibility."[20] The Bretton Woods system was viewed as the foundation both of the United States's postwar prosperity *and* its security, reflecting the Open Door's multidimensional—economic, strategic, ideological—character.

In building the postwar international economic system, America's economic self-interest obviously was a factor. During World War II, with the Depression still a fresh memory, U.S. officials were concerned with the postwar economic challenges of maintaining full employment and utilizing fully America's vast industrial capacity while converting to a peacetime economy.[21] Washington believed that America's postwar economic health—and its domestic political stability—were tied to its ability to export both capital and goods—especially to Europe. Thus, Washington pushed for the Bretton Woods system, because "stabilization of finance and monetary markets increased demand for American exports, created jobs at home, and safeguarded foreign investment."[22]

At the same time, U.S. planners thought intensively about America's specific postwar Open Door interests on the Continent, and they anticipated the policies that the United States would follow once the war ended. As early as autumn 1939 prominent outside consultants were advising the State Department's postwar planners that America's Open Door interests necessitated postwar Europe to be integrated economically—but *not* politically.[23] Planners feared that—regardless of whether Germany or Britain prevailed—the United States might be shut out of postwar Europe economically, and they were determined to keep the Continent open to U.S. economic penetration.[24] Washington also realized that postwar Europe likely would be devastated, and that to banish the twin nightmares of postwar Europe lapsing into both autarky and political and social turmoil, the United States would have to help resuscitate the Continent economically.[25] Finally, State Department planners—and their outside advisers in the business and financial communities—realized that to achieve America's postwar Open Door aims in Europe, German industry would have to be revived, and Germany somehow would have to be reintegrated politically and economically into Europe.[26] Thus, the outlines of America's postwar Western European grand strategy were taking shape during World War II. The United States had defined the key objectives of its postwar European grand strategy well *before* the cold war cast its shadow over U.S. foreign policy.

Security was the other key factor that impelled the United States to build the Bretton Woods system. Leading U.S. policymakers held a fundamentally Wilsonian view of American security. This was not fuzzy-minded idealism but a coherent—albeit dubious—framework for U.S. grand strategy. In looking ahead to the postwar world, U.S. officials—influenced strongly by the so-called lessons of the past drawn from the 1930s—believed a clear link existed between an open international economic system and a stable and peaceful world order. As Patrick J. Hearden observes:

> American leaders believed that a vast array of commercial restrictions and discriminatory trade practices had contributed both to the onset of the Great Depression and to the start of World War II. They hoped that a freer flow of trade, with all countries having equal access to raw materials and commodity markets around the globe, would provide the foundation for a peaceful and prosperous family of nations.[27]

The most notable proponent of this viewpoint was Cordell Hull.

U.S. policymakers largely blamed the outbreak of World War II on the policies of economic nationalism—autarky, state-directed trading, rival trade blocs—that had been prevalent during the 1930s. According to Hull, "wars were often largely caused by economic rivalry conducted unfairly," as states pursued nationalist policies of territorial conquest, trade advantage, and exclusive control over key raw materials and trade routes.[28] As U.S. policymakers saw it, economic nationalism fueled fierce geopolitical competitions between great powers and, as World War II seemingly demonstrated, invariably led to war. In an open international trading system, however, states would not need to capture resources and markets forcibly. As Hull put it, "unhampered trade dovetailed with peace," and it was impossible to "separate the idea of commerce from the idea of war and peace."[29] The United States pushed for an open international economy, because Washington feared, as a February 1944 State Department memo put it, that its failure to do so would cause a

> revival, in more intense form, of the international economic warfare which characterized the twenties and thirties. The development of sound economic relations is closely related to security. . . . Past experience makes clear that close and enduring cooperation in the political field must rest on a sound foundation of cooperation in economic matters.[30]

In Washington, "past experience" also led officials to see a link between economic nationalism and the kind of totalitarianism and militarism that had taken root in Germany and Japan before World War II.

In fact, U.S. policymakers believed there was a vicious cycle at work. Economic nationalism depressed world prosperity, and economic distress, in turn, caused domestic political turmoil, which allowed totalitarians and militarists to seize power. As Hull put it, "A people driven to desperation by unemployment, want, and misery is a constant threat of disorder and chaos, both internal and external. It falls easy prey to dictators and desperados."[31] Internal upheaval caused instability in the international political system, because it spawned revolutions and wars of aggression.[32] Washington also regarded economic nationalism as a source of ideological contagion that threatened America's security—which was seen to rest on both political liberalism and an open international economy. As Hull declared in a November 1938 speech, "I know that the withdrawal by a nation from orderly trade relations with the rest of the world inevitably leads to regimentation of all phases of national life, to the suppression of human rights, and all too frequently to preparations for war and a provocative attitude toward other nations."[33] The United States would prevent a replay of the 1930s by fostering an open postwar international economic system. It would strengthen the domestic political position of elites in other countries that, both for reasons of economic interest and ideology, would pursue foreign and economic policies compatible with U.S. interests.

In addition to spurring the United States to lay the foundations for an open postwar international economic system, America's war-induced relative power gains also prompted a "dramatic change in the military's definition of U.S. security requirements."[34] The pre-1939 doctrines of continental, or hemispheric, defense were discarded. "After 1945," Mark Stoler observes, "military planners defined U.S. security in global and indivisible terms whereby events anywhere in the world were considered potentially threatening and therefore of concern to the armed forces."[35] During World War II—*before* the Soviet Union became the dominant factor in U.S. military planning—U.S. strategists had concluded that defending its global postwar interests meant that America's strategic frontiers would have to pushed far beyond the Western Hemisphere. Already looking ahead to possible postwar conflicts, top military officers argued that "we prefer to fight our wars in someone else's territory," and—as they have done on and off ever since—they flirted with adopting preemptive or preventive military postures.[36] U.S. planners concluded that the United States needed a far-flung postwar network of air bases in the Atlantic (Iceland and Greenland), North and West Africa, the Middle East, and the Pacific.[37] These bases would allow the American homeland to be defended in depth and serve as staging points to project U.S. power into Eurasia.[38] America's postwar network of overseas air bases, and transit and landing rights, was intended to ensure that the United States would not be stopped by water from projecting its power into Europe, East Asia, and the Middle East to prevent any potential rival—whether a resurgent Germany or Japan, or the Soviet Union—from attaining hegemony in Europe or Asia, or threatening America's Open Door interests by cutting off access to Eurasian markets and raw materials.[39]

As World War II drew to a close, U.S. expansion was reflected in a whole new set of interests as the nation geographically extended its military, political, and economic reach. For example, U.S. Open Door muscle flexing to bring about "regime change" was nothing new in the Caribbean, Mexico, or Central America. But it was new in Western Europe, where, after World War II, the United States—for Open Door reasons—shaped political outcomes, especially in France and Italy, to prevent Communist parties from coming to power.[40] Fears that revolutionary upheaval in Europe would bring Communist governments to power *long preceded* the cold war: as early as fall 1939, U.S. policymakers "feared that socialists or communists might come to power and close the doors of the continent against U.S. commerce."[41] In furtherance of its policy, the United States used economic assistance, political support for noncommunist parties of the democratic Center and Center Left, propaganda, co-optation of intellectual elites (especially on the democratic Left), and covert actions by intelligence and political operatives. The degree of U.S. involvement in postwar Western European politics was unprecedented; not only had U.S. interests grown but so had the nonmilitary means at Washington's disposal to defend them.

During and immediately after World War II, for economic and strategic reasons, the United States for the first time projected its power and influence into the Middle East.[42] Oil drove America's Middle East involvement (though the United States also wanted to penetrate the region commercially and obtain the use of airfields for military and civilian purposes). The need to protect U.S. access to Middle Eastern oil generated a new postwar set of security and political commitments.[43] During the war, key U.S. officials recognized that control of oil would be an important postwar strategic interest. As Navy Secretary James Forrestal wrote to Secretary of State Edward Stettinius Jr. in December 1944:

> The prestige and hence influence of the United States is in part related to the wealth of the Government and its nationals in terms of oil resources, foreign as well as domestic. It is assumed, therefore, that the bargaining power of the United States in international conferences involving vital materials like oil and such problems as aviation, shipping, island bases, and international security agreements relating to the disposition of armed forces and facilities, will depend in some degree upon the retention by the United States of such oil resources.[44]

During the war, as America's stakes in the Arab Middle East deepened, Washington also came to regard Greece, Turkey, and Iran as strategically important.[45]

In 1946–47 America's growing involvement in the eastern Mediterranean and the Middle East was driven both by its interest in Middle Eastern oil and by its fears of the Soviet Union. Distrust of Soviet intentions led the United States to establish a permanent naval presence in the Mediterranean (in fall 1946) and, in 1947, to provide military and economic assistance to Greece and Turkey. Moreover, as U.S.-Soviet tensions escalated, the Middle East assumed a growing military importance as a base to wage a strategic bombing campaign against the Soviet Union in the event of war.[46] Nevertheless, even without the Soviet threat, the United States almost certainly would have been drawn into these areas.[47] America's regional strategic objectives—gaining control over Middle Eastern and Persian Gulf oil, and establishing the United States (at Britain's expense) as the region's dominant power—were fixed during World War II, well before U.S. policymakers became concerned about the Soviet threat.[48]

U.S. Unipolar Grand Strategy in the 1940s

As John Lewis Gaddis has observed, "Few historians would deny, today, that the United States did expect to dominate the international scene after World War II, and that it did so well before the Soviet Union emerged as a clear and present antagonist."[49] In other words, the United States sought extraregional hegemony. Even during World War II, U.S. policymakers were laying the grand strategic foundations of a postwar international system in which U.S. power would be predominant. Even during World War II, and its immediate aftermath, the United States aspired to be the preponderant power in the international system, and to make sure that there were no rivals that could challenge it.[50]

America's most fundamental war aim during World War II was to reduce *permanently* the power of Germany and Japan.[51] The U.S. goal of preventing Germany and Japan from re-nationalizing their security and foreign policies—in plain English, keeping them down geopolitically—was in place before the cold war, and transcended it once it began. Washington was determined "to prevent a recrudescence of German militarism and to see that the Germans never again menace the other peoples of Europe and the world."[52] Hence, the United States would not "accept any arrangement, provisional or permanent, which would permit Germany to re-emerge as a military power in its own right."[53] Similarly, even in 1954, when Washington had come to accept that cold war exigencies might make Japanese rearmament necessary, Japan still was to be constrained by U.S. power. U.S. air and naval dominance in East Asia would serve as "adequate safeguards against the recrudescence of Japanese military power as an aggressive force."[54] To attain global hegemony, the United States was equally concerned with reducing the power of its allies.[55] And, notwithstanding the wartime myths about the Anglo-American "special relationship," during World War II Washington took dead aim at Britain. The United States was determined to knock Britain from its great power perch and remove it as a possible postwar peer competitor, thereby completing the interwar period's unfinished geopolitical transition from British to American global hegemony.

Here, Washington employed a two-pronged strategy. The Treasury Department sought to coerce the British into accepting a postwar international financial system based on currency convertibility that would make Britain financially dependent on the United States. The State Department sought to wrest control of key raw materials sources—like Middle Eastern oil—from Britain and to pry open the British Empire's protected markets by compelling London to abandon its imperial trade system.[56]

The predatory nature of U.S. economic strategy is illustrated by America's wartime policy in the Middle East, where Washington sought to replace Britain as the dominant regional power. For example, the United States sought an oil concession in Iran, Britain's most important source of overseas oil, while keeping British oil interests out of Saudi Arabia, which was regarded as an American preserve.[57] The suspicions engendered by U.S. attempts to expand its influence in Iran led Roosevelt and Churchill to exchange the famous "sheep's eyes" telegrams, in which each asserted—disingenuously on the American side—that they had no designs on the other's Middle Eastern oil interests.[58]

As Robert Hathaway observes, "The vast oil reserves of the area provided incentive enough for an expanded role there, but the authorities in Washington were also interested in postwar military and commercial air rights, communications routes, and the possibility of new trade relationships."[59] Indicative of U.S. intentions was the 1944 intelligence gathering mission of Maj. Carleton S. Coon of the Office of Strategic Services (the OSS was the key wartime U.S. intelligence agency). In his report, Coon presciently argued that the United States would have three vital postwar interests in the region: "oil, Airbases, and Future Markets." He concluded that, given these interests, the United States would have a postwar "security problem" in the Middle East and that "this means in particular *security from our present allies,* almost all of whom have fingers in the Moslem pie and who have shown themselves particularly anxious to keep us out."[60]

During the war, the United States also sought to crack open the British Empire's protected markets. As Richard Aldrich comments:

> [This American interest] was given a heightened profile by the sudden arrival of numerous Americans in regions such as South and South East Asia where, prior to the war, the American presence had been relatively small. The course of the war awakened Washington to the commercial importance of a region with raw materials and with a large population which constituted actual or potential markets of great value.[61]

Throughout the war, Washington used the mantra of "anticolonialism" as a bludgeon against London's imperial preference trade system.[62] The United States was equally interested in gaining the economic and political upper hand over London in markets that were not part of the British imperial trade system.[63]

Washington's belief that London's imperial trade practices were a barrier to U.S. economic ambitions predated World War II. During the 1930s, the imperial preference system (adopted at the 1932 Imperial Economic Conference at Ottawa) was a constant source of friction in Anglo-American relations.[64] World War II afforded the United States the economic weapons to open the door to imperial markets, capture Britain's nonimperial export markets, and transform Britain into a financial ward of the United States.[65] Washington used what Robert Hathaway aptly describes as "coercive liberality" to force Britain to conform its policy to American wishes.[66]

Article VII of the Master Lend-Lease Agreement was a particularly powerful club. U.S. Lend-Lease aid enabled Britain to prosecute the war against the Axis, but it also "became the main instrument of American foreign economic policy, and the main source of grievance to its wartime ally."[67] To receive Lend-Lease assistance, London was forced to endorse the U.S. Open Door vision of a nondiscriminatory, multilateral postwar international economic order. Lend-Lease was not a "free gift"; Washington expected repayment, not in money or goods "but in a commitment to America's conception of the post-war world economy."[68] More important, the Master Lend-Lease Agreement imposed stringent wartime limits on the foreign exchange and gold reserves London could accumulate—a serious matter for a nation that would be dependent on imports of raw materials and foodstuffs for its postwar economic recovery—and also limited British exports.[69]

As Robert Skidelsky accurately observes, during the 1941 Anglo-American Lend-Lease negotiations, and later during the Bretton Woods talks, both London and Washington were "jockeying for post-war position."[70] In their discussions with the Americans about the postwar international economic system, the British were ever mindful of the straitened economic circumstances they would face at the end of the war. To pay off its debts, Britain would need to export, but its ability to do so would be crimped severely by its foreign exchange difficulties (which would hamper its ability to import the raw materials its export industries needed). Given the stark economic realities it would face when the war ended, Britain was wary about accepting Washington's recipe of open markets, nondiscrimination, and currency convertibility. Although London accepted the American vision of the postwar economy in principle as a long-term goal, it argued that Britain needed a postwar adjustment period to recover its economic and financial footing before free trade, nondiscrimination, and convertibility could be adopted as the bases of its own economic policy.[71]

At Bretton Woods, a compromise seemingly was struck between the United States and Britain. In return for Britain's assent to Bretton Woods, Washington gave London an escape clause allowing it to impose trade restrictions and foreign exchange controls if its postwar balance of payments problems persisted. The United States also promised to make a substantial postwar loan to London. During the Anglo-American loan negotiations, the United States reneged on the key commitments it had made to London at the time of Bretton Woods. The Anglo-American loan negotiations were contentious from the beginning, not least because the United States insisted that the loan be repaid with interest. London believed the loan should be interest-free in recognition of Britain's disproportionate economic sacrifices for the Allied cause. British officials regarded the U.S. demand for interest as "usury." The negotiations almost collapsed when the United States demanded as a loan condition that London abrogate the Bretton Woods escape clauses. Despite their prescient forebodings about the economic repercussions, the British were forced to promise that import controls would be ended (at the end of 1946) and that sterling would become freely convertible (as of mid-1947). The British were forced to accept Washington's terms, because Britain desperately needed the money and lacked the power to resist U.S. demands.[72]

During World War II, London entertained few illusions about U.S. intentions. The U.S. challenge to Britain's economic interests was clear, and monitoring it was one of the primary wartime tasks of British intelligence.[73] Lord (John Maynard) Keynes, Britain's chief negotiator for Lend-Lease, Bretton Woods, and the postwar loan, tried to ensure that U.S. wartime assistance did not become a lever to reduce postwar Britain to an American satellite.

"America," he said, "must not be allowed to pick out the eyes of the British Empire."[74] Throughout the war, his goal was to secure "the retention of enough assets to leave us capable of independent action" in the postwar world.[75] He was not successful.

David Dimbleby and David Reynolds have suggested that at World War II's end, the United States did not have to wrest power from Britain. A commanding postwar preeminence, they say, just fell into America's lap as a result of Britain's weakness.[76] Historians have documented amply that the "collapse of British power" had been ongoing since the latter part of the nineteenth century—a fact well understood during World War II by U.S. policymakers.[77] Nevertheless, Washington wasn't going to take any chances. To fulfill its aspirations of postwar global hegemony, the United States needed to ensure that Britain would be an adjunct, rather than a rival, to American power. Thus, as Gabriel Kolko observes, "it was crucial, in the American view, that Britain emerge from the war neither too weak nor too strong, but amenable to American direction on the larger issues."[78] Warren F. Kimball has observed that Washington was "remarkably willing and even eager" to use its economic power to break the British Empire and "obtain British compliance with [the U.S.] view of how the world's economy should be structured."[79] This coercive use of U.S. economic might was intended to achieve a *geopolitical* result: in the postwar world, "the leverage of American economic strength" was used—Keynes's hopes notwithstanding—precisely to deprive London of the freedom "to act independently."[80]

* * *

World War II produced a major change in the distribution of global power. The combined effect of the increase in America's absolute power and the decline of Britain, France, Germany, and Japan produced a dramatic gain in U.S. relative power, and led to the expansion of U.S. interests and ambitions militarily, politically, economically, and ideologically. During World War II and immediately thereafter, the United States reached for global hegemony. U.S. officials held a "unipolar" conception of America's strategic interests, and were determined to throttle Germany and Japan and to transform Britain from a world power into an appendage of the United States. Of course, there was one other obstacle to America's postwar hegemonic ambitions: the Soviet Union.

CHAPTER THREE

U.S. Grand Strategy and the Soviet Union, 1945–1953

When World War II ended, the Soviet Union was the only obstacle to U.S. global hegemony, and in the first postwar decade Washington's principal grand strategic goal was to secure that hegemony by removing the Soviet Union as a peer competitor. The United States emerged from the war in a position of unparalleled geopolitical preeminence, and the scope of America's interests expanded concomitantly, and, indeed, had done so while the war still was ongoing. Once the war ended, Washington's perceptions of the Soviet threat to those interests began to grow. As a result, U.S. and Soviet interests collided (or were perceived to collide by American officials) in Europe, the Middle East, and Northeast Asia, which contributed to the intensification of postwar Soviet-American tensions that culminated in the cold war.

I begin this chapter with a brief overview of the long-running debate about the cold war's origins. Using extraregional hegemony theory as an interpretative tool, I bring a fresh perspective to this controversy. To illustrate the expansionist dimensions of U.S. grand strategy, I examine three aspects of America's Soviet policy in the decade following 1945. First, I explore the U.S. attempt to gain the Soviet Union's acceptance of an "open sphere" in Eastern Europe. Second, I describe Washington's aim of eliminating the Soviet Union as a rival by rolling back its Eastern European empire, transforming its domestic political system, and reducing its external power. Finally, I discuss Washington's decision to divide Germany rather than seeking agreement with Moscow on German unification.

Who (or What) "Caused" the Cold War?

Few subjects have engaged American diplomatic historians and political scientists as deeply as that of the cold war's origins. The cold war orthodoxy, and the neo-orthodoxy that emerged after the cold war's end, put the blame for the cold war squarely on the Kremlin's shoulders. These two schools depict the cold war as a Manichaean struggle in which—thanks to America's exer-

tions—freedom and democracy triumphed over the Soviet Union's evil, totalitarian political system.[1] The orthodox and neo-orthodox explanations of the
cold war's origins share a common flaw: the United States is left out of the
picture. Orthodox and neo-orthodox scholars tell us an awful lot about Soviet grand strategic aims and ambitions (or at least those scholars' *interpretations* thereof) and about the effects (or what they *claim* were the effects) of
Communist ideology and Stalin's personality on Soviet policy. In their story
of the cold war, the United States is a passive actor—responding only in self-
defense when provoked by Soviet actions. These accounts of the cold war's
origins don't tell us much at all about *America*'s grand strategic aims and ambitions, and how these were shaped by U.S. policymakers' Open Door worldview.[2] They are similarly silent in explaining how Moscow's strategy was
shaped by Washington's grand strategic choices.

This, of course, is a simplistic way of looking at international politics. It
takes two to tango. Thus, for structural realists, the post–World War II rivalry
between the United States and the Soviet Union, in itself, requires little explanation. In the bipolar world that existed after 1945, it was inevitable that
there would be competition, and friction, between the international system's
only two great powers.[3] For neorealists, neither the Soviet Union nor the
United States "caused" this competition. Rather, it was determined structurally. What was not foreordained, however, was the form this rivalry would
take.

As we know, the cold war became a highly militarized, ideologically viru-
lent, and global struggle. It hardly is self-evident that it had to be so, however.
"Within a bipolar structure of power," Deborah Welch Larson has written,
"the United States and the Soviet Union could have defined their relationship in a variety of ways."[4] Postwar relations between Washington and
Moscow might have evolved in the more traditional mold of great power relations, in which competition is dampened by mutual restraint, legitimate security interests are accommodated, and spheres of influence are recognized.
In the 1945–47 period, some U.S. officials and foreign policy commentators
urged that Washington adhere to traditional approaches to great power
diplomacy in its dealings with the Moscow.[5] Instead, after 1945, America's
pursuit of extraregional hegemony exacerbated tensions with the Soviet
Union. Because of their extravagance, and because they pushed the United
States to seek extraregional hegemony, America's Open Door–driven grand
strategic ambitions foreclosed the possibility that the Soviet-American competition could be modulated.[6]

Could the Cold War Have Been Avoided?

Would it have been possible to manage the post-1945 Soviet-American rivalry
as a traditional great power rivalry? The unsatisfying orthodox/neo-ortho-

dox answer is that "as long as Stalin was running the Soviet Union" the cold war was "inevitable."[7] International politics, however, is not a morality play. Liberalism's conceits notwithstanding, there is no compelling evidence that states' external policies are determined by the nature of their domestic political systems. Even states led by tyrannical dictators, and with bad domestic systems, often pursue realpolitik foreign policies, and, perforce, relations with such states can be managed by the traditional techniques of great power diplomacy.

It is far from clear that Moscow's policies after 1945 were the outward projection of either Stalin's megalomania or the Soviet Union's totalitarian domestic political system. Indeed, as Walter LaFeber observes, "However Stalin acted inside Russia, where he had total control, in his foreign policy during 1941–1946 he displayed realism, a careful calculation of forces, and a diplomatic finesse that undercut any attempt to explain away his actions as paranoid."[8] Although there is still much we do *not* know from the Soviet archives, enough is known for leading historians to have concluded that the Kremlin's policy in the immediate postwar years was cautious and ambiguous, not expansionist or aggressive.[9] Stalin and the Soviet leadership were well aware that the Soviet Union's catastrophic wartime losses and the enormous disparity between U.S. and Soviet material capabilities counseled against pursuing a confrontational policy toward the United States.

As great powers usually do, in the 1945–47 period the Soviet Union adopted a mixed policy of cooperation and competition.[10] To be sure, the Soviets pursued traditional Russian imperial interests in the eastern Mediterranean and Iran; sought security in Eastern Europe by clamping down on Poland, Romania, and Bulgaria; and competed with Washington for influence in Germany. Yet at the same time, as Melvyn Leffler wrote in the early 1990s, the Soviets

> demobilized their armies and withdrew from important areas. In 1945 and 1946 they pulled their troops out of northern Norway and Bornholm, Denmark, established acceptable governments in Austria and Finland, allowed free elections in Hungary and Czechoslovakia, discouraged revolutionary action in France, Italy, and Greece, endeavored to maintain acceptable relations with the Chinese nationalists, and evacuated their forces, however belatedly, from Iran and Manchuria.[11]

Simply put, in World War II's aftermath Soviet behavior across the chessboard did not reflect the orthodox/neo-orthodox caricature (shared by many U.S. decision makers following World War II) of the Soviet Union as a predatory, aggressive, ideologically motivated state bent on attaining world domination.

The wartime, and immediate postwar, debates in Washington about U.S.-Soviet relations pitted two diametrically opposed perceptions of the Soviet

Union. What Daniel Yergin has called the "Yalta axioms"—which were embraced by President Franklin D. Roosevelt—"downplayed the role of ideology and the foreign policy consequences of authoritarian domestic practices, and instead saw the Soviet Union as behaving like a traditional Great Power within the international system, rather than trying to overthrow it."[12] The Yalta axioms postulated that postwar great power collaboration between Moscow and Washington, based on a spheres of influence approach, was possible. Conversely, the "Riga axioms"—which viewed "the Soviet Union as a world revolutionary state, denying the possibilities of coexistence, committed to unrelenting ideological warfare, powered by a messianic drive for world mastery"—held that the Kremlin could be handled only by resisting implacably its expansionist designs.[13]

Following Roosevelt's death, the Truman administration flirted briefly in 1945 with the Yalta axioms.[14] However, President Harry S Truman repudiated Secretary of State James F. Byrnes's attempt to establish a cooperative relationship with the Soviets at the December 1945 Moscow foreign ministers conference, and during the first three months of 1946 Washington decisively embraced the so-called cold war consensus based on the Riga axioms.[15] First articulated in U.S. diplomat George F. Kennan's "Long Telegram" and in former British prime minister Winston S. Churchill's equally significant "Iron Curtain" speech delivered at Fulton College, Missouri, the cold war consensus was synthesized in the September 1946 report to Truman by his advisers Clark Clifford and George Elsey.[16] The Clifford/Elsey report portrayed the Soviet Union as a rapacious power bent on world domination, with which the adjustment of conflicting interests through diplomacy was well-neigh impossible, because "the language of military power" was the only language that Moscow understood.[17] The United States should meet the Soviet threat, they recommended, by flexing its military and economic muscles and making "it unmistakably clear that action contrary to *our conception of a decent world order* will redound to the disadvantage" of the Soviet Union.[18] From 1946 on, U.S. policymakers translated the Riga axioms underlying the cold war consensus into a grand strategy that defined U.S. interests expansively; wove together geopolitical, military, economic, and ideological concerns; and aimed at maximizing America's relative power vis-à-vis the Soviet Union.

The United States's core objectives toward the Soviet Union reflected the marriage of geopolitics and the Open Door—a marriage consummated during World War II, *before* the Soviet Union came to be perceived by U.S. officials as an adversary. The paramount threat to American interests—identified by U.S. officials as early as the period between the German invasion of Poland (September 1939) and the fall of France (June 1940)—was that the outcome of the war would cause the United States to be locked out of Europe economically either as a result of a German victory or the coming to power of Communist parties as a result of political and social upheaval following a prolonged war. Europe's closure, it was feared, not only would affect America's prosperity but conceivably could transform its own domestic system by forcing the adoption of an autarkic, state-planned economy.[19] Thus, even before the United States entered the Second World War as an active belligerent, Washington determined that its main strategic goal was to prevent either a single, ideologically hostile power or a coalition of ideologically hostile states from dominating Eurasia. In this sense, America's postwar grand strategy was "counterhegemonic," but with an important Open Door twist that reflected Washington's fears about the economic and ideological ramifications of the Continent's closure to the United States.

As its policy toward Moscow evolved in 1945–46, the United States wanted to maintain a favorable distribution of power by preventing Eurasian industrial power (western Germany, Western Europe, and Japan) and natural resources (Middle Eastern oil, Southeast Asian raw materials) from falling under Moscow's control.[20] U.S. policymakers feared that "with these resources, the Soviet Union would be able to overcome its chronic economic weakness, achieve defense in depth, and challenge American power—perhaps even by military force."[21] The U.S. goal of preventing Moscow from dominating Eurasia may appear, at first blush, to track with traditional interpretations, like John Mearsheimer's, of the counterhegemonic stance of the United States toward Europe. In fact, it was far more ambitious than that. Had Washington's objective simply been to keep Eurasia's power centers out of Moscow's hands, it could have fostered the reemergence of Western Europe (and/or Germany) and Japan as *independent* poles of power in the international system; that is, as actors under neither Washington's nor Moscow's control. The counterhegemonic denial of Eurasian resources to the Soviet Union could have been attained through an offshore balancing strategy based on multipolarity. However, following World War II the United States had a far more ambitious set of grand strategic objectives.

In the immediate post–World War II years Western Europe, Germany, and Japan were too debilitated from the war to reclaim their prewar roles as independent poles of power, but, they might have done so within a relatively short period of time. Washington, however, rejected this, even as a long-term alternative. One reason was the fear that Western Europe, Germany, and Japan would bandwagon with the Soviet Union. More important, however, America's main grand strategic aim was to secure its global hegemony by bringing these potential poles of power into its own orbit and thereby prevent them from emerging as challengers to U.S. predominance. The United States wanted to harness—or, as Leffler puts it, "co-opt"—their power in furtherance of its own grand strategic objectives.[22] By integrating "Western Europe, West Germany, and Japan into a U.S. led orbit," the United States aimed to secure its "preponderant influence in the international system."[23] American strategy reflected Washington's abhorrence of traditional multipolar great power politics, which it regarded as inimical to U.S. interests. U.S. policymakers were committed to preventing the "re-nationalization" of Japan, Western Europe, and Germany, and to ensuring that they did not adopt independent ("neutralist" or "third force") foreign and security policies.[24]

How well founded was Washington's fear of postwar Eurasia's closure? Here, to understand why Soviet-American frictions mushroomed into the cold war, it is necessary to disentangle the objective threat to U.S. interests posed by Moscow's policies from Washington's own grand strategic ambitions. Throughout 1945, the prevailing view in Washington was that the Kremlin's policies in Eastern Europe, the eastern Mediterranean, and Manchuria were essentially defensive.[25] However, the cold war consensus that took root in Washington in early 1946 reflected a dramatic change in U.S. perceptions. This shift cannot be explained, however, by any *objective* change in Soviet capabilities and intentions: "American assessments of Soviet short-term military intentions had not altered; Soviet military capabilities had not significantly increased; and Soviet foreign policy positions had not changed."[26] During the 1945–1948 period, the risk of Soviet military action in Western Europe was, as U.S. policymakers recognized, virtually nil.[27] Moreover, there is plenty of evidence that during this period, Moscow realized both its weakness vis-à-vis the United States and that the Soviet Union "could not sustain the stress of another war."[28]

Although Washington did not fear Soviet military action, it did fear that the Soviets would gain control over Eurasia by capitalizing on the geopolitical, economic, and social dislocations caused by World War II. U.S. policymakers knew the Kremlin was not the cause of postwar turbulence, but they feared that Moscow would exploit it.[29] In particular, Washington feared that Communist parties would come to power by taking advantage of Western Europe's postwar malaise, and that nationalists in colonies throughout the world would harness Communist ideology to throw off Western rule. Certainly U.S. officials worried about these possibilities, because they postulated the subservience of local Communist parties to Moscow, and they also feared that key parts of Eurasia would bandwagon with the Soviet Union rather than balancing against it. Importantly, however, U.S. apprehensions about the effects of postwar turmoil would have existed even if there had been no perceived Soviet threat. After all, during the twentieth century's first four decades, it had become abundantly clear that Washington believed that its Open Door interests were gravely menaced by political instability, social revolution, and nationalism—even more so, when combined. No doubt, following World War II, the Soviet Union exacerbated Washington's fears in this regard, but they would have existed anyway (as, indeed, they existed even in 1939–40—and in 1917–1918).

The fact that America's basic—Open Door—grand strategic interests had been set in place before the cold war illuminates an important point: changed U.S. assessments of the Soviet Union from 1946 onward had less to do with Moscow's intentions and aspirations than with Washington's.[30] The scope of U.S. interests expanded greatly during World War II, and, consequently, U.S. policymakers defined the threats to those interests very broadly. There was an important paradox at the heart of U.S. grand strategy: "the growth of American power did not lead to a greater sense of assuredness, but rather to an enlargement of the range of perceived threats that must urgently be confronted."[31] Washington did not come to view the Soviet Union as "a threat" because of Moscow's intentions or capabilities—or its actions. As Leffler observes, U.S. policymakers simply "disregarded numerous signs of Soviet weakness, moderation, and circumspection."[32] For the United States, the Soviet Union came to be seen as a threat simply because it existed.

In the 1946–48 period, the Open Door and geopolitics converged and caused the United States to define its interests "in terms of Western control and American access to the resources of Eurasia outside the Soviet sphere."[33] To accomplish this objective, the United States embarked on what Leffler describes as a "risk-taking" grand strategy. Rather than being driven by the need to counter Soviet hegemony, this strategy aimed at establishing America's own postwar hegemony—especially in Western Europe. The outlines of America's early postwar grand strategy are well known. Militarily, the United States ringed the Soviet Union with strategic airbases, and, in 1948, it entered into the negotiations that culminated in 1949 in the North Atlantic Treaty. The March 1947 Truman Doctrine bolstered America's interests by extending military and economic assistance to Greece and Turkey. Most important, on the Continent the United States set out to stabilize Western Europe politically and economically through the Marshall Plan—which also required the United States to resuscitate West Germany's economy and integrate it into a U.S.-dominated Western European security and economic framework.

U.S. policymakers understood that their grand strategy would heighten Moscow's insecurity and provoke Soviet counterreactions.[34] For example, U.S. officials apprehended correctly that initiatives like the Marshall Plan— and the absorption of an economically revived West Germany into a U.S.-dominated Western Europe—would cause the Soviets to respond *defensively* by tightening their grip on Eastern Europe and eastern Germany.[35] And this is exactly what happened. For Stalin, the Marshall Plan—which prompted the establishment of the Cominform (September 1947) and the consolidation of Soviet control over Eastern Europe—was "a watershed," because he saw it as a "large-scale attempt by the United States to gain lasting and preeminent influence in Europe."[36] Scott D. Parrish points out that until summer 1947 Stalin still wanted to pursue a policy of detente toward the United States. "The Marshall Plan, however, radically changed Stalin's calculus," Parrish observes, "and led him to shift away from this more moderate line and to adopt a strategy of confrontational unilateral action to secure Soviet interests."[37] The Marshall Plan was perceived as triply threatening by the Kremlin. First, it was perceived as creating an anti-Soviet bloc by incorporating a resurgent Germany into the U.S. system.[38] Second, Washington structured it to prevent the Soviet Union from partaking in the Plan's benefits.[39] Third, and most important, it seemed intended to facilitate attainment of U.S. Open Door objectives in Eastern Europe. The Soviets reacted defensively to the Marshall Plan because they perceived it as "an attempt to penetrate the economies of eastern Europe, dilute the Soviet sphere, and reorient them westward."[40] U.S. officials similarly realized that the creation of a separate West German state and the North Atlantic Treaty also would be seen as threatening by the Soviets. Indeed, the Soviet blockade of Berlin was a defensive reaction to Washington's decision to proceed with currency reform in the western occupation zones, a measure the Kremlin rightly saw as step toward Germany's division and western Germany's incorporation into a U.S.-led Western European bloc.[41]

In the 1946–1949 period, U.S. officials confidently moved forward with this strategy because they understood that U.S. power dominated the postwar international system, and that, accordingly, the Soviet Union would not forcibly oppose the United States.[42] Fortified by its immense military and economic capabilities, the United States embraced a very broad conception of U.S. national interests, including

> a strategic sphere of influence within the Western Hemisphere, domination of the Atlantic and Pacific oceans, an extensive system of outlying bases to enlarge the strategic frontier and project American power, an even more extensive system of transit rights to facilitate the conversion of commercial air bases to military use, access to the resources and markets of most of Eurasia, denial of those resources to a prospective enemy, and the maintenance of nuclear superiority.[43]

It is hard to disagree with Leffler's conclusion that, to understand how the cold war began, "the breadth of the American conception of national security that emerged between 1945 and 1948" must be appreciated.[44] Indeed, following World War II Washington effectively equated national security with American global hegemony: "American leaders—moved by a traditional missionary impulse, convinced of their global responsibility, full of the self-confidence that comes of success, fundamentally unhurt by war in a wounded world—eagerly reached for their mandate of heaven."[45] In defining American objectives as broadly as they did, however, U.S. officials left very little room in their vision of the postwar world for the Soviet Union's legitimate great power security interests, or even for its survival as a peer competitor of the United States.

Keeping Eastern Europe's Door Open

If the United States had wanted postwar relations with the Kremlin to unfold along the lines of traditional great power diplomacy, Eastern Europe was the place were it should have implemented such a policy. This was a region in which Moscow, extending back into czarist times, had unquestionable strategic interests—and in which the United States had none. Indeed Roosevelt, Truman, and their senior advisers all recognized—at least up to a point— that the Soviet Union had legitimate security interests in Eastern Europe.[46] Moreover, even as World War II was being fought, policymakers in Washington understood that, when the war ended, the Soviets would control the region and the United States would have limited leverage to influence postwar events there.[47] Yet, when the war did end, the United States wanted Eastern Europe to remain open to American economic and ideological penetration. Washington's hopes for establishing a cooperative postwar relationship with the Soviet Union collided head-on with its stance on Eastern Europe.[48]

Washington and Moscow defined Soviet interests in Eastern Europe very differently. The United States acknowledged—or so the argument has been made—that the Kremlin had a legitimate interest in ensuring that the Eastern European states followed external policies that would bolster Soviet security.[49] However, Washington did not believe that Moscow's security needs required the Soviet Union to exercise control over the region's domestic political systems—hence, U.S. opposition to granting the Soviets an "exclusive"—closed—sphere of influence in the region. On the other hand, Moscow believed that its external security could be guaranteed only by maintaining firm internal control over the Eastern European states.[50] In 1945– 1947 the Truman administration put the onus on the Kremlin to reconcile Soviet security requirements with America's Open Door interests and ideals.[51] In doing so the United States ran the risk of causing the very rupture with Moscow that U.S. officials claimed they wished to avoid.

The United States was *not* prepared to use military force to compel the Soviet Union to accept an open sphere of influence in postwar Eastern Europe. But, in contrast to FDR, Truman and his senior advisers came to believe that the United States possessed diplomatic, economic, and political options to weaken the Soviet Union's stranglehold on that region and to keep it open to American influence.[52] After July 1945, U.S. officials believed that the shadow of the U.S. monopoly in atomic weapons would loom over postwar U.S.-Soviet relations.[53] In short, U.S. policymakers believed that the United States was strong and the Soviet Union was weak, and that taking a firm stance would create a cooperative postwar relationship on terms largely defined by the United States.[54]

The United States made several efforts to get Moscow to agree to an open sphere of influence in Eastern Europe. First, notwithstanding its deliberate ambiguity, Washington interpreted the Yalta Declaration on Liberated Europe as a clear-cut Soviet commitment to allow democracy in Eastern Europe, especially in Poland. However, when its Polish policy threatened to cause a rupture with Moscow the Truman administration backed off. Second, notwithstanding the outcome on Poland, at the September 1945 London foreign ministers conference the United States pressed hard to get the Soviet

Union to open up Hungary, Romania, and Bulgaria by refusing to recognize those governments diplomatically until democratic elections were held and open trade policies were accepted. Inevitably, the clash between U.S. aims and Soviet interests in Eastern Europe caused estrangement between the United States and Moscow, not least, because, for Washington, the Open Door opened only in one direction. The United States wanted Eastern Europe to remain open to American economic and political penetration, but it excluded the Soviet Union from having a meaningful role on the Allied Control Commissions in Italy and Japan, and also sought to keep Communist parties out of power in Western Europe.[55]

Why did the United States attempt to force the Soviets to accept an open sphere of influence in Eastern Europe? Strategic considerations surely were a factor, especially the concern that the Soviet Union's war-fighting ability would be enhanced if Moscow absorbed Eastern Europe's resources. Economic factors also played a role, although Eastern Europe was not, in a direct sense, economically important to the United States. However, Western Europe was an integral—indispensable—component of the postwar Open Door economic system that the United States aimed to construct. And U.S. officials were concerned that if Eastern Europe was absorbed into a closed, Soviet-controlled economic sphere, Western Europe would be cut off from the region that had been a key prewar supplier of raw materials and agricultural products. Moreover, because they were committed reflexively to an Open Door world, U.S. officials recoiled at the prospect of any part of Eurasia being closed to the United States.[56] The prospect of a postwar world where large portions of Eurasia were incorporated into autarkic Soviet and British economic blocs was anathema to U.S. policymakers, because it would hinder the attainment of U.S. postwar Open Door objectives and threaten a replay of 1930s-style economic nationalism.[57]

Even more important than these tangible factors, however, for U.S. policymakers Soviet behavior in Eastern Europe became a "litmus test" of the Kremlin's postwar intentions.[58] This test was one that Moscow could not pass, however, because American and Soviet interests in Eastern Europe were not symmetrical.[59] For the Soviets, exercising control over postwar Eastern Europe was the key to security. And for the Kremlin, "control" meant putting in place "friendly" governments that would be subservient to Soviet policy. Based on its interwar experiences this was simply good strategic sense, because the Kremlin feared that an open Eastern Europe once again could become a platform for an attack on the Soviet homeland.

The Americans, of course, didn't see the world the same way the Kremlin saw it. For Washington, the Soviet Union's refusal to allow free elections, open trade, and liberalism's other accouterments to take hold in Eastern Central Europe suggested that the Kremlin was committed to following an ideologically driven, expansionist postwar policy.[60] Moreover, in Eastern Europe Soviet security requirements clashed with America's universalist objectives—and the American vision of an Open Door world was nothing if not universalist. As Geir Lundestad observes, postwar U.S. policymakers believed that America's interests legitimately extended to all corners of the globe, and that those of the Soviet Union (and Britain) did not.[61] America's universalist ambition to incorporate Eastern Europe into an Open Door world was based on the assumption that its security interests would be served if democratic governments could be established there and if the region was not closed economically.[62] Thus, postwar U.S. security interests were determined not merely by tangible geopolitical and strategic factors but also but ideology. U.S. policymakers "wanted a world safe both for liberal democracy and liberal capitalism," and, therefore, it was for the "best of reasons" that the United States opposed Soviet attempts to close off Eastern Europe.[63]

Finally, Eastern Europe was an integral part of America's strategic aim of eliminating the Soviet Union as a peer competitor. Washington hoped that an open Eastern Europe would be a springboard for bringing about regime change—"de-Bolshevikization"—in the Soviet Union.[64] U.S. policymakers had concluded by 1946 that "the very existence of the Soviet Union threatened American security."[65] They believed that "free access for American economic power would in turn help to create and sustain political predominance. The American demand for free elections in eastern Europe was considered by American policy-makers as much a means to such economic and political ends as a philosophic or moral end in and of itself."[66] The lingering question about American policy is whether it backfired.

Because of their importance to Soviet security, there was never a snowball's chance in hell that the inner ring of states on the Soviet Union's borders—Poland, Romania, Bulgaria—could have remained "open." However, during the period from the end of the war through 1947, the Soviet Union did tolerate a considerable degree of political pluralism in Czechoslovakia and Hungary (and occupied Austria), and (throughout most of 1946) allowed significant political pluralism in its German occupation zone. The Kremlin cracked down on these vestiges of openness as a defensive response to America's offensive strategy in Europe. Had the United States followed a different policy—a great power/spheres of influence policy—the course of events in those places *might* have been different. However, by seeking to keep Eastern Europe "open," American policy helped cause the postwar U.S.-Soviet relationship to escalate from a great power rivalry into the cold war.[67] U.S. policymakers should have known that U.S. policy toward Eastern Europe was a litmus test in reverse, heightening the Kremlin's insecurity and deepening its suspicions of *American* intentions. Washington's pursuit of an open Eastern Europe suggests that, because the United States enjoyed a huge superiority in power, it did not need to be overly concerned about how Moscow would respond to American policy.[68]

ELIMINATING THE SOVIET THREAT

One thing we know now for sure is that from the end of World War II until the early 1950s U.S. policymakers wanted to neuter the Soviet Union as a peer competitor. Washington aimed to accomplish this task by rolling back the Soviet sphere of influence, reducing drastically the Soviet Union's power relative to that of the United States, and bringing about a regime change in the Kremlin. President Roosevelt apparently believed that the Soviet Union's domestic system would be transformed gradually and peacefully by American economic power and the appeal of American values into something approaching a liberal democracy.[69] Roosevelt's successors also wanted regime change in the Soviet Union, but unlike FDR they were unwilling to let events take their course. This is unsurprising. As N. Gordon Levin and Ronald Powaski have argued, from the time of the Russian Revolution U.S. policymakers were inclined to regard the Communist regime as fundamentally illegitimate, and this belief (the Riga axioms) was deeply ingrained in the U.S. Foreign Service during the interwar years—especially among those young officers who would become key Soviet experts during World War II and the postwar period.[70]

During the late 1940s and early 1950s, U.S. grand strategy aimed at bringing about the collapse of Soviet power.[71] This strategy was based on Washington's belief in America's superior power and an assumption that the Soviet Union's domestic political system was fragile.[72] The goal of eliminating the Soviet Union as a peer competitor was formally adopted in November 1948 in National Security Council (NSC) 20/4, which stated that U.S. *peacetime* goals toward the Soviet Union were

> to reduce the power and influence of the USSR to limits which no longer constitute a threat to the peace, national independence and stability of the world family of nations[and] bring about a basic change in the conduct of international relations by the government in power in Russia, to conform with the purposes and principles set forth in the UN charter.[73]

In the event of war, the objectives set forth in NSC 20/4 included the termination of control of the Soviet Union by the Communist Party and the creation of postwar conditions that would "prevent the development of power relationships dangerous to the security of the United States and world peace."[74] NSC 20/4 postulated that, with or without a hot war, the United States would, by eliminating the Soviet Union as a great power rival, remove the only barrier standing between the United States and its goal of global hegemony.

As Gregory Metrovich demonstrates, the peacetime objectives of NSC 20/4 were more than rhetoric; during the late 1940s the United States engaged in a covert campaign against the Soviet Union, including an attempt to weaken Moscow's control over Eastern Europe.[75] Instead of advocating a defensive containment strategy, NSC 20/4 "focused . . . on the steps necessary to eliminate the Soviet threat altogether."[76] Notwithstanding his reputation as the author of the containment doctrine, Kennan was the primary architect of this "rollback" strategy. At the same time that he was arguing in public that a patient strategy of defensive containment would result in the mellowing of Soviet power, behind closed doors Kennan was advocating an active, offensive strategy intended to bring about a radical diminution of Soviet power.[77] The objectives of NSC 20/4—rolling back Soviet power from Eastern Europe, fomenting regime change inside the Soviet Union, and eliminating the Soviet Union as a peer competitor—were reaffirmed forcefully in April 1950 in NSC 68.[78]

NSC 68 called for the United States to amass "clearly preponderant power" in the international system, and made it clear that, for its authors (primarily Paul Nitze), "preponderant power" and global hegemony were synonymous.[79] NSC 68 made no attempt to disguise the offensive nature of American grand strategy; as LaFeber dryly observes, its policy objectives "were not overburdened with modesty."[80] NSC 68 rejected the idea that "containment" was a static, or passive, grand strategic posture that aimed merely at repelling Soviet geopolitical thrusts or deterring the Kremlin.[81] Rather, NSC 68 stated, containment was "a policy of calculated and gradual coercion." In implementing containment, U.S. power would be used muscularly "to attain the fundamental purpose of the United States, and foster a world environment in which our free society can survive and flourish," and not simply for the "negative" purpose of "resisting the Kremlin design."[82] The question, of course, was what it would take for the United States to achieve this objective.

NSC 68 provided an unequivocal answer: the United States should seek victory over the Soviet Union by adopting a grand strategy that "would check *and roll back* the Kremlin's drive for world power."[83] Simply put, NSC 68 stipulated that the ultimate aim of U.S. grand strategy was, by means short of hot war, to eliminate the Soviet Union as a peer competitor by using preponderant U.S. power to force the retraction of Soviet influence and control from regions beyond the borders of the Soviet Union, and, ultimately, to bring about regime change inside the Soviet Union itself.[84] U.S. "policy and actions," NSC 68 declared, must "be such as to foster a fundamental change in the nature of the Soviet system," because until this change occurred the United Sates could "expect no lasting abatement" of the cold war.[85]

NSC 68 did not propose that the United States achieve military victory over the Soviet Union. It did assert, however, that a massive increase in U.S. military capability was needed to support the risk-taking grand strategy it recommended.[86] Once the United States had attained an overwhelming—"preponderant"—power advantage over the Soviet Union, Washington could wield its clout and thereby "change the world situation by means short of war in such a way as to frustrate the Kremlin design [for world domination] and hasten the decay of the Soviet system."[87] Confronted with the preponderant power of the United States—and with its own grip in Eastern Europe, and even on the Soviet Union, weakened by U.S. covert operations—Moscow would realize that it could not prevail in a long-term competition in the face of superior U.S. resources.[88]

Reflecting the prevailing view among U.S. officials—notably Secretary of State Dean Acheson, who believed the United States should only "negotiate" with Moscow once it had achieved a "situation of strength"—NSC 68 inveighed against conducting serious talks with the Kremlin.[89] Once the United States attained the "preponderant power" specified in NSC 68, Acheson wrote, "they [the Soviets] may then be willing to recede."[90] Skeptical about the efficacy of diplomacy, NSC 68 explicitly ruled out a spheres of influence approach as a basis for a U.S.-Soviet settlement, saying it would foster German or Japanese "neutrality." This would benefit the Soviets and undercut the United States, because, as NSC 68 put it, "the idea that Germany or Japan or other important areas can exist as islands of neutrality in a divided world is unreal, given the Kremlin design for world domination."[91] Other states had only two choices: they could either align themselves with the United States or oppose it. Independence from Washington was tantamount to opposition, which is why the United States wanted to keep a tight leash on Germany, Japan, and Western Europe rather than risk a deal with the Soviets that might allow them to emerge as autonomous poles of power. Rather than seeking dangerous diplomatic agreements with Moscow, the United States would build up its strength, at which point, NSC 68 suggested, "the Kremlin [would] be compelled to adjust" and the cold war would end on America's terms.[92] Soviet power would be broken, it would no longer would be a peer competitor, and the United States would fulfill its global hegemonic ambitions.[93]

THE DIVISION OF GERMANY

It has frequently been argued that Germany's postwar division was the logical—inevitable—basis for the postwar U.S.-Soviet relationship in Europe.[94] Far from being inevitable, however, Germany's division resulted from deliberate policy choices made by Washington.[95] Between 1946 and 1953, the United States and the Soviet Union might have agreed on German reunification, but the United States closed the door on a reunified Germany. On the one hand, Washington's German policy was affected by the U.S.-Soviet relationship, and Germany became a focal point of the superpower rivalry. At the same time, America's German policy also was driven by Open Door considerations that existed quite apart from the dynamics of the Soviet-U.S. rivalry. Both the cold war and non–cold war dimensions of Washington's postwar German policy illustrate the hegemonic nature of America's postwar grand strategy. The U.S. decision to divide Germany—and even more its rejection of Soviet reunification overtures in 1952 and 1953—underscore that Washington had turned its back on engaging in great power diplomacy with Moscow. In its non–cold war dimension, U.S. postwar German policy points to the primacy of Open Door concerns over cold war considerations.

The U.S. decision to divide Germany was rooted in the intricacies of the reparations question—which, in turn, was related to postwar U.S. economic assistance for Soviet reconstruction—and the ambiguous accord reached at the July 1945 Big Three summit meeting at Potsdam. At Potsdam, the Big Three (Truman, Churchill, and Stalin) had contradictorily agreed both to treat Germany as a single economic unit and to allow each of the occupying powers to extract reparations from its own zone.[96] In 1945, the Soviet Union obviously was interested in obtaining material aid to facilitate its postwar recovery from the enormous devastation it sustained during World War II. As it became increasingly clear to Moscow that a hoped-for postwar reconstruction loan from the United States would not be forthcoming, the Soviets focused their attention on German reparations as a means of rebuilding their nation. Washington opposed having Germany pay reparations from current production, because it was unwilling to subsidize either German reparations (which necessitated the importation of goods vital to rebuild German industry and food and clothing for German workers) or occupation costs.[97] Hence, the United States insisted on the "first charge" principle, which meant that any revenues earned by German exports would be used to defray the costs of necessary imports rather than for reparations.[98]

Even as World War II was drawing to a close many key U.S. policymakers had decided that western Germany's integration into the postwar liberal, multilateral economic order was imperative, because western Europe's stabilization and economic revival was linked to it. This also affected the Soviet stake in German reparations. For example, western Europe desperately needed German coal for its recovery.[99] Germany's coal industry could not be gotten up and running, however, without first importing large amounts of goods. Again, the United States did not want to foot the bill for these imports, so here too the first-charge principle was invoked.[100] The decision to revive Germany's coal industry was made *before* Potsdam. It reflected the paramountcy of America's Open Door interests—which required that German resources be used for western Europe's reconstruction rather than for reparations—and their priority over U.S.-Soviet relations.[101] At the time the decision was made, it was not directed against the Soviet Union, but, over time, U.S.-Soviet differences on the reparations issue marked increasingly sharp differences about Germany's future.[102]

A critical fork in the road was reached in mid-1946 when the United States and Britain fused their respective occupation zones to create the so-called Bizone.[103] In part, the Bizone was created because Washington and London were concerned about the occupation's mounting financial burdens, but it also reflected the growing tension in Soviet-American relations and worries about Western Europe's political and economic stability. In creating the Bizone, Washington implicitly rejected the option of treating Germany as a single economic—or political—entity.[104] The Soviets reacted strongly, because they understood the effect would be to close the door on obtaining reparations from western Germany.[105]

U.S.-Soviet differences came to a head at the March/April 1947 foreign ministers conference in Moscow. There, the Soviets again pressed the case for treating Germany as a single economic unit and their claim for reparations from current production in the western zones (including access to Ruhr resources). The Soviets also proposed that Germany be reunified, neutralized, and demilitarized. Like the Americans, the Soviets feared the possible reemergence of Germany as an independent great power. While the Americans feared a Soviet-German alliance, the Soviets fretted that the United States would incorporate western Germany into a U.S.-led anti-Soviet grouping. The Kremlin's fears were well founded. At the Moscow conference, the United States spurned Soviet overtures on German unification, because it had decided to secure its grip on western Germany by integrating it with Western Europe.[106] This decision made explicit what had been implicit at Potsdam and in the decision to create the Bizone: for the United States, western Germany's contribution to Western Europe's economic rehabilitation was more important than the Soviet Union's need for reparations.[107] Rather than having western Germany go to work to rebuild the Soviet Union, Washington wanted to put western Germany to work rebuilding Western Europe, thereby furthering U.S. Open Door aims in Western Europe.

After the Moscow summit, the United States did not formally renounce the goal of German reunification, but from then onward U.S. German policy gathered momentum step-by-step, each step confirming the basic U.S. decision that a divided Germany was preferable to a reunified one. Fundamentally, that decision was not driven by U.S.-Soviet tensions but reflected that the United States "had developed a quite independent preference for German partition."[108] Although the Open Door interests driving Washington's German policy were not related to the cold war, they contributed to the deterioration in U.S.-Soviet relations. Because the U.S. goal of reviving Western Europe economically was accorded more importance than relations with Moscow, in Washington "there was no willingness to analyze how" U.S. policy "might be affecting Soviet behavior or to explore positions that might offer a basis for compromise."[109]

The Marshall Plan confirmed that Western European economic reconstruction—and perforce German economic revival—was the paramount objective of U.S. European policy.[110] German economic rehabilitation led, in turn, to the 1948 decisions to implement currency reform in western Germany and to lay the foundations for a West German state. At the same time, the need to reassure Western Europeans that Germany would not once again threaten their security led the United States to make a continental commitment militarily and to embed West Germany in an integrated Western Europe. Each of these steps served to solidify both Germany's division and Europe's, and to deepen the cold war. But Washington was less worried about these consequences than about the possibility that the Kremlin would throw a monkey wrench into its policy by making the United States an offer it couldn't refuse on German reunification. The American ambassador to Moscow, Walter Bedell Smith, neatly summarized U.S. policy in a December 1947 letter to Gen. Dwight Eisenhower: "The difficulty under which we labor is that in spite of our announced position we really do not want nor intend to accept German unification in any terms that the Russians might agree to, even though they seemed to meet most of our requirements."[111] Although Smith's was clearly the dominant view in Washington, before the creation of the West German state and the signing of the North Atlantic Treaty, the State Department's internal policy formulation process presented the Truman administration with a final chance to reconsider the thrust of its European grand strategy.

In an August 1948 State Department Policy Planning Staff paper (PPS 37)—with the Berlin blockade and negotiations on the North Atlantic Treaty and creation of a West German state as a backdrop—George F. Kennan reviewed Washington's German policy and recommended that the United States sound out Moscow's willingness to strike a deal on German reunification.[112] Kennan acknowledged that there were real risks in such a settlement, but he argued that there would be a big upside, because Soviet forces would be withdrawn to the east into Poland or the Soviet Union itself. This would enhance Western Europe's security. Even more important, Kennan believed that reunifying Germany was the only way to avoid what he called "the congealment of Europe along present lines."[113] If the United States went ahead with its plans to create West Germany, he warned, the Continent irrevocably would be divided into U.S. and Soviet zones of control. And if that happened, Kennan predicted, "it would be hard—harder than it now is—to find 'the road back' to a united and free Europe."[114] On the other hand, a reunified Germany would "keep things flexible for an eventual retraction of Soviet power and for the gradual emergence from Soviet control, and entrance into a free European community, of the present satellite countries."[115] Having analyzed the pros and cons of both courses of action Kennan recommended that the United States try to reach a settlement with the Soviet Union that would lead to German reunification.[116]

Kennan's views, of course, failed to carry the day inside the policy councils of the Truman administration. However, there were at least two other opportunities when a deal *might* have been reached with the Soviets on German reunification: the so-called Stalin peace note in 1952, and a Soviet initiative in 1953, shortly after Stalin's death. On each occasion, Washington rejected the German reunification option for essentially the same reasons that Kennan's proposal had been rejected: concerns about German domestic politics; concerns about a reunified Germany's external policies; the relationship of U.S. German policy to American strategy vis-à-vis the Soviet Union; and the relationship of U.S. German policy to American Open Door objectives in Western Europe.

Importantly, both Kennan and those U.S. officials who opposed German reunification had the same goal: ensuring development of what U.S. officials often called "the right kind of Germany."[117] U.S. officials were extremely skeptical about West Germany's commitment to democracy.[118] They feared that West Germany would slide back into authoritarianism (or worse, go Communist). There were also worries that revived German nationalism could affect West Germany's external orientation and lead to a Rapallo-like Soviet-German alignment (the Treaty of Rapallo was the 1922 rapprochement between Weimar Germany and the Soviet Union whereby the Continent's two post–1919 outcast great powers came together diplomatically in an attempt to counter the postwar ascendance in European affairs of Britain and France).[119] Alternatively, a nationalist West Germany might slide into "third force" neutralism.[120] The specter of resurgent German nationalism meant, High Commissioner John J. McCloy observed, that the United States was locked in a "struggle for the soul of Faust."[121] Where Kennan and his colleagues differed was on what to do. Kennan believed that the West Germans would never accept Germany's division and that a West German state would "become the spokesman of a resentful and defiant nationalism directed" against the United States."[122] However, most U.S. officials came to the opposite conclusion: a reunified Germany would be dangerous. These policymakers knew that the United States controlled "the best part of Germany" (as Walter Lippmann described it), and they were not about to risk having it slip from their grasp. For them, the only solution to the German problem was to consolidate West German democracy, quell German nationalism, contain German power, and tether Germany firmly to the West by integrating West Germany into Western Europe.[123]

American opposition to German reunification in the late 1940s and early 1950s illuminates the hegemonic impulses that drove postwar U.S. grand strategy, and demonstrates the interplay of the Open Door and cold war dimensions of that strategy. With respect to U.S. Open Door objectives, division facilitated Germany's integration into Western Europe, because the Western Europeans were less threatened by a "truncated Germany" than by a reunified one.[124] By the same token, because of lingering worries that a resurgent West Germany might cause Western Europe to backslide into destabilizing power politics, U.S. hegemony—including a permanent U.S. military presence—was necessary to contain Germany, reassure the Western Europeans, and maintain peace on the Continent.[125] This was another reason for Washington to oppose German reunification, because any deal with the Soviets on Germany was certain to be predicated on mutual U.S. and Soviet military disengagement from Europe.[126]

Finally, Germany's neutralization was the sine qua non of any possible U.S.-Soviet deal on reunification. However, this raised important issues for Washington. First, U.S. officials worried that Germany's neutralization would have a demonstration effect, encouraging other states in Western Europe to adopt a "neutralist" orientation—that is, to break free of American tutelage.[127] Second, a reunified Germany would be free to follow an independent foreign and security policy, which could only lead to bad results—a Germany once again running amok on the Continent, or aligning with Moscow—and pull the rug out from under Washington's hegemonic strategy in Western Europe.[128] Here, as Secretary of State Dean Acheson put it, Washington's Open Door objectives in Western Europe were too important to be sacrificed on the altar of German unity.[129] Third, reunification could lead to Germany's reemergence as an independent great power on the Continent.[130] As Leffler puts it, U.S. officials "were not interested in making a unified Germany the linchpin of a third force in world affairs."[131]

Of course, as Acheson said in 1949, the United States always was ready to reunify Germany "if the circumstances are right."[132] The "right" circumstances meant reunification on American terms, including guaranteed free elections, the continuing presence of American troops in Europe, reunified Germany's economic integration into Western Europe, and its membership in the U.S.-designed Western European security architecture.[133] As Acheson said, if negotiations on German reunification took place, the United States could not "accept any proposal which would prohibit or limit the right of a unified Germany, or a Western Germany, to join the West and contribute to Western European defense."[134] Thus, for U.S. officials, the fundamental precondition for German reunification was, as Acheson put it, a change of heart by the Soviets and the willing alteration of their policy—something that Washington knew was not in the cards.[135] At the same time, both the Truman and Eisenhower administrations believed that by acting as a magnet that would pull both eastern Germany and Eastern Europe westward, a West Germany successfully embedded in Euro-Atlantic structures could be a powerful lever with which to pursue Washington's Soviet strategy, which aimed at the retraction of Soviet power.[136]

Was there an exit ramp from the cold war? If so, it was Germany. Had they been able to agree on German unification, the Soviet Union and United States could have disengaged mutually from Central Europe with two big payoffs for the United States. First, a reunified Germany would have allowed the United States to implement an offshore balancing strategy pursuant to which Germany—not the United States—would have balanced against (or contained) Soviet power in Europe. Second, in contrast to the roll-back fantasies expressed in NSC 20/4 and NSC 68, U.S.-Soviet mutual disengagement would have resulted in the *actual* retraction of Soviet power from Eastern Europe, which would have bolstered Western Europe's security. With the superpower confrontation in the heart of Europe defused, the Kremlin might have been willing to accept—as it did in Austria, Hungary, and Czechoslovakia in 1946–1947—a "Finlandized" Eastern Europe.

Could Germany have been reunified in the first decade following World War II? Certainly between 1946 and 1949 there were opportunities had the United States been willing to explore them.[137] Again, in 1952 and 1953 the Soviet Union made diplomatic overtures on the subject. There is an ongoing debate about whether the 1952 and 1953 proposals represented a real chance to achieve Germany reunification.[138] There is too much we still do not know to reach a definitive conclusion about the sincerity of Moscow's overtures. But we know this: the United States was not in the least bit interested in probing the Kremlin's position and testing "the relative strength of the Soviets' preference for settlement versus socialism in negotiations" about Germany.[139] Washington categorically had decided that German reunification would not serve U.S. interests—unless, of course, the Kremlin capitulated and accepted reunification on the basis of Washington's maximalist conditions.[140] For the United States the Open Door in Western Europe was more important than rolling back Soviet power in Eastern Europe.[141] U.S. policy provides one answer to the question of whether 1952 and 1953 were "lost opportunities" to achieve German reunification. They were neither lost nor opportunities, because the United States was not interested in German reunification.

* * *

Extraregional hegemony theory is a useful tool with which to reexamine the cold war's origins. Seen through its lens, it is apparent that America's hegemonic ambitions contributed hugely to the fact that U.S.-Soviet frictions escalated into the cold war. The hegemonic ambitions driving America's postwar grand strategy were evidenced in the U.S. attempt to force Moscow to accept an "open sphere" of influence in Eastern Europe, in NSC 20/4 and NSC 68, and in America's German policy. Washington's German policy is important in another respect, too, because it underscores that America's Open Door aims in Western Europe were more important than reaching an agreement with the Soviet Union on German reunification, which might have precluded the Continent's division.

This brings us to perhaps the most important truth about America's postwar European grand strategy: fundamentally, it was driven by the Open Door, not by cold war concerns. Although U.S. policy toward the Soviet Union was affected by Washington's Open Door policy, the Soviet Union was only a secondary—not the primary—factor in America's postwar European grand strategy. Thus, even if the Soviet Union had not existed, after World War II, America's Open Door aims on the Continent would have led to the establishment of U.S. hegemony in Western Europe.

CHAPTER FOUR

The Open Door and American Hegemony in Western Europe

In this chapter I explain why, in the late 1940s, the United States established its hegemony over Western Europe. I begin by focusing on the Open Door—economic and ideological—dimensions of America's postwar Western European grand strategy. Then I discuss the military and security aspects of America's postwar European grand strategy. Boiled down to basics, mine is a two-pronged argument. First, as I have already made clear, America's post–World War II Western European strategy was driven primarily by Open Door imperatives and not by cold war exigencies. Second, it was the Open Door's *logic* that required the United States to exercise hegemony over postwar Western Europe, because the United States could attain its Open Door objectives in Europe only by acting as a stabilizing hegemon on the Continent.

My argument is, in a sense, "counterfactual," because I contend that even if there had been no Soviet threat to Western Europe—actual or perceived—the broad outlines of Washington's grand strategy on the Continent would have pretty much resembled the strategy that it followed from the end of World War II until 1990, and which it has continued to pursue since the Soviet Union's collapse. It is important, however, that my argument not be misconstrued. I am not arguing that America's Open Door economic aims in Western Europe did not affect the cold war (or vice versa). Obviously, they did. The Marshall Plan and the American decision to divide Germany were big steps toward Europe's final division into rival Soviet and U.S. spheres and the downward spiral in U.S.-Soviet relations.[1] My argument is simply that the Open Door economic objectives underlying America's European grand strategy existed prior to and independently of cold war considerations, a point nicely made by Carolyn Woods Eisenberg: "In reality, the Truman administration's concern about European recovery predated the Soviet-communist threat, and would have existed anyway. Even during wartime, the State Department planning committees had emphasized reconstruction and the establishment of a multilateral trading order on the Continent."[2]

71

The Grand Strategic Logic of the Open Door

To grasp the complexity of America's post–World War II continental grand strategy, it is necessary to unpack the Open Door's logic. U.S. strategy rested on a fundamental premise: that America's postwar prosperity was linked to Western Europe's economic revival. Moreover, for economic—and political—reasons U.S. policymakers wanted to supplant Western Europe's prewar division into national markets with a single, integrated market. There also was an important ideological dimension to America's Open Door strategy in Europe. After World War II, Washington fostered Western Europe's economic recovery to ensure its political and social stability, specifically by preventing Communist parties from coming to power, because it feared such regimes would sabotage America's Open Door strategy by adopting autarkic (or nationalist) economic policies. If the forces of closure triumphed, the United States would be isolated in an ideologically hostile world, with possibly portentous implications for America's own core values. To ensure that domestic political conditions in Western Europe were conducive to its Open Door interests, the United States, as Alan Milward notes, used the economic leverage it wielded through the Marshall Plan to forge a Western European political consensus in favor of liberal political values.[3]

Before Western Europe could integrate economically, the predicate security conditions had to be created. Specifically, the United States needed to prevent postwar Europe from becoming "re-nationalized"—from backsliding into its traditional pattern of great power politics—lest the resultant instability prevent the United States from realizing its Open Door economic objectives. The Open Door thus was the motor for America's postwar continental commitment: to realize its Open Door goals, the United States needed to keep the peace in Western Europe by acting as that region's hegemonic stabilizer. At the same time, U.S. policymakers invested the economic Open Door with a key security dimension, because they believed that economic integration and interdependence would contribute to peace and stability in Europe. Economic nationalism, or autarky, was believed to fuel great power competition and cause war.[4] Here, the security and economic aspects of America's Open Door strategy in Europe led back to the Open Door's ideological component.

U.S. ECONOMIC INTERESTS IN
POSTWAR WESTERN EUROPE

After World War II the United States set out to reconstruct Western Europe. Even though U.S. economic well-being did not objectively depend on trade with Western Europe, policymakers in Washington *believed* that America's prosperity was tied to its access to export markets abroad—especially in Western Europe, which accounted for nearly a third of U.S. exports (but only for

1.3% of its GDP).[5] As Undersecretary of State for Economic Affairs Will Clayton said, "We need markets—big markets—in which to buy and sell."[6] U.S. officials were haunted by the specter of the Great Depression, and it was an article of faith that exports and an open international economy would be vital to America's postwar economic health and political stability. Postwar Western Europe's ability to serve as a vital export market was in doubt, however, because the Western European countries were suffering from a "dollar gap." Simply put, they lacked enough dollars to buy American products.[7]

The optimal solution would have been for the Western Europeans to increase their exports to the United States. However, they were in no position to do so, because the Continent's export capacity had been crippled by wartime economic dislocations. Much of Western Europe's industrial plant and infrastructure (especially transportation networks) had been heavily damaged. Economic recovery also was constricted by the disruption of the complex pattern of prewar intra-European trade, which exacerbated the dollar gap.[8] Moreover, to jump-start their economic recoveries, the Western European states were forced to deplete their scarce dollar reserves purchasing products and raw materials from the United States that, under normal economic conditions, they would have purchased from one another. Finally, Western Europe's economic recovery—and its ability to earn dollars by exporting—was hamstrung by low productivity (stemming in part from obsolete plants), bottlenecks caused by raw material scarcities, and malaise in the labor force caused by inflation and food shortages.[9] The apparent gravity of Western Europe's economic condition was underscored by the famously harsh winter of 1946–47, which appeared to have stopped Western Europe's 1946 economic recovery dead in its tracks. Doubtless, the bad weather exacerbated the economic crisis, but it did not cause it. The causes were the dollar gap and the very structure of Western Europe's political economy, which was still organized along national lines.

Western Europe's dollar shortage had implications both for America's economic prosperity and for Washington's Open Door grand strategy. U.S. policymakers worried about the economic consequences of (in Paul Nitze's words) a "bankrupt world"—that is, a world lacking dollars to buy American products.[10] U.S. officials *believed* the United States would suffer economically unless the dollar gap was solved and Western Europe was revived. As an April 21, 1947 report of the State-War-Navy Coordinating Committee (SWNCC) pointed out, "A substantial decline in the United States export surplus would have a depressing effect on business activity and employment in the United States."[11] Moreover, the report observed, should a drop in U.S. exports coincide with a U.S. recession—which the Council of Economic Advisers expected within the coming year—"the effect on production, prices, and unemployment might be most serious."[12]

Fears that Western Europe's dollar gap would adversely impact America's own economic health reinforced Washington's concern that the Continent's foreign exchange shortage could undermine the broader postwar U.S. Open Door objective of constructing an open, multilateral international economic system. As the SWNCC report observed, "The great weight of evidence indicates that even the current volume of United States foreign financing, and particularly its distribution between countries, is not adequate to the accomplishment of either world economic stability and the type of world trading system which is the object of our trade policy, or of our political objectives in several critical countries."[13] To ensure its own economic well-being and create an open international economic system, the SWNCC report concluded, the United States would have to increase its foreign economic assistance substantially. However, for that assistance to be efficacious economically while simultaneously advancing broader U.S. objectives, it would have to be tied to Western Europe's economic and political integration.[14]

The Marshall Plan—formally known as the European Recovery Program (ERP)—was Washington's dramatic response to Western Europe's economic crisis. Although the Marshall Plan came to be invested with cold war implications, its underlying impetus was to promote U.S. Open Door interests in Europe.[15] U.S. officials perceived that America's own economic well-being—and broader Open Door ambitions—were threatened by Europe's crisis.

In the initial study prepared in May 1947 by the newly formed State Department Policy Planning Staff, its director, George F. Kennan, argued that Communist subversion was not the cause of Western Europe's economic travails. Those, he said, resulted "in large part from the disruptive effect of the war on the economic, political, and social structure of Europe, and from a profound exhaustion of physical plant and of spiritual vigor."[16] Although Kennan recognized that U.S. security could be threatened if Western European Communist parties successfully exploited the Continent's economic malaise, he argued that the main thrust of U.S. assistance to Europe "should be directed not to the combating of communism as such but to the restoration of the economic health and vigor of European society."[17] Washington should correct the misimpression engendered by the Truman Doctrine that "the United States approach to world problems is a defensive reaction to communist pressure and that the effort to restore sound economic conditions in other countries is only a by-product of this reaction and not something we would be interested in doing if there were no communist menace."[18]

Two months later, in July 1947, Kennan reiterated that Washington's interest in aiding Western Europe's economic recovery transcended the Communist threat and was independent of it: "The United States people have a very real economic interest in Europe. This stems from Europe's role in the past as a market and as a major source of supply for a variety of products and services."[19] Although certain costs would be imposed on the United States if it helped Western Europe to recover economically, these would, he observed, be outweighed by the economic benefits.[20] By the same token, if Western Europe remained mired in recession, the risk to America's economic well-being would be considerable, because "past experience has taught us that the U.S. cannot achieve full prosperity in a world of depression."[21] These concerns were echoed by Undersecretary of State Will Clayton, who, after acknowledging the "awful implications" of Western Europe's political, economic, and social disintegration for the "peace and security of the world," cut to the economic bottom line, stating that "the immediate effects on our domestic economy would be disastrous: markets for our surplus production gone, unemployment, depression, a heavily unbalanced budget on the background of a mountainous war debt."[22]

America's postwar international economic policies—the Marshall Plan, building an open international economic system—required the United States to do what it had not done during the 1930s: assume the mantle of hegemonic leadership of the international economic system by acting as the world's lender, and buyer, of last resort.[23] U.S. officials understood that the Marshall Plan was only a stopgap, because the United States could not indefinitely pump dollars into Western Europe.[24] When Marshall Plan assistance ran out, there was a risk that trade between the United States and Western Europe would slump, with baleful consequences:

> Domestic and foreign production would be reduced; American exports and foreign imports would fall and become subject to increasing restrictions designed to safeguard foreign monetary reserves; sources and markets would be governed less and less by competition; standards of living would drop; and employment abroad and at home, especially in export industries, would suffer.[25]

To prevent these outcomes, over the longer term the United States would have to meet Western Europe's need for dollars by buying more of its products, which required "a change in our traditional attitude toward imports, and a willingness to place the economic interests of the nation as a whole . . . above the special interests of political groups which may have to face increased competition from abroad."[26]

THE OPEN DOOR AND WESTERN EUROPEAN ECONOMIC INTEGRATION

Beyond solving the dollar gap, America's Open Door economic interests also were deemed to require Western Europe's economic integration. The United States wanted to promote "unification"—which for U.S. officials meant creation of a "large single economic unit in Europe"—and to establish supranational institutions to superintend Western Europe's economic integration.[27] Specifically, U.S. policymakers believed a large, single market would be more efficient than a Europe divided into national markets and would permit the Western Europeans to increase productivity—and attain a higher rate of economic growth—by reaping the advantages of specialization, achieving a more optimal allocation of resources and taking advantage of economies of scale.[28] Paul Hoffman, director of the Economic Cooperation Administration (ECA)—the U.S. government agency charged with administering the Marshall Plan—spelled out the link between a large, integrated, competitive market and U.S. economic objectives in Europe: "Europe could not be self-supporting until it had made great progress towards unity and until there was a wide, free, competitive market to lower costs, increase efficiency, and raise the standard of living."[29]

Conversely, Washington held that a Western Europe organized on narrow, national economic lines would be inefficient, because Western Europe's "existing trade barriers (a) clog the flow of Europe's trade and (b) will set an uneconomic pattern for any reconstruction efforts."[30] As the British Foreign Office observed, Washington attached "importance to avoiding the perpetuation of uneconomic rivalries between the countries of Europe."[31] By promoting Western Europe's economic unity, integration would eliminate "the small watertight compartment into which Europe's pre-war and present economy is divided."[32]

American officials also feared that the persistence of national economies in Western Europe could cause the Continent to revert to 1930s-style economic nationalism and autarky. This could fuel political rivalry and geopolitical instability on the Continent, and threaten America's interlinked strategic, and Open Door, interests.[33] By surmounting what Washington regarded as Western Europe's archaic division into multiple sovereign states through integration and supranationality the United States aimed to banish the specter of nationalism that had made the Continent, in the minds of U.S. policymakers, the "cockpit" of "power clashes" and the "breeder of wars."[34] U.S. policymakers, as Michael Hogan observes, held a "world view rooted in political conviction as well as in economic interests," which explains why they regarded economic integration as a policy that would cause the giving way of "national rivalry to rapprochement, economic autarky to economic regionalism and, then, to a multilateral system of world trade."[35] For economic and strategic reasons, therefore, the United States supported Western Europe's step-by-step process of economic integration beginning with the European Payments Union, then the European Coal and Steel Community, and ultimately the creation of the European Common Market by the 1957 Treaty of Rome.

The Interplay of Economics, Ideology, and Security

In the immediate aftermath of World War II, U.S. policymakers worried that Communist governments could come to power in Western Europe—especially in France or Italy. Washington had three concerns. First, American officials feared the economic consequences if such regimes addressed the dollar gap by adopting nationalist economic policies, including state-directed economic planning, import limits, foreign exchange controls, and preferential bilateral trade agreements.[36] Second, Washington feared the geopolitical consequences of a return to prewar economic nationalism, which might presage a reprise of 1930s-style power politics that, in the minds of U.S. officials, had been the prime cause of World War II.[37] Washington's concerns were expressed by ambassador to France David Bruce, who worried about "a return to the worst continental type of autarchy, with each nation retiring behind its national boundaries, as they have so frequently and tragically in the past."[38]

Finally, although these concerns would have shaped U.S. policy even if there had been no cold war, rising tensions with Moscow heightened them. Communist governments in Western Europe might enter into bilateral trade arrangements with the Soviet Union and drift into Moscow's orbit. If this happened, the result could be a Soviet-directed "continental system" that would exclude the United States economically from Western Europe.[39] The United States would then be compelled to respond to Western Europe's closure by adopting its own state-directed economic policy. As Will Clayton put it, "We would have to reorder and readjust our whole economy in this country if we lost the European market."[40]

Importantly, Washington's apprehensions about an autarkic Western Europe tied to Moscow were not primarily military in nature. That is, Washington did not fear that a continental hegemon would be able to threaten the United States by mobilizing the resources of the European continent. Rather, just as had been the case in 1939–40 (and, arguably, in 1917–18), U.S. policymakers were concerned that America's core values at home—the American way of life—would be imperiled if an *ideologically* hostile great power dominated the Continent and closed it to the United States. Not only would the United States be forced to regiment its own economy to cope with an autarkic Europe but it would also be forced—or so it was believed—to maintain a vastly increased military establishment during peacetime. As a State Department memo said, "The change in the power relationships involved would force us to adopt drastic domestic measures and would inevitably require great and burdensome sacrifices on the part of our citizens."[41] The United States would have to become a "garrison state" to defend its core values.[42] The change in the configuration of power in Europe would jeopardize American democracy and its free market economic system. "Geopolitical considerations provided the *connecting tissue* between foreign economic distress and the prospective decay of liberal capitalism at home."[43] The defense of America's core values required that Europe be kept open, both economically and ideologically.

U.S. policy toward France illustrates the interaction between Open Door economic interests and U.S. security concerns. Because France was seen as the linchpin of America's European grand strategy, the United States determined that it would have to support France economically in order to forestall the French Communist Party (PCF)—which was banking on its ability to exploit the political discontent engendered by economic hardship—from coming to power.[44] Well before the Marshall Plan, in May 1946, the United States extended France a package that included a $650 million loan from the Export-Import Bank, cancellation of France's $2.8 billion Lend-Lease debt, and other economic help.[45] The aid package was finalized on the eve of France's national elections; Washington wanted to influence the outcome by bolstering the non-Communist Center and Center-Left parties.[46]

After World War II, the United States used diplomatic and military sticks, as well as economic carrots, to make sure that the Communists did not come to power in France or in other important Western European countries. It did not hesitate to intervene in French domestic politics. As Marshall said, "It is of prime importance that the French people be made to realize the essential necessity for France's own good of developing a strong, unified and cooperative non-Communist government."[47] The United States made clear to the French and Italian governments that Marshall Plan aid would be withheld if the Communists were allowed to join the ruling coalitions.[48] As Melvyn Leffler observes, "Once having encouraged the expulsion of the Communists from the governing coalitions of France and Italy, American officials were determined to keep them out lest they hamstring the initiatives desired by the United States."[49] Finally, if necessary, the U.S. was prepared to use raw military power—either directly or indirectly by threatening to intervene militarily—to keep the Communists out of power in France and Italy.[50]

DOMESTIC POLITICAL STABILITY
IN POSTWAR WESTERN EUROPE

The U.S. goal of keeping the Communists out of power in postwar Western Europe illustrates how intertwined the political and economic Open Doors were and how both fused with American strategic concerns. Keeping Western Europe open economically led the United States to pursue political stability by helping Western Europe get back on its feet economically. The Marshall Plan was designed specifically to act as a political balm and to prevent the Communists from making political gains.[51] By promoting increased productivity and economic growth—creating "stable abundance" (in Hogan's phrase)—the United States aimed to alleviate the divisive politics of redistribution that had bitterly split Western European politics along social and class lines before and after World War II. As Michael Hogan and Alan Milward each have pointed out, through the Marshall Plan the United States ambitiously sought not only to reconstruct Western Europe's economies but to reorder their domestic politics. The United States used the Marshall Plan to forge a political consensus in Western Europe in support of liberal values.[52]

U.S. policymakers believed that sustained economic growth would lead to pluralist democracy.[53] "At a certain level of *per capita* national income," Milward observes, "a set of political and social values would emerge akin to those in the United States and, in a world made safe for democracy, communism would appear as a political and economic anachronism."[54]

Beyond the worries about economic closure was a deeper, more pervasive ideological anxiety. The Open Door always has required—as it still does—*openness* not only to American trade and investment but equally to American political ideals, values, and culture. America's security, prosperity, and domestic stability have required an Open Door *world*. Following World War II, the darkest fear of U.S. policymakers was—as it arguably had been in 1917 and 1941—that if the forces of closure triumphed on the Continent, the United States would be left alone in an ideologically hostile world.

To head off possible ideological isolation, the United States—in today's inside-the-Beltway jargon—sought to "shape the international environment" by planting America's liberal political ideology in the Old World's political soil. This objective transcended the cold war. As the U.S. diplomat Charles Bohlen put it in July 1948, "The present world situation is not viewed primarily as a struggle between the United States and Russia. The United States is interested not only in the military revival of Europe but also in its cultural, spiritual, and economic restoration, so that, in general there can be created the kind of world in which the people of the United States would like to live."[55] Even the archrealist Kennan dreaded the possibility that the United Sates could be left isolated ideologically. If the United States lost Western Europe, he said, "We would be placing ourselves in the position of a lonely country, culturally and politically. To maintain confidence in our own traditions and institutions we would henceforth have to whistle loudly in the dark. I am not sure that whistling could be loud enough to do the trick."[56]

The Marshall Plan aimed to keep Western Europe open politically as well as economically, to keep the United States from becoming a "lonely country" ideologically. The Marshall Plan reflected U.S. policymakers' belief that "values would follow aid, rather as in previous centuries trade had been thought to follow that flag, and that these values would deeply influence the political development of the European countries in a favorable direction."[57] It aimed to create a political grouping—a "stable, loyal political bloc"—of Western European states that would share America's political, economic, social, and cultural values.[58]

THE PRIMACY OF THE OPEN DOOR

Although U.S. Open Door ambitions existed independently of the cold war, it is an open question whether policymakers could have rallied congressional and public support for their policies absent the Soviet, and Communist, "threats." When Truman administration officials tried to sell Congress on the

Marshall Plan by pointing to the economic benefits the United States would reap from creation of a single large, integrated Western European market, its sales pitch tended to fall flat. On the other hand, "the words that were really electrifying up on the Hill were 'Communist threat,' and that was theme that the salesmen [Truman administration officials lobbying for the Economic Cooperation Act, the Marshall Plan bill] tended to return to again and again as they worked the halls of Congress."[59] However, as Michael Hogan observes, in truth "American leaders had goals besides Communist containment, goals that would have shaped their diplomacy regardless of the perceived Communist menace."[60] Cold war considerations were superimposed on the already extant Open Door foundations of American strategy. When U.S. officials defined American interests, Open Door concerns were never far from the surface. One can point to innumerable statements like those of George C. Marshall and Will Clayton that stressed that, although Western Europe's economic collapse could have adverse effects geopolitically, it would also be very harmful to American prosperity.[61] Or, as a 1950 State Department report stated, even if the "strengthening of the non-Soviet world" was a "more important" reason for the United States to revive Western Europe economically and embed it in an open international economic system, the United States nevertheless had "a large measure of economic self-interest in such a development."[62] What these statements demonstrate is this: If the cold war concerns had been removed from the equation, U.S. Open Door economic interests would have remained, and these would have shaped America's European strategy.

Economic interests—and the concomitant geopolitical need for stability and the ideological need for an "open" international system in which U.S. core values would be secure—impelled the United States to revive Western Europe and to incorporate it into the postwar international economic order.[63] The cold war heightened the importance of these interests, but it did not cause them.[64] Here it is important to remember that all of the Open Door's components *predated* the cold war: the perceived link between American prosperity and overseas economic expansion; the need for stable governments abroad that would favor openness rather than closure; the fear that autarky abroad would have inimical economic and strategic consequences for the United States; the belief that geopolitical stability was a prerequisite for an open international economy; and the conviction that the United States could be prosperous and free only in a world molded by America's political, economic, and cultural values. Moreover, America's Open Door objectives in Western Europe were the same in 1945 as they had been after 1918, when it had sought to "integrate markets, expand trade, and stimulate growth" in Western Europe to ensure American prosperity and stabilize the Continent.[65] Given the "lines of continuity" linking Washington's Open Door goals in Europe after the two world wars, there is every reason to believe—or, more correctly, no reason not to believe—that the United States would have pursued those objectives even in the absence of a clash with the Soviet Union.[66]

America's Role as Regional Stabilizer

Following World War II, U.S. policymakers viewed Western Europe's traditional balance of power security architecture as a "firetrap" that had involved the United States in two world wars, and as Undersecretary of State Robert Lovett said, Washington was going to make certain that this firetrap was not rebuilt.[67] Just as postwar U.S. officials regarded as unhealthy a Western Europe fragmented economically along national lines, during both the Truman and Eisenhower administrations Washington viewed Western Europe's division into sovereign nation-states as the primary source of the instability that had caused two world wars. Warning of the risks if Western Europe returned to its traditional geopolitical patterns of behavior, Secretary of State John Foster Dulles stated in 1953, "Surely there is an urgent, positive duty on all of us to seek to end that danger which comes from within. It has been the cause of two world wars and it will be disastrous if it persists."[68] Thus, U.S. policymakers were determined that "European security must be built on a much sounder basis than in the past."[69] The kind of Western Europe central to postwar U.S. grand strategic objectives was one in which the freedom of the Western European states to act as sovereign national entities would be severely constrained. In the realm of security, as well as that of economics, the U.S. sought to curb the power of Western Europe's states by fostering integration.

AMERICA'S GERMAN DILEMMA AND THE IMPERATIVES OF "SINGLE CONTAINMENT"

The biggest challenge facing Washington was what to do about Germany. The conventional wisdom is that America's post–World War II Western European grand strategy was—as Wolfram Hanreider famously described it—one of *double* containment; that is, containment of both the Soviet Union and Germany.[70] With the cold war's onset, Washington wanted to add the economic and, eventually, military resources of a revived Western Europe—especially of West Germany—to the anti-Soviet coalition. However, because the prospect of a revived Germany aroused obvious fears in Western Europe, U.S. policymakers needed to figure out how "to reconcile the economic and security imperatives underlying American policy: Germany's revitalization had to be harnessed to the causes of European recovery and Soviet containment without restoring its prewar hegemony or reinvigorating the economic autarky that had twice led to world war."[71] Hence, the description of American strategy as "double" containment. Yet we should not be blinkered by the cold war: the United States would have had to contain Germany even if there had been no Soviet threat, and no cold war.[72] Put another way, had the United States not needed to pursue a European grand strategy based on double containment, the Open Door's logic would have impelled Washington to adopt a strategy of *single* containment directed at Germany.[73]

The German Problem and West European Economic Revival Germany and its long-standing rivalry with France was the most specific manifestation of the West European "firetrap." France and Germany were the two most important states in postwar Western Europe, but they had been at each other's throats three times in seventy years. When World War II ended, the last thing France—and the other Western European states that had been victims of German aggression—wanted was to see Germany back on its feet either economically or geopolitically. U.S. policymakers, too, were also concerned, and they were no less resolved than their French counterparts to keep Germany in check.[74] A State Department paper nicely summarized Washington's thinking about Germany: "the right kind of Germany" would be an important "economic and political asset to the West," but the "wrong kind of Germany"—a Germany in which nationalist forces were ascendant—would be an "imminent danger" to American interests in Europe.[75] Consequently, Washington was "fully determined to end the German menace once and for all."[76]

Yet, as U.S. policymakers recognized, Western Europe's postwar economic recovery was linked to a rejuvenated German economy.[77] Germany still "was the pivot of the continent's international trade and payments and the driving force in its technological advance."[78] If Germany remained down and out economically, Western Europe would be unable to regain its economic footing. Yet, given the worrisome geopolitical implications, for U.S. officials the fact that Germany was Western Europe's economic motor could not be viewed as anything other than a "bitter economic reality."[79]

Even while World War II was ongoing, U.S. policymakers realized that Western Europe's postwar economic fate was linked to Germany's. The decision to revive the German economy was made for Open Door reasons, and, as Carolyn Woods Eisenberg makes clear, it "predated the East-West rift."[80] Washington understood clearly that without a productive German economy, the Marshall Plan stood no chance of succeeding, and the United States would be unable to realize its Open Door goals. In 1947 Secretary Marshall, Navy Secretary Forrestal, and Secretary of War Robert Patterson concurred "that Germany must cooperate fully in any effective European plan, and that the economic revival of Europe depends in considerable part on recovery in German production—in coal, in food, steel, fertilizer, etc., and on efficient use of such European resources as the Rhine River."[81] Indeed, it has been argued, notably by John Gimbel, that, far from being a response to the Soviet Union or the cold war, the Marshall Plan's real purpose was to make Germany's economic reconstruction politically acceptable (in both the United States and in Western Europe) by presenting it as a *Western European* economic recovery program.[82] For the Open Door policy to work in Western Europe, however, Washington had to reassure France—which U.S. policymakers considered "the keystone of continental Europe"—that Germany's economic resurgence would not result in the restoration of German predominance in Europe.[83]

Resolving the Franco-German Rivalry At the end of World War II, the primary concern of French policymakers was to reduce Germany's relative power advantage over France, constrain German independence, and enhance French influence in Europe.[84] France's German policy during the early postwar years conflicted with Washington's.[85] Whereas American aims in Europe required Germany's economic rehabilitation, France's security required that Germany be kept down.[86] Indeed, Germany's defeat seemingly paved the way for France to reassert its own ambitions for continental preeminence and to defang permanently its rival across the Rhine by following policies similar to those it had pursued from 1919 to 1924, including territorial annexations in the Rhineland, the Ruhr, and the Saar.[87] In contrast to the post–World War I period, the outcome of World War II appeared to offer some prospect that the French could be successful the second time around. As Alan Milward observes, Germany's unconditional surrender in 1945 was viewed "as an opportunity not to be missed. Germany was to be permanently weakened by being turned once more into a weak confederation of states with no central institutions."[88]

The flip side of Paris's post-1945 strategy of weakening Germany was strengthening France economically. In 1945–46 France aimed to obtain German coal and iron ore by dismembering Germany, which would kill two birds with one stone.[89] If the Rhineland, Ruhr, and Saar could be detached from Germany, Paris would be able to gain control over the coal and iron ore it needed to build up its own industrial base while weakening permanently Germany's industrial and military potential. However, Paris's annexationist strategy ran directly counter to Washington's policy of reviving Germany's economy to kick-start trade within Western Europe, and the French were forced to abandon it.

Although compelled to give up on annexation, France sought to attain its security and economic objectives through other means. The postwar French economic plan—the Monnet Plan, named after its architect, Jean Monnet—was more than a roadmap for France's industrial modernization and revival. It also had important strategic implications and, as Hogan notes, was designed to make "France, rather than Germany, the economic and political hub of the European system."[90] In essence, the Monnet Plan aimed at France supplanting Germany as Western Europe's leading steel producer.[91] Paris sought to cripple German industry once and for all by using the postwar occupation to dismantle many German steel mills and impose stringent controls on the output of Germany's remaining steel industry. At the same time, the Monnet Plan called for expanding French steel production capacity so that French steel exports would displace Germany's, with France becoming the prime supplier to the rest of Western Europe.

To facilitate the vastly expanded steel output called for by the Monnet Plan, France sought privileged access to West German coal and coke.[92] "Far from being based on a liberal internationalism," Milward observes, "the Monnet Plan was based on the crudest possible expression of mercantilist principles. It was aimed at seizing German resources in order to capture German markets."[93] Simply put, the Monnet Plan's objective was to enable France to absorb Germany's economic base and thereby "shift political power from Germany to France permanently, and thereby guarantee French security after the occupation ended."[94] As with its annexationist strategy, France's Monnet Plan clashed with Washington's Open Door strategy. This became especially apparent when the United States launched its Marshall Plan initiative.

The Marshall Plan confirmed an important shift in Washington's German policy, which reflected interlocking Open Door concerns and cold war exigencies. Instead of working with the Soviets to administer Germany as a single entity, Washington decided that American interests would best be furthered by Germany's division and western Germany's economic integration with Western Europe.[95] U.S. officials believed that a revived *West* German economy was the indispensable engine of Western European economic recovery, a view summed up in a State Department policy paper: "There can be no satisfactory future for Europe unless . . . the productive forces of Germany can again play a constructive part in the European economy."[96] Because the "predominant desire" of U.S. policymakers was, Eisenberg observes, "to use the German economy to create a free trading system in Western Europe," Washington had no patience with those—notably France—who regarded German economic revival as a security threat.[97]

The Marshall Plan compelled France to adjust its German policy. Washington's linked decisions to divide Germany, resuscitate western Germany's economy, and create a West German state made the Monnet Plan's German policy no longer viable. Paris, therefore, had to come up with new approaches, because even as the cold war intensified France continued to regard Germany as the primary threat to its security.[98] France adopted a dual-track policy. First, to control Germany, William Hitchcock notes, France abandoned its heavy-handed policy of coercion in favor of more subtle strategies, such as economic integration, regional planning, and political cooperation.[99] Second, France demanded—and received—military guarantees from the United States that it would be protected against German aggression. These military commitments made possible the pursuit of a policy of institutionalized collaboration and economic integration with Germany.

By 1948, U.S. and French policies began to converge. Officials in Washington understood that the United States could not achieve the Marshall

Plan's Open Door objectives without alleviating French apprehensions about Germany.[100] The source of French fears was clear to the Americans: "The crux of the problem is French concern over Germany's rapidly reviving economic power and the high level, relative to France, which it must be allowed to reach if it is to become self-sustaining."[101] To implement its policies, therefore, the United States needed to "take all possible steps to allay French fears consistent with conditions which would give Germany a chance for economic recovery."[102] Washington realized that Franco-German cooperation was key to Western Europe's stability.[103] Although Western Europe's political, economic, and security integration was the preferred American strategy for resolving the German problem—and for stabilizing the Continent—before integration could proceed the United States had to address France's security concerns. As Lewis Douglas, the influential U.S. ambassador to Britain, argued, if "assured of long-term United States defensive cooperation against German aggression . . . the French would relax in their attitude regarding German industry and reconstruction."[104]

Because the cold war dominates accounts of America's postwar European grand strategy, it is easy to overlook that the U.S. security commitment on the Continent was driven as much—indeed, arguably, more—by the need to reassure France that it would not again fall victim to German aggression than it was by concern with the Soviet threat. The 1948 Brussels treaty (Treaty of Economic, Social and Cultural Collaboration and Collective Self-Defence)— to which Britain, France, and the Benelux countries were signatories—was directed against Germany, not the Soviet Union. The impetus for the Brussels pact was British foreign secretary Ernest Bevin's January 1948 call for a "Western European Union." U.S. officials welcomed Bevin's initiative, because, as George F. Kennan put it, it was the only "hope of restoring the balance of power in Europe without permitting Germany again to become the dominant power."[105] At the end of February 1948, Marshall indicated that Washington would guarantee French security against Germany. France would be secure, he said, as long as U.S. occupation forces remained in Germany, and, given the deterioration in relations with the Soviet Union, he predicted that U.S. troops would remain in Germany for an "unforeseeable and indefinite duration, thus offering protracted security guarantees and establishing a firm community of interests."[106]

In early 1948 the three Western Allies met in London to concert their plans to incorporate western Germany into the Marshall Plan. The London meeting resulted in the announcement of the intention to create a federal state in western Germany, establish international control over the Ruhr, and set up a military security board to ensure that West Germany remained demilitarized. To secure French assent to the London agreement, the United States told Paris that U.S. troops would remain in Germany "for a long time."[107] The 1949 North Atlantic Treaty was designed in large part to assure France that it would not be menaced by a revived Germany, a fear that deepened with the impending end of the Allied occupation and the creation of the Federal Republic of Germany. For Washington, a—arguably, *the*—key goal of the North Atlantic Treaty was to assure the French that they would not be left alone to face Germany.[108] Ambassador Bruce said the United States would need to give France "binding security commitments looking far into the future," and, as Acheson acknowledged, this is what the North Atlantic Treaty was intended to do.[109]

By the late 1940s, the cold war's shadow came to loom over America's Western European grand strategy. Hence, America's policy of "keeping the Russians out" became entangled with its goal of "keeping the Germans down." The cold war forced Washington to deal with the complex issue of German rearmament and caused U.S. officials to worry that a renascent Germany would either play off the United States against the Soviets or align with Moscow in the hope of attaining reunification.[110] These issues were what double containment was all about. Yet the contours of U.S. strategy were shaped before the Soviet-American confrontation heated-up. Fundamentally, U.S. strategy was driven by the logic of the Open Door, which would have required that the United States "keep the Germans down" with or without the cold war. It was the Open Door that dictated that the United States had to stabilize Western Europe in order to facilitate the Continent's economic recovery and integration. It was the Open Door, not the cold war, that dictated that the United States address French concerns about German power. For Washington, Franco-German reconciliation was, as Klaus Schwabe observes, "a value, independently of the Cold War."[111] To gain French acceptance of German recovery Washington was compelled to make a long-term military commitment to Western Europe.[112] As Kennan said, the United States had "no intention of permitting Germany to become again a threat" to Western European stability, and to this end it would maintain troops in Germany until such time as ironclad safeguards were in place to prevent a resurgence of German military power.[113] Washington was under no illusions about what its role as Western Europe's hegemonic stabilizer entailed. As a 1949 State Department paper put it, the United States was pledged "not to withdraw from Europe until the peace is secure. And we shall neither evade nor withdraw from whatever obligations must be undertaken in order to maintain that peace *in perpetuity*."[114]

IMPLEMENTING AMERICAN HEGEMONY IN EUROPE THROUGH SUBORDINATION

America's military presence in Western Europe was the necessary condition for achieving the U.S. goal of European integration.[115] For U.S. policymakers, European integration had a double meaning: economic integration was the key to the realization of America's Open Door policy in Europe, and European political integration was a mechanism for ensuring that postwar

Western Europe would remain geopolitically stable. The United States regarded integration as the antidote to the two main threats to postwar Western Europe's stability: the specific problem of Germany, and the larger fear that postwar Europe would revert to its traditional pattern of multipolar security competitions.[116]

For U.S. policymakers, the lesson of 1914 and 1939 was clear: unless reined in, Germany, because of its population and economic strength, would become the preponderant power again in Europe. In facilitating Germany's economic revival, U.S. policymakers had no intention of allowing Germany to become a geopolitical rogue elephant capable of disturbing Europe's geopolitical equilibrium.[117] The solution was to "de-nationalize" Germany by integrating it into a wider Western European framework. As Kennan wrote, "Germany became a problem child in Europe only since it has begun to think in national terms, that is, since it has become a Reich . . . it will continue to be a problem, and an insoluble one, as long as its affairs are approached on a nationalist basis. There is no solution of the German problem in terms of Germany; *there is only a solution in terms of Europe*."[118] Integrating Germany into Western European political, economic, and military institutions would smother its ability to adopt an independent security policy.[119]

U.S. policymakers promoted the creation of supranational economic institutions in postwar Europe as a means of solving the problem of German power. As Kennan and Murphy argued, if integration was the only feasible solution to the German problem, an integrated Western Europe into which Germany could be fitted had to be created.[120] The impetus for initiatives such as the 1950 "Schuman Plan"—named after French foreign minister Robert Schuman—to create a European Coal and Steel Community really came from Washington, not from Western Europe.[121] The United States championed economic integration as a means of diluting Germany's control over its own economy, which furthered two important goals. First, Germany's key industries and resources were made available to serve the broad economic interests of Western Europe. Second, economic integration prevented Germany from transforming its economic muscle into military power and making a new bid to dominate Europe. For the United States, integration was "designed to prevent the resurgence of former tensions and conflicts among the free nations of Europe and against any future revival of aggressive militarism."[122] Indeed, integration was so central to resolving the German problem that Kennan and his colleague Robert Murphy said, "If this closer association of the other European countries were not called for by other requirements, it would be called for by their *common interest in handling the German problem alone*."[123]

PREVENTING MULTIPOLAR INSTABILITY WITHIN
EUROPE THROUGH INTEGRATION

For the United States, the biggest threat to peace and stability in Western Europe was the region's potential reversion to multipolarity, which would lead to renewed security competitions and, possibly, war and thereby undermine U.S. Open Door economic interests.[124] The kind of Western Europe central to postwar U.S. grand strategic objectives, therefore, was one in which the freedom of the Western European states to act as sovereign national entities was constrained tightly. The U.S. diplomat Charles Bohlen cut to the heart of the U.S. de-nationalization strategy when he said "our maximum objective should be the general one of making common European interests more important than individual national interests."[125] Indeed, as Geir Lundestad observes, integration's attractiveness was precisely that it "would do away with old-fashioned nationalism" in Western Europe.[126] Attaining integration and unity was an explicit goal of U.S. policy from the Marshall Plan onward.[127] However, when they spoke of integration leading to Western European unity, U.S. policymakers really meant they wanted to tie the hands of the Western European states—especially France and Germany—so tightly that they would be unable to pursue independent, national policies in economic or security affairs.[128]

The United States pushed for European integration to ensure that "divisive nationalist trends" did not reemerge.[129] When U.S. policymakers invoked—as they often did—the specter of European "disunity," the were using the term as a code word for the possibility that Europe would backslide into its traditional, multipolar pattern of security relations.[130] The United States, in Dulles's words, saw Western European integration as a means "to create a situation where the Western nations will cease this suicidal strife in which they have been engaged in recent centuries."[131] By persuading the Western Europeans to "pool" their military and economic sovereignty, Washington aimed to strip them of the capacity to take unilateral, national action.[132] As Kennan put it, the United States wanted Western Europe integrated on terms that "would automatically make it impossible or extremely difficult for *any member*, not only Germany, to embark upon a path of unilateral aggression."[133] For the United States, the utility of institutions like NATO, the European Defense Community (EDC), the European Coal and Steel Community, and the Common Market was that they could help to constrain the Western Europeans.[134] As the State Department said, the United States hoped that "cautious initial steps toward military, political, and economic cooperation will be followed by more radical departures from traditional concepts of sovereignty."[135] U.S. officials sought to use institutions to subordinate the individual interests of the Western European states to the overarching interests of the Atlantic community, because they believed that a "partial surrender" of sovereignty in the realm of security would "become a driving force toward further unification in Western Europe."[136]

NATO—and the Atlantic Community concept to which it was central—became the linchpin of the U.S. strategy of preventing the reemergence of European multipolarity. Through NATO and the Atlantic Community, and its Military Assistance Program, Washington made certain that Western European integration was harnessed to U.S. interests. The integration of Western European defense under an American supreme commander was intended to ensure that the Europeans did not return to defense policies based on purely national armies.[137] Western European integration was a means to prevent any Western European state from acquiring the military capability to support autonomous national security policies, and, more specifically, it was the preferred instrument to control the military power of a renascent Germany.[138]

The question of constraining Germany militarily became acute as the cold war intensified, especially after the outbreak of the Korean War in June 1950. Yet, even as U.S. grand strategy came to be increasingly dominated by cold war concerns, U.S. officials never lost sight of the purely Western European dimension of the German problem and its relation to the Open Door. Once the decision to revive Germany economically was implemented, Washington was keenly aware that German power was growing rapidly and that it threatened to upset the precarious Franco-German balance on which the realization of America's Western European objectives seemed to hinge.[139] The Franco-German relation was at the forefront of American concerns. According to McBride, who transcribed the minutes of a foreign ministers meeting, Dulles believed that "the history of the past two hundred years in Europe showed that *Western Europe would tear itself to pieces unless the Franco-German problem were resolved.* He said the results of the European wars had been a decline in the power and influence of Western civilization."[140] Thus, he said six months later, "As we see it, the post-war planning of Western Europe is designed to correct some of these serious mistakes of the past and to *create a situation where the Western nations will cease this suicidal strife* in which they have been engaged in recent centuries."[141] Because of its Open Door aims, the United States had foremost to solve the Franco-German problem and keep peace in Europe—a point underscored by Dulles himself.[142] To accomplish these tasks, the State Department Planning Staff observed, the United States needed to foster the emergence of "an integrated Europe in which German participation is so hedged by safeguards that it cannot develop into hegemony."[143] NATO and the abortive EDC were the instruments through which Washington sought to accomplish this goal.

From the outset, the North Atlantic Treaty—which morphed into the North Atlantic Treaty Organization in 1950—was conceived of as more than a bulwark against the Soviet Union. It was intended to be a defensive alliance to "resist aggression, whatever its source," and specifically as a safeguard that would ensure that Germany could not "again plunge Europe into war."[144] German rearmament would frighten France (and the other Western European states) and imperil America's own strategic objectives in Western Europe.[145] So the trick, Acheson observed, was to incorporate German military power into Western Europe's defense "without disrupting anything else we were doing and without putting Germany into a position to act as the balance of power in Europe."[146] The answer was to absorb German military power into a broader Western European framework, by embedding its forces in supranational structures. In Acheson's words, Washington realized "only too well that we must not recreate a German national army which would be independent and a powerful separate force," and, therefore, German forces were to be organized "so that they could not function alone and separately."[147] At a minimum, the West Germany military would not be allowed to have an independent general staff, and "the dependent nature of German forces" would be maintained by preventing West Germany from building up an arms industry under its national control.[148] At a maximum, West Germany's contribution to NATO was to be incorporated into the proposed European Defense Community.

The EDC was conceived of as the security counterpart to the ECSC. The idea was to permit NATO to draw on West German troops for Western Europe's defense without fueling the rise of a German military phoenix that could threaten America's Open Door interests in Western Europe or imperil French–Western European security. As Dulles put it, Western Europe's security required a German contribution, and the EDC was an "orderly way to bring it about so Germany can be tied solidly to the West and at the same time not be a potential danger."[149] The EDC reflected the U.S. preference for a federal approach to European integration and security.[150] The United States, Kevin Ruane observes, was the strongest supporter of the EDC, because it was "seen in Washington as a vehicle for realizing the wider American goal of a United Europe."[151] The idea behind the EDC was simple: the West European states composing the EDC would appoint a common defense minister and raise a multinational Western European army, which would be placed under NATO command. Germany's military power would be controlled by limiting German units to regimental size and embedding them in larger divisional-level formations with other Western European troops. The EDC, the State Department Policy Planning Staff noted, went hand in hand with economic integration in addressing the German question: "The new German armed forces, whether in a realized EDC or otherwise, must be subject to supra-national organs of control and not be permitted to develop as a national army under national control."[152] Although the EDC foundered in 1954 on the shoals of French domestic politics, its larger purposes were realized when the London so-called Nine-Power Conference (September–October 1954) approved the proposals put forward by British foreign secretary Anthony Eden as an alternative to the EDC approach to West German rearmament.[153] Although the Eden plan eschewed the EDC's federal approach to integrating a rearmed West Germany, it nonetheless achieved the same desired result of constraining Bonn's ability to take unilateral national actions in the realm of security.

Although the EDC was designed—against a cold war backdrop—to solve the issue of German rearmament through integration, it also was intended to serve the broader purpose of America's postwar European strategy: preventing Western Europe's reversion to multipolarity by diluting the sovereignty—in today's terminology, de-nationalizing—of all Western European states in defense and economic policy. Washington favored measures "which would tend to increase intradependence within the European community and its close association with and *dependence upon the broader Atlantic community.*"[154] U.S. policymakers promoted the EDC because it was based on the voluntary surrender of sovereignty by the Western European states and because they believed it would thus be a spur to further integration.[155] Washington similarly used NATO—and especially the Supreme Allied Commander Europe (SACEUR)—to foreclose the possibility that the West European states would re-nationalize their security policies.[156] The last thing Washington wanted was a Western Europe—or a West Germany—organized militarily on the basis of separate national armies under the control of the individual nations.[157]

In his famous December 1953 threat to undertake an "agonizing reappraisal" of U.S. policy toward Europe if France did not ratify the EDC, Dulles gave voice to U.S. concerns about Western Europe reverting to its bad old habit of multipolar power politics, and about the relationship between West European integration and U.S. interests in Europe:

> Much has been done to make Western Europe a healthy and co-operating area but decisive steps remain to be taken. These steps must involve something more than treaties between sovereign states. Mere promises for the future are not enough to bury a past so replete with bitter memories. The need is for Europe to move onward to more complete and organic forms of union. . . . If, however, the European Defense Community should not become effective, if France and Germany remain apart so that they will again be potential enemies, then there would indeed be grave doubt as to whether Continental Europe could be made a place of safety. That would compel an agonizing reappraisal of basic United States policy.[158]

Dulles's threat to reconsider America's European strategy was a bluff. Although some U.S. policymakers—notably Dwight Eisenhower—hoped that some U.S. forces eventually could be brought home, during the Truman and Eisenhower administrations complete U.S. military disengagement from Europe never was seriously considered.[159] Withdrawal was not a realistic option precisely because it was America's role as Western Europe's hegemonic pacifier—and the concomitant presence of U.S. troops—that kept the Western Europeans from returning to the kind of multipolar, nationalist security rivalries that would have been fatal to America's Open Door interests.[160] In particular, the structures the United States promoted aimed at the "single containment" of Germany.[161]

NATO was central to America's postwar European grand strategy, because quite apart from containing the Soviet Union, it was the means by which the United States ensured that Western Europe would remain stable geopolitically. Consequently, U.S. policymakers knew that there was a big risk in justifying NATO primarily in cold war terms. As Acheson noted, NATO was much more than a "medium term mil[itary] coalition to cope with the present Sov. threat."[162] If NATO was perceived as being essentially an anti-Soviet alliance, the Soviets could, by following a détente policy, undercut the ostensible rationale for NATO and for the U.S. military commitment to Europe.[163] Some four decades before the cold war's end, U.S. policymakers recognized the dilemma the United States would face if the superpower confrontation in Europe cooled. John C. Hughes, the U.S. permanent representative to the North Atlantic Council, observed that "NATO must be more than a mere military alliance to survive beyond the immediate threat of military aggression. . . . NATO must be more than a military coalition, otherwise it would be at the mercy of any plausible Soviet peace offensive."[164] To make certain that NATO could outlive the waning of the Soviet threat, Hughes argued that Washington would have to take "imaginative steps designed to develop North Atlantic Community which holds out to the peoples composing it hope for objectives broader and more lasting than deterring or repelling military aggression."[165] U.S. policymakers never intended that NATO should go out of business if the cold war ended. Given NATO's centrality to America's hegemonic strategy in Europe, Washington could not afford to have NATO go away just because the Soviet threat did. In the early 1950s, the United States intended to remain in Europe permanently, even if the threat of Soviet aggression disappeared, and this tells us an awful lot about the actual nature of America's grand strategic ambitions on the Continent. It tells us that the United States never contemplated following the offshore balancing strategy of coming home from Europe after the Soviet challenge had been disposed of.

* * *

Following World War II, America's European grand strategy was driven by its Open Door ambitions, and it would have been even if there had been no rivalry with the Soviet Union. U.S. policymakers believed that America's prosperity was linked to its access to Western European markets. There was more to the Open Door than economic interests, however: the Open Door strategy in Europe had crucial ideological and security dimensions as well. As a consequence, Washington promoted Western European political and economic stability to thwart the forces of closure and autarky from coming to power.

Officials were convinced that the safety of America's core values required that Western Europe be open to U.S. economic and ideological penetration.

The Open Door's logic also compelled the United States to take on the responsibility of acting as Western Europe's hegemonic stabilizer. Germany was at the root of U.S. strategy, because to make its economic rehabilitation palatable to the Western Europeans the United States needed to reassure them that they would not again fall victim to German aggression. To facilitate its role as Western Europe's stabilizer, the United States promoted Western European integration for security, as well as economic, reasons. Through integration, Washington also sought to prevent a reversion to destabilizing multipolarity by "de-nationalizing" Western Europe, and thereby making war impossible among the Western European states. Moreover, by using integration to subordinate the Western European states to an "Atlantic Community" dominated by the United States, Washington consolidated its hegemonic role on the Continent. There also was another aspect to America's hegemonic strategy in Europe: the United States wanted to prevent the emergence of an independent, Western European pole of power in the international system.

CHAPTER FIVE

The Containment of Europe: American Hegemony and European Responses

In addition to acting as Western Europe's regional stabilizer (or "pacifier"), the United States also sought to prevent the emergence of an independent pole of power on the Continent. America's hegemony on the Continent triggered Western European attempts to counterbalance U.S. power. In arguing that the Western Europeans have attempted to "balance" against U.S. hegemony, I am not suggesting that they believed that the United States posed an immediate, or existential, threat to their security. However, they have believed that the hard power asymmetry between the United States and Western Europe threatened important Western European security, political, and economic interests. For the Western Europeans, creating an independent pole of power has been a way of regaining autonomy over their own geopolitical destiny. If, in a unipolar world (and throughout the postwar era the non-Soviet world was unipolar), creating an independent pole of power to constrain a hegemon and creating the capability to act independently of it isn't counter-hegemonic balancing, it's hard to see what would constitute balancing behavior.[1] That the Western Europeans regarded America's hegemonic power as threatening should not be surprising, because Western European perceptions of the United States have always been far more ambivalent than most U.S. policymakers and foreign policy scholars care to admit.[2]

The first half this chapter is devoted to discussing the most important of these efforts, French president Charles de Gaulle's challenge to the United States's Western European hegemony. The U.S. reaction to De Gaulle's attempt to create an independent Western European counterweight to U.S. power is an important test of extraregional hegemony theory: if the United States had been pursuing an offshore balancing strategy toward the Continent, it should have welcomed the emergence of an independent pole of power in Western Europe to which it could have passed on the responsibility for defending Western Europe from the Soviets.

The second half of this chapter discusses America's European grand strategy from the end of the cold war to the present. The question I set out to answer is why the United States remains committed to maintaining its European hegemony and to acting as the region's stabilizer. If the United States truly was an offshore balancer, it should have brought its troops home from Europe when the cold war ended. Today, if the United States is following an offshore balancing grand strategy, it should welcome the efforts of the European Union to build an independent European military capability, to which Washington can devolve the responsibility for the Continent's defense. In fact, however, Washington has opposed the EU's bid for strategic autonomy and has sought to undermine the EU's "state building" process.

A Hegemon's Dilemma

At first blush, it seems difficult to reconcile America's postwar policy of reconstructing Western Europe with extraregional hegemony theory. After all, instead of trying to maintain its immense post-1945 relative power advantage over war-ravaged Western Europe, the United States chose to help the Western Europeans get back on their feet economically. Analyzing U.S. policy, Arthur Stein has suggested that the United States faced "the hegemon's dilemma" in the late 1940s with respect to Western Europe.[3] The hegemon's dilemma is choosing between competing logics of economics and security—between the logics of absolute gain and relative gain.[4] U.S. Open Door economic interests in reviving trade and creating an open international economic system pushed Washington to provide generous assistance to spur Western Europe's economic recovery. However, in the long term Western Europe's revival would diminish America's power relative to the Continent. A restored Western Europe inevitably would be a latent independent pole of power in international politics and a potential challenger to U.S. hegemony.

During the twentieth century, the United States *ostensibly* fought two big wars in Europe to prevent a single power (Germany) from dominating the Continent and mobilizing its resources to challenge the United States geopolitically in the Western Hemisphere. Since the 1940s, Washington has performed a delicate balancing act. For Open Door reasons, as we have seen, the U.S. encouraged Western Europe's integration into a single market. At the same time, however, the last thing U.S. policymakers wanted was for economic integration to cause the kind of political unification that could result in the emergence of a new pole of power on the European continent—whether in the guise of a resurgent Germany or of a politically united Europe. "Washington," observes Frank Costigliola, "always feared that a unified Europe—if it were truly independent—could be dangerous."[5] Here, the well-known quip that NATO was created to "keep the Russians out, the Germans down, and the Americans in" misses the mark. From Washington's standpoint, NATO's primary raison d'être was to keep America in—*and on top*—so that Germans could be kept down, the Europeans could be kept from being at one another's throats militarily, and also so that they could be kept from uniting politically and balancing against the United States.

U.S. strategists always understood that in pushing for Western European integration and "unity" there was the danger of creating the geopolitical equivalent of Frankenstein's monster.[6] Washington had no intention of allowing the emergence of a politically unified Europe capable of breaking free of U.S. tutelage.[7] More to the point, because they believed that the United States had the instruments of power and persuasion to keep the Western Europeans in line, postwar U.S. policymakers did not believe that the United States actually faced a hegemon's dilemma.

First, Washington believed the Soviet threat would keep Western Europe firmly tethered to the United States.[8] Second, U.S. policy was designed to keep an integrated Western Europe in check geopolitically by enfolding it within America's hegemonic embrace in a U.S.-dominated Atlantic Community.[9] As Secretary of State Dean Acheson said, "Unity in Europe requires the continuing association and support of the United States."[10] The State Department Policy Planning Staff made the same point: "If there is to be an effective organization of Europe, it will have to be set in a framework which assures continuous and responsible leadership by the United States."[11] Referring to the link among NATO, the Atlantic Community, and European integration, Acheson wrote that "in all these fields basic criterion from US viewpoint is, of course, extent to which any given action by Eurs promotes or prejudices US security and basic interests. North Atlantic community, which finds increasingly concrete expression in NATO, is accordingly framework within which we seek maximum development of common action in pursuit of basic objectives common to North America and Western Europe."[12] Simply put, as David Calleo observed, in the postwar era, from Washington's standpoint, the "Atlantic Community" always meant that the United States led and Western Europe followed.[13]

By anchoring Western European integration within the Atlantic Community structure that it dominated, the United States sought to prevent the Western Europeans from becoming an independent geopolitical "third force." As Secretary of State Dean Acheson and Undersecretary of State Robert Lovett told President Truman, "An increased measure of Continental European integration can be secured *only* within the broader framework of the North Atlantic Community. This is entirely consistent with *our own desire to see a power arrangement on the Continent which does not threaten us* and with which we can work in close harmony."[14] Acheson stated with crystal clarity the U.S. strategic intention of keeping Western Europe subordinated to U.S. hegemony when he adverted to the necessity of forging a "well-knit large grouping of Atlantic states within which new EUR grouping can develop, thus ensuring unity of purpose within the entire group and *precluding possibility of Eur Union becoming third force or opposing force.*"[15] In plain English, U.S. grand strategy sought to subordinate an integrated Western Europe to U.S. hegemony and to prevent the emergence on the Continent of an independent pole of power that could challenge Washington's predominance in Euro-Atlantic affairs.

The Gaullist Challenge to American Hegemony

The 1956 Suez Crisis was a watershed in Western European attitudes toward U.S. hegemony. Forced into a humiliating retreat from the Suez Canal by U.S. economic coercion, Britain—which in the late 1940s had aspired to become a third force in global politics capable of balancing against the United States—abandoned its claim to great power status and opted instead to maintain influence with Washington through the Anglo-American "special relationship." Suez had the opposite effect on the Continent. There, the crisis focused French and West German attention on the need for a Western European counterweight to U.S. power. As William I. Hitchcock recounts, West German chancellor Konrad Adenauer and French premier Guy Mollet were meeting in Paris on November 6, 1956, at the height of the Suez Crisis (and the simultaneous turmoil in Hungary). Shortly after Adenauer exclaimed it was time for Europe to unite "against America," Mollet excused himself to take a phone call from British prime minister Anthony Eden, who informed Mollet that, under U.S. pressure, London had decided to call off the Anglo-French invasion of the Suez Canal. When a crestfallen Mollet returned to the meeting room and conveyed the content of the telephone conversation to his guest, Adenauer consoled him by saying, "Now it is time to create Europe."[16]

Indeed, in the late 1940s and 1950s the founding fathers of today's European Union hoped that the European Coal and Steel Community and then the Common Market would be the embryo of a united Europe that could act as a geopolitical and economic counterweight to the United States. Thus, Geir Lundestad notes:

> Although they wanted the two sides of the Atlantic to cooperate more closely, in a more general sense it was probably also the desire of most European policymakers to strengthen Western Europe vis-à-vis the United States. This could be done economically by supporting the Common Market and politically by working more closely together on the European side.[17]

Even Jean Monnet, author of the Schuman Plan that proposed the ECSC and the "father" of European integration, first toyed with the idea of an Anglo-French federation in the late 1940s, because he saw that it could be the first step in constructing a Western European bloc capable of standing apart from both the Untied States and the Soviet Union.[18] However, it was not until Charles de Gaulle became president of France in 1958 that Western Europe took concrete measures to balance against American hegemony.

AMERICAN HEGEMONY AND THE
GAULLIST ALTERNATIVE

During the early and mid-1960s, de Gaulle mounted a strong challenge to American hegemony in Europe, which, as Frederic Bozo has put it, arrayed Washington's "Grand Design" of a Western Europe snugly embedded within the U.S.-dominated Atlantic Community against de Gaulle's "Grand Ambition" of a "European Europe."[19] These competing visions of Western Europe's role pitted the Gaullist aim of creating a Western Europe strategically independent of the United States against a U.S. policy driven, in Bozo's words, by "an internationalism both idealistic and hegemonic."[20]

De Gaulle's Grand Ambition was shaped by two underlying factors. First, a perceived shift in the strategic nuclear balance between the United States and the Soviet Union appeared to place in doubt the credibility of Washington's pledge to defend Western Europe, if necessary, with nuclear weapons.[21] Second, there was the problem of American hegemony, which was viewed in Paris as both European and global in nature. De Gaulle was well versed in the realities of international politics and believed that, because of its overwhelming power, the United States was driven "automatically" to extend its influence and "to exercise a preponderant weight, that is to say, a hegemony over others."[22] This was especially true in transatlantic relations. Moreover, following Washington's showdown with the Soviet Union in the 1962 missile crisis, De Gaulle concluded *then* that the world had become "unipolar"—dominated by a hegemonic America.[23]

By 1961, De Gaulle believed that Western Europe had recovered from World War II's ravages and was ready to reemerge as an independent pole of power in the international system—and that a revitalized France was prepared to assume the mantle of leadership in a European Europe. His Grand Ambition was a clear response to American hegemony; it was made up of five key elements—each of which challenged Washington's vision of U.S.-West European relations. First, de Gaulle opposed the integration of the French— and Western European—militaries into the U.S.-led NATO structure. As he saw it, an "integrated" Europe was an adjunct of U.S. power rather than an autonomous player in international politics. For de Gaulle it also was unacceptable for Washington to be the Continent's federator and protector, because these roles should be played by the Western Europeans themselves.[24] Second, De Gaulle opposed supranational approaches to Western European integration. France's aborted Fouchet Plan—which aimed to transform the European Economic Community (EEC) from a common market into a Western European organization with a common defense and foreign policy—rejected supranationalism in favor of an intergovernmental approach that recognized, and preserved, the sovereignty of the EEC's six members.[25] Third, De Gaulle believed that for both strategic and diplomatic (prestige) reasons, France needed to possess an independent national nuclear force.

Fourth, Gaullist policy envisioned a close Franco-German axis as the foundation for the Europeanization of Western European defense and the construction of an independent West European pole of power in international politics. Finally, de Gaulle aimed to overcome Europe's cold war division and—through a policy toward Moscow of "detente, entente, cooperation"—break the superpowers' condominium over Europe by replacing the "Yalta system" with a Europe united from "the Atlantic to the Urals."

The so-called American Grand Design for Western Europe was the mirror image of the Gaullist Grand Ambition.[26] Whereas Paris opposed the NATO concept of military integration, Washington viewed NATO as the linchpin of a strategy that would integrate Western Europe—not just militarily, but also politically and economically—within a U.S.-dominated Atlantic Community.[27] As Costigliola observes, Washington "talked community, but practiced hegemony."[28] The Fouchet Plan threatened this objective, which is why the United States opposed it. Echoing the concerns Dean Acheson had expressed a decade earlier, Washington feared that "a European Union acting in the defense domain might become a bloc within NATO and consequently contest U.S. leadership."[29] In contrast to De Gaulle—who had concluded that France needed its own nuclear weapons because strategic nuclear parity between the superpowers had eviscerated the U.S. nuclear guarantee to Western Europe—the Kennedy and Johnson administrations reached precisely the opposite conclusion. In Washington, strategic nuclear parity meant that NATO's strategy for Western Europe's defense needed to be based on "flexible response" (by upgrading the Alliance's conventional forces and decreasing its reliance on strategic nuclear weapons). That strategy, in turn, required that the United States exercise centralized control over NATO nuclear weapons. For the United States, the prospect of Western European states—France, or worse, Germany—having independent nuclear forces was anathema. Whereas Paris wanted a European Europe based on a Franco-German axis, Washington was determined to anchor—and contain—West Germany within the NATO/Atlantic Community structure. Finally, in contrast to de Gaulle—who aimed at breaking the cold war stalemate—the United States wanted to preserve the status quo in Europe (tacitly cooperating with Moscow to do so), and to thus choke off independent Western European initiatives toward the Soviet Union and East Central Europe. In contrast to the Gaullist approach, Washington wanted to bipolarize détente—thereby keeping management of the East-West relationship firmly in U.S. hands—and keep it focused on issues of concern to the two superpowers (primarily arms control agreements pertaining to strategic nuclear weapons).

Given the big difference in the way Paris and Washington looked at the world, the Franco-American tensions of the early and mid-1960s were inevitable. Washington saw French policy for what it was: a direct assault on the post–World War II hegemony that the United States had established over Western Europe.[30] Specifically, by raising the prospect of multipolarity within

Europe *and* of Western Europe's emergence as an independent pole of power in international politics, de Gaulle's Grand Ambition threatened to undermine the two cornerstones of America's Western European grand strategy.

U.S. FEARS OF MULTIPOLARITY WITHIN EUROPE

Just as it had during the late 1940s and early 1950s, during the 1960s the United States continued to fear that Western Europe would revert to destabilizing multipolarity. Whereas America's strategy was to *de*-nationalize Western Europe, de Gaulle's strategy explicitly sought to *re*-nationalize French (and European) security policy. Anticipating the apprehensions of their post–Cold War counterparts, U.S. policymakers in the 1960s feared that France's re-nationalization strategy would trigger a geopolitical chain reaction. If Paris pursued a sovereign national security policy, other Western European powers—especially Germany—would do the same. As John J. McCloy said, "He [de Gaulle] was stimulating nationalism which would breed more nationalism."[31] For Washington, "nationalism" was a code word for a return to Europe's historic pattern of great power behavior.

A multipolar, re-nationalized Western Europe would undermine America's Open Door interest in regional peace and stability. As the U.S. ambassador to France, Charles Bohlen, put it, de Gaulle was "convinced that nineteenth century nationalism is motor force of international affairs. Effective manipulation of these nationalistic forces could result in serious erosion of American position."[32] In June 1963, after de Gaulle had challenged U.S. primacy by concluding the Franco-German treaty (Treaty of Elysée) and vetoing Britain's application to join the Common Market, Undersecretary of State George Ball said, "Never, at any time since the war—and this is the main point—has Europe been in graver danger of back-sliding into the old destructive habits—the old fragmentation and national rivalries that have twice brought the world to disaster in the past."[33] What George Ball called old-style "competitive nationalism" was a threat to the American vision of "European unity"—that is, an integrated, de-nationalized, and stable Europe subordinate to the United States.[34] Indeed, the core ambition of Washington's Grand Design was to create an Atlantic Community that "would link America to an 'integrated' Europe—meaning free from national ambitions deemed to be archaic."[35]

U.S. FEARS OF WESTERN EUROPE'S EMERGENCE AS AN INDEPENDENT POLE OF POWER

Washington's other big concern was de Gaulle's stated ambition to create an independent pole of power in Western Europe. President Kennedy noted that if de Gaulle succeeded, U.S. leverage over Europe could wane, because the Western Europeans, having staged a vigorous postwar recovery, no longer were dependent on the United States economically. Acknowledging that "the European states are less subject to our influence," Kennedy went on to say "if the French and other European powers acquire a nuclear capability they would be in a position to be entirely independent and we might be on the outside looking in."[36] "Here," comments Bozo, "we are at the heart of the Franco-American misunderstanding. Despite its rhetoric on the subject since the early 1950s, the interest of the United States consisted in avoiding Europe of the Six [the Common Market] being transformed into an autonomous strategic entity that would radically modify the givens of the transatlantic situation and would compromise U.S. preeminence in Europe."[37] Rather than welcoming the opportunity to act as an offshore balancer—and pass responsibility for the Continent's defense to the Western Europeans—the United States regarded the prospect of an independent pole of power as a dangerous challenge to U.S. primacy in Europe. Thus, unsurprisingly, Secretary of State Dean Rusk denounced the idea of a European third force as a "delusion."[38] Rusk told French ambassador Herve Alphand that the idea of a Western European third force "touched a sensitive nerve," and he denounced as "fallacious" the notion that Western Europe could achieve a status equal to the United States and Soviet Union.[39]

The United States did not oppose a French-led third force because of worries that Western Europe would adopt an equidistant posture between the United States and the Soviet Union in the cold war. Rather, the United States objected to the very notion of a Western Europe able to stand on its own, free from U.S. control. "We were concerned," Kennedy explained, "about whether there was to be a wholly separate, independent force unrelated to American responsibility and interest."[40] The United States found de Gaulle's policies so objectionable because, as Bohlen put it, de Gaulle was seeking to create a "European Europe under French leadership capable of functioning as third great concentration of international political force," a project inherently counter to U.S. interests.[41]

U.S. REACTION TO THE FRANCO-GERMAN TREATY

During the early and mid-1960s, de Gaulle mounted two specific challenges to America's European primacy: his bid to forge an independent Western European pole of power based on a Franco-West German alliance, and his attempt to build a French nuclear force. Throughout the 1960s, U.S. strategists fretted constantly that if Paris successfully lured West Germany out of the "Atlantic" (that is, U.S.) orbit, such a Euro-centric strategic axis "would fragment Europe and divide the Atlantic world."[42] In plain English, it would shatter U.S. hegemony on the Continent. Washington's worst nightmare seemed to become a reality when, on the heels of the transatlantic crisis precipitated by France's veto of Britain's bid to join the Common Market, West German chancellor Konrad Adenauer and President de Gaulle signed the Franco-German treaty on January 22, 1963.[43]

The treaty was the centerpiece of the Gaullist vision of a European Europe, and it also evidenced Adenauer's disenchantment with U.S. policy, which stemmed from the Kennedy administration's handling of the 1961–62 Berlin crisis. The crisis underscored growing doubts about the credibility of America's extended deterrence strategy and of Washington's commitment to German reunification.[44] Washington's passive acquiescence in the erection of the Berlin Wall and subsequent bilateral negotiations—correspondence between Kennedy and Nikita Khrushchev and the parallel talks that Secretary of State Dean Rusk conducted separately with Soviet foreign minister Andrei Gromyko and with the Soviet ambassador to the United States, Anatoly Dobrynin—suggested to Adenauer (correctly) that the United States and the Soviet Union were tacitly cooperating to stabilize the postwar status quo in Central Europe at Germany's expense.[45] With good reason, Adenauer feared that the two superpowers would agree to a deal that ratified Germany's division, recognized (at least de facto) the German Democratic Republic, confirmed the Oder-Neisse line as Germany's eastern border, and foreclosed any possibility of West Germany becoming a nuclear power.

Washington reacted with alarm to the Franco-German treaty because it challenged NATO's role as the primary instrument of West European security and thus was a direct assault on U.S. hegemony in Western Europe. Indeed, top U.S. policymakers, including Kennedy and Rusk, believed that the treaty was intended to force the United States out of Europe.[46] It's not surprising that the U.S. moved decisively to eviscerate it.[47] Washington played hegemonic hardball—as Bozo says, "putting Bonn's back against the wall"—to compel West Germany's renunciation of treaty language that suggested that Western Europe's defense could be based on a Franco-German alliance, rather than on NATO.[48] The United States told Bonn it had to choose either Paris or Washington as its security guarantor.[49] As Marc Trachtenberg observes, U.S. officials also told the Germans that if they chose the United States, "it would have to be on American terms."[50] America's "terms" were acceptance of U.S. hegemony in Western Europe. "Top American officials," notes Trachtenberg, "made it clear that they intended to take the lead and that Europe, especially Germany, would have to follow."[51]

To whip Bonn back into line, Washington followed a two-pronged strategy. First, the United States threatened that if Bonn did not irrevocably commit itself to the United States and NATO, the United States would withdraw from Europe militarily and wash its hands of responsibility for West Germany's defense. As Rusk said, "If Europe were ever to be organized so as to leave us outside, from the point of view of these great issues of policy and defense, it would become most difficult for us to sustain our present guarantee against Soviet aggression. We shall not hesitate to make this point to the Germans if they show signs of accepting any idea of a Bonn-Paris axis."[52] Second, underscoring its anger over the treaty, Washington intervened in West German domestic politics to vitiate it. This "major American intervention in German internal politics" included U.S. prompting of leading West German politicians to speak out against Adenauer's foreign policy and collaboration with the "Atlanticist" wing of the ruling Christian Democratic/Christian Socialist coalition to secure Bundestag passage of a treaty preamble reaffirming the primacy of West Germany's commitment to NATO, and to accelerate Adenauer's retirement and replacement as chancellor by the more pliable Atlanticist Ludwig Erhard.[53]

THE GERMAN NUCLEAR QUESTION

De Gaulle's nuclear policy posed a twin threat to U.S. strategy. First, Washington saw France's push to build an independent nuclear deterrent (*force de frappe*) as part of Paris's drive to establish an independent West European pole of power. Second, U.S. strategists believed that de Gaulle's nuclear renationalization strategy would cause the "German question" to resurface. Washington responded to both of these strategic challenges with its ill-fated proposal to create a NATO multilateral nuclear force (known as the MLF).[54]

Keeping the West Germans from becoming an independent nuclear power was a "fixed point" of U.S. policy.[55] In this respect, U.S. policy represented the German prong of "double containment." A nuclear-armed Gaullist France was a bad outcome, but a "Gaullist" West Germany—armed with its own national nuclear force—would be even worse.

Given the apparent nuclear aspirations of West German "Gaullists" like Franz-Josef Strauss (the defense minister until late 1962), the Kennedy administration's fear that West Germany would go nuclear was not unfounded. Here, Washington was especially concerned that there would be a "demonstration effect" if France acquired its own nuclear weapons. The West Germans would say, "If others can have nuclear weapons, why can't we?" Understandably, Washington was concerned that France's pursuit of an independent nuclear capability would spur Bonn to go down the same path. If Germany did go nuclear, it would "throw into disarray" Washington's efforts to promote European integration and to strengthen the Atlantic Community.[56] So, with the proposed multilateral force (MLF), Washington aimed to scuttle the French plans for a nuclear force in the hope that this would quell any West German ambitions about acquiring its own national nuclear capability.[57] For the same reason—notwithstanding Kennedy's decision to give Britain Polaris missiles at his December 1961 Nassau meeting with Prime Minister Harold Macmillan—Washington also hoped that London's nuclear deterrent ultimately would be subsumed into the MLF, and thus disappear as a purely national force.

Washington believed the MLF would kill two birds with one stone. First, by refusing to help Paris develop its own national nuclear forces, the United

States sought to drive up the cost of going it alone in the hope that France ultimately would abandon its bid for nuclear independence and join the U.S.-controlled MLF.[58] If France (and, eventually, Britain) gave up their independent nuclear forces, Washington believed, West Germany would be content to remain without a national deterrent of its own. As Pascaline Winand puts it, Washington sought to "bring the French and British nuclear forces down to the same level in order to thwart the political and nuclear ambitions of both nations. Equality . . . would forestall the divisive forces of French and British nationalism and prevent the most divisive force of all from reemerging: German nationalism."[59]

Second, by allowing the Germans to participate in the MLF—over the use of which Washington retained a veto—West German demands for nuclear "equality" would be satisfied, thus further reducing Bonn's incentive to strike out on its own version of nuclear Gaullism.[60]

THE THREAT TO AMERICAN HEGEMONY
FROM A NUCLEAR EUROPEAN EUROPE

Washington's other big worry was that de Gaulle's nuclear policy would create an autonomous Western European defense capability. An independent pole of power would undercut the U.S. policy of "organizing Europe along lines consistent with US interests."[61] The MLF, however, would prevent Western Europe's independence. As Kennedy said, "It is through the multilateral concept that we increase the dependence of the European nations on the United States and tie these nations closer to us."[62]

The MLF was part and parcel of the U.S. strategy of maintaining its continental primacy by promoting the creation of a de-nationalized, integrated Western Europe enfolded into the U.S.-dominated Atlantic Community. In contrast to de Gaulle's European Europe based on the nation-state, "the MLF was specifically directed against the nation-state."[63] As National Security Advisor McGeorge Bundy noted, if the United States continued to encourage "movement toward European integration and Atlantic partnership," the negative consequences of France's independent nuclear policy could be "contained and limited."[64] Deane R. Hinton, the State Department's director of Atlantic Political-Economic Affairs, hit the nail on the head with respect to the de-nationalizing role European integration played in U.S. strategy. "The United States always has felt," he said, "that the Community structure tended to moderate nationalistic excesses."[65] As George Ball observed, de Gaulle's policies endangered the American strategic design for Europe, because, if Paris succeeded, "the achievement of a unified Europe and a dynamic Atlantic Community would be indefinitely postponed."[66]

NATO was the keystone of U.S. strategy, and Washington believed that the Alliance confronted an extant challenge in the French nuclear program and the Franco-German treaty and a potential one if the Soviet threat to Western

Europe ever was perceived to diminish. Indeed, a central thrust of de Gaulle's grand strategy was to bring about a relaxation of tensions with Moscow that would end the cold war—and with it, the so-called Yalta system. If successful, the cold war rationale for American hegemony on the Continent would be undermined fatally.

For Washington, the way to counter these threats was to reinvigorate the "Atlantic Community." Arguing that the United States should forge stronger economic and other links with Western Europe, George Ball observed that "the new relationships should go beyond purely military bonds to encompass political and economic matters, since the military relationship was based purely on fear which could prove to be a transitory phenomenon."[67] NATO would have important work to do even if the cold war receded, and the United States had to ensure it would outlive the East-West confrontation in Europe.

The United States could not afford to have NATO and the overarching Atlantic Community weakened, because they were the key to ensuring its fundamental interest on the Continent: making it safe for the Open Door by maintaining peace *within* Western Europe. As the Pentagon put it, "the preservation of the political stability and security of Western Europe" was "important to our national security."[68] Referring to the purported "lesson" of the two world wars, the Pentagon observed that, quite apart from the cold war, it was "very clear that the United States is needed in Europe" to create a political environment permitting "a secure and easy relationship among our friends in Western Europe."[69] As Rusk said, the U.S. military presence was pivotal to stability within Western Europe: "Much progress has been made. But without the visible assurance of a sizeable American contingent, old frictions may revive, and Europe could become unstable once more."[70] Similarly, Dean Acheson observed in the mid-1960s that, as the vehicle for America's stabilizer role in Western Europe, "NATO is not merely a military structure to prepare a collective defense against military aggression, but also a political organization to preserve the peace of Europe."[71] As had been the case in the 1950s, U.S. policymakers during the Kennedy and Johnson administrations were determined that NATO would outlive the cold war.

After the Cold War: A Seamless Continuity of American Grand Strategy

More than fifteen years after the cold war NATO is still in business and U.S. troops are still in Europe (albeit in much-reduced numbers from their peak cold war levels). This is something that needs explaining. After all, leading neorealist scholars predicted that, as a consequence of the Soviet Union's demise, NATO would unravel and U.S. military power would be retracted from Europe.[72] But it hasn't happened yet. On the contrary, in 1997, NATO expanded by admitting to membership three former Soviet satellites: Poland,

Hungary, and the Czech Republic. In March 2004, the Alliance completed a second round of expansion, admitting seven former Communist states, including the Baltic states, which formerly had been part of the Soviet Union itself.

Not only has the Alliance outlasted the cold war, but—not coincidentally—the United States continues to be the preponderant power in European security affairs. The obvious question, then, is why have predictions of NATO's demise and an American pullback from Europe not been fulfilled? One answer—John Mearsheimer's—is to say that the last fifteen years are an anomaly, not a predictor of America's early twenty-first century grand strategy. U.S. troops are still in Europe, he says, mostly because of inertia, and it is unrealistic to have expected that the United States would walk away from Europe "overnight."[73] Give it a bit more time and American power will be retracted from Europe as the United States reverts to an offshore balancing strategy.[74]

My answer is different. No one should hold their breath in anticipation of a U.S. military pullback from Europe (or from East Asia), because on the Continent the United States is—as it has been since the early 1940s—pursuing a grand strategy of extraregional hegemony, not an offshore balancing strategy. The driving force behind U.S. European grand strategy has not been "counterhegemony"—blocking the bids of other would-be European hegemons—but the goal of imposing America's own hegemony on the Continent. Offshore balancers neither seek extraregional hegemony nor act as regional stabilizers.[75] Therefore, evidence that America's European grand strategy is driven by the aims of perpetuating its hegemony on the Continent and maintaining regional stability would cast doubt on the claim that the United States has acted as an offshore balancer and support the case that the United States is an extraregional hegemon.

PERPETUATING AMERICAN HEGEMONY

The sudden collapse of Soviet power beginning in late 1989 seemingly swept away the foundations on which America's European grand strategy had been based for more than four decades. For the first time since the late 1940s, the United States was in a position to reexamine its commitment to Europe from the ground up.[76] As we know, this did not happen. Doubts that arose in the cold war's immediate aftermath about whether U.S. alliances could—or should—remain intact vanished quickly. Policy analysts argued that NATO should be invested with new missions: preventing power vacuums and instability, providing "reassurance," and promoting the spread of democracy and free markets into East Central Europe.[77] How can the continuation of the American commitment to Europe and the survival of NATO after the Soviet Union's collapse be explained?

In retrospect, perhaps it is not surprising that U.S. military power was not withdrawn from Europe after the end of the cold war. During the early 1970s, West Germany's Ostpolitik compelled the Nixon administration to consider what would happen to NATO—and to U.S. hegemony on the Continent—if the cold war status quo was revised drastically.[78] Ostpolitik was a direct challenge to America's Western European grand strategy, which held that Germany's division was the prerequisite for a stable Soviet-American relationship on the Continent and for U.S. hegemony in Western Europe.[79]

U.S. policymakers clearly understood Ostpolitik's implications. Washington could live with a modestly successful Ostpolitik, because a reduction of tensions in Central Europe would lower the risk of a superpower clash. But if the West Germans attained Ostpolitik's long-term objectives, the Nixon administration feared that the U.S. position in Europe could be jeopardized seriously. Merely by pursuing reunification, there was a risk that Bonn "could be inclined to view its policies in the East, rather than the West, as the most promising road to unity, and there could be some diminution of its ties in the West."[80] Moreover, if West German policy led to a real reduction in cold war tensions, "the internal cohesion of the Alliance might be far more difficult to maintain." The worst-case scenario was that if Ostpolitik produced a breakthrough in Bonn's relations with Moscow, East Berlin, and the Warsaw Pact states, "the role and influence of the United States in Europe can be expected to decline." The Nixon administration had no more intention than its predecessors—or successors—of allowing America's hegemonic role in Europe to be undermined. The administration therefore looked beyond the cold war and reformulated America's European interests in such a way that they would endure even if the cold war ended. Thus, in the early 1970s, U.S. policymakers were preparing the arguments for keeping NATO in business that would be advanced by officials and analysts after 1989.

At the top of the list was the Open Door. Unsurprisingly, Nixon administration officials believed that an immutable U.S. objective in Europe was "a secure and friendly environment for American investments in Europe and for the operation of trans-national corporations based on American capital, and the assurance of a mutually profitable trade relationship with Western Europe in the first instance but encompassing in time the entire continent."[81] Thus, as NSSM 84, prepared during the first Nixon administration, argued, U.S. forces performed important tasks unrelated to the cold war.[82] U.S. troops, NSSM 84 noted, "promote West European integration" and "contribute to political stability in and among West European countries."[83] In other words, America's role as the Continent's hegemonic stabilizer was what kept the Western Europeans from being at each other's throats. The American presence in Europe also served "to discourage pressures for nuclear proliferation" and to "provide a framework for German security and an *acceptable* German defense effort."[84] That is, U.S. forces still were needed to keep the

Germans down. And in case anyone missed the point, NSSM 84 made it with crystal clarity:

> The US commitment to Europe contributes to a stable relationship between those European countries into whose wars we have been drawn twice in this country [*sic*]. Our force presence is reassuring to those NATO Allies who would be uneasy about German domination without the balance provided by the US.[85]

Through NATO, the United States would continue to ensure that Germany would be contained and that the security policies of the West European states would remain de-nationalized. Even if the day for double containment passed, the United States would have to stay on in Europe to contain Germany, and it could use the German threat to rationalize the perpetuation of its preponderance in Western Europe. U.S. policymakers never entertained the idea of "coming home" from the Continent. Rather, they invoked the same reasons for the United States to exercise hegemony over post–cold war Europe as they had used to make the case for exercising hegemony over Western Europe after World War II.

NATO's POST–COLD WAR CENTRALITY

The European security arrangements that emerged after 1989 were not inevitable. There was no a priori reason to assume that the United States would maintain a military presence after Soviet power receded from East Central Europe, that NATO would survive once the Warsaw Pact began to dissolve or that a reunited Germany would be tied to an American-led alliance rather than being unaligned.

Prior to 1989, most observers probably would have made exactly the opposite predictions had they been asked to describe what a post–cold war Europe would look like. There was every reason to assume that the United States would withdraw its military forces from Europe and that once the conflict that brought them into being faded away, both cold war alliances would disappear and be replaced by a new European security architecture. Indeed, before 1989, many observers, especially Europeans, had argued that the dissolution of both blocs was a necessary precondition for ending Europe's division.[86] Those who envisioned German reunification as a realistic possibility invariably believed it could only happen if both superpowers militarily disengaged in Central Europe and if a unified Germany was attached neither to Washington nor to Moscow.[87]

When the cold war ended, however, U.S. policymakers were determined that America's European grand strategy would not be changed in any major way.[88] They did understand, however, that by removing the rationale for America's presence, the Soviet Union's collapse threatened Washington's hegemonic role in Europe.[89] President George H. W. Bush pretty much admitted this. When asked in December 1989, immediately after his Malta summit with Soviet president Mikhail Gorbachev, if the cold war was over, he responded: "If I signal to you there's no Cold War, then you'll say, 'Well, what are you doing with troops in Europe?' I mean, come on!"[90] Far from planning to leave Europe, the Bush I administration wanted to preserve America's hegemony in Europe and to keep NATO—the instrument through which Washington exercised its continental preeminence—in business. As Philip Zelikow and Condoleeza Rice, both of whom served as Bush I administration foreign policy officials, observe:

> [The Bush I] administration believed strongly that, even if the immediate military threat from the Soviet Union diminished, the United States should maintain a significant military presence in Europe for the foreseeable future. . . . The American troop presence thus . . . served as the ante to *ensure a central place for the United States as a player in European politics.* The Bush administration placed a high value on retaining such influence, underscored by Bush's flat statement that the United States was and would remain 'a European power.' . . . *The Bush administration was determined to maintain crucial features of the NATO system for European security even if the Cold War ended.*[91]

As the National Security Advisor Brent Scowcroft has written, "Whatever developed with respect to the Cold War," the United States "had to continue to play a significant role in European security," and "the vehicle for that role *must* be NATO."[92]

The Clinton administration similarly was resolved to preserve NATO and to ensure that the United States remained a "European power." The Clinton foreign policy team determined that the United States would have to reinvent NATO, investing the Alliance with new roles and missions that would provide a convincing rationale for keeping it in business.[93] Secretary of State Madeleine Albright's views on this subject encapsulated those of the Clinton administration and much of the U.S. foreign policy establishment. As one official who served under her recounts:

> [Albright believed that] America was a European power. It had fought the Cold War not only to defeat communism but to win the peace as well. . . . Albright firmly believed that *America's interest and role in Europe transcended the Soviet threat,* but that the Alliance had to be reshaped if it was to survive. She believed that NATO needed to be transformed and modernized to meet the challenges of the next fifty years—and the U.S. needed to do so at a time when many questioned whether it was needed at all or if the United States should even remain in Europe.[94]

Using phraseology reminiscent of Voltaire's comment about God, Albright said, "Clearly if an institution such as NATO did not exist today, we would want to create one."[95]

The Soviet Union's collapse made plain that, as Albright and her advisers believed, America's post–cold war European interests transcended Communism and the Soviet threat.[96] But there was nothing new here, because, as I have already demonstrated, since the end of World War II America's most fundamental interests on the Continent were unrelated to cold war concerns. These interests required the United States to don the mantle of hegemon and stabilizer in postwar Europe. Had the cold war not happened, U.S. policymakers in the late 1940s would have reached a similar conclusion to Albright's—that American Open Door interests required a continental commitment—and they would have acted on it.

THE BUSH ADMINISTRATION AND GERMAN UNIFICATION

Prior to November 1989 the Bush I administration articulated the U.S. goal of achieving a "Europe whole and free." This was just rhetoric, however. The last thing the administration wanted was a reunified Germany. Such a Germany would pose a double threat to U.S. hegemony in Europe. First, it would undermine the primary publically articulated rationale—Europe's cold war division—for U.S. predominance on the Continent. As Scowcroft observed, from Washington's standpoint "the status quo was the basis of postwar stability and peace in Europe. Why disrupt the situation with unnecessary talk of reunification?"[97] Second, a reunified Germany could plunge Europe back into multipolar power politics and possibly emerge as a challenger to U.S. hegemony. Thus, when events thrust German reunification to the top of the international agenda, the U.S. goal was to "anchor" Germany to NATO and thereby prevent a reunified Germany from following an independent foreign or security policy or acquiring nuclear weapons.[98] Washington created the so-called Two Plus Four diplomatic process to forestall Bonn from undermining U.S. interests by cutting a separate deal with Moscow on reunification.[99] U.S. officials believed that unless tied down securely by NATO, a reunified Germany would be a geopolitical loose cannon in Europe.[100] Such a "re-nationalized" Germany would trigger a renewal of security rivalries on the Continent and cause dangerous instability that would threaten U.S. interests in Europe.

The U.S. insistence on keeping Germany tied to NATO also had another dimension. The United States was determined to take advantage of a weakened Soviet Union to marginalize Russia as a future player in European security and ensure that it could not challenge America's global dominance. By playing hardball with the Kremlin in negotiating the post–cold war settlement in Europe, Washington was taking advantage of America's vastly increased relative power (the result of Soviet weakness) to achieve "a fundamental shift in the strategic balance" by compelling Moscow to accept a U.S.-imposed settlement, as if it had "suffered a reversal of fortunes not unlike a catastrophic defeat in a war."[101] Indeed, the United States was so resolved to have its way on German reunification that it was prepared to risk a backlash within the Soviet Union against Gorbachev and his reforms.[102]

To be sure, the United States wanted Moscow "to accept this result and believe they retained an appropriate, albeit diminished, role in European affairs."[103] Washington suggested cosmetic changes in NATO's declaratory policy to make it "appear" to Moscow that the Alliance was no longer a threat to the Soviet Union's security.[104] And U.S. officials tirelessly lectured the Soviets on why *they* would be better off if a reunified Germany were part of NATO.[105] The Soviets countered by arguing that a reunified Germany should either belong to both the Warsaw Pact and NATO or to neither of them.[106] Washington summarily dismissed any idea of compromise on a reunified Germany's NATO membership. As President George H. W. Bush said: "The Soviets are not in a position to dictate Germany's relationship to NATO. What worries me is talk that Germany must not stay in NATO. To hell with that! *We prevailed, they didn't*. We can't let the Soviets snatch victory from the jaws of defeat."[107] Washington's reassurances to Moscow that the United States "was not forcing Germany into NATO" were disingenuous.[108] In fact, as Scowcroft said in May 1990, the issue of Germany's full NATO membership was "not negotiable," because the United States already had decided that this was the only acceptable basis for reunification.[109] As Secretary of State James Baker told Foreign Minister Eduard Shevardnadze: "If push came to shove, we were going to admit a unified Germany into NATO over Soviet objections."[110] When the Berlin Wall came down, Washington flexed its bulked-up muscles to compel the Kremlin to accept a one-sided resolution of the German question.

THE EXPANSION OF U.S. POWER IN EUROPE

During the 1990s, the United States further exploited its cold war victory and consolidated its hegemonic role in Europe by twice enlarging NATO. Without countervailing Soviet power, there was nothing to prevent the United States from capitalizing on its increased relative power by expanding the scope of its influence in Europe both territorially and ideologically. Geographically, the Alliance's enlargement projected American power into a region that traditionally had fallen within Russia's strategic orbit, well outside of Washington's geopolitical purview (or, indeed, even its strategic radar screen). The United States pushed for the Alliance's enlargement, despite Moscow's strenuous objections and notwithstanding that this repudiated assurances given the Soviet Union during the German reunification negotiations.[111] The Clinton administration repeatedly stated that NATO's first round of enlargement was not directed against Russia.[112] This did not allay Moscow's fears, however.[113] Similarly, although the Kremlin was under no illusions about the inevitability of NATO's second round of expansion, Russia made clear that the Alliance's second enlargement threatened its security.

NATO's formal enlargement in the 1990s was only part of the expansion of U.S. power. Washington's post–cold war policy has been one of "double enlargement": not only extending NATO's geographical scope but broadening its mission to encompass regions beyond the Alliance's boundaries.[114] The Clinton administration asserted that, in the post–cold war era, America's, and NATO's, strategic concerns extended to Europe's peripheries, including the Baltic states, Ukraine, the Caucasus and Central Asia, North Africa, and the Balkans.[115] The Bush II administration has been similarly committed to the Alliance's double enlargement.

Double enlargement confirmed America's post–cold war role as Europe's stabilizer. In this role, the United States has sought to prevent the reemergence of new great powers within Europe that could cause European security affairs to become "re-nationalized." The stabilizing post–cold war U.S. military presence in Europe "reassured" the Europeans that they need not fear one another and, thereby, prevented Europe from relapsing into its bad old habit of power politics.[116] Washington also deemed it imperative to prevent "instability" on Europe's periphery—emanating from ethnic and national conflicts like those in the Balkans—from "spilling over" into its core.[117] If that happened, America's Open Door interests would be imperiled. As the Continent's stabilizer, the United States could not afford to ignore small wars in the periphery. Such conflicts, U.S. policymakers believed, had a tendency to mushroom into big ones, and history—so they claimed—demonstrated that the United States invariably is drawn into Europe's wars.[118]

The United States also has broadened its influence in Europe by imposing its preferred ideology, values, and political institutions beyond its traditional sphere of influence in Western Europe. Soviet power had frustrated Washington's post–World War II hopes of keeping East Central Europe open to America's economic and ideological influence. The collapse of Soviet power, however, meant that the United States now could bring East Central Europe inside the Open Door world, just as the United States had brought postwar Western Europe into its orbit some four decades earlier. In this respect, NATO's geographic enlargement advanced the Clinton administration's aim of "enlarging the zone of democracy" by consolidating the fledgling free market democracies of Poland, Hungary, and the Czech Republic. As President Clinton said, "We want all of Europe to have what America helped build in Western Europe—a community that upholds common standards of human rights, where people have the confidence and security to invest in the future, where nations cooperate to make war unthinkable."[119] The retraction of Soviet power presented the United States with the opportunity to build a post–cold war Europe based on America's liberal political and economic ideals. As Undersecretary of Defense Walter Slocombe put it, "We have the possibility to build a system in Europe—and indeed the entire world—organized on the model of what we used to call the Free World, that of liberal market democracies living in peace with their neighbors."[120] During the

1990s, the United States took advantage of the collapse of Soviet power to replicate throughout the Continent the political, economic, and security structures it constructed in Western Europe after World War II.[121]

Far from fading into decrepitude, NATO's importance to the United States was undiminished. The Alliance advanced several interconnected U.S. objectives: it forestalled the rise of European power centers that could challenge U.S. preponderance; it provided stability for the Continent by keeping the lid on Europe's latent geopolitical rivalries; and, by stabilizing the Continent's core and its peripheries, it created the security framework for the Open Door. In short, post–cold war NATO was the instrument through which the United States perpetuated its hegemonic role in Europe. This remained true even after 9/11, notwithstanding the Bush II administration's preference for seeking support from "coalitions of the willing," rather than NATO, for its military operations in Afghanistan and Iraq.[122] Washington's chilly response to Europe's attempts to develop autonomous military capabilities has made crystal clear both NATO's continuing centrality in U.S. grand strategy and that the United States has no intention of surrendering its hegemonic prerogatives in Europe.

MAINTAINING AMERICA'S EUROPEAN HEGEMONY

Since the late 1990s, Washington has attempted to derail the European Union's plans to create, through the European Security and Defense Policy (ESDP), military capabilities outside NATO's aegis. U.S. policy illuminates the drive for extraregional hegemony underlying America's European grand strategy. Washington wants to prevent Europe's "decoupling" from NATO to preclude the EU (or a subgroup thereof) from emerging as an independent pole of power. America's goal is to preserve NATO's primacy in Euro-Atlantic security affairs, and thus maintain U.S. hegemony on the Continent.

From the moment the cold war ended, the Europeans manifested "stirrings of independence bordering on insubordination" that reflected their growing restiveness with U.S. dominance of transatlantic relations.[123] At its Cologne (January 1999) and Helsinki (December 1999) summits, the EU took an important step toward military autonomy by adopting the European Security and Defense Policy.[124] ESDP is envisioned as the backbone of an independent European security policy, one developed by Europeans without U.S. input. At their November 2000 meeting, the EU's defense ministers gave . ESDP concrete expression by announcing plans to create a sixty-thousand strong Rapid Reaction Force (RRF).[125] The EDSP and the RRF fanned a sharp disagreement between the United States and the EU about how far the "Europeanization" of the Continent's defense should go. Immediately prior to the EU's December 2000 Nice summit, European Commission president Romano Prodi, French president Jacques Chirac, and French prime minister

Lionel Jospin all indicated that, although it would draw on European military assets also earmarked for NATO, the RRF would be an autonomous European force—the embryo of an EU army—with a chain of command, headquarters, and planning staff separate from NATO.[126]

The U.S. reaction to the RRF was swift and hostile. Speaking at a NATO defense ministers' meeting in Brussels just prior to the EU's Nice summit, the outgoing Secretary of Defense, William Cohen, declared that if the EU created an independent defense capability outside the Alliance's structure, NATO would become a "relic of the past."[127] Cohen's comments were a toned-down version of internal Pentagon discussions advocating that the United States respond to the EU's approval of the RRF by withdrawing its own military presence from Europe.[128] Foreshadowing the views of the Bush II administration, several days after the Nice summit, John Bolton, who shortly would become undersecretary of state during the Bush II administration's first term, described the RRF as "a dagger pointed at NATO's heart."[129] Like its predecessor, the Bush II administration has tried to keep Europe's defense capabilities tightly bound to NATO by diverting European defense efforts away from ESDP and the RRF and focusing them instead on building up a NATO Response Force.[130]

Since the end of World War II, as we have seen, the United States has supported European integration for its own strategic, political, and economic reasons.[131] However, U.S. support for European integration always has been conditioned on its taking place only within the framework of an overarching—and *American*-dominated—"Atlantic Community."[132] The United States has never wanted a truly equal Western Europe, because such a Europe not only would be independent of the United States but might exercise that independence in ways that clash with U.S. interests.[133] The EU's move toward strategic self-sufficiency, therefore, is regarded by Washington as a threat to NATO and, perforce, to U.S. preponderance in Europe.[134]

U.S. policymakers' reaction to ESDP and the RRF reflects long-standing U.S. fears that an equal and independent Europe would throw off Washington's tutelage and Washington's pervasive suspicion that ESDP and the RRF are the "camel's nose in the tent"—that they will become rivals to NATO in European security affairs.[135] From Washington's perspective, EDSP can only have one acceptable purpose: creating a European "pillar" of NATO that will enable the Europeans to share more of the burdens of the continent's defense. As Secretary of State Madeleine Albright said in 1998, ESDP is "a very useful way to think about *burden sharing*."[136] Other senior Clinton administration officials made clear that, for the United States, ESDP must be based on "the principle that these institutions should be the European pillar of a strong trans-Atlantic alliance and not separate and competing entities."[137] As Frederic Bozo suggests, the United States regards all European steps toward autonomy "with reticence bordering on hostility" and is incapable of accepting any European defense effort that it does not control.[138]

To block ESDP from undercutting NATO, the Clinton administration proclaimed the so-called Three Ds: ESDP must not diminish NATO's role, duplicate NATO's capabilities, or discriminate against NATO members that do not belong to the EU.[139] Implementation of the "Three Ds"—especially the nonduplication and nondiminishment proscriptions—would foreclose the EU from ever achieving strategic autonomy and would ensure Europe's continuing security dependency on United States. This is because the United States has a virtual monopoly on NATO military capabilities in such key areas as intelligence, advanced surveillance and reconnaissance systems, power projection, and precision guided munitions.

Transatlantic frictions arising from European efforts to build an independent military capability flared again during the Iraq War. For many European policymakers and analysts, the key "lesson learned" from the Iraq War is that Washington will pay little heed to European views on international political issues unless Europe can back up its voice with real military capabilities. Taking advantage of the EU's "variable geometry," which allows for structured, or enhanced, cooperation among subgroupings of the EU's membership—the EU version of "coalitions of the willing"—as the invasion of Iraq was winding down in April 2003, France and Germany (along with Belgium and Luxembourg) met to lay the foundations for an independent European military capability—including a European military headquarters—built around the Franco-German core of "Old" Europe.[140] French president Jacques Chirac explicitly said the purpose was to enable Europe to constitute a pole of power capable of playing its role in a multipolar system and of balancing the United States.[141] Predictably, Washington reacted coolly to this initiative. In October 2003, the U.S. ambassador to NATO, Nicholas Burns, called the EU's plan to develop an independent military capability "one of the greatest dangers to the transatlantic relationship."[142]

Some will look at declining U.S. force levels in Europe and suggest that the era of U.S. hegemony on the Continent has passed. This would be shortsighted, however. For sure, the number of U.S. troops in Europe has gone down from the cold war peak, and the Bush II administration is mulling plans to redeploy U.S. forces in Europe. Under the administration's current plan, when the U.S. commitment to Iraq ends—whenever that may be— some units deployed in Europe will be based in the continental United States and the remaining forces in the "New" Europe rather than in Germany. When it comes to American hegemony in Europe, however, numbers of U.S. troops there and base locations do not begin to tell the story.

The United States still controls the levers of military power in Europe. The NATO supreme command and the crucial Mediterranean regional command (North Africa and the Near East) are always held by U.S. officers whose chain of command goes to the Pentagon and White House. Within NATO, the United States still holds a virtual monopoly on military capabilities that are key to waging modern high-intensity conventional warfare. And, unlike the EU, the United States has the ability to project military power over great distances. Moreover, the United States can—and does—hamstring EU attempts to build a transnational European defense industry—especially by withholding important technologies. The United States has opposed the proposed European defense procurement agency, which is intended to facilitate the growth of an integrated European arms industry.[143] The U.S. can—and does—encourage European NATO members to concentrate individually on carving out "niche" military capabilities that will complement U.S. power, rather than potentially challenging it.

Finally, Washington can—and does—engage diplomatically in a game of "divide and rule" to thwart the EU's political unification process. For example, the United States has been pushing hard for the EU's enlargement—and especially the admission of Turkey—in the expectation that a bigger EU will prove unmanageable and, hence, unable to emerge as a politically unified actor in international politics. Similarly, the United States promoted NATO expansion in the hope that the "New Europe" (Poland, Hungary, the Czech Republic, and Romania), which—except for Romania (which is to join the EU in 2007)—simultaneously joined both the EU and NATO in spring 2004, will advocate Atlanticist interests over European ones within the EU and, thereby, form a counterweight against French and German aspirations for a united Europe capable of counterbalancing American hegemony. For the United States, a Europe that speaks with many voices is optimal, which is why it is trying to do what it can to ensure that the EU's "state-building" process fails, thus ensuring that a united Europe never emerges as an independent pole of power.[144] Finally, the United States has continued to remind the rest of Europe—sometimes delicately, sometimes heavy-handedly (as in President George W. Bush's speech in Prague during the November 2002 NATO summit)—that it still needs a hegemonic America to act as Europe's pacifier and stabilizer in order to "keep the Germans down."

* * *

The United States's resistance to Western European challenges to its continental hegemony refutes the notion that the United States has been acting as an offshore balancer with respect to Europe. By the early 1960s, at the latest, the United States could have passed the buck for Western Europe's defense to the Europeans. The U.S. commitment to defend Western Europe not only was expensive but dangerous, because it could have caused the United States to become embroiled in a nuclear war with the Soviets. Far from welcoming de Gaulle's attempt to create an independent Western European pole of power, however, the United States acted to preserve its hegemony over Western Europe. The story of America's post–cold war European grand strategy is a classic example of more of the same—or "déjà vu all over again." What is striking is its familiarity, not its novelty. As Leffler points out, when World

War II ended U.S. policymakers believed that "neither an integrated Europe nor a united Germany . . . must be permitted to emerge as a third force or a neutral bloc."[145] *Plus ça change, plus c'est la même chose.* The United States today is pursuing the same European grand strategy that it pursued during the cold war and the foundations of which were laid during World War II.

CHAPTER SIX

Liberal Ideology and U.S. Grand Strategy

Several years ago, David Stiegerwald suggested that in the cold war's wake, Wilsonianism—shorthand for the projection abroad of America's liberal ideology—had been rehabilitated and had reclaimed its central role in the shaping of U.S. grand strategy.[1] In truth, however, Wilsonianism did not need to make a comeback after the Soviet Union's demise, because with respect to U.S. grand strategy it never had gone away, although its role was obscured by the geopolitical aspects of the Soviet-American rivalry. The Soviet Union's collapse, however, lifted the realpolitik veil from American grand strategy and exposed to clear view its liberal ideological foundation.

Today, U.S. policymakers believe, as they have since the early twentieth century, that the United States can be safe only in an Open Door world—a world shaped by America's liberal ideology; and it is the Open Door, not the pressures exerted by the international system, that is the motor of America's quest for extraregional hegemony. The conventional wisdom is that liberalism has peace-promoting effects, which is why the political and economic Open Doors constitute the backbone of U.S. grand strategy. However, as I demonstrate in this chapter, the conventional wisdom is wrong. Far from bolstering U.S. security, America's liberal ideology leads to overexpansion, unnecessary military interventions abroad, and, occasionally, involvement in otherwise avoidable wars. Liberalism's consequences for U.S. grand strategy, in other words, are pernicious, not peace producing.

The Liberal Foundations of American Overexpansion

Liberal ideology shapes both the way policymakers define U.S. interests and their perception of threats to those interests. This linkage among ideology, interests, and threats explains a fundamental paradox of American grand strategy. It may be true, as John Lewis Gaddis has suggested, that paranoia is an occupational hazard for great powers.[2] One would think, however, that the United States would be an exception to this rule. At least since the early

118

twentieth century, the United States has been the most secure great power in modern international history. Since America's great power emergence, it is fair to say that U.S. policymakers never truly have believed that America's territorial integrity or its regional hegemony in the Western Hemisphere seriously have been menaced.[3] Even in the post-9/11 era, terrorism does not pose an *existential* threat to the American homeland. Yet, U.S. foreign policy elites traditionally have been afflicted by a pervasive sense of U.S. vulnerability, which is, as William Appleman Williams observed, a byproduct of "American exceptionalism" (the belief that, because of its domestic political system and ideology, the United States is a singular nation). Because of this perceived singularity America has had "a deep sense of being alone" and of being "perpetually beleaguered."[4]

From the beginning, America's grand strategy has been based on the premise that the one sure means of reducing U.S. vulnerability is by gaining absolute security.[5] In the decades following 1783, when the United States was weak, it sought absolute security by trying to insulate itself from Europe's great power rivalries. However, since the beginning of the twentieth century—when the relative capabilities of the United States increased and it emerged as a great power—the attainment of absolute security has been linked to the establishment of an Open Door world. The formidable hard power of the United States meant that it no longer was constrained to adopt a limited definition of its national interests, and the construction of an Open Door world became a seemingly feasible grand strategic objective for the United States to pursue.[6]

In seeking absolute security by achieving an Open Door world, the goal of U.S. grand strategy is nothing less than to "shape the international environment." U.S. officials have adopted an ideological, de-territorialized definition of America's security requirements, which focuses on "threats" to American core values that ideological or economic closure abroad would pose to liberalism at home. Given this broad definition of U.S. security requirements, it is unsurprising that policymakers always are quick to see even improbable dangers as imminent ("or grave and gathering") threats. As Robert Johnson explains, in contrast to concrete territorial threats to the nation's security, threats to world order generate a pervasive anxiety "that has at its center the fear of the unknown. It is not just security, but the pattern of order upon which the sense of security depends that is threatened."[7] By definition, any strategy that equates security with the defense of de-territorialized "milieu goals"—like openness—rather than with tangible strategic factors—like geography and the distribution of power—is open ended, because it is impossible to fix a point beyond which America's security interests are not implicated.[8]

U.S. grand strategy is both ambitious and expansionary precisely because it is predicated on the belief that the health of America's core values at home is linked to the maintenance of an Open Door world abroad. Liberalism imposes a logic on U.S. grand strategy that causes overexpansion: it defines U.S. interests expansively; those interests are believed to be threatened potentially by events anywhere, which engenders "domino theory" thinking; maintenance of an Open Door world requires the United States constantly to demonstrate its credibility; and, because the United States must fight when its territorial security is not obviously endangered—or, more correctly, obviously is not endangered—U.S. policymakers usually must resort to threat inflation to justify U.S. intervention abroad.

The Political Open Door and American Overexpansion

Walter LaFeber has observed that "America's mission" of extending democracy worldwide is not altruistic. Rather, "it grew out of the belief that American liberties could not long exist at home unless the world was made safe for democracy."[9] U.S. officials worry that turmoil *anywhere*—even events in the distant reaches of the periphery—could spark a geopolitical chain reaction that spirals out of control and culminates in "a strangulating constriction of an open world environment."[10] Of course, there is a dark side to America's mission: the belief that the United States can be secure *only* in an Open Door world of ideologically like-minded states. Louis Hartz correctly identified the source of this belief when he described the effects of "liberal absolutism" on American politics.[11]

Notwithstanding its unquestioned position as the "hegemonic ideology" in America, Hartz argued that liberalism nonetheless has been deeply insecure about its dominant role in U.S. domestic politics. Consequently—and ironically in view of the prevailing understanding that tolerance is intrinsic to liberalism—as a political philosophy American liberalism is *in*tolerant of competing political ideologies.[12] And it has sought preemptively to discredit, and suppress, them in order to maintain its domestic intellectual and ideological ascendancy. American liberalism operates the same way abroad as it does at home. American liberalism assumes that to be secure domestically it must extirpate hostile ideologies abroad; it can remain hegemonic at home only by attaining hegemony abroad. American liberalism is, therefore, the hegemonic ideology at home and the ideology of hegemony abroad—and it is the fountainhead of America's imperial ambitions.

An Open Door world is American liberalism's way of replicating in foreign affairs the same ideological preeminence it has enjoyed within the United States. In other words, the United States—and American core values—can be secure only by eliminating all external sources of ideological contagion. In this respect, the distinction between America's foreign and domestic policies long has been blurred—if not, indeed, erased. As Lloyd C. Gardner notes, the key assumption underlying U.S. grand strategy is that "America must have a favorable climate for its institutions to thrive, and perhaps even for them to survive."[13] President Franklin D. Roosevelt declared: "If the United States is to have any defense, it must have a total defense. We cannot defend ourselves a little here, and a little there."[14] Echoing FDR, Kennedy and Johnson's Secretary of State Dean Rusk neatly captured the synthesis between absolute security and America's liberal ideology when he remarked that "the U.S. is only safe to the extent that its total environment is safe."[15] One of Rusk's predecessors, Cordell Hull, claimed that if the United States was left alone in an ideologically inhospitable world, "the sphere of our international relationships would shrivel until we would stand practically alone among the nations, as a self-contained hermit state."[16] Similarly, during the height of the cold war, Walt W. Rostow and Max Milliken linked the survival of liberalism at home with fostering democracy and economic development in the Third World: "We have, in short, a major and persistent stake in a world environment predominantly made up of open societies; for with modern communications it is difficult to envisage the survival of a democratic American society as an island in a totalitarian sea."[17] There is an obvious escape path from this nightmare of ideological isolation. By exporting democracy the United States can kill two birds with one stone: it can assure itself that it won't be alone in a hostile world, and it can eliminate the ideologies that are said to threaten the Open Door world on which American security purportedly depends.

Just as American policymakers fear that "democracy in one country" would not be viable, they also believe that a world of many democracies will be peaceful and stable.[18] And, at least since Woodrow Wilson's time, U.S. policymakers have subscribed to liberal ideology's claim that "bad" states—that is, nondemocracies—are the cause of bad things in international politics, like war and instability. Robert E. Osgood nicely captured liberalism's take on American strategy: "War is wicked, it must be caused by wicked men; therefore, convert the misguided, and peace will reign."[19] Distilled to its essence, this is what the so-called democratic peace theory is all about.

As a *theory* of international politics, the democratic peace theory carries little weight.[20] It rests on dubious grounds methodologically.[21] More important, it is not valid empirically. Democratic states *have* gone to war with other democracies, and in crises democracies are just as prone to making military threats against other democracies as they are against nondemocracies.[22] However, democratic peace theory has a lot of clout in policymaking because it plays to the Wilsonian predispositions of U.S. strategists and provides the United States a handy pretext for intervening in the internal affairs of regimes it considers troublemakers. Thus, far from being a theory of peace, democratic peace theory causes the United States to act like a "crusader state."[23] America's crusader mentality springs directly from liberalism's intolerance of competing ideologies and the concomitant belief that—merely by existing—nondemocratic states threaten America's security and the safety of liberalism at home. According to Wilsonian precepts, the best way to deal with such states is to use American power to bring about regime change.[24] The belief that the United States can only be safe in a world of liberal democracies creates real, and often otherwise avoidable, friction between the United States and nondemocratic states.

The March 2003 invasion of Iraq—and the Bush II administration's subsequent commitment to fostering a democratic transformation throughout the Middle East—illustrates how U.S. grand strategy is skewed by liberal ideology.[25] Attributing the terrorist threat to the United States to the failure of democracy to take root in the Middle East, President Bush committed the United States to "a forward strategy of freedom in that region."[26] Pursuant to that strategy, the export of democracy to Iraq is viewed as the spearhead of a regionwide democratic transformation.[27] Both President Bush and Secretary of State Condoleeza Rice have made clear their belief that, while it is a formidable and prolonged challenge—a "generational commitment"—the Middle East's successful democratization is crucial to U.S. security.[28]

U.S. policymakers believe America's values are good for the United States and right for the rest of the world, and that, in self-defense, Washington has the right to impose them on others.[29] Of course, U.S. officials don't put it quite so bluntly. On the contrary, like President George W. Bush, they often go to great lengths to deny that democratic enlargement and nation building are motivated by the desire to impose specifically American values on others.[30] Whether or not U.S. policymakers really believe their protestations is an open question. But hardly anyone else believes them, and for good reason, because Wilsonian liberalism self-consciously rests on the conviction that the United States is a model for the world and that its values and institutions are superior to everyone else's. This means, however, that the United States perforce is intolerant of cultures and political systems different from its own.[31] The inclination to universalize liberal democracy puts the United States on a collision course with others whose ideologies, institutions, and values differ from America's, and it causes Washington to regard world politics as a Manichean struggle between good and evil, rather than as a contest between rival powers with conflicting national interests.[32]

The Bush II administration's visions of an "axis of evil" and "outposts of tyranny" are merely the most recent examples of this recurring pattern in American grand strategy. Ending evil may be a worthy aspiration for ministers of the cloth, but it is a dangerous—and open-ended one—for ministers of state. Even theologians—Reinhold Neibuhr was a good example—know that in real life evil cannot be eradicated, because it is as much a part of the human condition as is goodness. A grand strategy based on moral absolutism is a prescription for conflict, not for peace. In contrast to a realpolitik-based grand strategy—which, precisely because it is nonideological, allows for the possibility that competing interests can be reconciled diplomatically—liberal ideology is a barrier to diplomatic accommodation between the United States and nondemocratic states.[33]

Nondemocratic states know—and have known long before March 2003—that the United States is willing to use its hard power to impose its liberal institutions and values on them. This tends to create self-fulfilling prophecies, because it causes states that might not otherwise have done so to become "threats." When the United States challenges the very legitimacy of existing nondemocratic regimes, the effect is to increase *their* sense of isolation and vulnerability. States and regimes are highly motivated to survive, so it's no surprise that, in self-defense, others respond to U.S. offensive use of liberal ideology by adopting strategies that give them a chance to do so, including asymmetric strategies such as acquiring weapons of mass destruction and supporting terrorism.

Another grand strategic consequence of U.S. democracy-promotion efforts is that these often generate instability abroad. Again, Iraq is a good example. Convinced that the Middle East already is so turbulent that nothing the United States does will make things worse, the Bush II administration professes indifference about the destabilizing potential of democratic transitions in the region.[34] President George W. Bush declared that the United States will not accept the status quo in the Middle East and that "stability cannot be purchased at the expense of liberty."[35] Although it's unlikely the United States can purchase real democracy in the Middle East at any price, it is likely that by attempting to do so Washington will end up buying a lot more turmoil in the region. Indeed, radical Islamic groups see the U.S. push to democratization as a path for seizing power.[36] The odds are high that U.S. efforts to export democracy will backfire, because even if democracy should take root in the region, it is not likely to be *liberal* democracy. Illiberal democracies usually are unstable, and they often adopt ultranationalist and bellicose external policies.[37] In a volatile region like the Middle East, it is anything but a sure bet that newly democratic regimes—which by definition would be sensitive to public opinion—would align themselves with the United States. Moreover, if new democracies should fail to satisfy the political and economic aspirations of their citizens—precisely the kind of failure to which new democracies are prone—they easily could become far more dangerous breeding grounds for terrorism than are the regimes now in power in the Middle East.

The last thing the United States should want to do is risk causing even more upheaval in the Middle East—where, it has been said, "the real alternatives are chaos or autocracy."[38] Although there are a lot of governments in that region with which it is distasteful to do business, the devil one knows is better than the devil one doesn't. And, unpalatable though it may be, a great deal of stability—or at least less instability—usually can be bought by dealing with nondemocratic regimes than by attempting to transform them. On this point, the Bush II administration's characterization of Iraq as a "central front in the war on terrorism" is disingenuous. Before the United States decided to invade Iraq in March 2003 in order to overthrow Saddam Hussein, Iraq had no connection at all to the war on terror. It was America's policy of imposing regime change that destabilized Iraq and made it a cauldron of "terrorism" (or insurgency). French president Jacques Chirac got it right—a conclusion confirmed by U.S. intelligence officials—when he said that the invasion of Iraq had caused an increase in terrorism and made the world less safe than it would have been had Saddam Hussein been left in power.[39]

As Robert W. Tucker has observed, once a great power goes beyond traditional balance-of-power considerations and makes others' domestic political systems the litmus test of its own security, its interests cease to be *national* interests and instead become *imperial* in nature.[40] By this standard, America's liberal ideology clearly is inherently imperial: it postulates that nondemocracies are "threats" and that, therefore, the United States has the right to intervene in other states' domestic politics. Thus, in April 1993 President Bill Clinton declared that to keep the peace it is no longer sufficient to focus on the balance of power among states. American "policies must also focus on relations within nations, on a nation's form of governance, on its economic structure, on its ethnic tolerance. These are of concern to us for they shape how these nations treat their neighbors as well as their own people and whether they are reliable when they give their word."[41] Liberal ideology postulates that to be secure the United States must continue to expand until it has established an Open Door world by replicating its liberal institutions and values abroad. Thanks to liberalism, there is "a potentially limitless dimension" to the American conception of "national" security.[42]

The Economic Open Door and American Overexpansion

Liberal ideology implies that international economic openness is the natural order of things in international politics and that economic openness, having emerged from a kind of geopolitical parthenogenesis, causes peace and stability. However, this is far from being true. International economic openness occurs *only* when a hegemonic power acts deliberately to establish and maintain the kind of stable international security order that is needed for economic interdependence to take root and flourish.[43] An open international economic system requires an absence of geopolitical turbulence in vital core regions; the existence of stable governments that will keep domestic economies open to foreign trade and investment; secure trade routes; and access to—and stability in—the peripheries. Firms that engage in overseas trade and investment don't like instability.[44] Hence, patterns of foreign trade and investment are not dictated simply by profit margins and expected rates of return. Rather, as John Gallagher and Ronald Robinson observed, these patterns are shaped by the prevailing security order in the international political system:

> Economic expansion . . . will tend to flow into the regions of maximum opportunity, but maximum opportunity depends as much upon political considerations of security as upon questions of profit. Consequently, in any particular region, if economic opportunity seems large but political security small, the full absorption into the extending economy tends to be frustrated until power is exerted upon the [region] in question.[45]

Since 1940, this is exactly what the United States has done: it has used its military power to create a stable international order that is safe for the economic Open Door. Put another way, America's economic interests abroad have acted as a magnet by pulling in U.S. military power to defend those economic stakes.

For U.S. policymakers, the fundamental threat to the economic Open Door is "instability." In 1937, President Franklin D. Roosevelt warned that "if the world outside our borders falls into the chaos of war, world trade will be completely disrupted."[46] This also was the view of U.S. policymakers during the cold war—and it remains so. Since 1990, U.S. officials have argued that "the U.S. cannot prosper amid chaos and conflict."[47] As Secretary of Defense Dick Cheney said in 1992, the United States is part of an open international economic system that "cannot thrive where regional violence, instability, and aggression put it in peril."[48] "Instability," President Clinton's defense secretary William Cohen said, "destroys lives *and markets*."[49] In concrete terms, instability could result in the economic closure of Europe and East Asia.

U.S. military forces are not in Europe and East Asia because Washington is worried about preventing the rise of hegemons in those regions; rather, they are there to keep the Open Door open by preventing regional instability—especially revived great power rivalries—that could lead to closure.[50] U.S. grand strategy rests on the premise that the United States must act as the regional stabilizer in order to make war "unthinkable" in Europe and East Asia, because America's prosperity purportedly is linked inextricably to these core regions.[51] Defending the Open Door also requires the United States to ensure that its allies in the core regions will have access to markets and raw material sources in the peripheries. That is, the United States remains responsible for defending the perceived interdependence of the core and the periphery. The U.S. commitment to the Persian Gulf and the wars the United States fought against Iraq in 1991 and 2003 are prime examples. Moreover, the United States also must use its military power in the peripheries—and often in areas adjacent to them—to ensure that geopolitical turbulence does not "spill over" and affect economic relations in the core. Left unchecked, local conflicts in the periphery will spread and have far-reaching consequences—because "every big war started as a small war the world did not care enough to do something about."[52] Hence, U.S. strategy is wedded to a posture of taking early—or even preemptive—steps against looming instability, rather than reacting to it. As National Security Advisor Samuel R. Berger put it, "Our engagement not only can fend off an existential threat—it reduces the likelihood of such a threat emerging in the first place."[53]

U.S. policymakers are concerned especially about preventing the consequences of re-nationalization, which reflects their belief that America's role as regional stabilizer is what keeps the major states of Europe and East Asia from being at one another's throats. In the argot of U.S. national security planners, "re-nationalization" refers to the possibility of any of America's key European or East Asian allies—Germany, the EU, Japan, or South Korea—breaking free of Washington's strategic embrace and developing the capability to follow their own autonomous foreign and security policies.

U.S. forces are in Europe and East Asia to prevent the kind of "security vacuums" that could lead to re-nationalization. Security vacuums "could make countries there feel vulnerable, which in turn could lead to excessive military capabilities and an unsteady balance of one against another" and cause "regional rivalries" that "could lead to tensions or even hostilities."[54] Indeed, without America's stabilizing presence, Europe and East Asia "could unravel into unrestrained military competition, conflict, and aggression."[55] In plain English, U.S. policymakers fear that key regions will lapse back into multipolar instability that could affect U.S. Open Door economic interests. If any of the major powers in Europe and East Asia acquire the military capabilities to defend themselves unaided by the United States, their neighbors will feel threatened, latent "security dilemmas" will resurface, and a cycle of rising tensions and arms races (possibly including nuclear proliferation) will be triggered. According to the *2001 Quadrennial Defense Review,* America's stabilizing role in international politics "provides a general sense of stability and confidence, which is crucial to the economic prosperity that benefits much of the world"; and its alliances and its security commitments "underpin the political stability on which the prosperity of civilized nations is built."[56]

Re-nationalization is the code word U.S. strategists use to denote a reversion to multipolarity. Because they believe multipolarity is inherently destabilizing—and hence inimical to economic openness—the goal of U.S. grand strategy in Europe and East Asia is countermultipolarity, not "counterhegemony."[57] To stymie multipolar tendencies, U.S. grand strategy aims to "reassure" its European and East Asian allies that they do not have to worry about taking care of their own security. In addition to protecting them against external threats, the United States will protect them from one another and defend their interests in the peripheries. Simply put, a core premise of U.S. grand strategy is that it is better for the United States to defend its allies than it is for them to stand on their own two feet.

By opposing multipolarity and assuming the primary responsibility for its allies' security based on its monopoly of advanced military capabilities, the United States accomplishes two key grand strategic objectives: it neutralizes allies' incentives to acquire the kinds of military capabilities that would put them in the same league as the United States, and it regulates their external behavior by preventing them from acting independently of Washington in security policy. American security guarantees are intended to assure U.S. allies that Washington will defend them against all comers and thereby convince them that they do not need to acquire the kind of military power they would need to defend themselves, and that, perforce, would enable them to act independently of the United States.[58] The economic Open Door invests U.S. grand strategy with an imperial, as well as hegemonic, dimension. A second-century BC Roman statesman observed that "our people have now gained power over the whole world by defending their allies."[59] The United States has followed a similar route to geopolitical dominance: by defending its allies, the United States has gained power over the world—or, at least, the parts of it that matter strategically.

There is, of course, a big difference between defending America's own territorial security and protecting the interests of allies. Great powers are willing to risk a lot to defend themselves, but allies and adversaries alike frequently doubt whether a great power will incur similar risks to defend others. Consequently, the success of America's "reassurance" strategy hinges on others' perceptions that U.S. security guarantees are credible. Putting its allies at ease isn't so easy, though. The United States must convince them it will defend *their* interests, even when those interests are disconnected from U.S. territorial security, or—as with the defense of Western Europe during the cold war—when defending them is so risky to the United States as to possibly appear to others (allies and adversaries alike) as irrational.[60]

The entire fabric of American grand strategy would unravel if U.S. allies no longer felt reassured by Washington's security umbrella. If the credibility of U.S. commitments to regional stability is questioned, that "in turn could cause allies and friends to adopt more divergent defense policies and postures, thereby weakening the web of alliances and coalitions on which we rely to protect our interests abroad."[61] Hence, credibility is viewed by U.S. decision makers as a vital interest.[62] To establish its credibility, however, the United States often is forced to intervene in conflicts where its own interests are not at stake.[63] Indeed, Robert McMahon has noted that this explains a paradox: the United States tends to intervene most frequently "in areas of demonstrably marginal value to core U.S. economic and security interests."[64] Precisely by being willing to fight in such places, the United States, or so policymakers believe, establishes its credibility.[65] Of course, it's not so easy for U.S. policymakers to explain to domestic audiences why the United States must intervene in regions of marginal strategic value, or why it must act before there is any obvious threat to U.S. interests. This is why, as John A. Thompson puts it, threat exaggeration—which includes the frequent invocation of domino imagery—is an American foreign policy tradition.[66] As Jerome Slater observes, notwithstanding the cold war's end, the domino theory retains its vitality in U.S. strategic thought. There are two reasons for this.

First, the United States remains overwhelmingly powerful, which tempts it to define its security interests extravagantly. Second, the Wilsonian ideology that underpins U.S. foreign policy has inculcated a belief that the United States has an obligation "to provide world leadership for global order, collective security, democracy, and capitalism."[67]

Coupled with the need to prevent turmoil from spilling over from the peripheries into the core, the need to maintain American credibility leads inexorably to the expansion of U.S. security commitments. Although some proponents of U.S. hegemony, notably Robert J. Art, argue that hegemony only requires selective, limited U.S. commitments in areas of core strategic concern, this evidently is not true. The United States continually is forced to expand the geographical scope of its strategic commitments. Core and periphery are—or, more correctly, are perceived to be—interdependent *strategically*. However, while the core is constant, the "turbulent frontier" in the periphery is always expanding.[68] U.S. policymakers fear what *might* happen—falling dominoes and closure—if the United States does not intervene and broaden its defensive perimeters. Thus, the United States finds itself extending its security frontier ever farther into the periphery. There is, however, no obvious stopping point to this process, which tends to become self-perpetuating, because "expansion tends to feed on itself in order to protect what is acquired."[69] Each new defensive perimeter is menaced by turmoil on the other side of the line, which requires yet another outward push of the security frontier.[70] America's security frontiers are, in reality, frontiers of *in*security.[71] Two examples of this dynamic are the origins of U.S. involvement in Indochina and the interventions in the Balkans.

INDOCHINA

America's involvement in Indochina in the late 1940s and early 1950s—the first step down the "path to Vietnam"—is a good example of how the link between economic openness and grand strategy not only requires the United States to defend its allies from direct threat but to guarantee their economic access to the periphery.[72] Following World War II, the United States had no significant economic interests in Southeast Asia. However, that region was potentially important to Japan as a market and as source of food, oil, rubber, and tin. (Southeast Asian resources were also of some importance to Britain and Western Europe.)[73] The United States became involved in Indochina to defend Japan's (and Western Europe's) economic stakes in Southeast Asia.[74]

Following World War II, Washington deliberately fostered Japanese economic interests in Southeast Asia, after concluding, in the later 1940s, that cold war strategic imperatives required Japan's economic recovery. In reviving Japan's economy, the main challenge was to find alternatives to its prewar reliance on Chinese markets and raw materials. U.S. policymakers determined that the best solution was to reorient Tokyo's trade toward Southeast

Asia and to create economic "interdependence" between that region and Japan.[75] However, Southeast Asia was "convulsed with turmoil," and Washington feared that the conflicts in Malaya and French Indochina would result in Japan being cut off economically from the region.[76] Thus, although Southeast Asia was "at best of secondary significance" to the United States economically, it became involved in the region to ensure that it was kept open economically to Japan.[77]

The origins of U.S. involvement in Indochina also illustrate how domino concerns fuel the expansion of U.S. strategic interests. Other places in Southeast Asia—especially Malaya and the Dutch East Indies—were much more important economically to Japan (and the Western Europeans) than Indochina. The United States became involved there because the Truman and Eisenhower administrations feared the "domino theory" consequences for Southeast Asia of a Communist victory.[78] If the Indochina domino toppled, Washington believed, Japan and Western Europe would be cut off successively from key raw materials and the region's markets would be closed to Japan. As President Eisenhower said, if Indochina fell it would lead to the loss of "that region that Japan must have as a trading area" with the result that Japan "will have only one place in the world to go—that is, toward the Communist areas in order to live."[79]

Although Indochina's intrinsic strategic value was minimal, it became important because Washington viewed it as a firewall to prevent the more economically vital parts of Southeast Asia from falling under Communist control. The United States crossed the most crucial threshold on the path to the Vietnam War in the early 1950s, when Washington concluded that the strategic requirements of economic openness—specifically Southeast Asia's economic importance to Japan and Western Europe—necessitated that containment be extended to that region.[80] The progressive U.S. entanglement in Indochina that culminated in the Vietnam War was the logical consequence of Washington's commitment to the economic Open Door.

THE BALKANS

The U.S. military interventions in the Balkans (Bosnia in 1995, Kosovo in 1999) are another example of how the perceived American interest in economic openness leads to overexpansion. The parallels between Indochina and the Balkans are striking—notwithstanding that, unlike the perceived interdependence between Japan (and Western Europe) and Southeast Asia in the late 1940s and early 1950s, the Balkans' economic importance to Western Europe was nil and there was no geopolitical threat there that corresponded to Washington's (mistaken) belief that the Vietminh were the agents of a monolithic, Kremlin-directed Communist bloc. The case for intervention was even less compelling strategically in the Balkans than in Indochina. Nevertheless, the rationales for U.S. intervention in Bosnia and Kosovo relied on arguments similar to those used to justify U.S. involvement in Indochina in the early 1950s.

The United States intervened in Bosnia (1995) and Kosovo (1999) for three tightly interconnected reasons. First, in its role as Europe's regional pacifier, the United States acted to maintain European stability by preventing the Balkan crisis from snowballing from the Continent's periphery into its core. Second, the United States was concerned to maintain the economic Open Door. Finally, the United States intervened in the Balkans to maintain the viability of the NATO alliance as the instrument through which the United States exercises its European hegemony.

Concern about instability spilling over from the Balkan periphery to the European core weighed heavily on the minds of U.S. policymakers. Explaining his decision to deploy U.S. troops in Bosnia, President Clinton declared: "The stability and security of Europe is of fundamental important interest to the United States. The conflict in Bosnia is the most dangerous threat to European security since the end of World War II. If the [Dayton] negotiations fail and the war resumes, there is the very real risk that it could *spread beyond Bosnia*, and involve Europe's new democracies, as well as our NATO allies."[81] In fact, U.S. apprehensions about spillover effects were not confined only to the Balkans but encompassed East Central Europe, another area where the United States had had no discernible security interests. After the Soviet Union's collapse, Washington regarded both of these areas as actual or potential breeding grounds for instability that could affect the West European core. By expanding NATO's membership and area of responsibility into the Balkans and East Central Europe, the United States aimed to stabilize those areas. Washington's concerns show how the economic Open Door produces a kind of grand strategic bootstrapping. Had Washington not acted as Europe's stabilizer, or so U.S. officials believed, Western Europe might have re-nationalized. And a "re-nationalized" Western Europe—one beset with political rivalries and security competitions—would have been an inhospitable environment for the economic Open Door.

The economic Open Door was the second reason the United States intervened in the Balkans and extended NATO into East Central Europe. U.S. officials were quite candid in stating that by imposing order there, they would be opening the door for American business to penetrate these regions. Secretary of Defense William Cohen justified NATO enlargement as a means of bringing to Central and Eastern Europe the same kind of stability that Western Europe has enjoyed since the end of World War II, and thereby opening up those regions to investment. Speaking to a group of businessmen, he observed that "you are not about to make investments in areas that are not stable or profitable."[82] U.S. policymakers also believed that America's prosperity was inextricably linked to Europe's. As Deputy Secretary of State Strobe Talbott declared, "The well-being of the United States depends in large measure on what happens in Europe—the U.S. will not prosper without an economically vibrant Europe; the U.S. will not be safe without a secure and peaceful Europe."[83] In this context, it is unsurprising that U.S. policymakers argued that the United States had to intervene in the Balkans to preserve the economic Open Door in Europe, which—or so they said—would be affected if turmoil there spilled over into Western Europe. Senator Richard Lugar urged U.S. intervention in Bosnia because "there will be devastating economic effects in Europe of a spread of war and, thus, the loss of jobs in this country as we try to base a recovery upon our export potential."[84] William Odom, former director of the National Security Agency, explicated the perceived significance of the link between America's economic stakes in Europe and its strategic interests on the Continent: "Failure to act effectively in Yugoslavia will not only affect U.S. security interests but also U.S. economic interests. Our economic interdependency with Western Europe creates large numbers of American jobs."[85] Similarly, in making the case for the Kosovo war, President Clinton said that to be prosperous the United States needed a Europe that was secure enough to be a good trading partner and to purchase American exports. As he put it, "If we're going to have a strong economic relationship that includes our ability to sell around the world, Europe has got to be a key. . . . That's what this Kosovo thing is all about."[86]

Finally, Washington viewed the Balkan crisis as a direct challenge to America's credibility and to NATO's.[87] Here, the Balkan interventions are another example of how the economic Open Door renders U.S. grand strategic commitments open ended in scope. They demonstrate why America's hegemonic grand strategy cannot be implemented on the basis of selective, limited commitments to key regions: U.S. policymakers invariably believe that events in strategically marginal places are important tests of America's credibility (or its "will" or "resolve"). This is especially true when demonstrating to allies that the United States will honor its security commitments, because U.S. credibility is the key to Washington's countermultipolarity and reassurance strategy. As Robert Art puts it, because "events on the periphery of areas central to American interests" might affect U.S. allies, the United States often is compelled to intervene to maintain the credibility of its alliances—even though its own security is unaffected by these events.[88] Concerns about alliance cohesion and credibility can compel U.S. intervention even when the issues are nonstrategic (so-called humanitarian interventions) and take place in the periphery rather than the core.

Art's own writings illustrate the impossibility of implementing America's hegemonic grand strategy selectively by confining U.S. commitments only to strategically "vital" areas in the core. For example, in 1991, before the Balkan crisis, Art argued that the *only* U.S. security concern in Europe (and East Asia) is to prevent great power war, because only conflicts of that magnitude could negatively affect economic interdependence. "In contrast," he wrote, "wars among the lesser powers in either region (for example, a war between Hungary and Romania over Transylvania) would not require American involvement."[89] Yet, in 1996, in the midst of the Balkan crisis, Art said U.S. intervention in Bosnia—by any standard, a "war among lesser powers"—was now necessary because the Balkan war had implicated NATO's cohesion and viability and raised doubts about America's leadership and its willingness to remain engaged in Europe.[90] Absent continued U.S. involvement in European security matters, Art argued, NATO would be unable to perform its post–cold war tasks: maintaining a benign security order conducive to Western Europe's continuing politico-economic integration; containing resurgent German power; and preventing the West European states from renationalizing their security policies.[91] Art's views are broadly shared by the policymaking community. What makes them especially important, however, is that they demonstrate that even the "selective engagement" version of U.S. hegemony extends America's frontiers of *in*security well beyond the core regions where U.S. interests are said to be centered.

America's liberal ideology holds that political and economic Open Doors cause peace and stability. In the real world, however, liberalism does not cause peace. Rather, it is America's hard power that creates the conditions in which democracy can spread and economic openness can occur, and thereby help to bolster the peace and stability underwritten by U.S. hegemony. As Defense Secretary Cohen put it:

> Peace and stability are the very cornerstones of prosperity. When our diplomats and military forces combine to help create stability and security in a nation or region, that same stability and security attracts investment. Investment generates prosperity. And prosperity strengthens democracy, which creates more stability and more security.[92]

Cutting through the circular logic of this "virtuous circle," the bottom line is that stability and peace—specifically the Pax Americana—are the preconditions for ideological and economic openness.

In claiming that democracy and economic openness cause peace, liberal international relations theory has pointed the causal arrows in the wrong direction. With respect to democracy, the causal arrow actually goes this way: American hegemony causes (supposedly) peace, and peace, in turn, leads to democracy.[93] The story with respect to the economic Open Door is the same: liberalism's causal arrow points 180 degrees in the wrong direction, and U.S. policymakers know it.[94] Since World War II, U.S. strategists have conceded that the stability provided by U.S. military engagement abroad is the "oxygen" without which there could be no economic openness.[95]

There is no stand-alone liberal peace. American power is what keeps the world—or parts of it—from being closed to the United States ideologically and economically. The realization of American liberalism's aspirations—in the guise of the political and economic Open Doors—requires the United States to establish its hegemony in key regions. Consequently, liberalism's grand-strategic consequences—overextension, military intervention, and war—are contrary to those claimed by liberal international relations scholars. The central role of the Open Door—and liberal ideology—in America's hegemonic grand strategy raises two important questions. First, is American hegemony sustainable over the long term, or is it likely to trigger a counterhegemonic backlash against the United States? Second, does the pursuit of hegemony and an Open Door world pay off for the United States as advertised by increasing its security, or could the United States gain more security by pursuing an alternative grand strategy?

CHAPTER SEVEN

The End of the Unipolar Era

The Soviet Union's collapse transformed the distribution of power in the international system from bipolarity to unipolarity. However, during the 1990s international relations scholars, strategists, and foreign policy commentators were divided on whether America's post–cold war hegemony could be sustained over the long haul or was merely a "unipolar moment."[1] Fifteen years after the cold war, U.S. hegemony clearly has proved to be more than momentary, but the debate about its future is far from settled. Whether American hegemony can be sustained, and for how long, are open questions. Moreover, whether hegemony is a wise grand strategy for the United States —whether its benefits exceed its costs—also is a contested issue.

There are three main schools of thought on how long American can maintain its present hegemony. Unipolar optimists believe that American hegemony will last for a very long time and that it is beneficial for the United States and for the international system as a whole. Unipolar agnostics believe American hegemony might last for a time, but they are uncertain whether it will. They are alert to the possibility that others could balance against the United States and less sanguine than unipolar optimists about American hegemony's long-run prospects. Nevertheless, they believe that the duration of American preponderance can be extended somewhat *if* the United States follows wise policies that allay other's fears of U.S. power. Finally, unipolar pessimists believe that American hegemony, at best, will last only for another decade or two. They believe both that U.S. hegemony will trigger a counter-hegemonic backlash against the United States and that the costs of preserving America's waning preponderance outweigh the benefits.

Unipolar Optimism and Unipolar Agnosticism

Unipolar optimism's core claim is a "tipping point" argument: that if a great power becomes so powerful that others cannot challenge it, balance-of-power politics essentially comes to an end. Thus, as William C. Wohlforth argues, the predictions of balance-of-power theory do not hold in a unipolar world, because "there is a threshold concentration of power in the strongest state that makes a counterbalance prohibitively costly."[2] According to unipolar optimists, America's hard power has surpassed this threshold, which means that other states cannot counterbalance the United States, because they lack the capabilities to do so. Simply put, the sheer magnitude of America's military, technological, and economic power is an imposing entry barrier that discourages would-be "peer competitors" from even attempting to compete geopolitically against the United States.

Unipolar optimists also argue that U.S. hegemony magnifies the collective action problems that invariably affect the timeliness and efficiency of counterbalancing.[3] Because U.S. hard power capabilities are so formidable, no other state is powerful enough to act as a magnet—and as a protective shield against U.S. reprisals—for others who might want to organize a coalition to counter U.S. hegemony.[4] In the absence of a "coalition magnet," it is difficult to assemble a group of states possessing enough hard power to confront the United States successfully, because states that might otherwise be tempted to balance against the United States are vulnerable to being singled out as potential rivals and being punished by the hard fist of U.S. power. Any state that attempts to counterbalance the United States on its own runs the risk that it will be taken down by the United States preventively, before it becomes strong enough to contest U.S. hegemony.

There is nothing new about preventive war as a tool of grand strategy, and, just as "clipping" a rival is always an option in the Mafia, it always is an option for hegemons worried about rising challengers.[5] However, seldom has this option been brandished so openly—and enthusiastically—as it has been by the United States during the Bush II administration. The invasion of Iraq demonstrates that Washington is willing to back up its words with deeds. Nothing in the logic of the Bush II administration's *National Security Strategy* suggests that preventive military action will be used *only* against rogue states or terrorists; indeed, its logic applies even more forcefully to rising great powers that might challenge U.S. hegemony in the future. The *National Security Strategy* states that the United States will prevent any other state from "surpassing, *or even equaling*, the power of the United States."[6] To accomplish this aim, the United States will maintain overwhelming military superiority so that it "can dissuade other countries from initiating future military competitions" against the United States, and, if necessary, to "impose the will of the United States . . . on *any* adversaries."[7] In this perspective, Iraq was—and doubtless was intended to be—a shot across the bow of America's potential great power rivals: Don't even think about messing with the United States.[8]

Unlike their optimistic counterparts, who believe the long-term perpetuation of U.S. hegemony is a geopolitical slam dunk, unipolar agnostics acknowledge the *possibility* that, under certain conditions, others could balance against the United States, but they don't believe that such counterbalancing is inevitable. Whether others oppose U.S. hegemony depends on how the United States exercises its power. By acting wisely and with restraint, Washington can defuse concerns others might have about U.S. power and thereby negate any incentives they may have to engage in counterbalancing.[9] On the other hand, if the United States uses its hegemonic power in a ham-fisted manner, others will be spurred to balance against the United States, and American hegemony will end sooner than it might otherwise.

To support their contention that the United States can avoid what heretofore has been the fate of hegemons, unipolar agnostics blend hegemonic stability theory, neoliberal institutionalism, and balance-of-threat theory and distill them into a series of "if . . . then" predictions about the effects of U.S. hegemony. Others will not balance against the United States, they say, if the United States provides public goods to the international system; acts as an offshore balancer; avoids posing an existential threat to the second-tier major powers; focuses its strategic attentions elsewhere (terrorists, rogue states) rather than on the second-tier major powers; acts multilaterally instead of unilaterally and is considerate of other states' interests; and is a liberal democratic hegemon.

U.S. hard power represents the coercive dimension of American hegemony. Hegemonic stability theory, on the other hand, purportedly illustrates the benevolent aspect of U.S. preponderance.[10] Hegemonic stability theory usually is associated with international political economy, and its core claim is that to function effectively the international economic system needs a dominant power to perform key tasks: providing a stable reserve currency and international liquidity; serving as a lender and market of last resort; and making, and enforcing, the "rules of the game." Hegemony (or, at least, *liberal* hegemony) is a good thing, because the hegemon's actions confer systemwide benefits. The logic of hegemonic stability theory also can be extended from the realm of political economy to other aspects of international politics, including security. As Robert Gilpin has noted, a hegemonic power not only establishes the rules and norms of international order but also uses its military power to stabilize the international system (or at least its key geographic regions).[11] According to both variants of hegemonic stability theory, others will cooperate with a "benign" hegemon because they benefit from the collective goods the hegemon provides. That is, other states will "bandwagon" with America's "benevolent" hegemony. As John Ikenberry puts it, bandwagoning with a hegemon is "an attractive option when the lead state is a mature, *status quo* power that pursues a restrained and accommodating grand strategy."[12]

Hegemonic stability theory highlights the fact that Washington has many military, economic, and diplomatic arrows in its grand strategic quiver that can be—and are—employed as inducements to ward off potential challenges to its preeminence.[13] On the military side, the United States has considerable leverage that can be wielded to maintain its hegemony. Most important, perhaps, is the fact that U.S. military power offers a protective shield for states in unstable regions, which is a strong incentive for them to bandwagon with the United States—or, less charitably, to free-ride by passing the buck for maintaining their security to the United States.[14] At least as important, U.S. military power helps provide the geopolitical prerequisites for an open international economy: stability in key regions and secure access to what Barry Posen calls the "global commons" of sea, air, and space—the media through which global communications are transmitted and through which goods and people move.[15] The United States also has lots of economic and financial carrots to offer other states, which either can be withheld from those that contest American hegemony or given as rewards to those that accept it. For example, the United States remains—for the time being—the world's most important market, access to which is crucial for others' export-oriented economies, and as hegemonic stability theory predicts, as the reigning global hegemon the United States provides the international economic system with important collective goods from which many states benefit.[16]

Unipolar optimists and agnostics believe that balance-of-threat theory bolsters U.S. preponderance. In contrast to Waltzian balance-of-power theory, which argues that states balance against *power*, balance-of-threat theory claims that others balance against the state that poses the greatest *threat* to their security.[17] Balance-of-threat theory holds that the mere asymmetry of power in a hegemon's favor does not, ipso facto, constitute a threat to others' security, because the state posing the greatest threat to others is not necessarily the strongest state in the system. According to Stephen M. Walt, "threat" is a function of several factors, including a state's aggregate power (determined by population, economic and military capabilities, and technological prowess); geographical proximity to others; its possession of offensive military capabilities; and aggressive intentions (or, more correctly, whether others *perceive* that the state harbors such intentions).[18]

Proponents of the balance-of-threat approach believe that, because of geography, America's hegemonic power is not inherently threatening to other states.[19] The main reason for this is the asserted "off-shore" nature of American power: the United States cannot easily project its power into Eurasia, so other major states need not really worry too much about the United States.[20] Geography purportedly neutralizes the threat of U.S. hegemony in a second way: while the United States is an ocean away, "the other major powers lie in close proximity to one another, they tend to worry more about each other than they do about the United States."[21] If Eurasia's major states build up their capabilities to balance against the United States, they run the risk that, as an unintended consequence, they will cause their neighbors to feel threatened, and thereby trigger the formation of *regional* power balances directed against *them*.[22] Because the major Eurasian powers must worry more about their neighbors than about the United States, their attention is diverted from any possible threat posed to them by U.S. hegemony. The same dynamic also allows the United States to adopt a divide-and-rule policy that plays off these powers against one another to ensure that they are too preoccupied defending themselves from one another to balance against the United States.[23]

According to some unipolar agnostics, yet another reason why the second-tier major powers have not engaged in hard-balancing against the United States is that they do not believe America's hegemonic power poses an existential threat: their sovereignty—at least up to now—has not been threatened by U.S. dominance.[24] Several factors are cited as reasons U.S. hegemony is not viewed as threatening. First, the United States is seen as a defender of the international system's territorial status quo. Second, although the United States is a quasi-imperial power, its empire rests on indirect control rather than on direct rule. Hence, unlike other imperial powers, the United States is not a predatory land-grabber. Moreover, in contrast to the great hegemonic powers of modern history—from the Hapsburg Empire under Charles V to Hitler's Germany—the United States does not need to annex other states' territory to enhance its wealth or its military capabilities. Finally, most of the second-tier major powers have secure, second-strike nuclear deterrent forces that serve to immunize their homelands from conquest. As T. V. Paul puts it, "Nuclear possession—in some instances, only in small numbers in comparison with the U.S.—offers assurance to the weaker great powers that their existence as independent powers will not be directly challenged by the hegemon similar to what European states experienced in the past at the hands of predatory imperial powers."[25] For all these reasons, it is claimed, compared to the European great powers, today's second-tier major powers have less incentive to balance against hegemonic power, because there is no real threat to their sovereign independence.[26]

A somewhat different take on balance-of-threat theory contends that others do, in fact, have sufficient latent capabilities to offset hegemonic American power. As Keir Lieber and Gerard Alexander argue, "Whether viewed in terms of combined populations, resources, economic power, or military strength, various combinations of Germany, France, Britain, Russia, China, and Japan—to name only a relatively small number of major powers—would have more than enough actual and latent power to check the United States."[27] Although the major Eurasian powers could counterbalance the United States, they say, these states have no *motivation* to do so because they are not threatened by it. This is because America's strategy—and its enmity—are focused primarily on terrorist groups (like al Qaeda) and rogue states such as Iran, North Korea, and, until March 2003, Saddam Hussein's Iraq.

Unipolar agnostics believe the United States needs to work hard at demonstrating to others the benevolence of its hegemony. Conceding that distance alone does not ensure that others will not come to view American hegemony as threatening, they worry that if the United States throws its hegemonic weight around recklessly, other states will wake up, smell the geopolitical coffee, and begin thinking about the dangers that U.S. preponderance poses to them. Hence, the United States "has an interest in not driving other states to abandon cooperation with the dominant state and move toward a strategy of resistance or balancing."[28] To ensure that others accept U.S. hegemony willingly rather than opposing it, unipolar agnostics recommend a number of measures the United States can take to reassure other states that they are not endangered by U.S. preponderance, including using force with restraint; avoiding unilateral military action; adopting a defensive realist military posture that eschews the acquisition of the kind of offensive capabilities that will cause others to fear for their security; acting multilaterally and allowing others to have a voice in how the U.S. exercises its power; and making concessions to others' interests to secure their cooperation (for example by signing the Kyoto treaty on climate change and joining the International Criminal Court).[29]

Unipolar agnostics believe that by working through multilateral institutions—that is, by voluntarily accepting constraints on its own power—the United States defuses others' fears of it hegemonic power. As Ikenberry puts it: "American hegemony is reluctant, open, and highly institutionalized—or, in a word, liberal. This is what makes it acceptable to other countries that might otherwise be expected to balance against hegemonic power, and it is also what makes it so stable and expansive."[30] By exercising its preponderance through multilateral institutions and accepting real—externally imposed—restraints on its power, the United States can demonstrate to others that its hegemony is benign, because it is based on mutual consent and give and take.[31] Moreover, according to unipolar agnostics, the fact that the United Sates is a *democratic* hegemon not only alleviates others' fear of America's hegemonic power but attracts others into the U.S. orbit. Charles Kupchan and Ikenberry have argued that the liberal democratic nature of America's domestic political system legitimates U.S. hegemony and simultaneously reassures others that the United States will exercise its power benevolently.[32]

The argument that the United States is a benevolent hegemon resonates with policymakers, as well as with scholars. As National Security Advisor Sandy Berger argued in a 1999 speech to the Council on Foreign Relations:

> We are accused of dominating others, of seeing the world in zero sum terms in which any other country's gain must be our loss. But that is an utterly mistaken view. It's not just because we are the first global power in history that is not an imperial power. It's because for 50 years, we have consciously tried to define and pursue our interests in a way that is consistent with the common good—rising prosperity, expanding freedom, collective security.[33]

Even President George W. Bush employed unipolar agnosticism's rhetoric in his January 2004 State of the Union speech by declaring "we have no desire to dominate, no ambitions of empire." The administration's *National Security Strategy* claims that the rest of the world will accept U.S. hegemony, because rather than using its "strength to press for unilateral advantage," the United States seeks to "create a balance of power that favors human freedom: conditions in which all nations and all societies can choose for themselves the rewards and challenges of political and economic liberty."[34] Like Berger, President George W. Bush simply was following in the footsteps of his father, President George H. W. Bush, who stated in his January 1992 State of the Union speech: "A world once divided into two armed camps now recognizes one sole and preeminent superpower: the United States of America. And they regard this with no dread. For the world trusts us with power—and the world is right. They trust us to be fair and restrained; they trust us to be on the side of decency. They trust us to do what's right." U.S. policymakers understand the reasoning that underlies unipolar agnosticism, and—with words, if not always with deeds—they have incorporated it into U.S. grand strategy. In the coming decades, the success—or failure—of America's hegemonic grand strategy will hinge on whether other major states believe that America's hegemonic power can be trusted.

The Illusion of American Hegemonic Exceptionalism

For the United States, a great deal rides on whether the post–cold war distribution of power that has prevailed in the last fifteen years is semipermanent (as unipolar optimists suggest), extendable for some time (as unipolar agnostics believe), or is merely a transitional period leading to the fairly rapid reemergence of a new balance of power. The historical record and balance-of-power theory suggest that the pursuit of hegemony is self-defeating. Yet, U.S. policymakers are wagering that the United States will succeed where others have failed, that *American* hegemony will be an exception to the heretofore ironclad rule that great powers that aspire to hegemony always are defeated. When the arguments for America's "hegemonic exceptionalism" are examined closely, it is clear there are no solid reasons for believing that the United States enjoys a privileged exemption from the fate of hegemons.

The balance-of-threat notion that the United States is a benevolent hegemon is unconvincing. This does not mean that balance-of-threat theory is devoid of utility, although it has a built-in problem because, rather than being distinguishable clearly, power and threat blend together. Still, when the international system is multipolar, balance-of-threat theory can be a useful analytical tool, because in a world of multiple great powers it is not always clear who threatens whom—or who threatens whom the *most*.[35] However, balance-of-threat theory's utility in a unipolar world is, at best, marginal. Unipolarity pretty much erases the distinction between balancing against threat vs. balancing against power, because the threat inheres in the very fact that hard power capabilities are overconcentrated in the hegemon's favor.[36] In a unipolar system, others must worry about the hegemon's capabilities, not its intentions.

To be sure, even in a unipolar world, not all of the other major powers will believe themselves to be threatened (or to be equally threatened) by the hegemon. But *some* of them *will* regard the hegemon's power—even that of the United States—as menacing. For example, although unipolar optimists and agnostics both like to say U.S. hegemony is nonthreatening because U.S. power is "offshore," this manifestly is not the case. In Europe, East Asia, and the Middle East, American power is both onshore (or lurking just over the horizon in East Asia) and in the faces of Russia, China, and the Islamic world. Similarly unconvincing is the argument that U.S. hegemony won't be challenged because the major Eurasian powers will be too busy competing against one another to balance against the United States. This argument is myopic historically and unsound theoretically. If the past teaches us anything, it is precisely that when faced with a hegemon, at least some of the other great powers put their intramural differences on the back burner and coalesce to counterbalance against it. There is no reason to think that America's hegemony will prove to be an exception to the rule.

Unipolar agnostics claim that by acting multilaterally—and being considerate of other states' interests—the United States can establish its credentials as a benevolent hegemon and insulate itself from counterbalancing. This argument misses the point. The very hallmarks of international politics—anarchy, self-help, competition—mean that, in the realm of security, unilateral strategies are always the default option of great powers. As John Mearsheimer says, "States operating in a self-help world almost always act according to their own self-interest and do not subordinate their interests to the interests of other states, or to the interests of the so-called international community. The reason is simple: it pays to be selfish in a self-help world."[37] Smart policymakers in other states know this, and they understand the implications with respect to U.S. behavior.

Prophylactic multilateralism cannot inoculate the United States from counterhegemonic balancing, because no fig leaf is big enough to cover up the fact of U.S. power. Moreover, what the feisty Brooklyn Dodger manager Leo Durocher said about baseball is also true in international politics: nice guys finish last. A great power does not become a hegemon by acting nicely to others—and they know it. The United States can profess a due regard for others' interests and a commitment to multilateralism, but everyone knows that whenever it chooses to do so it can break free from multilateralism's constraints and use its power unilaterally to others' detriment.[38] Hence, in a unipolar world, others must focus on the hegemon's capabilities (which, more or less, are knowable), not its intentions (which are difficult to ascertain and can change).[39] If, by some chance, other states did not know this before (and it's pretty clear that many of them did), they know it after the U.S. invasion of Iraq.

Finally, just because the United States is a democracy doesn't mean that others won't fear its hegemonic power. When important geopolitical interests are on the line, realpolitik, not regime type, determines great power policies. The fact that U.S. power is unbalanced—and that Washington is so little constrained—means that, whenever it believes its interests dictate, the United States can throw the purported strictures of democratic benevolence out the window and act as hegemons typically have acted. Indeed, since the end of the cold war, the nature, and scope, of America's hegemonic ambitions have become increasingly apparent even to its liberal democratic allies. The post–cold war policies of the United States have caused other states to have second thoughts about whether it really is a status quo power. And the fact that the United States is a democratic hegemon does nothing to cause nondemocratic states (either second-tier major powers or lesser-ranking regional powers) to regard the United States as a benevolent hegemon.

In international politics benevolent hegemons are like unicorns—there is no such animal. Hegemons love themselves, but others mistrust and fear them—and for good reason. In today's world, others dread both the over-concentration of geopolitical weight in America's favor and the purposes for which it may be used:

> No great power has a monopoly on virtue and, although some may have a great deal more virtue than others, virtue imposed on others is not seen as such by them. All great powers are capable of exercising a measure of self-restraint, but they are tempted not to and the choice to practice restraint is made easier by the existence of countervailing power and the possibility of it being exercised.[40]

While Washington's self-proclaimed benevolence is inherently ephemeral, the hard fist of American power is tangible. Hence, others must worry constantly that if U.S. intentions change, or if a multilateral United States reverts to unilateralism—as arguably has happened under the Bush II administration—there is a good chance that they are going to get whacked.

Coming to Grips with Balancing in a Unipolar World

The unipolar optimists and agnostics are wrong: contrary to their claims, there has been considerable counterbalancing by other states against U.S. hegemony since the Cold War's end. There are two reasons why unipolar optimists and agnostics have overlooked these counterbalancing efforts. First, to date, these efforts to offset America's current preponderance of power have failed to result in a new equilibrium in the distribution of power in the international system. That is, there has been balancing, but a "balance" of power has not been restored. Second, unipolar optimists and agnostics have missed the evidence of counterbalancing against U.S. hegemony since the early 1990s because they have adopted an unduly narrow definition of balancing behavior.

To understand what has happened geopolitically since the cold war's end and to make an informed judgment about what likely will happen in coming years, it is necessary to come to terms with the very concept of "balancing." What does it mean to balance? Although balancing is the most ubiquitous form of great power grand strategic behavior, it is not always clear which actions qualify as balancing and which do not.[41] As Randall Schweller points out, "Although arguably the most frequently used term in international politics, balancing remains an ambiguous concept."[42] In a similar vein, Jack Levy has observed that there is a great deal of disagreement about how balancing behavior should be defined and exactly what kinds of outcomes balance-of-power theory predicts.[43]

Fundamentally, balancing is a countervailing strategy.[44] States balance when power is overconcentrated, because power asymmetries mean the weaker states are at risk of being dominated by the strongest one. In most of the literature, balancing means "hard"—military—balancing against *existential* threat, the danger that weaker states can be invaded and conquered by the stronger power.[45] States try to preserve their territorial integrity by deterring the stronger power—or defeating it if deterrence fails—through buildups of their own military power ("internal balancing") and/or by entering into counterhegemonic coalitions with other states ("external balancing").[46] Given the nature of the threat posed by a *rising* hegemon, the tendency to define balancing in hard military terms as a response to existential threat is understandable. However, while hard balancing is always at the core of international politics, defining balancing behavior so narrowly fails to capture the geopolitical dynamics in the current era of U.S. hegemony.

The current unipolar distribution of power in the international system is unprecedented in the history of the modern (post-1500) international state system: for the first time, the international system is dominated by an *extant* hegemon. Consequently, we need to rethink how we define balancing, because counterbalancing against an *actual* hegemon is much more complex than balancing against a *rising* one. To be sure, even in a unipolar world there should be some hard—military—balancing against the hegemon. And there is. For example, Beijing's ongoing military modernization and buildup is driven by the realization that the United States and China are on a possible collision course over Taiwan and are competing with increasing intensity to control scarce resources—particularly oil. At the same time, in a unipolar world, the difficulty of challenging an extant hegemon has given rise to new forms of balancing. Thus, in today's unipolar era, we should, and do, see others responding to U.S. preponderance by engaging in terrorism, soft balancing, opaque balancing, and semi-hard balancing.[47]

TERRORISM

Strictly speaking, terror attacks such as those mounted by al Qaeda are not balancing, because, in realist international relations theory, balancing is a form of *state* behavior. However, in the case of Osama bin Laden and al Qaeda, terrorism often is an asymmetric strategy pursued by groups that are not states but would like to control one (in this case, Saudi Arabia). Balancing's core concept is the idea of a counterweight, specifically the ability to generate sufficient capabilities to match—or offset—those of a would-be, or actual, hegemon. Although nonstate terrorist organizations like al Qaeda lack the material capabilities to engage in this kind of counterbalancing, their behavior reflects some of the key attributes of balancing. Beyond connoting the creation of a counterweight, balancing also signifies opposition, or resistance, to a hegemon. Although groups like al Qaeda cannot counterbalance American hegemony, they are engaged in a related form of behavior: *undermining* U.S. hegemony by raising its costs to the United States. Deplorable though they are, from this perspective al Qaeda's attacks on the American homeland and U.S. interests abroad are attempts to attain its own clearly defined geopolitical objectives of removing the U.S. military presence from the Persian Gulf, forcing Washington to alter its stance in the Israeli-Palestinian dispute, and causing internal unrest that culminates in the overthrow of conservative Arab regimes aligned with the United States. In other words, while its actions may not fit the strict definition of counterbalancing, al Qaeda has sought to undermine U.S. hegemony and thereby compel changes in America's hegemonic regional strategy in the Persian Gulf and Middle East.

SOFT BALANCING

Soft balancing is a concession to the disparity in military power between the United States and other major states in today's international system.[48] Soft balancing relies on diplomacy—conducted through ad hoc coalitions or through international institutions—and, rather than challenging U.S. hegemony directly, it seeks to constrain the United States and limit Washington's ability to impose its policy preferences on others. The key idea underlying soft balancing is that by coordinating their diplomacy and lending one another mutual support, soft balancers can gain outcomes vis-à-vis the United States that they could not obtain by acting separately. To date, soft balancing has taken two forms. First, the second-tier major powers have cooperated—either through informal ententes or by creating organizational structures—to rein in America's exercise of hegemonic power. Examples include periodic summit meetings (Sino-Russian, Franco-Russian, Sino-Indian-Russian) that pledge cooperation to restore multipolarity, and the Shanghai Cooperation Council, created by Moscow and Beijing to coordinate efforts to resist the intrusion of U.S. power into Central Asia.[49] The second-tier major powers also engage in "binding" strategies that seek to enmesh the United States in international institutions, to ensure that it is restrained by international law and norms of permissible great power behavior. However, as the combined efforts of France, Germany, and Russia to use the United Nations to prevent the March 2003 U.S. invasion of Iraq demonstrate, binding is an ineffective means of constraining U.S. hegemony (although perhaps marginally more successful as a means of delegitimizing U.S. unilateral actions). This does not mean, however, that soft balancing is unimportant. After all, grand strategy is about utilizing the key instruments of a state's power—military, economic, and *diplomatic*—to advance its interests and to gain security. Diplomacy invariably is an integral component of counterbalancing strategies. Thus, soft balancing's real significance is that, if states learn that they can work together diplomatically in standing up to the United States, the groundwork may be laid for future coalitions that will be able to engage effectively in hard balancing, or semi-hard balancing, against the United States.

OPAQUE BALANCING

The very fact of U.S. hegemony is a powerful disincentive for states to engage in open, aggressive counterbalancing. Yet, because mere soft balancing in itself cannot constrain the United States, those states that want to offset American hegemony ultimately must find some way to match U.S. hard power capabilities. The trick is to do so without becoming the object of American enmity. One way to do so is to engage in an opaque form of internal balancing. Rather than undertaking an overt arms buildup aimed at the United States, major powers might try first to close the capabilities gap with the United States by concentrating on building up—and catching up—economically and technologically. Opaque balancing is inherently ambiguous, because it is difficult to determine whether its underlying purpose is to develop a state's civilian economy or to lay the groundwork for an eventual military challenge to U.S. hegemony. This very ambiguity, however, reduces the risk that opaque balancers will be the targets of preventive U.S. military action.

China and Russia are good illustrations. Clearly, both states today are accommodating themselves to U.S. preponderance, and, because it benefits them economically, they are integrating into the U.S.-dominated international economic system. This does not mean, however, that their long-term grand strategic intentions are benign. In today's unipolar world, states like China and Russia are bandwagoning with the United States in the short and medium term to spur their economic growth. But looking down the road, they aim to convert their economic gains into the military capabilities they need to contest American preponderance. As Mark Brawley puts it:

Since economic ties can deliver benefits to both parties, the weaker power might hope to survive in the short run by allying with the hegemonic power, but add to its current economic base as well. If current economic gains can be converted to military power in the future, the bandwagoning state might improve its power potential so that it could reassert its autonomy at some point in the future.[50]

States like China and Russia are following the timeless strategy of those that are relatively weak today but expect to be relatively strong tomorrow: lying low in the weeds and waiting for the opportune moment—when the trends in the relative distribution of power are more favorable—to balance openly against the United States. Other examples of opaque balancing are joint military cooperation (such as the fall 2005 Sino-Russian exercises) and arms sales (sales of advanced Russian weaponry to China, for example, and the prospective lifting of the EU's arms embargo on China).[51] The Sino-Russian maneuvers are opaque balancing because they are not clearly directed at any other states, and also because China has conducted joint exercises with India, a strategic rival. Arms sales are opaque balancing because it is often difficult to tell whether they are motivated by commercial or by strategic imperatives.

"SEMI"-HARD BALANCING

In a unipolar world, an existential threat posed by the hegemon's power is not the only incentive for second-tier major powers to counterbalance by building up their military capabilities. America's hard power also poses a nonexistential "soft threat": a threat to the autonomy and interests of potential adversaries and U.S. allies alike. Because of its dominant position, the United States can exercise its power to "shape the international system" in ways that promote U.S. interests while simultaneously curbing others' freedom of action and undercutting their interests, especially in regions like the Middle East/Persian Gulf where the interests of the United States and the second-tier major powers could diverge. Moreover, second-tier major powers that are beneficiaries of U.S. protection have reason to hedge against future American unwillingness to continue its regional stabilizer role in Eurasia.

For these reasons, the second-tier major powers have strong motivation to engage in "semi"-hard balancing by building up their own military capabilities, even if they have little reason to apprehend that America's hegemonic power threatens their sovereign existence. By investing themselves with the capability to act autonomously of the United States in the realm of security, the second-tier major powers can constrain the United States, gain bargaining leverage, acquire the means to force the United States to respect their interests abroad rather than running roughshod over them, and ensure they can take care of themselves if the United States withdraws its security umbrella. This kind of balancing is "semi"-hard because it is not explicitly directed at countering a U.S. existential threat.[52] At the same time, however, semi-hard balancing is a form of insurance against a United States that may someday exercise its power in a predatory and menacing fashion or decide to abandon them strategically. In a unipolar world, the creation of new poles of power in the international system—even by U.S. allies—is, in itself, semi-hard balancing against hegemonic power. De Gaulle's challenge to U.S. hegemony in the early 1960s was a clear example. Obviously, France did not fear a U.S. invasion. De Gaulle did fear, however, that Europe had surrendered its military and diplomatic independence to Washington, and his strategy aimed to constrain U.S. power and regain Europe's autonomy by creating a new pole of power in the international system that was independent of U.S. control. The European Union's current "state-building" effort—including its creation of a common foreign and security policy backed up by independent military capabilities and an integrated European defense industry—also is a form of semi-hard balancing against American hegemony.

How American Hegemony Will End

Although other forms of balancing—terrorism, soft balancing, opaque balancing, and semi-hard balancing—have been features of the unipolar era, balance-of-power realists erred in predicting that hard balancing against the United States quickly would restore equilibrium to the distribution of power in the international system. Balance-of-power realists failed to appreciate fully the "duality of American power" in a unipolar world.[53] They did not give due weight to the fact that the second-tier major powers would face conflicting pressures both to bandwagon with a hegemonic United States and to balance against it. Similarly, balance-of-power realists did not foresee that virtually all the possible counterbalancers had internal problems that constrained their ability to engage in effective hard balancing against the United States. Russian power was weakened by the geopolitical and economic consequences of the Soviet Union's collapse. Japan's economy was stagnant from the early 1990s until the early 2000s. Germany's economy was severely burdened by the costs of reunification. And China and India were focused on developing their economies.

In retrospect, it is not surprising that the second-tier major powers chose to avoid confronting the United States head on while it was at the zenith of its power, but this doesn't mean that great power politics has been banished permanently from the international system. Even the most robust unipolar optimists admit that *eventually* peer competitors will emerge and that their counterbalancing strategies will succeed in offsetting U.S. hegemony. Similarly, it is not surprising that, in the short term, the second-tier major powers have chosen to pursue mixed strategies of cooperation with and competition against the United States. This does not imply that they are reconciled to continuing U.S. hegemony, however. Rather, they have chosen to lie low and reap the benefits of free-riding on America's military and economic coattails while simultaneously engaging in other (nonhard and semi-hard) forms of balancing until the time is ripe to challenge U.S. hegemony more directly.

Viewed properly, the real debate about the future of American hegemony has been miscast. The issue is not whether other states can, or will, balance against U.S. hegemony. They are, and have been since the cold war's end. Similarly, the issue is not whether American hegemony will end. Even unipolar optimists and agnostics admit that someday it will end. The key question is *when* it will end. On this point, the unipolar pessimism of the balance-of-power theorists is not misplaced. There are good reasons to believe that the unipolar era will end within the next decade or two. Indeed, the foundations of U.S. hegemony already are eroding due to the interaction of external and internal factors. First, unipolar optimism notwithstanding, the distribution of power in the international system will shift as new great powers (or "peer competitors") emerge to challenge the United States. Second, by succumbing to the "hegemon's temptation," the United States will become increasingly overextended abroad. Third, fiscal and economic constraints increasingly will impinge on Washington's ability to maintain America's overwhelming military advantage, and, as the U.S. military edge declines, other major states will be emboldened to engage in hard balancing against the United States.

Balance-of-power theory is good at predicting that power balances will form whenever too much power is concentrated in the hands of a single great power, but it is less useful in predicting how long it will take for this to happen.[54] When the cold war ended, balance-of-power theorists were wrong in predicting that unipolarity would give way quickly to multipolarity. In part, they underestimated the geopolitical effect of the Soviet Union's collapse, which meant there were no other states with the capabilities to step into the vacuum the collapse created and act as counterweights to American power.[55] In other words, balance-of-power theorists failed to appreciate the obstacles to restoring equilibrium in the global distribution of power that would obtain in a unipolar system.

This analysis has been challenged by Leiber and Alexander, who maintain that over the last fifteen or so years the other major powers *have* possessed the capabilities to redress the imbalance of power that favors the United States but have chosen not to do so. For several reasons, this is a shaky argument. First, although, in the abstract, a counterhegemonic coalition might have been assembled against the United States during that time, such a grouping could be effective only if virtually all the states Lieber and Alexander mention—Germany, France, Britain, Russia, China, and Japan—joined. The collective action impediments to such a coalition are virtually insuperable, however—the geopolitical equivalent of drawing an inside straight in poker.[56] If the coalition members did not all hang together, they would hang separately, and each would be fearful that the others would defect and leave it exposed to U.S. retaliation. Second, this coalition is an example of the fallacy of composition: by aggregating the power potential of each of these states, a formidable-looking coalition is created—*on paper.* But wars are not fought on paper, and it's doubtful that the military effectiveness of such a coalition would have come close to matching that of the United States. Especially in today's era of high-tech conventional warfare, the military effectiveness of coalitions requires joint training and doctrine; an agreed-upon strategy and a mechanism to coordinate it; common logistics; and interoperability of weapons systems and command, control, and communications systems. The coalition hypothesized by Lieber and Alexander fails to meet any of these indicators of military effectiveness. Finally, contrary to what Lieber and Alexander argue, it's pretty clear that since 1990 some states *have* regarded U.S. hegemony as threatening. For example, Russia was vehemently opposed when Washington pushed for NATO's eastward expansion. Moscow had plenty of motivation to respond to this threat, but it didn't because it lacked the *capabilities* to do so.[57]

Although balance-of-power theorists were off with respect to the timing, now, even if somewhat belatedly, new great powers indeed are emerging, and the unipolar era's days are numbered. In its survey of likely international developments up until 2020, the National Intelligence Council's report, *Mapping the Global Future,* notes:

> The likely emergence of China and India as new major global players—similar to the rise of Germany in the 19th century and the United States in the early 20th century—will transform the geopolitical landscape, with impacts potentially as dramatic as those of the previous two centuries. In the same way that commentators refer to the 1900s as the American Century, the early 21st century may be seen as the time when some in the developing world led by China and India came into their own.[58]

In a similar vein, a study by the Strategic Assessment Group concludes that already both China (which, according to *Mapping the Global Future,* by around 2020, will be "by any measure a first rate military power") and the European Union (each with a 14 percent share) are approaching the United States (20 percent) in their respective shares of world power. Although the same study predicts the EU's share of world power will decrease somewhat between now and 2020, China and India are projected to post significant gains. In other words, the international system today already is on the cusp of multipolarity and is likely to become fully multipolar between now and 2020.[59]

It is unsurprising that, as balance-of-power theory predicts, new great powers are rising.[60] The potential for successful counterhegemonic balancing always exists in a unipolar system, because hegemony is not the equivalent of what used to be called "universal empire."[61] A unipolar system still is made up of sovereign states, and even if none of them have the short-term capacity to counterbalance the hegemon, invariably some of these states—which I term "eligible states"—have the potential to do so. Differential economic growth rates determine which actors in the international system are eligible states.

The distribution of power in the international system never is static, because some states are gaining relative power while others are losing it. A hegemon's grip on preponderance begins to loosen when the relative power gap between itself and some of the others starts narrowing appreciably. When that gap closes enough, an inflection point is reached where the hegemon's hard-power capabilities no longer are an effective entry barrier to others' emergence as peer competitors. As Gilpin puts it, "The critical significance of the differential growth of power among states is that it alters the cost of changing the international system and therefore the incentives for changing the international system."[62] The redistribution of power in the international system caused by differential growth rates invariably has important geopolitical consequences: time and again relative "economic shifts heralded the rise of new Great Powers which one day would have a decisive impact on the military/territorial order."[63]

In a unipolar world, eligible states have real incentives to transform their latent capabilities into actual hard power. Given the anarchic nature of the international political system, eligible states can gain security only by building themselves into counterweights to the hegemon's power. In this sense, unipolar systems contain the seeds of their own demise, because the hegemon's unchecked power, in itself, stimulates eligible states, in self-defense, to emerge as great powers. The emergence of new great powers erodes the hegemon's relative power, ultimately ending its dominance. Thus, from the standpoint of balance-of-power theory, "unipolarity appears as the least stable of international configurations."[64] The two prior unipolar moments in international history—France under Louis XIV and mid-Victorian Britain—suggest that hegemony prompts the near-simultaneous emergence of several new great powers and the consequent transformation of the international system from unipolarity to multipolarity.

It can be argued, of course, that these examples are not germane to predicting the future of American hegemony. By any objective measure, the United States today is far more dominant in international politics than were late seventeenth-century France and Victorian Britain. Still, the lessons of the two prior unipolar moments should not be discounted. Because it often is difficult to assess the actual distribution of power accurately, policymakers' *perceptions* of the balance of power are as important—often more so—than objective reality.[65] With the advantage of hindsight, we can debate whether late seventeenth-century France or Victorian Britain were in fact hegemonic.[66] At the time, however, leaders of eligible states *did* perceive that the distribution of power in the international system was unipolar, and, because they regarded this as menacing, they engaged in internal and external balancing to counter the hegemon's preponderant power.

FROM BANDWAGONING TO BALANCING

Up until now, other states have foregone *overt* counterbalancing because they benefit from American hegemony. However, Washington's ability to provide other major states with collective goods—in both the security and economic spheres—is a wasting asset. Although other states have relied on U.S. security guarantees to protect them against regional rivals and instability, the credibility of America's extended deterrence commitments is increasingly problematic. As other major states experience growing doubts about whether they can count on the United States to protect them, they will move—and, indeed, in some cases already have—to acquire military capabilities so that, if necessary, they can defend themselves without U.S. assistance.[67] When other major states build up militarily as a hedge against abandonment by the United States, they open a second avenue to multipolarity. Regardless of how multipolarity comes about—as the result of balancing against the United States, or as a result of others arming themselves as a hedge against regional rivals—the consequences for America's hegemonic grand strategy are the same. Precisely because multipolarity is antithetical to the Open Door world that the United States seeks, the aim of American grand strategy is to prevent the other major powers—even U.S. allies—from gaining autonomy in the realm of security.

The economic dominance of the United States also is increasingly waning, which means that other states increasingly will have fewer reasons to bandwagon with the it. The situation in East and Southeast Asia is a striking illustration. China is emerging as the motor of the region's economic growth. While the United States has been preoccupied with the war on terrorism and Iraq, China has used its burgeoning economic power to extend its *political* influence throughout East and Southeast Asia. Because their own prosperity is more and more closely tied to their relations with China, South Korea and the most of the states in Southeast Asia are gradually slipping into Beijing's political orbit.[68] In the future, these states are likely to bandwagon with China, not the United States. Given the increasing risk that the United States and China are headed for a military showdown over Taiwan's future, Beijing's increasing regional economic clout is likely to have important geopolitical repercussions. The United States may be in for a rude shock in such a crisis, because many of the states in Southeast Asia that it would look to for support may either cast their lot with China or remain neutral. Indeed, even Australia—traditionally a staunch U.S. ally, but now linked closely to China economically—has suggested that it might not support the United States in a future Taiwan crisis.[69]

With stunning rapidity, China has emerged as a dominant factor in the global economy and is spearheading East Asia's drive to displace the United

States as the locus of economic and technological leadership in the international economy.[70] This trend, which includes China's great power emergence, highlights an important paradox of hegemonic stability theory. Over time, a liberal hegemon becomes the victim of the very open international economic system it put in place, because openness facilitates the diffusion of economic, technological, and organizational skills to other states, which causes the hegemon to lose its "comparative advantage" over them.[71] This dynamic is too frequently overlooked in current discussions of U.S. grand strategy (and trade policy). The perverse grand strategic consequence of America's hegemonic role in the international economic system is that by acting in accordance with hegemonic stability theory's dictates, the United States is helping to accelerate a change in the relative distribution of power in the international system. As America's relative economic power wanes, others will have decreasing incentives to bandwagon with the United States. The ongoing redistribution of global power is bringing forward the day when eligible states will be strong enough economically to challenge U.S. preponderance militarily.

AMERICA'S LOOMING STRATEGIC OVEREXTENSION

If, as is probable, several new great powers emerge more or less simultaneously in the coming decades, the United States almost certainly will become strategically overextended. (The same result could obtain even if the United States had to deal with threats posed by multiple major regional powers—what U.S. strategists call "near-peer" competitors—in Europe, East Asia, and the Middle East.) If new great powers emerge simultaneously in different regions of the globe, the United States would confront a situation similar to that which Britain faced between 1880 and 1900. During this period neither Germany, the United States, nor Japan emerged as a power capable of challenging Britain *globally*. But their simultaneous rise in three areas of vital strategic concern to Britain—Western Europe, East Asia, and the Western Hemisphere—signaled the relative decline of British power and confronted London with a strategic challenge that it could meet only by accommodating the United States and Japan and conceding their respective preeminence in the Western Hemisphere and East Asia.

There is another road to U.S. overextension: the United States could succumb—and, arguably, has—to the "hegemon's temptation." The hegemon's temptation is caused by the *im*balance of power in its favor. Conscious both of its overwhelming military superiority and of the fact that no other great powers are capable of restraining its ambitions, a hegemon easily is lured into overexpansion. When it comes to hard power, hegemons have it, and seldom can resist flaunting it—especially when the costs and risks of doing so appear to be low.[72] Thus, we should expect a unipolar hegemon to initiate many wars and to use its military power promiscuously. From this perspective, it is not surprising that since the cold war the United States has—in addition to Afghanistan and Iraq—intervened in such peripheral places as Somalia, Haiti, Bosnia, and Kosovo while simultaneously extending its military reach into Central Asia, the Caucasus region, and East Central Europe (all areas never previously viewed as ones where the United States had important interests).

The very nature of hegemonic power predisposes dominant powers to overexpand in order to maintain their leading position in the international system. As Gilpin observes, a hegemon earns its prestige—others' perceptions of the efficacy of its hard power capabilities—by using military power successfully to impose its will on others.[73] When a hegemon wields its military power conspicuously, others are put on notice that the prudent course of action is to accommodate its dominance rather than challenging it. In effect, hegemons believe that the frequent use of force has a potent deterrent, or dissuasive, effect on other states. Clearly, U.S. policymakers believe this to be the case. Thus, after extolling the displays of America's military virtuosity in Afghanistan and Iraq, Secretary of Defense Donald Rumsfeld declared that those wars should be a warning to other states: "If you put yourself in the shoes of a country that might decide they'd like to make mischief, they have a very recent, vivid example of the fact that the United States has the ability to deal with this."[74] There is, of course, a paradox to the hegemon's temptation: overexpansion leads to "imperial overstretch" and counterhegemonic balancing—the combined effect of which is hegemonic decline. Strategically, hegemons usually end up biting off more than they can chew.

It is a truism that economic strength is the foundation of hegemonic power. A strong economy provides the resources that can be converted into military power and generates the wealth to pay for the extensive military apparatus necessary to maintain the hegemon's dominant position. But here—more acutely—hegemons confront a problem that traditionally has perplexed the statesman of great powers: striking the proper balance between public and private investment in the domestic economy, domestic consumption, and investment in military power. On the one hand, because they are expected to provide welfare as well as national security, modern states constantly face the dilemma of allocating scarce resources among competing external and domestic policies. At the same time, grand strategists must be cognizant of the danger that overinvesting in security in the short term can weaken the state in the long term by eroding the economic foundations of national power.[75] Finding the right balance between security and economic stability is a timeless grand strategic conundrum.[76]

Paul Kennedy's 1987 book *The Rise and Fall of the Great Powers* ignited an important debate about the sustainability of American hegemony. In a nutshell, Kennedy argued that the United States was doomed to repeat a familiar pattern of hegemonic decline, because the excessive cost of military commitments abroad was eroding the economic foundations of American power. An important backdrop to Kennedy's book was the so-called twin deficits: endless federal budget deficits and a persistent balance-of-trade deficit. As a result, the United States had quickly gone from being the leading creditor state in the international economic system to being the leading debtor, and had became dependent on inflows of foreign—especially Japanese—capital. As Gilpin noted (also in 1987), the inflow of Japanese capital "supported the dollar, helped finance the [Reagan] defense buildup, and contributed to American prosperity. More importantly, it masked the relative economic decline of the United States."[77] The late 1980s debate about possible American decline was terminated abruptly, however: first, by the Soviet Union's collapse, and then by U.S. economic revival during the Clinton administration, which also saw the yearly federal budget deficits give way to annual budget surpluses.

The economic vulnerabilities that Kennedy pinpointed did not disappear, however. Once again, the United States is running endless federal budget deficits and the trade deficit has grown worse and worse. In contrast to the late 1980s (when Japan was the problem), today America's biggest bilateral trade deficit is with China ($162 billion in 2004 according to U.S. government figures—more than twice as much as the second biggest bilateral trade deficit, $75 billion with Japan). Moreover, China also has emerged as a major U.S. creditor. According to the Treasury Department, it now is the number-two investor in U.S. Treasury bills ($242 billion, compared with Japan's $683 billion). The United States still depends on capital inflows from abroad—to finance its deficit spending, to finance private consumption, and to maintain the dollar's position as the international economic system's reserve currency. Because of the twin deficits, the underlying fundamentals of the U.S. economy are out of alignment. The United States cannot live beyond its means indefinitely. Sooner or later, the bill will come due in the form of higher taxes and higher interest rates. And, as the United States borrows more and more to finance its budget and trade deficits, private investment is likely to be crowded out of the marketplace, with predictable effects on the economy's long-term health. In a word (or two), the United States is suffering from "fiscal overstretch."[78]

Economically, the United States is looking at the same problems in the early twenty-first century that it faced in the 1980s (and which had been building since the early 1960s). Except this time the long-term prognosis is bleaker, because there are two big differences between now and then.[79] First, during the cold war, Japan (and, during the 1970s, West Germany) subsidized U.S. budget and trade deficits as a quid pro quo for U.S. security guarantees. It will be interesting to see whether an emerging geopolitical rival like China—or, for that matter, the European Union—will be as willing to underwrite U.S. hegemony in the coming decades. Second, big changes on the economic side of the ledger make America's long-term economic prospects problematic. The willingness of other states to cover America's debts no longer can be taken for granted. Already, key central banks are signaling their lack of confidence in the dollar by diversifying their currency holdings.[80] There are rumblings, too, that the Organization of Petroleum Exporting Countries (OPEC) may start pricing oil in euros, and that the dollar could be supplanted by the euro as the international economy's reserve currency. Should this happen, the ability of the United States to sustain its hegemony would be jeopardized.[81] The domestic economic picture is not so promising, either. The annual federal budget deficits are just the tip of the iceberg. The deeper problem is the federal government's huge unfunded liabilities for entitlement programs that will begin to come due about a decade hence.[82] Increasingly, defense spending and entitlement expenditures are squeezing out discretionary spending on domestic programs. Just down the road, the United States is facing stark "warfare" or "welfare" choices between maintaining the overwhelming military capabilities on which its hegemony rests or funding discretionary spending on domestic needs and funding Medicare, Medicaid, and Social Security.[83]

During the past fifteen years or so since the Soviet Union's collapse, the United States was able to postpone the need to grapple with the painful issues Paul Kennedy raised in 1987. However, the chickens are coming home to roost, and those questions soon will have to be faced. Gilpin's 1987 description of America's grand strategic and economic dilemmas is, if anything, even more timely today:

> With a decreased rate of economic growth and a low rate of national savings, the United States was living and defending commitments far beyond its means. In order to bring its commitments and power back into balance once again, the United States would one day have to cut back further on its overseas commitments, reduce the American standard of living, or decrease domestic productive investment even more than it already had. In the meantime, American hegemony was threatened by a potentially devastating fiscal crisis.[84]

At some point, the relative decline of U.S. economic power that is in the offing will bring American hegemony to an end. In the shorter term, however, the United States can prolong its hegemony *if* Americans are willing to pay the price in terms of higher taxes, reduced consumption, and the curtailment of domestic programs. But there is a treadmill-like aspect to preserving U.S. hegemony, because perpetuating American dominance will hasten the weakening of the economic base on which it rests.

CRUMBLING ENTRY BARRIERS,
NEW RIVALS, AND THE END

As a hegemon, the United States is very much like a corporation enjoying a monopoly in the marketplace. Monopolists and hegemons have one thing in common: they don't like competition, and both seek to erect formidable entry barriers that discourage the emergence of rivals. The United States almost certainly will find it increasingly difficult to maintain the entry barrier—its overwhelming military dominance—that, so far, has prevented the emergence of great power challengers to its hegemony. Since the cold war, the United States has shown every sign of succumbing to the hegemon's temptation, and Iraq—along with the simultaneous designation of Iran and North Korea as enemies—has highlighted the mismatch between America's hegemonic ambitions and the military resources available to support them. To maintain its dominance, the U.S. military will have to be expanded, because it is too small to meet current—and likely future—commitments.[85] No one can say for certain how long significant U.S. forces will remain in Iraq (and Afghanistan), but it's safe to say that substantial numbers of troops will be there for a long time. At the same time, in addition to the ongoing war on terror (and the concomitant requirements of homeland defense), the United States faces possible future conflicts with North Korea, Iran, and China.

The cost of maintaining the hard power capabilities—both quantitative and qualitative—needed to sustain U.S. hegemony and of fighting the kinds of wars that hegemons invariably fight to affirm their dominance will become ever more onerous. Yet, if the United States is unable to maintain is military dominance, the entry barrier that heretofore has kept new great powers from emerging and challenging U.S. hegemony will begin to crumble, and challengers will come to believe that they can leap over the previously insurmountable barrier to great power status. Indeed, when that inflection point is reached, the strategic calculus for eligible states changes, because the costs of great power emergence and counterbalancing decrease and the payoffs for doing so increase. At that point, instead of acquiescing to unipolarity, eligible states will adopt grand strategies of great power emergence and counterhegemonic—hard—balancing.[86] Here, there is an important feedback loop at work: internal constraints on America's hegemonic power trigger an external shift in the international distribution of power, which in turn exacerbates the effects of U.S. fiscal and strategic overstretch. This is the geopolitical reality that the United States likely will confront in the next two decades.

* * *

American hegemony cannot be sustained indefinitely. In fact, even hardcore unipolar optimists acknowledge that eventually new great powers *will* emerge, and when they do there is a good chance that they will challenge—

or "balance" against—the United States. Perhaps sooner than they would have us believe. When unipolar *optimists*—who supposedly believe America's hegemonic power will be unchallengeable far into the future—embrace the policy line of unipolar agnostics and urge the United States to practice "magnanimity and restraint in the face of temptation" by acting multilaterally and being nice to other states, they betray both an unspoken anxiety about the durability of U.S. hegemony and a fear that it will provoke precisely the kind of geopolitical backlash that they say cannot happen (or, at least, cannot happen for a long time to come).[87]

At the end of the day the debate pitting unipolar optimists and agnostics against unipolar pessimists is about the related questions of timing and costs. How long can the United States keep the world unipolar? Do the benefits of perpetuating unipolarity outweigh the costs of doing so? In 1993, I suggested that by 2010 unipolarity would give way to multipolarity.[88] In contrast, in 1999 Dartmouth professor William C. Wohlforth—the foremost unipolar optimist—stated that American hegemony was then a decade old and "that *if* Washington plays its cards right, it *may* last as long as bipolarity."[89] The post–World War II bipolar era lasted forty-five years (1945–90). So by Wohlforth's calculations, U.S. preponderance would last until around 2030. The difference in our predictions about how long American hegemony would last was only about twenty years. Twenty years may seem like a long time, but it isn't—especially for strategists, who are paid to look beyond the events of the day and think about how the state's interests will be affected over the longer term by shifting power configurations.

Two historical examples illustrate how much can change geopolitically in twenty years. In 1918–20, Germany was defeated and seemingly shackled by the Treaty of Versailles, but twenty-two years later Germany was ascendant on the Continent. In 1896, a "splendidly isolated" Great Britain was acknowledged as the dominant world power. Twenty years later, the rise of German, American, and Japanese power had eroded Britain's global power position and forced a profound change in British grand strategy, including the entente with France and the consequent "continental commitment" that sucked London into World War I.[90] Far from being splendidly isolated, Britain was enmeshed in the horrors of trench warfare, and its soldiers were being slaughtered in the futile July 1916 Somme offensive. The change in Britain's geopolitical fortunes between 1896 and 1916 is a reminder that a state's position of dominance in international politics can melt away with unexpected rapidity.

The handwriting is on the wall. The United States enjoys no privileged exemption from the fate of hegemons. Indeed, since the early 1990s, there *has* been ongoing balancing against American hegemony. This includes not only terrorism, opaque, and semi-hard balancing, but, in China's case, a determined effort at hard balancing against American hegemony by building up its own military capabilities. Unipolar optimists conflate balancing with the attainment of balance in the international system (that is, a more or less equal distribution of power among the great powers). "Balancing" is a grand strategy pursued by individual states. States that balance seek to create counterweights to a hegemon's power and to ultimately bring about a realignment in the distribution of power in the international system—a "balance of power", if you will. It is important, however, not to conflate balancing (which is behavior at the unit level) with the actual attainment of balance (which is a systemic outcome). The fact that unipolarity has not yet given way to a new distribution of power does not mean that there has been an absence of balancing against the United States since the cold war ended. Rather, it means that balancing behavior by other states has not yet produced the desired systemic outcome.

At the same time, it doubtless is true that it will take some time for others' balancing efforts to realize their intended outcome. Although the United States, contrary to my 1993 prediction, *probably* will not be challenged by great power rivals as early as 2010, it is even more doubtful that U.S. hegemony will endure until the early 2030s. Is it worthwhile paying the price to hang onto unipolarity for, *at best,* another two decades? Given that American hegemony is destined to end sooner rather than later and that the costs of trying to "shape the international system" to America's liking will rise (even as the benefits of doing so diminish), it would make more sense grand strategically for the United States to retrench and husband its resources for the long haul. The United States can do this by adopting an offshore balancing grand strategy.

CHAPTER EIGHT

The Strategy of Offshore Balancing

I hope that the debate about America's grand strategic alternatives may be broadened by outlining an offshore balancing strategy and explaining why it would be better than hegemony. Recently, Barry Posen has argued that the only real grand strategies that the United States can choose from are two different approaches to hegemony that he attributes, respectively, to the Bush II and Clinton administrations: "primacy" and "selective engagement."[1] Posen's characterization of America's strategic choices is not persuasive, however, because in the realm of grand strategy the United States has more than just these two alternatives from which to choose.[2] There are four ideal-type grand strategies that the United States could adopt: primacy (hegemony), selective engagement, offshore balancing, and isolationism. In principle, selective engagement is distinguishable from primacy (and, therefore, not a variant of hegemony), and offshore balancing is distinguishable from isolationism (though both are what Robert Art calls "free hand" strategies). In *practice*, however, the lines separating primacy from selective engagement and offshore balancing from isolationism easily can be blurred.

Hegemony and selective engagement differ in their approach to the balance of power in Eurasia (Europe and Asia considered as one continent). Hegemony seeks to maintain an *imbalance* of power in Eurasia in America's favor. Selective engagement *ostensibly* seeks to maintain a multipolar distribution of power. However, hegemony and selective engagement both require an ongoing forward U.S. military presence in Eurasia, and both assume that unless deterred by U.S. power Eurasian great power wars will spread and drag in the United States. Selective engagement differs from hegemony in its intent, however, because it does not deliberately seek to amass overwhelming hard power to enable the United States to *impose* its will on other states. In *practice, however, selective engagement tends to look a lot like hegemony for two reasons. First, it similarly seeks to promote the political and economic Open Doors abroad. Second, although it ostensibly seeks to safeguard the United States by preventing the emergence of a Eurasian hegemon, selective engagement requires the United States to do more than simply maintain a balance of power in Eurasia. Here, selective engagement is marred by a big internal contradiction: to keep Eurasian wars from starting in the first place, and to keep Eurasia open economically and ideologically, it substitutes American power for a balance of power. Selective engagement requires the United States to follow the same kind of policies as hegemony—opposing multipolarity, preventing U.S. allies from re-nationalizing their security policies, and fighting wars of credibility—which is why, although they differ in conception, the two grand strategies resemble each other closely in prescription and practice.

Offshore balancing rests on a very different set of premises. It posits that the *only* American strategic interest at stake in Eurasia is preventing the emergence of a Eurasian hegemon, and rejects the notion that Eurasian great power wars inevitably draw in the United States. In principle, offshore balancing also is different from isolationism. Unlike offshore balancing, an isolationist approach to grand strategy assumes that the balance of power in Eurasia is irrelevant to U.S. security, because even a Eurasian hegemon could not threaten the United States. In practice, however, the two strategies can appear to be similar. First, neither offshore balancing nor isolationism holds that U.S. interests require it to use military power to preserve economic or ideological openness in Eurasia. Second, both offshore balancing and isolationism posit that, most of the time, Eurasian great power wars can be contained, and confined, without involving the United States. Third, although offshore balancing concedes that a Eurasian hegemon *might* threaten the territorial security of the American homeland, there are circumstances when it might *not*. Finally, today, at least, there is no rising hegemon in Eurasia that necessitates an ongoing U.S. military presence there, which means that for all practical purposes the current grand strategic prescriptions of offshore balancing and isolationism look very much alike.

Hegemony versus Offshore Balancing

An offshore balancing grand strategy would have four key objectives: (1) insulating the United States from possible future great power wars in Eurasia; (2) avoiding the need for the United States to fight "wars of credibility" or unnecessary wars on behalf of client states; (3) reducing the vulnerability of the American homeland to terrorism; (4) maximizing both America's relative power position in the international system and its freedom of action strategically. Unlike America's current hegemonic grand strategy, offshore balancing is a multipolar—not a unipolar—strategy, and therefore it would accommodate the rise of new great powers while simultaneously shifting, or devolving, to Eurasia's major powers the primary responsibility for their own defense. In this respect, not only is offshore balancing a strategy of devolution but it also is a strategy of *deflection*. By drawing back from Eurasia, and refraining from pushing others around, the United States gives them a lot less reason to push back. Rather than focusing their grand strategic attention on the United States, they would pay more attention to their neighborhood rivals. As an offshore balancer, the United States could maximize its relative power effortlessly by standing on the sidelines while other great powers enervate themselves in security competitions with one another.

Offshore balancing and hegemony give very different answers to four key questions about U.S. grand strategy. First, how valid is the "magnet theory," which holds that U.S. involvement in Eurasian great power wars is inevitable? Second, can the United States, at any acceptable cost and risk, prevent a return to multipolarity in Eurasia, and would its interests be harmed or served by such a development? Third, does the United States need to maintain a permanent military presence in Eurasia to maintain international economic openness and access to Persian Gulf oil? Fourth, is the rise of a Eurasian hegemon *invariably* a threat to U.S. security?

IS THE "MAGNET THEORY" VALID?

The assertion that the United States invariably is drawn into major overseas conflicts does not hold water. The United States can remain on the sidelines during Eurasia's great power wars, and often has done so. Since the United States became independent in 1783, great power wars have been waged in Europe in 1792–1815 (actually at least *seven separate* great power wars involving France and various opponents), 1853–55, 1859–60, 1866, 1870, 1877–1878, 1914–1918, and 1939–1945.[3] Before Pearl Harbor, there was one great power war in East Asia (the 1904–5 Russo-Japanese War). The United States has been involved in three of these wars, but it safely could have remained out of at least two of the wars in which it fought. In 1812, hoping to conquer Canada while the British were preoccupied with the Napoleonic Wars, the United States *initiated* war with Britain.[4] Similarly, the United States—arguably with disastrous consequences—*chose* to enter World War I, even though it was not attacked and its security was not threatened.

An interesting counterfactual study awaits on what would have happened had the United States not intervened in 1917.[5] A strong argument can be made that the war would have ended in a compromise peace. Indeed, in fall 1917—half a year *after* the United States entered the war—British prime minister David Lloyd George showed interest in a peace feeler orchestrated by German foreign minister Richard von Kuhlmann. However, the British government decided not to pursue a compromise peace, largely because they concluded that U.S. intervention would tilt the military balance against Germany. For London, there was no point in settling for a compromise peace when Britain could fight on and—with American help—win a decisive victory.[6] Indeed, once the United States entered the war, during the Allies' crisis year of 1917, President Wilson poured cold water on the very idea of peace negotiations.

Prior to the U.S. declaration of war, Wilson had argued that a compromise "peace without victory" was the key to postwar international stability. Once the United States was in the war, however, Wilson changed his tune. As David Stevenson, a noted historian of the First World War, says, after April 1917, Wilson's "goal became peace *through* victory, Germany's defeat becoming essential for a successful settlement."[7] It fairly can be said that the United States really got sucked into World War I *after* Wilson took the United States into the conflict. In April 1917, Wilson believed that the United States could leave the heavy lifting of fighting the German army to the Allies and limit its involvement to providing the Allies with war matériel and loans and to fighting a naval war against German submarines in the Atlantic. But the United States was "sucked in deeper than it had anticipated" and had to make an all-out commitment to fighting in Europe, because it underestimated Germany's power and overestimated that of the Allies (especially France and Russia).[8]

Had World War I actually ended with a compromise peace the First World War probably would have ended before the revolutions that destroyed the German, Austro-Hungarian, and Russian empires, and thereby destabilized postwar Central Europe. Moreover, a compromise peace might not have sown the seeds of social and economic unrest that facilitated Hitler's rise to power. Had such a peace occurred, would a second great war have been waged in Europe? Probably. But, if so, it would have been a much different war than World War II—without Hitler, and without the Holocaust—and it might have been a war the United States could have avoided.

A related argument invoked repeatedly in support of hegemony is that U.S. "isolationism" in the 1920s and 1930s had disastrous consequences and that it would have a similar effect in the future. Here, two points should be made. First, top U.S. diplomatic historians have debunked the notion that the United States followed an isolationist policy during the 1930s.[9] Second, and more important, the United States did *not* become involved in the Pacific War with Japan because it followed an "isolationist" policy but rather because it adopted a forward policy of assertively defending its perceived East Asian interests (especially in China) from Japanese encroachment. U.S. policymakers—notably, but not only, Secretary of State Cordell Hull—believed that Japan had to be opposed because it "intended to create a self-sufficient trading bloc that would be a mockery of the American principles of the Open Door."[10] With respect to the European war of 1939–41, it is similarly true that U.S. strategy was not "isolationist." In fact, the United States shrewdly followed an offshore balancing strategy. In 1939–1940, the United States stood on the sidelines in the reasonable expectation that Britain and France could successfully hold Germany at bay—an expectation shared by British, French, *and* German strategists alike. When France was defeated stunningly in the brief May–June 1940 campaign, the United States continued to offshore balance, by staying out of the fighting in Europe while furnishing military equipment and economic assistance to Britain and (after June 1941) the Soviet Union. In 1941, the United States also fought a limited liability naval war against German U-boats in the Atlantic to make sure its assistance got through to the British and Russians. Had Germany not declared war on the United States several days after Pearl Harbor, Washington might have persisted in that strategy indefinitely.

The historical record does not support the claim that European and Asian wars invariably compel the United States to intervene. The United States does not get "sucked into" Eurasian wars. Wars are not forces of nature that magnetically draw states into conflict against their will. Policymakers have volition. They *decide* whether to go to war.[11] The United States could have followed an offshore balancing strategy and probably remained out of both world wars (and certainly out of World War I). However, although America's interests would have allowed it to remain safely on the sidelines, America's ambitions—and its ideology—caused it to become involved in these conflicts. In this sense, far from enhancing America's security, the grand strategic internationalism to which those ambitions have given rise has contributed to American *in*security.

AMERICA'S EURASIAN ALLIANCES:
TRANSMISSION BELTS FOR WAR

Although rare, great power wars do happen. Indeed, there are many reasons to believe another Eurasian great power war might break out in the next several decades. The United States *does* have a choice grand strategically. It can maintain its Eurasian military commitments in the hope of preventing such a war, or it can pull back its forward presence from Eurasia and rely on a multipolar regional power balance to block the emergence of a hegemon. If the United States sticks with its current grand strategy and fails to stop the outbreak of great power war in Eurasia, it will be automatically swept up in the fighting—regardless either of its degree of interest in the conflict or the costs and risks of involvement. As an offshore balancer, on the other hand, the United States would have the ability to intervene in a war if its security interests necessitated that it do so, but it might also be able to stay out of a war altogether if they didn't.

The evolving situation in East Asia best illustrates the dangers inherent in America's hegemonic grand strategy, and offshore balancing's corresponding advantages. East Asia is regarded by U.S. strategists as especially salient to U.S. interests because of its economic dynamism and because the region's geopolitical rivalries may spawn new great powers. As a recent RAND Corporation study argues, the "pivotal long-term" U.S. objective in East Asia is to "preclude the rise of a regional or continental hegemon" in order "to prevent the United States from being denied economic, political, and military access to an important part of the globe" and "to prevent a concentration of resources that could support a global challenge to the United States on the order of that posed by the former Soviet Union."[12] To achieve these objectives, the United States must prevent "in Asia the growth of rivalries, suspicions, and insecurities that could lead to war" and trigger changes in the distribution of power both regionally and globally.[13] This is a challenging grand strategic task for the United States, because the potential for future conflict is high in East Asia, where there are a number of extant rivalries that could intensify. Leaving aside (for the moment) the United States and China, important rivalries in the region include China vs. Japan, China vs. India, and Korea vs. Japan. Russia is a wild card that could align either with or against China, or find itself on a collision course with Japan. More immediately, there are other dangers in the region, specifically the threat posed by North Korea both to South Korea and to Japan.[14]

America's hegemonic strategy holds that in East Asia (and in Europe) the United States must (1) protect U.S. allies from "rogue states" armed with nuclear weapons or other weapons of mass destruction; (2) remain in Eurasia to prevent great power rivalries from erupting into war by providing regional deterrence and reassurance; and (3) underscore the credibility of its commitments by fighting in defense of its allies if deterrence fails. This is potentially a high-risk strategy. Its viability hinges on a key question: How credible are American security guarantees in East Asia?

America's East Asian strategy is most immediately challenged by North Korea. Although Pyongyang claims it has nuclear weapons, it is uncertain whether it actually does. If it does not presently have them, however, it certainly is close to having some weapons in hand, and—unless something happens either diplomatically or militarily to interrupt its weapons development program—its arsenal could grow considerably during the next few years. Moreover, Pyongyang currently has ballistic missiles capable of delivering nuclear warheads against targets in South Korea and Japan, and it could have some intercontinental missile capability in a decade or so. The North Korean regime's unpredictability, its nuclear ambitions, and the military standoff along the 38th parallel between North Korean forces and U.S. and South Korean troops make the peninsula a volatile place. Conflict is not inevitable, but neither is it unimaginable.

If diplomacy fails to bring about a North Korean agreement to dismantle its nuclear weapons, the United States may decide to strike preemptively in an attempt to destroy Pyongyang's nuclear facilities.[15] It is impossible to know whether this would spark an all-out war on the peninsula. On the other hand, fearing it might be the target of such strikes or a U.S. campaign to bring about regime change, North Korea might lash out irrationally in ways that confound the predictions of deterrence theory. Given that the American homeland currently is not vulnerable to North Korean retaliation, the U.S. deterrent umbrella *should* dissuade Pyongyang from using nuclear weapons to attack civilian or military targets in South Korea or Japan. Whether North Korea *actually* would be deterred, though, is a huge unknown. Three things are known, however. First, if North Korea has nuclear weapons, U.S. troops in South Korea, and possibly in Japan, are hostages.[16] Second, even a nonnuclear conflict on the peninsula would be costly to the United States (notwithstanding the fact that the United States ultimately would prevail on the battlefield). Third, U.S. troops in South Korea act as a trip wire, which ensures that, if war does occur, the United States automatically will be involved.

Preventing great power war in East Asia is an even more daunting challenge to America's hegemonic grand strategy. China's rapid ascendance illustrates concretely why America's hegemonic grand strategy increasingly carries with it risks that the United States need not—and should not want to—incur. There is a long-standing antagonism between Japan and China, which are natural competitors for dominance in East Asia. In both countries, nationalist sentiment is growing, and has been inflamed by recent events. This is, in short, a—perhaps *the*—paradigmatic example of the kind of relationship that America's regional pacifier role is supposed to prevent from escalating into a full-blown security competition (or worse). To prevent Japan from re-nationalizing militarily, however, the United States must reassure Tokyo that it can deter China, and, if deterrence fails, defend Japan and its interests. To maintain the credibility of its security commitment to defend Japan, and to contain China, the United States also must defend Taiwan. Whether America's security guarantees to Japan and Taiwan are credible— and whether Washington should want to honor them if called on to do so— are open questions, however. Here, America's hegemonic grand strategy in East Asia poses—or soon will—the same kinds of questions about extended deterrence that the United States confronted during the cold war.

During the cold war, the United States sought to deter a Soviet strategic nuclear attack on Western Europe by extending its strategic nuclear umbrella to cover its NATO allies. However, deterring attacks on overseas allies and their interests—"extended deterrence"—is not so easy.[17] The reason is straightforward: "One of the perpetual problems of deterrence on behalf of third parties is that the costs a state is willing to bear are usually much less than if its own territory is at stake, and it is very difficult to pretend otherwise."[18] The logic of extended deterrence in a nuclear world is simple: if push comes to shove, it's better that one's allies be conquered than for one's homeland to be destroyed. Nuclear weapons magnify the self-help imperative that is at the core of international politics. For nuclear great powers, it's foolish to risk your existence for the sake of allies. Yet, extended deterrence cannot work unless both potential challengers and the defender's allies are convinced that the defender's commitment is credible.[19]

For the United States during the cold war, making extended deterrence credible was the rub. Threats to commit suicide are inherently *incredible*— in both senses of the term. To reassure the Western Europeans and deter the Soviets, the United States was forced to adopt a very dangerous strategic posture on the Continent. In essence, the United States—to use Thomas C. Schelling's image—"threw the steering wheel out of the car," in a deliberate attempt to tie its hands so that a Soviet *conventional* attack on Western Europe would have escalated virtually automatically to a strategic *nuclear* exchange between the superpowers. In other words, U.S. strategy was designed to ensure that Washington would do reflexively what it would not do rationally. Of course, the cold war in Europe never became hot. This does not mean, however, that extended deterrence worked. Rather, America's security commitment to Western Europe never was tested, because there is no credible evidence suggesting that during the entire period from the end of World War II to the Soviet Union's collapse that the Kremlin ever planned to initiate a war of conquest against Western Europe. Of course, it is a good thing that the United States security guarantee to Western Europe was not tested by the Soviet Union, because the United States would have paid a horrendous price for honoring it. For precisely this reason, extended deterrence was a contentious issue that repeatedly stretched NATO's cohesion to the breaking point.

Throughout the cold war, the Western Europeans never were confident that the United States would use nuclear weapons on their behalf. Just as important, because they understood the risks to their own country, *U.S.* policymakers equally were uncertain whether, if it had been put to the test, the United States would have done so. Thus, for example, in 1959 Secretary of State Christian Herter stated, "I can't conceive of the President of the United States involving us in an all-out nuclear war unless the facts showed clearly that we are in danger of devastation ourselves, or that actual moves have been made toward devastating ourselves."[20] Herter's remarks caused a furor in Western Europe.[21] Twenty years later, in Brussels, speaking (supposedly off the record) at the annual meeting of the Institute for International Strategic Studies, former Secretary of State Henry A. Kissinger—echoing Herter's concerns—asked, "Don't you Europeans keep asking us to multiply assurances we cannot possibly mean, and that if we do mean, we should not want to execute, because it would destroy our civilization?"[22] Playing devil's advocate, it could be argued that, notwithstanding U.S. and Western European doubts about the credibility of the U.S. commitment, extended deterrence really did "work" during the cold war in the sense that it dissuaded the Soviets from attacking Western Europe. If so, it should work in East Asia both to deter China and reassure Japan. This counterargument is not a strong one, however, because the strategic context has changed significantly since the cold war. Perhaps the most important change is that, as Robert Jervis has observed, "few imaginable disputes will engage vital U.S. interests."[23] There is a crucial link between intrinsic value to the United States of what is being protected, the likely risks and costs of going to war if deterrence fails, and the credibility of America's extended deterrence commitments.[24] Here, the key question is whether the likely stakes in a future U.S.-China showdown—Taiwan, the Senkaku Islands (claimed by both Beijing and Tokyo), or contested claims to the reputedly mineral-rich South China Sea underwater seabed—rise to the same level of grand strategic importance for the United States as Western Europe purportedly did during the cold war.

Taiwan, the Senkaku Islands, and the disputed waters of the South China Sea may be important—for substantive and symbolic reasons—to China and Japan, but they have no *intrinsic* strategic value to the United States. Preserving Taiwan's independence or vindicating Japan's claims in the East and South China Seas confers no "value-added" to America's own security. This greatly impairs the credibility of America's commitments to Taiwan and Japan, because, in a crisis, motivational asymmetries would shift the "balance of resolve" in China's favor.[25] For sure, in the case of Taiwan, China is very highly motivated to reclaim what it regards as its own territory, which means that China is likely to be willing—or will *believe* that it is willing—to take more risks to reincorporate Taiwan than the United States will be to prevent Beijing from doing so.[26]

Since the cold war, the strategic context affecting extended deterrence has shifted against the United States in other ways. For one thing, during the cold war the respective U.S. and Soviet spheres were demarcated clearly, which reduced the chances for a superpower clash. Moreover, both superpowers exercised considerable control over their major allies and thus were at minimal risk of being chain-ganged into a conflict—that is, getting dragged into a war in which their own interests were not directly implicated because of the actions of an ally or client.[27] In contrast, today, instead of the cold war's clearly delineated spheres of influence, East Asia's likely flashpoints are contested gray areas, which increases the chances for conflict. In addition, because states increasingly have greater latitude to pursue their own foreign and security policy agendas than was the case during the cold war, there is a real risk of the United States being dragged into a war because of a protected state's irresponsible behavior. A good illustration is the current Taipei regime's flirtation with declaring the island's independence from China—a move that Beijing says would compel a forcible Chinese response—which poses a real danger that the United States could be ensnared in a major war by the risk-taking behavior of its Taiwanese client state.[28]

As China's military power—conventional and nuclear—increases, the potential risks to the United States of coming to Taiwan's (or Japan's) defense also are increasing. The spring 1996 crisis between China and Taiwan is illustrative. During the crisis—which China provoked by conducting intimidating military exercises in an attempt to influence Taiwan's presidential elections—a Chinese official said that unlike the Formosa Strait crises during the 1950s, China now was a nuclear power, and the U.S. nuclear deterrent therefore could not prevent Beijing from using force against Taiwan, because U.S. decision makers "care more about Los Angeles than they do about Taiwan."[29] This comment illustrates an important point: Taiwan matters more to China than it does to Washington (and one hopes Los Angeles matters more to U.S. officials than does Taipei). In a showdown over Taiwan, the United States would be engaged in *extended* deterrence to prevent China from attacking. Beijing, however, would be engaged in *direct* deterrence to prevent U.S. intervention in what it regards as an internal Chinese matter. Beijing's 1996 threat was, of course, hollow, but now that China is on the verge of possessing a survivable nuclear retaliatory capability, it is becoming quite real.

It could be argued that the United States would not have to risk involvement in a potential future conflict over Taiwan, or over Japanese interests in the East and South China Seas, because they are peripheral to America's own vital security interests. This overlooks the fact that America's hegemonic grand strategy *requires* the United States to defend its allies when they are attacked *and* to stand firm in the peripheries to demonstrate its credibility. As Robert Art puts it, "The defense of allies, even if infrequent, strengthens America's reassurance role"; if the United States failed to defend its allies, its commitment in East Asia (and in Europe) "would lose its effectiveness and its beneficial effects would evaporate."[30] The paradox of America's hegemonic grand strategy is that it compels the United States to risk war over strategically unimportant places to prove—to allies and adversaries alike—that it will fight to defend stakes that are important. Indeed, according to the perverse logic of America's hegemonic strategy, the less important a place is to U.S. interests, the more important it is to defend it.

America's hegemonic grand strategy is based on incorrect premises about credibility and reputation. Jonathan Mercer has shown, for example, that whether a state stands firm in a current crisis seldom affects its reputation for resoluteness in future showdowns with other potential rivals, because others rarely predict a state's future behavior based on its actions in previous crises.[31] Similarly, empirical research has cast serious doubt on one of hegemony's key assumptions, namely that the United States must fight in the peripheries to establish its credibility and its commitment to defend its core interests.[32] Incorporating these insights, in contrast to America's present grand strategy, offshore balancing would rest on the premise that concrete vital interests should determine U.S. commitments, not the reverse.[33] An offshore balancing strategy would recognize that when America's intrinsic stakes in a specific crisis are high—and its military capabilities are robust—neither adversaries nor others will question its resolve. By the same token, offshore balancing posits that when the United States fails to intervene in peripheral areas, others will not draw adverse inferences about its willingness to defend truly vital interests.

FROM DETERRENCE AND REASSURANCE
TO DEVOLUTION

Proponents of U.S. hegemony like to say that America's military commitments in Eurasia are an insurance policy against the purportedly damaging consequences of a Eurasian great power war by preventing it from happening in the first place or limiting its harmful effects if it does happen. This is a dubious analogy, because insurance policies neither prevent, nor limit, damage to policyholders. Rather, they compensate the policyholder for damage incurred. Even on its own terms, however, the insurance policy argument is not persuasive. Both Californians and Floridians know that some types of insurance are either unaffordable or unobtainable at any price. The chances of the "Big One"—a catastrophic earthquake on the San Andreas Fault—jolting Los Angeles or San Francisco, or a Force 5 hurricane making a direct hit on Miami, are small. But if either were to happen the consequences could be catastrophic, which is why insurance companies don't want to offer earthquake and hurricane insurance. Prospective great power wars in Eurasia represent a similar dynamic: the risk of such a war breaking out may be low, but if it does it could be prohibitively expensive for the United States to be involved.

Rather than being instruments of regional pacification, today America's alliances are transmission belts for war that ensure that the U.S. would be embroiled in Eurasian wars. In deciding whether to go war in Eurasia, the United States should not allow its hands to be tied in advance. For example, a non–great power war on the Korean Peninsula—even if nuclear weapons were not involved—would be very costly. The dangers of being entangled in a great power war in Eurasia, of course, are even greater, and could expose the American homeland to nuclear attack. An offshore balancing grand strategy would extricate the United States from the danger of being entrapped in Eurasian conflicts by its alliance commitments.

Offshore balancing is a strategy of burden *shifting*, not burden sharing. As such, it would devolve to other states the costs and risks of their defense. From the late 1940s to the present U.S. alliance commitments have turned geostrategic logic on its head, because these commitments have imposed the greatest burdens—both economically and in terms of danger—on the alliance partner (the United States) whose security is least at risk. In World War II's immediate aftermath, it made sense for the United States to allow Western Europe and Japan to shelter *temporarily* under its strategic umbrella while they got back on their feet. Today, however, there is no inherent reason why the United States should be compelled to bear the costs or run the risks of shielding other states from direct attack or protecting their overseas interests from regional turmoil. Western Europe, Japan, and South Korea, for example, have the economic and technological wherewithal to provide fully for their own security. However, by promising its allies that it will defend them,

America's current hegemonic grand strategy gives them strong incentives to free ride on the back of U.S. security guarantees. An offshore balancing strategy would shift strategic responsibilities to where they properly belong: from the United States to those allies whose interests and security are most immediately implicated.

By devolving full responsibility for their defense to U.S. allies, offshore balancing would take advantage of the unique geostrategic advantages that allow the United States to benefit from multipolarity, exercise a free hand strategically, and avoid being automatically engulfed in Eurasian conflicts because of its alliance commitments. As an offshore balancer, the United States would reap security advantages from a reversion to multipolarity. The United States is far removed from powerful rivals and shielded from them both by geography and its own hard power. Consequently, as an insular great power, the United States is far less vulnerable to the effects of "instability" than are the major powers of Eurasia, and it could—and should—insulate itself from possible future Eurasian great power wars. For the United States, the risk of conflict and the possible exposure of the American homeland to attack, rather than arising from any direct threat to the United States itself, derive directly from the overseas commitments mandated by hegemony's all-encompassing definition of U.S. interests.

Of course, proponents of current U.S. grand strategy will object that, by retracting its security umbrella, the United States will create Eurasian security vacuums that will cause re-nationalization and a reversion to destabilizing multipolarity.[34] Ironically, however, America's hegemonic grand strategy is failing in this respect already, because re-nationalization is occurring gradually, even though the United States is acting as a regional stabilizer. On its present grand strategic course the United States will end up with the worst of both worlds: notwithstanding the U.S. military presence, Eurasia is becoming more multipolar and more volatile. This means that instead of increasing the chances of peace, its alliances expose the United States to the rising probability of becoming entrapped in a future Eurasian war.

Just as their West European counterparts did during the cold war, America's major Eurasian allies understand the dilemmas of extended deterrence in a nuclear world. In 1961, French president de Gaulle told President Kennedy that Europe could never believe that the United States really would risk the destruction of New York in order to save Paris.[35] Today, U.S. allies have similar—well-founded—doubts about whether the United States would risk Seattle or Los Angeles to defend Tokyo or Taipei. America's Eurasian allies are starting to re-nationalize because they understand that the credibility of U.S. security guarantees is eroding. Instead of foregoing military autonomy (re-nationalizing) they have every reason to make sure they can defend themselves if they are abandoned by the United States. The result is that security competitions of increasing intensity—like that between China and

Japan—are taking place even though the U.S. military presence in East Asia is supposed to prevent them from happening.

Japan is a good example of the kind of creeping re-nationalization now occurring in East Asia. While still wedded to the United States, in recent years Tokyo has become increasingly concerned that, at some point, it "might face a threat against which the United States would not prove a reliable ally."[36] In 1998, for example, U.S. failure to warn Tokyo of an impending North Korean missile test (which overflew Japanese airspace) galvanized doubts about U.S. reliability and jolted the Japanese government into procuring its own reconnaissance satellites. In the last several years, Japan has become extremely worried about China's military buildup. In response, Japan is moving toward dropping Article 9 of its American-imposed constitution (which imposes severe constraints on Japan's military policy), building up its own forces, and quietly pondering the possibility of becoming a nuclear power.[37] In other words, incrementally Japan is laying the foundation for its emergence as an independent pole of power. As Naval War College East Asian security expert Jonathan Pollack puts it:

> Even though Japanese actions appear embedded in the prevailing framework of the bilateral relationship with the United States, the evidence of shifting directions is palpable. American policymakers as well as Japan's neighbors will increasingly deal with a leadership far more willing and able to chart its own course, with a far clearer concept of Japan's long-term national interests.[38]

South Korea—looking ahead to the peninsula's eventual reunification—also is laying the foundation for its strategic decoupling from the United States. In recent years, Seoul's military strategy has deemphasized its land force capabilities (which should receive priority if its defense program is driven primarily by the threat from the North), in favor of building up its naval and airpower. As one leading expert has put it, rather than investing in countering a North Korean threat that "could well diminish over time and that might disappear altogether," during the twenty-first century's first decade "the peninsular focus of Korean national security policy will be increasingly supplanted by more of a regional orientation."[39] Here South Korea is following the same strategy as Japan: both "are seeking to diversify their political-security options rather than depend exclusively on the United States or assume the forward deployment of U.S. military power in perpetuity."[40]

There is nothing the United States can do that will fully reassure its allies that Washington will protect them. Recognizing this, America's allies—especially in East Asia—have every incentive to do exactly what U.S. strategy is supposed to prevent them from doing: re-nationalize and emerge as autonomous poles of power—which will unravel the entire fabric of America's hegemonic grand strategy.[41] Instead of vainly attempting to stem the tide of onrushing multipolarity, as an offshore balancer the United States would implement an orderly devolution of security responsibilities—including managed proliferation of nuclear weapons—to the potential great powers (and regional ones like South Korea) that heretofore have sheltered under America's extended deterrence umbrella.[42] Given that managed proliferation would involve politically stable states that are capable of building secure, second-strike retaliatory forces, it would not be destabilizing. On the contrary, because the deterrence provided by national deterrent forces is more credible than extended deterrence provided by a distant protector, Eurasia probably would be more stable—not less—if, acting as an offshore balancer, the United States went forward with strategic devolution.[43] In any event, given the nature of the evolving Eurasian security environment, for the United States it would be better and safer to let other states defend themselves.

Assessing the Consequences of U.S. Disengagement

America's current hegemonic grand strategy is predicated on the belief that U.S. disengagement will adversely affect three crucial American interests. First, regardless of whether a Eurasian hegemon emerges, disengagement would increase the chances of security competitions and wars that "could disrupt America's Eurasian trade and investment."[44] That is, disengagement would impact U.S. economic Open Door interests adversely. Second, disengagement increases the risk that America's access to Persian Gulf oil will be cut off. Third, disengagement could result in the emergence of a Eurasian hegemon that would menace U.S. security. These are not compelling arguments, however.

STRATEGY AND THE INTERNATIONAL ECONOMY

The economic Open Door is a central pillar of America's hegemonic grand strategy. For proponents of hegemony (and selective engagement) it is, independent from the need to prevent a Eurasian hegemon, a stand-alone rationale for permanent U.S. military engagement in Eurasia. Many of the core assumptions on which America's hegemonic strategy rests stem from the perceived need to maintain an international political and security order that provides a hospitable climate for an open international economic system. America's hegemonic grand strategy is based, however, on a logically inconsistent set of assumptions: that the U.S. simultaneously is dominant in terms of military and economic power and economically "interdependent" with the international economy. Now, for sure, the United States is connected to the global economy. But, in economic and strategic terms, it is not especially *vulnerable* to possible disturbances of peacetime economic intercourse that could be caused in the future by a major war or other forms of international instability. In fact, precisely because it is so powerful economically in relative terms, the opposite is true. Building on this insight, an offshore balancing strategy would not require that the United States maintain its military commitments in Europe and East Asia for the purpose of defending international economic openness.

The fear that the United States could be hurt economically by war or instability is overhyped, as Eugene Gholz and Daryl Press have demonstrated in an important article.[45] Using "strategic adaptation theory," they demonstrate that, as a general rule, nonbelligerent great powers are only minimally affected by wartime disruption of international trade, capital flows, and overseas direct investment. Indeed, far from being hurt economically, noncombatant great powers "can often find ways to profit from instability and war by selling to the belligerents, by expanding sales to markets formerly served by belligerents, by lending money at lucrative rates, and by buying up overseas assets that belligerents liquidate to raise money for the war."[46] In other words, although major wars do impose adjustment costs on the economies of noncombatant great powers, market mechanisms create new opportunities to prosper, and these are pounced upon.

Great powers that remain on the sidelines during major wars are well positioned to increase their national wealth during a conflict. This illustrates a well-known fact about international economics: states with big economies have more options than smaller states.[47] As Gholz and Press point out, noncombatant great powers have important advantages that enable them to make the adjustments necessary to be economic winners during wartime.[48] The historical record backs up their argument. During the period of its neutrality, from 1914 to 1917, the United States profited from World War I in a number of ways.[49] The United States went from being a net debtor in 1913 to being a net creditor by the war's end, and New York began displacing London as the world's leading international financial center. At the same time, U.S. manufacturers profited by selling their products to the belligerent powers and also by capturing foreign markets that the belligerent powers were forced to abandon as their economies switched to a war footing. U.S. firms also expanded their direct investments abroad by purchasing—at fire-sale prices—assets that the belligerents were forced to sell to finance their war efforts. In the event of a future great power war, the United States is well positioned to repeat its World War I experience.

At the end of the day, economic calculation and strategic logic suggest that if great powers go to war in Eurasia, defending economic openness is not a compelling reason for U.S. intervention. Although it's unclear whether the United States would profit or lose economically in a future great power war, it is clear that, either way, "the trade and financial effects of a foreign war . . . would likely be very small."[50] If the United States doesn't stand to be hurt much economically—if at all—from a future great power war, there is no reason for it to run the risks and bear the costs of its current hegemonic grand strategy, the main aim of which is to defend the economic Open Door from war and instability.

America's hegemonic grand strategy, as Gholz and Press point out, is expensive and inefficient economically, because "the costs of maintaining overseas stability are an order of magnitude higher than the plausible costs of distant turmoil."[51] The United States pays a lot more to defend the economic Open Door than it stands to lose if the Open Door is shut temporarily in a future great power war. As Gholz and Press point out:

> Each year the United States spends approximately $150 billion on the military beyond the requirements of protecting core U.S. national security interests, and this extra spending prevents at most a few billion dollars of cost to the United States from overseas instability and economic disruption. Protecting the U.S. economy from disruptions is not a sound reason for high levels of defense spending or global military activism.[52]

The United States is tied to a hegemonic grand strategy that is both expansive—in terms of ambitions and commitments—and expensive. All grand strategies involve trade-offs. In return for relief from the risks and burdens of hegemony—the likelihood of being drawn into unnecessary wars and the certainty of defense budgets much higher than they need to be to defend core U.S. interests—an offshore balancing strategy would accept the risk that the United States could suffer a slight diminution of its wealth if multipolarity leads to intense great power security competitions, or war, in Eurasia.

Proponents of America's hegemonic grand strategy have sought to rebut the argument that the economic Open Door is not a compelling reason for the United States to maintain its security commitments in Eurasia.[53] Essentially, their case rests on three main counterarguments. First, in a variation on the "magnet theory," it is asserted that when great power wars break out in Eurasia, it is impossible for the United States to cease economic intercourse with at least some of the belligerents, which inevitably drags the United States into war. This is a very dubious argument, and the historical examples that its proponents cite do not support their case. The United States was not dragged into the wars of the French Revolution and Napoleonic wars because of its trade with the belligerents. America's full-blown involvement—the War of 1812—occurred because the United States sought to take advantage of Britain's preoccupation with France to pursue its expansionist ambitions in Canada.[54] Proponents of hegemony also point to the two world wars as another example of the United States being dragged into war because of its economic ties with the belligerents. This is a very difficult claim to fathom.

For sure, before December 7, 1941, the United States was involved in an undeclared naval war with Germany in the Atlantic. But U.S. naval operations were driven by military-strategic concerns, not economic ones: ensuring that German U-Boats did not cut off the flow of war matériel from the United States to Britain and the Soviet Union. In the Pacific, economic considerations did contribute to the onset of war. Here, however, it was not trade that led the United States into war but rather Washington's decision to use economic statecraft as a weapon of coercive diplomacy against Tokyo. The series of U.S. embargoes imposed on Japan in 1940–41 were intended to force Tokyo either to accede to U.S. conditions for a diplomatic settlement or, after June 1941, to divert Japan from attacking the Soviet Union by compelling it to refocus its strategy on securing oil and other raw materials in Southeast Asia.[55]

The historical record also fails to support the argument that the United States was dragged into World War I because of its financial and mercantile ties to the Allies.[56] When Germany declared unrestricted submarine warfare on January 31, 1917, the United States broke off diplomatic relations with Berlin. Beyond that, however, President Wilson did nothing. The sinking of Allied merchant ships (even with the loss of American lives) provoked no response from the American people, and no action from Wilson. What did inflame pro-war sentiment in Congress and among the American public, however, was publication on March 1, 1917 of the so-called Zimmermann telegram. The telegram—which was intercepted and decoded by British naval intelligence and passed to the U.S. ambassador to England on February 24—was a note from the German foreign minister to the Mexican government proposing an alliance against the United States and holding out the return to Mexico of the territories it had lost to the United States in 1848. Of course, the Germans were in no position to do anything to help Mexico (which had plenty of problems of its own with the Wilson administration). In other words, the German proposal was pie-in-the-sky, but it made an impression on Americans and Wilson and galvanized the United States to declare war with Germany.

If trade really determined the decision about entering the European conflict, the United States still had several options short of going to war. It could have opted for armed neutrality (a course of action briefly considered, but rejected, by Wilson). It could have prevented U.S. banks from lending money to the Allies. It could have required the Allies to ship their purchases of food and war matériel from the United States in their own ships. Or, given that the British blockade of Europe impinged on U.S. trade—and violated international law—at least as much as Germany's U-boat campaign, the United States could have gone to war with Britain. The United States did none of these things. To be sure, during the interwar period, revisionist historians like Charles Tansill and Charles Beard argued that the United States went to war because American banks had loaned so much money to the Allies that the United States would have been hurt if Germany had won the war.[57] Very few historians hold to this view today, however. As David Stevenson points out, in making his decision to take the United States into the

Great War, Wilson was not concerned with protecting American trade with, or loans to, the Allies, because he and his advisers expected the Allies to win the war.[58] Far from being dragged into war by its trade with the Allies, Wilson *chose* to take the United States into war so that he could wield America's power at the peace conference and force both the Allies and the Germans to accept a postwar international order based on the Open Door and America's liberal ideology.

If we assume, just for the sake of argument, that the magnet effect was a factor leading to U.S. involvement in Eurasian wars before 1945, nuclear weapons have changed the geopolitical equation since then. There are many imponderables about nuclear strategy. Nuclear weapons today *probably* would deter war between nuclear-armed great powers in Eurasia. On the other hand, because of the stability-instability paradox (the standoff at the strategic nuclear level makes it more thinkable for nuclear-armed great powers to fight limited, conventional wars against one another), nuclear deterrence might allow great powers to begin wars in the hope that they would be fought with conventional weapons only. However, in a conventional conflict between nuclear-armed great powers, the risk of escalation would be omnipresent. Precisely because of these unknowns, American grand strategy should maximize U.S. autonomy, because the last thing the United States should want is to be caught in the cross fire of a nuclear war fought by Eurasian great powers. If the United States adopts an offshore balancing grand strategy, it simply is not the case that the United States would be sucked into a war between Eurasian great powers. A nuclear conflict in Eurasia cannot leap the Atlantic or Pacific oceans and engulf the United States *unless* the United States is embroiled from the outset because of its forward military presence in Eurasia. In a nuclear world, it would be irrational to risk being involved in such a conflict for economic reasons (and, probably, for *any* reason).

A second contention advanced by proponents of American hegemony is that the United States cannot withdraw from Eurasia because a great power war there could shape the postconflict international system in ways harmful to U.S. interests. Hence, the United States "could suffer few economic losses during a war, or even benefit somewhat, and still find the postwar environment quite costly to its own trade and investment."[59] This really is not an economic argument but rather an argument about the consequences of Eurasia's political and ideological, as well as economic, closure. Proponents of hegemony fear that if great power wars in Eurasia occur, they could bring to power militaristic or totalitarian regimes. Here, several points need to be made. First, proponents of American hegemony overestimate the amount of influence that the United States has on the international system. There are numerous possible geopolitical rivalries in Eurasia. Most of these will not culminate in war, but it's a good bet that some will. But regardless of whether Eurasian great powers remain at peace, the outcomes are going to be caused more by those states' calculations of their interests than by the presence of U.S. forces in Eurasia. The United States has only limited power to affect the amount of war and peace in the international system, and whatever influence it does have is being eroded by the creeping multipolarization under way in Eurasia. Second, the possible benefits of "environment shaping" have to be weighed against the possible costs of U.S. involvement in a big Eurasian war. Finally, distilled to its essence, this argument is a restatement of the fear that U.S. security and interests inevitably will be jeopardized by a Eurasian hegemon. This threat is easily exaggerated, and manipulated, to disguise ulterior motives for U.S. military intervention in Eurasia.

A third claim by advocates of U.S. hegemony is that, even if historically valid, the argument advanced by proponents of grand strategic restraint—like Press and Gholz—is of doubtful relevance in today's world. Thus, Art concedes that the United States may well have turned a "profit" economically from World War I between 1914 and 1917, but questions whether it could do so in a future Eurasian war, because the United States is far more embedded in the international economy today than it was in 1914 and hence has more to lose. Although the percentage of the American GDP that is made up of imports and exports has approximately tripled since World War I, the patterns of U.S. trade and investment are much more diversified than they were then, which means the United States is far better placed to withstand the economic disruption that could be caused by a war in Europe or East Asia. According to the United States Department of Commerce, in 2000 23 percent of U.S. merchandise exports went to Europe, 35 percent to Asia, and 39 percent to the Western Hemisphere (mostly to Canada and Mexico). If a war should break out in Eurasia in coming decades it is unlikely to engulf both Europe and East Asia, which means that the United States would not be crippled economically, because it still would be able to trade with one of these regions plus the Western Hemisphere. Precisely because its export markets, and sources of imports, are diversified, no single overseas region is crucial to America's economic well-being.

Advocates of hegemony (and selective engagement) also seem to have a peculiar understanding of international economics and convey the impression that international trade and investment will come to a grinding halt if the United States abandons its current grand strategy—or if a Eurasian great power war occurs. This is not true, however. If the United States abandons its current grand strategic role as the protector of international economic openness, international economic intercourse will not stop, even in time of great power war.[60] If the United States were to adopt an offshore balancing grand strategy, its own and global markets would adapt to the new political and strategic environment. Firms and investors would reassess the risks of overseas trade and investment, and over time investment and trade flows would shift in response to these calculations. Instead of being diminished, international trade and investment would be diverted to more geopolitically secure regions, and these "safe havens"—especially the United States—would be the beneficiaries. Finally, the assumption that a Eurasia dominated by a hegemon would be closed economically to the United States is dubious. A Eurasian hegemon would have a stake in its own economic well-being (both for strategic and domestic political reasons), and it would be most unlikely to hive itself off completely from international trade.

The bottom line is that the arguments of hegemony's proponents are not convincing. Great power wars in Eurasia don't happen often, and when they do, America's economic stakes in Eurasia have never sucked it into war against its will. Doubtless, at some point in the coming decades great power war again will occur in Eurasia. When it does, the United States is uniquely well positioned to weather any economic disruption that might ensue. The United States benefits economically from great power peace in Eurasia, but Eurasia is at peace most of the time—and will be regardless of the presence of U.S. troops—and most of the time U.S. trade with Eurasia will not be affected by great power turmoil. In this sense, it is far from clear that any economic benefit accrues to the United States from its military commitments in Eurasia. Simply put, regardless of whether American troops are playing a hegemonic—"stabilizing"—role, most of the time the United States is going to be able to reap the benefits of economic exchange with Eurasia. On the other hand, U.S. forces in Eurasia do not ensure the continuance of peace (just as their withdrawal would not mean the inevitable outbreak of war). What the U.S. forward presence does do, however, is expose the United States to automatic entanglement in a future great power war in Eurasia, regardless of whether its interests seriously are implicated by the conflict. In a nuclear world, this is something the United States should want to avoid. The aim of American grand strategy should be to preserve America's freedom to decide whether its interests require it to intervene in a Eurasian war and, if so, to determine the extent of its military involvement.

OIL, THE OPEN DOOR, AND AMERICAN GRAND STRATEGY

When it comes to economic Open Door justifications for maintaining a forward U.S. military presence abroad to ensure regional stability, access to oil—especially Persian Gulf oil—is a special case. Advocates of both hegemony and offshore balancing agree that—under present conditions—the United States has important interests in the Gulf that must be supported by U.S. military power. However, they disagree on two key questions. First, how deeply does the United States need be involved militarily and politically in the Gulf? Second, what is the likelihood of an oil stoppage severe enough to seriously damage the U.S., and global, economies?

There are two main threats to U.S. oil interests. First, there is the danger of a single power in the Gulf region consolidating its control over the majority of the world's oil reserves. The fear that Iraq would control both Kuwaiti and Saudi Arabian oil reserves, as well as its own, was the nightmare scenario invoked by U.S. policymakers as one of the rationales for the 1991 Persian Gulf War. An "oil hegemon" in the Gulf would be in a position to raise oil prices and use oil as an instrument of political coercion. Yet, although the United States does have an interest in preventing the emergence of a Persian Gulf oil hegemon, the risk of such a development is low, because the three largest states in the Gulf—Saudi Arabia, Iraq, and Iran—lack the military capabilities to conquer each other. This was true even before the Gulf War, or the Iraq War. Thus, when Iraq went to war with Iran in September 1980, the conflict ended in a prolonged, bloody stalemate. Similarly, from the end of the Gulf War in 1991 until the U.S. invasion in March 2003, Iraq posed no military threat to Saudi Arabia (or Iran).

On the other side of the coin, because of its overwhelming military capabilities compared to the "big three" Gulf powers, the United States easily could deter any of them from launching a war of conquest. In 1990, for example, the United States was able to dissuade Saddam Hussein from using Kuwait as a platform for conquering Saudi Arabia by inserting airpower and a limited number of ground forces (as a trip wire) into Saudi Arabia, and by imposing an economic embargo on Iraq.[61] This policy of containment and deterrence worked in 1990—and still was working in March 2003.[62] To make sure no Gulf oil hegemon emerges in the future, Washington should make it clear that it would respond militarily to prevent a single power from gaining control over a majority of the region's oil capacity. However, a deterrence strategy does not require a substantial U.S. military presence in the region, because the United States today (in contrast to 1990) can back up its deterrent threat with long-range airpower and sea-based cruise missiles.

Domestic instability in a major oil-producing state is another threat to U.S. interests in the Gulf. In the form of civil unrest, instability could temporarily reduce the flow of oil from an affected country and drive up prices. However, because the oil industry is globally integrated, other oil producers would increase their own production to make up for the lost capacity. Thus, any spike in oil prices would be temporary, and lost supplies would be replenished by other producers. In fact, past experience shows that this is precisely what happens when internal instability in an oil-producing state causes a temporary disruption in oil supplies.[63] Instability in any of the Gulf oil producers, of course, could bring a hostile regime to power. Here, there are two things to keep in mind. First, it is unlikely that U.S. military intervention could forestall such an event, and indeed it might make things worse. Second, the economic consequences of such an event are exaggerated. In an integrated, global oil market it is immaterial whether a hostile regime would sell oil directly to the United States. Because oil is fungible, all that matters is that such a regime make its oil available to the market. The chances of a hostile regime embargoing its oil are very low. All the major oil producers in the

Gulf are economically dependent on their oil revenues. Even if a hostile regime in the Gulf wanted to embargo oil shipments to the United States or the West, it could not long do so without shooting itself in the foot economically. Moreover, if a hostile regime chose to behave in an economically irrational fashion by sacrificing income to achieve political or economic objectives, markets would adjust. Higher oil prices caused by an embargo would lead oil-consuming states like the United States to switch to alternative energy sources and use energy more efficiently, and also provide an incentive for other oil-producing states to increase the supply of oil in the market.[64] Simply put, in relatively short order the supply-demand equilibrium would return to the marketplace, and oil prices would return to their natural marketplace level.

There is a wild card, however: Saudi Arabia. Because Saudi Arabia is the world's largest oil producer and has the largest known oil reserves, if a hostile Saudi regime imposed an embargo or cut back drastically on production it would be difficult for the market to adjust, because other oil producers do not have the capacity to replace lost Saudi Arabian oil. A major long-term interruption of oil exports from Saudi Arabia would cause real economic damage to the United States and the other industrialized nations (although, over time, it would lead to the development of alternate energy sources that now are untapped because they cost more than oil). Given the political unrest percolating in Saudi Arabia, it's a good bet that in coming years the Saud monarchy may lose its grip on power. However, America's forward military presence in the Gulf does not offer a real solution to the possibility of a hostile regime coming to power in Saudi Arabia. Indeed, the U.S. military presence in the region serves to make things worse rather than better in this regard, because it is a lightning rod for Islamic fundamentalists like Osama bin Laden and al Qaeda. The U.S. invasion of Iraq and subsequent occupation have exacerbated the problem.

Access to oil is an important U.S. interest, and in some respects U.S. military power plays an important role in keeping the oil flowing from the Gulf. But there is no need for an on-the-ground U.S. military presence in the Gulf and Middle East. Over-the-horizon deterrence can prevent the emergence of a Gulf oil hegemon—and without triggering the kind of anti-American backlash that occurs when U.S. forces visibly are present in the region. Similarly, although its closure is a low-probability event, the United States has an important interest in making sure the Strait of Hormuz remains open. But this is a task that can be accomplished by U.S. naval power. Finally, domestic instability in the Gulf oil-producing states is a risk—especially in Saudi Arabia. But, as Secretary of State Condoleeza Rice acknowledged, the Gulf and the Middle East are going to be unstable regardless of what the United States does.[65] U.S. military power, and its heavy-handed political influence, are not an antidote to domestic instability in the region. On the contrary, they contribute to it. This suggests that the wisest policies for the United States are to reduce its footprint in the Gulf and the Middle East and formulate a viable long-term energy strategy that minimizes its vulnerability to the vicissitudes of that endemically turbulent region.

Quite apart from addressing the threat to oil supplies posed by regional instability, energy independence is a grand strategic imperative for another reason. Although there is always a margin of error in predictions, there does seem to be a growing belief among energy experts that while demand for oil is on the upswing, oil production capacity has just about maxed out. Consequently, it appears that there will be a widening gap in the future between demand and available supply.[66] A good part of this disequilibrium is caused by the rapid economic growth of China and India, which also are quickly emerging as great powers. This suggests that competition to control increasingly scarce oil supplies could be a potent source of great power security competition in coming decades.[67] This is another reason why the United States needs a sensible national energy strategy.

THE "DANGER" OF A EURASIAN HEGEMON

The received wisdom is that since the early twentieth century (at least), America's grand strategy has been counterhegemonic. That is, the United States has sought to prevent a single great power from achieving a Mackinderesque dominance of the Eurasian heartland, because a Eurasian hegemon would control enough hard power to threaten the American homeland. This fear is invoked by U.S. strategists, along with the economic Open Door and oil access concerns, as a reason that the United States cannot abandon its hegemonic grand strategy in favor of offshore balancing.

The prospect that a threatening hegemon will emerge in Eurasia is remote, and the United States does not need to maintain a permanent Eurasian military presence to guard against this possibility. The United States has three lines of defense against a potential Eurasian hegemon: regional power balances, distance, and its own military capabilities. Regional power balances are America's first line of defense against a rising Eurasian hegemon, and an offshore balancing strategy would rely on the balance-of-power dynamics of a twenty-first-century multipolar system to thwart a distant great power seeking Eurasian predominance. The major powers in Eurasia have a much more immediate interest in stopping a rising hegemon in their midst than does the United Sates, and it's money in the bank that some of them will step up to the plate and balance against a powerful, expansionist state in their own neighborhood. In a multipolar system, the question is not whether balancing will occur, but which state(s) will to do it. Here is where the logic of passing the buck comes into play.[68] Offshore balancing would aim to capitalize on the strategic advantages of America's insular position and pass the buck for stopping a Eurasian hegemon to those whose security would be most immediately jeopardized.[69] Insularity allows the United States to stand aloof from others' security competitions and engage in bystanding and buck-passing behavior that compels others to take on the risks and costs of counterhegemonic balancing in Eurasia.[70]

Offshore balancing is a hedging strategy. It recognizes that if regional power balances fail, the United States *might* need to intervene counterhege-monically, because a Eurasian hegemon *might* pose a threat to American security. However, an offshore balancing strategy would not assume that the rise of a twenty-first-century Eurasian hegemon *inevitably* would threaten the United States. There is a strong case to be made that the nuclear revolution has transformed the geopolitical context with respect to America's interests in Eurasia in two crucial ways. First, nuclear weapons have made the Eurasian balance less salient to the United States. Because of nuclear deterrence (and geography), fear that a future Eurasian hegemon would command sufficient resources to imperil the United States arguably is a strategic artifact of the prenuclear era.[71] Second, even as the impact of the Eurasian balance of power has declined as a factor in America's security, in a nuclear world the likely cost of U.S. intervention in a great power war in Eurasia has risen.

Any good strategy hedges against unknown (and unknowable) future contingencies. There are three reasons why an offshore balancing strategy would not rule out the possibility that, as the balancer of last resort, the United States might need to intervene to thwart the emergence of a Eurasian hegemonic challenger. First, the military-technological balance could shift to America's disadvantage. Second, a Eurasian hegemon might be able to use its power to coerce the United States diplomatically. Third, the United States might find it too uncomfortable psychologically to live in a world dominated by another power. Although any of these things is possible, none of them is very likely. For example, it's very difficult to imagine changes in military technology that could make the American homeland vulnerable to invasion. Even in the prenuclear age, the United States was virtually impregnable in the Western Hemisphere. Similarly, as long as the United States remains among the foremost great powers in terms of military capabilities and economic power, it's hard to see how it could be blackmailed diplomatically by a putative Eurasian hegemon. Finally, the fear of psychological isolation stems not from a realpolitik—or interest-based—conception of U.S. national security but from an expansive, de-territorialized conception of security stemming from Wilsonian ideology and concomitant political and economic Open Door concerns. Fear of American vulnerability in an ideologically hostile world reflects a fear of closure, not concerns about the balance of power.

It could be said—and has—that offshore balancing is another term for "isolationism." Leaving aside the question of whether the term "isolationism" is anything more than an epithet, offshore balancing is an insular grand strategy, but it is not an isolationist one. It acknowledges that there could be circumstances in which American vital interests mandate U.S. intervention in Eurasia, and it is a grand strategy that would maintain robust U.S. military capabilities. At the same time, however, offshore balancing would maintain a healthy skepticism about arguments that vital American interests invariably are implicated in Eurasian crises. The worst-case scenario view that America's security is menaced by potential Eurasian hegemons is deeply ingrained in the worldview of U.S. strategists who have an oddly unidirectional view of the "stopping power of water." Water, they say, prevents the United States from seeking extraregional hegemony in Eurasia, but for some reason water would not need keep a Eurasian hegemon from challenging the United States in its own backyard. Perhaps the reason some realists make such arguments is that they fear being tagged with the "isolationist" label. Understandably so, because without the driving fear of a Eurasian hegemon it would be hard to find a compelling realist justification for a permanent U.S. military involvement in Eurasia.

In the first decade of the twentieth century, for example, U.S. policymakers worried that Wilhelmine Germany would seize an island base in the Caribbean and use it as a springboard to invade the East Coast. The conventional (and ex post facto) realist explanation of U.S. entry into World War I is that U.S. leaders feared that a victorious Germany would be able to challenge U.S. primacy in the Western Hemisphere.[72] And, between the fall of France in June 1940 and the Japanese attack on Pearl Harbor, President Franklin D. Roosevelt told the American people that Germany would be able to project power into South America, from whence it could challenge America's regional hegemony. To these historical examples, John Mearsheimer adds his own hypothetical: a German victory in World War II, coupled with a rapid rise in Mexico's population and wealth in the early 1950s. In this scenario, Mexico and Germany would have been obvious allies, and Mexico "*might* even have invited Germany to station troops in Mexico."[73]

Each of these cases—historical and hypothetical—are examples of threat inflation: the threat is overstated, because the issues of geography and—especially—military capabilities are ignored. The Atlantic Ocean (like the Pacific) has constituted a formidable defensive barrier for the United States, not because it is liquid but because European peer competitors have lacked the capabilities to project power into the Western Hemisphere, and the United States has possessed the capabilities to prevent them from doing so. Put another way, water has not stopped European peer competitors from threatening the United States in the Western Hemisphere, but the U.S. Navy has stopped them dead in their tracks.

Pre–World War I American fears of a German threat to U.S. control of the Western Hemisphere were baseless.[74] Before Germany could have established naval power in the Western Hemisphere, it first would have had to get past the Royal Navy, and then it would have needed to defeat the U.S. Navy. Imperial Germany had the proverbial snowball's chance in hell of pulling off this geostrategic double play (especially since the German High Seas Fleet lacked the combat radius to operate outside of the North Sea).

The same can be said of the argument about U.S. entry into World War I. As already noted, the United States did not enter the war because Wilson and his advisers feared that the Allies were going to lose. On the contrary, they expected them to win the war, which "means that the strategic argument (that a German victory would imperil the western hemisphere)" was "not critical for Wilson."[75] The argument that the United States entered World War I for counterhegemonic or security reasons fell out of favor with historians decades ago.[76] Indeed, thinking counterfactually, if the United States had stayed out of the First World War and Germany had "won," it is difficult to conjure a plausible scenario where it would have won so decisively that Berlin could have compelled England to surrender, reduce, or destroy the Royal Navy, which would have remained an important barrier against the projection of German naval power across the Atlantic. In any event, once the 1916 naval construction program had been completed, the U.S. Navy would have been by far the strongest in the world. In the face of American naval power, it's hard to see how Germany could have projected enough power across the Atlantic to threaten U.S. security.[77] Moreover, after the bloodletting of World War I, it would have been some time before even a victorious Germany could have contemplated challenging the regional hegemony of the United States in the Western Hemisphere.

The claim that U.S. security was at risk between the fall of France and Pearl Harbor is also open to question.[78] For example, the pre–Pearl Harbor specter depicted by the pro-interventionists that Nazi Germany would leap from West Africa to the Brazilian bulge, and thence take on the United States in its own hemisphere, was vastly overdrawn, because Germany lacked the power projection capabilities to do so.[79] And the United States had the military capabilities to prevent Germany from doing so. This illustrates a more fundamental point: the arguments of American pro-interventionists notwithstanding, the United States was impregnable to attack from Eurasia. America's security did *not* hinge on the Eurasian balance of power.

After June 1940, of course, interventionists argued that Britain was America's last line of defense, and that if it fell the United States would be vulnerable to a German attack. But if America's physical security really had been tied to Britain's survival, it is curious that the United States did not enter the war when the British were on the ropes and Hitler's chances of winning a decisive victory were at their peak. Instead, following the fall of France, senior U.S. military officials opposed both the destroyers-for-bases swap with London and the diversion of war matériel to the British at the expense of America's own military buildup. As John Thompson has pointed out, during this period U.S. military planners rejected the pro-interventionist argument. They continued to believe in the viability of a hemispheric defense strategy and doubted that the United States could be challenged successfully in the Western Hemisphere even if Germany gained unchallenged hegemony in Europe. Two of America's leading civilian military strategists, Hanson W.

Baldwin and Nicholas Spykman, agreed that the United States could defend itself militarily even if Germany and Japan successfully subdued all of Eurasia.[80] Although Spykman qualified his argument by maintaining that the United States would be cut off from vital raw materials and ultimately would be strangled economically, he was a better strategist than he was a political economist.[81] In fact, the United States almost certainly could *not* have been done in by an economic embargo imposed by the victorious Germans and Japanese, because as Robert Art points out, "through a variety of measures—substitution, synthetic production, expanded domestic production, conservation, recycling, and imports from sources within the quarter sphere [Western Hemisphere]—the United States could have acquired what it needed."[82]

Mearsheimer's own hypothetical of a post–World War II alliance between Mexico and a victorious Nazi Germany is yet another example of how the threat of a Eurasian hegemon is overstated. First, the very logic of offensive realism—a state gains security by eliminating its rivals—means that the United States would never allow another state in the Western Hemisphere (either singly, or in concert with a peer competitor from another region) to become powerful enough to threaten its regional primacy. After all, if the United States was willing to undertake a preventive war against Saddam Hussein's Iraq—a state in a distant region that, at best, was a minor strategic annoyance and posed no plausible threat to the security of the American homeland—it would not hesitate to launch a preventive war against a regional upstart, like Mearsheimer's hypothetical Mexico, that threatened U.S. hegemony in the Western Hemisphere. If Mexico had ever tried to act as posited in Mearsheimer's hypothetical, it would have been a dead duck geopolitically. Moreover, if Germany had won World War II in Europe (as Mearsheimer's hypothetical assumes), the United States would not have been sitting by idly. Undamaged by the war, the United States presumably would have harnessed its enormous economic resources to maintain superior air and naval power, and a nuclear deterrent. It strains credulity to think that the United States would simply have stood aside and allowed Germany to "ferry" a large number of troops to Mexico and establish a major military presence there.

The fundamental problem with all these scenarios, both historical and hypothetical, is that distant peer competitors have never been able to do the one thing they would need to do to challenge the United States in its own neighborhood: move freely across the sea. Since the beginning of the twentieth century, the United States has been able to generate more than enough naval (and strategic air) power to stop dead in the water any distant rival that might attempt to take on the United States over here. And, if anything, since 1945 nuclear weapons have made America's regional primacy all but unassailable.[83] Rather than detracting from U.S. security, nuclear weapons enhanced it significantly. These overblown notions of American vulnerability to a Eurasian hegemon reflect an underlying worldview shared by U.S. policymakers and popularized by Wilson and FDR: that in the modern world, the United States lives perpetually under the shadow of war. This grand strategic narrative rests on two key assumptions. First, because of advances in modern military technology, others can acquire the means to inflict grave damage on the United States. Second, the world is shrinking. As a result, the argument goes, the United States itself is at risk and must involve itself in the security affairs of distant regions to ward off threats to the American homeland. These arguments have a very familiar ring, because they have been invoked by the Bush II administration to justify expanding the war on terror and the invasion of Iraq. Although a straight line connects the administration's grand strategic narrative with those of Wilson and FDR, the conception of American security embodied in these narratives always has been based on a deeply flawed premise. For, far from shrinking the world grand strategically, for the United States, modern weaponry—naval and strategic airpower, intercontinental delivery systems, and nuclear weapons—has *widened* it.

Proponents of offshore balancing are sensitive to the fact that the threat posed by potential Eurasian hegemons has often been exaggerated deliberately and used as a pretext for intervening in conflicts where America's security clearly has not been at risk. When policymakers use arguments about technology and a shrinking world to warn of American vulnerability, they are, as Michael S. Sherry notes, doing a lot more than simply depicting reality. They are trying to shape public perceptions and to create a new reality, which is why this narrative of U.S. national security is "an ideological construction, not merely a perceptual reaction."[84] To be blunt, U.S. officials often have invoked the specter of a Eurasian hegemon to rationalize the pursuit of America's own hegemonic, Open Door–driven ambitions. Although it is always possible that the threat of a Eurasian hegemon justifiably might compel U.S. intervention, whenever this argument is made to justify a specific intervention, red lights should flash and it should be scrutinized very carefully, because U.S. officials have cried wolf way too many times in the past.

Implementing Offshore Balancing

Today, unlike 1941 or the early cold war, no rising hegemon threatens Europe. Although China is a potential hegemon in East Asia, in Japan, India, Russia (and eventually, a reunified Korea) there also exists the foundation of a robust multipolar regional balance of power that could contain China without U.S. involvement. Simply put, in the early twenty-first century geopolitical conditions are far different from those that necessitated U.S. military engagement in Eurasia in World War II or immediately thereafter. In short, even as the risks of the ongoing presence of the United States in Eurasia—especially in East Asia—are rising, the need for U.S. military involvement no longer is pressing. Moreover, America's hegemonic strategy in the Persian

Gulf has given rise to a new kind of threat in the form of Islamic terrorism. Today, there are powerful reasons for the United States to eschew hegemony—and the strategic risks and economic burdens that go with it—and adopt an offshore balancing grand strategy. An offshore balancing grand strategy would look much different than America's current strategy.[85]

As an offshore balancer, the United States would leave NATO and retract its military power from Europe. Instead of opposing the European Union's plan to develop military capabilities that would permit it to emerge as an independent pole of power in the international system, the United States would support the EU's efforts. The United States would devolve to the EU fully responsibility for defending European interests both on the Continent and beyond it.

Likewise, the United States would terminate the mutual security treaty with Japan and facilitate Japan's acquisition of whatever kind of military capabilities Tokyo decides that it needs to function as an independent great power, including a secure second-strike nuclear deterrent and power projection capabilities that would permit Japan to protect its trade routes and its territorial claims in the East and South China Seas.

In addition it would avoid implementing an overtly confrontational policy toward China. It is hardly surprising (indeed, it parallels in many ways America's own emergence as a great power) that China—the largest and potentially most powerful state in Asia—is seeking a more assertive political, military, and economic role in the region and even challenging America's present dominance in East Asia. This poses no direct threat to U.S. security, however. Doubtless, Japan, India, Russia (and perhaps Korea) may be worried about the implications of China's rapid ascendance. But this is precisely the point of offshore balancing: because China potentially poses a direct threat to them—not to the United States—they should bear the responsibility of balancing against Chinese power. The United States should avoid policies that inflame Sino-American relations. That means a hand-off attitude with respect to China's internal policies. The United States lacks the power to transform China into a liberal democracy. Trying to do so serves only to poison relations with Beijing. Finally, Washington should declare unequivocally that the Taiwan issue is a purely internal Chinese matter. Taiwan's unresolved status is the legacy of a civil war that ended on the mainland in 1949. It is worth recalling that before the outbreak of the Korean War, Secretary of State Dean Acheson recommended that the United States extricate itself from the unfinished business of the Chinese civil war and leave Taiwan to its fate. More than a half-century later, the United States finally should do so. For the United States, going to war to defend Taiwan's self-styled independence makes sense only as a pretext for fighting a preventive war with China. This is something the United States should avoid. The United States should leave the containment of China to the emerging multipolar power balance in Asia.

187

As with China, the United States should stay out of Russia's internal affairs and be nonconfrontational, for the same reason: the United States cannot transform Russia into a free-market democracy. Washington's preaching does nothing more than make relations with Moscow more tense than they need to be. The United States also should recognize Moscow's legitimate sphere of influence in Russia's "near abroad," especially in Chechnya and Central Asia, where it is combating Islamic fundamentalism. The United States has an important interest in maintaining good relations with Moscow. Although—not for the first time in its history—Russia is down and out as a great power, it probably will bounce back, as it has in the past. For an off-shore balancing United States, Russia is a geostrategic linchpin because it could play a crucial role in three regional power balances: in Europe (vis-à-vis an EU superstate or a renascent Germany if the EU project fails); in East Asia (vis-à-vis China), and in the Persian Gulf/Central Asia.

As an offshore balancer, the United States would withdraw its troops from South Korea. The U.S. commitment to South Korea had a plausible strategic rationale during the cold war. However, there is no compelling justification for keeping U.S. troops on the peninsula today when a wealthy and techno-logically advanced South Korea is capable of defending itself from North Korea without assistance from the United States. The fact that U.S. policy-makers plan on maintaining a military presence on the peninsula even fol-lowing reunification—which, obviously, would remove the North Korean threat—is another piece of evidence proving that America's hegemonic am-bitions have always transcended the cold war (and its vestiges).

Another thing the United States would do as part of its offshore balancing policy would be to forego a strategy of perpetuating its dominance by seek-ing—as it presently appears to be doing—nuclear hegemony by building up a first-strike capability coupled with strategic missile defenses. Given the real-ity that terrorists, or hostile states like North Korea, could acquire nuclear weapons and long-range missiles, it makes sense for the United States to de-velop missile defenses, which potentially are a *real* form of insurance. How-ever, to reassure the other rising great powers that their security is not en-dangered by American hegemony, the deployment of a missile defense system should be coupled with a significant reduction of the U.S. strategic nuclear arsenal.

The United States would also work to reduce its dependence on imported oil and extricate itself from the Middle East. America's reliance on imported oil poses three dangers. First, there is the economic danger if the flow of oil is interrupted because Persian Gulf instability impacts the global oil market. Second, the U.S. presence in the Gulf—which is wholly attributable to con-cerns about access to cheap oil—fans Islamic terrorism against the United States. Third, if current indications are correct, the world is approaching an inflection point where increasing demand for oil will exceed oil production capacity. In large part, the increasing scarcity of oil is due to the increased demand for energy by China and India, both of which are rising great powers. Thus, in coming years, the quest for obtain secure supplies of oil could well become a major cause of geopolitical friction. Addressing these issues requires a multipronged policy.

With respect to energy security, the United States needs to formulate a viable national energy strategy. Market mechanisms usually work, but not always. And for the United States, energy is about grand strategy, not just economic theory. The United States should embark on a "Manhattan Project" to develop new energy sources that ultimately will render the Persian Gulf strategically and economically irrelevant. In the short term, the United States should impose an oil import tax to reduce oil consumption and to keep oil prices high enough to make the use of alternative energy sources economically viable. Serious consideration should be given to imitating China's current oil strategy and entering into long-term contracts with suppliers in more secure areas than the Persian Gulf (and Central Asia). The United States should aim to lock up the oil exports of its Western Hemisphere neighbors (and, as a regional hegemon, it should be prepared to flex its muscles with recalcitrant states like Venezuela).

To reduce the Islamic terrorist threat to the American homeland, the United States needs to restructure its Middle East policy. Except for its naval presence in the Strait of Hormuz, the United States should remove its military forces from the Gulf, including Iraq. The United States should refrain from causing even more regional instability by promoting democracy. At the same time, however, instead of propping up reactionary regimes in the region, the United States should be prepared to let "nature take its course." To offset the widespread anti-Americanism in the Islamic world, the United States should take a strictly evenhanded stance on relations between Israel and Palestine. The United States should support the creation of a viable Palestinian state and insist on the removal of all Israeli settlements from the West Bank.

An offshore balancing grand strategy must be implemented carefully. Because of the terrorist threat, the recommended changes in U.S. strategy toward the Gulf and Middle East should be put in place swiftly. On the other hand, because of the complexities and long-term strategic implications of an American shift to an offshore balancing strategy, U.S. military power should be retracted from Europe and East Asia gradually, and in consultation with the Europeans, Japanese, and Koreans. An orderly, phased U.S. withdrawal will give the Europeans, Japanese, and Koreans time to adjust to America's new grand strategy. As part of the change in grand strategy, the United States should be prepared to assist the Europeans, Japanese, and Koreans in building up their independent military capabilities through arms sales and technology transfers. Also, although the

United States will not maintain an ongoing forward military presence in Eurasia, it should seek to maintain close military contacts with the Europeans and the Japanese—and develop them with India and Russia—and conduct regular joint exercises. Because future geopolitical conditions might necessitate the reinsertion of U.S. military power into Eurasia, the United States should maintain a network of basing rights that can be used for this purpose should it become necessary. Finally, the adoption of offshore balancing is bound to result in the acquisition of nuclear weapons by Japan, Germany (either as a national nuclear force or as part of an EU nuclear force), and possibly Korea. The United States should relax its nonproliferation policy and help these states, and both India and Pakistan (which already have nuclear weapons), acquire the technology to build survivable forces, and to maintain secure command and control over their nuclear arsenals.

* * *

Advocates of hegemony claim that it is illusory to think that the United States can retract its military power safely from Eurasia. The answer to this assertion is that the risks and costs of American grand strategy are growing, and the strategy is not likely to work much longer in any event. As other states—notably China—rapidly close the gap, U.S. hegemony is fated to end in the next decade or two regardless of U.S. efforts to prolong it. At the same time, understandable doubts about the credibility of U.S. security guarantees are driving creeping re-nationalization by America's Eurasian allies, which, in turn, is leading to a reversion to multipolarity. In this changing geopolitical context, the costs of trying to hold on to hegemony are high and going to become higher. Rather than fostering peace and stability in Eurasia, America's military commitments abroad have become a source of *in*security for the United States, because they carry the risk of entrapping the United States in great power Eurasian wars.

The events of 9/11 are another example of how hegemony makes the United States less secure than it would be if it followed an offshore balancing strategy. Terrorism, the RAND Corporation terrorism expert Bruce Hoffman says, is "about power: the pursuit of power, the acquisition of power, and use of power to achieve political change."[86] If we step back for a moment from our horror and revulsion at the events of September 11, we can see that the attack was in keeping with the Clausewitzian paradigm of war: force was used against the United States by its adversaries to advance their political objectives.[87] As Clausewitz observed, "War is not an act of senseless passion but is controlled by its political object."[88] September 11 represented a violent counterreaction to America's geopolitical—and cultural—hegemony. As the strategy expert Richard K. Betts presciently observed in a 1998 *Foreign Affairs* article:

It is hardly likely that Middle Eastern radicals would be hatching schemes like the destruction of the World Trade Center if the United States had not been identified so long as the mainstay of Israel, the shah of Iran, and conservative Arab regimes and the source of a cultural assault on Islam.[89]

U.S. hegemony fuels terrorist groups like al Qaeda and fans Islamic fundamentalism, which is a form of "blowback" against America's preponderance and its world role.[90]

As long as the United States maintains its global hegemony—and its concomitant preeminence in regions like the Persian Gulf—it will be the target of politically motivated terrorist groups like al Qaeda. After 9/11, many foreign policy analysts and pundits asked the question, "Why do they hate us?" This question missed the key point. No doubt, there are Islamic fundamentalists who do "hate" the United States for cultural, religious, and ideological reasons. And even leaving aside American neoconservatives' obvious relish for making it so, to some extent the war on terror inescapably has overtones of a "clash of civilizations." Still, this isn't—and should not be allowed to become—a replay of the Crusades. Fundamentally 9/11 was about geopolitics, specifically about U.S. hegemony. The United States may be greatly reviled in some quarters of the Islamic world, but were the United States not so intimately involved in the affairs of the Middle East, it's hardly likely that this detestation would have manifested itself in something like 9/11. As Michael Scheurer, who headed the CIA analytical team monitoring Osama bin Laden and al Qaeda, puts it, "One of the greatest dangers for Americans in deciding how to confront the Islamist threat lies in continuing to believe—at the urging of senior U.S. leaders—that Muslims hate and attack us for what we are and think, rather than for what we do."[91] It is American *policies*—to be precise, American hegemony—that make the United States a lightning rod for Muslim anger.

Hegemony has proven to be an elusive goal for the great powers that have sought it. The European great powers that bid for hegemony did so because they were on a geopolitical treadmill. For them, it seemed as if security was attainable only by eliminating their great power rivals and achieving continental hegemony. And it is this fact that invested great power politics with its tragic quality, because the international system's power-balancing dynamics doomed all such bids to failure. The United States, on the other hand, has never faced similar pressures to seek security through a hegemonic grand strategy, and, too often, instead of enhancing U.S. security as advertised, America's hegemonic grand strategy has made the United States less secure. In the early twenty-first century, by threatening to embroil the United States in military showdowns with nuclear great powers and exposing the United States to terrorism, the pursuit of hegemony means that "over there" well may become over *here. Objectively,* the United States historically has enjoyed an extraordinarily high degree of immunity from external threat, a condition that has had nothing to do with whether it is hegemonic and everything to do with geography and its military capabilities. Consequently, the United States has, should it wish to use it, an exit ramp—offshore balancing—that would allow it to escape from the tragedy of great power politics that befalls those that seek hegemony. The failure of the United States to take this exit ramp constitutes the real tragedy of American diplomacy.

Conclusion

Since the early 1940s, the United States has pursued a grand strategy of extraregional hegemony. From the standpoint of neorealist theory, this is puzzling. The historical record shows that hegemonic grand strategies invariably have proved self-defeating, because they result in counterhegemonic balancing and/or imperial overstretch. Adding to the explanatory puzzle is that when employed as theories of grand strategy, both offensive realism and defensive realism predict that, instead of pursuing extraregional hegemony, the United States should have followed an offshore balancing grand strategy.

The puzzle is explained partially by the fact that America's geostrategic position in the international system is sui generis. Unlike Europe's great powers—which could attain security only by establishing hegemony on the Continent—the United States has not *needed* to seek security through extraregional hegemony. Because of military capabilities and geography, since its emergence as a great power, the United States has been extraordinarily secure. Moreover, before 1945 America's security was bolstered by the fact that Europe's great powers had to focus their strategic attention on threats close to home and were unable, therefore, to build up the power projection capabilities to seek extraregional hegemony.

Unlike Europe, the Western Hemisphere was a power vacuum rather than a multipolar system, which allowed the United States to attain regional hegemony. America's unique status as the only regional hegemon in the international system was a launching pad for U.S. pursuit of extraregional hegemony. The stopping power of water did not prevent the United States from extending its hegemony to Western Europe after World War II. Combined with military capabilities, water (or, more correctly, geography) often is a barrier to great power expansion, because it is difficult to project great power over long distances. However, the "stopping power of water" is not an ironclad rule. As America's experience demonstrates, distance is not invariably an insurmountable obstacle to the attainment of extraregional hegemony. The United States was able to establish its extraregional hegemony on the Continent after World War II because Western Europe was a power vacuum, the United States had overwhelming military capabilities, and it was the beneficiary of sheer good luck (the war ended with a massive U.S. military presence on the Continent).

The Open Door and America's Pursuit of Extraregional Hegemony

If security did not drive America's postwar pursuit of extraregional hegemony, what did? That question is best answered by extraregional hegemony theory, a neoclassical realist theory of U.S. grand strategy. After World War II, the presence of American military power in Europe, the shift in the distribution of power between the United States and Europe in America's favor as a result of the war, and America's hard power capabilities provided the opportunity and means for the United States to seek hegemony in Western Europe. But what were the motivations animating U.S. grand strategy? The answer is found at the domestic level: the economic and political Open Doors—in other words, America's liberal (Wilsonian) ideology—caused the United States to seek hegemony.

The Open Door is a complex set of linkages among economic and political (ideological) openness abroad, America's prosperity, and the security of its core values domestically. Since World War II, the Open Door has reflected what present-day U.S. policymakers call the virtuous circle (which is based on circular logic): international economic openness and the spread of American ideology abroad create peace and security for the United States, and the U.S. military presence in Europe, East Asia, and the Middle East creates the conditions that allow for international economic openness and the spread of American ideology. By the same token, the Open Door posits that closure abroad—either economic or ideological—would endanger the safety of America's core values at home by forcing the United States to adopt regimented economic policies and to become a garrison state. In essence, the Open Door substituted an open-ended, ideological, and de-territorialized definition of American security for a more traditional conception of security based on the international system's distribution of power. That is, it divorced the concept of security from defense of the American homeland and, instead, ultimately defined security ideationally (or, as Arnold Wolfers put it, in terms of "milieu goals").

The Open Door posits that the United States can be secure—that its domestic political and economic system can survive—only if it enjoys absolute security. Unsurprisingly, therefore, even as World War II was still being fought, U.S. postwar planners had concluded that the United States needed to aim for unipolarity. To this end, Washington used its economic leverage to reduce Britain to an adjunct to American power and its military muscle to ensure that Germany and Japan never again could reemerge as great powers. During the late 1940s and the 1950s, U.S. policymakers also aspired to eliminate the Soviet Union as a great power rival by fomenting internal dissension and "rolling back" the Soviet empire in East Central Europe. However, this aspiration—which never entirely disappeared as an element in America's cold war strategy toward the Soviet Union—ran up against the harsh realities of the nuclear revolution, and its realization had to be deferred.

Postwar U.S. grand strategy toward Western Europe was based on the perception that America's prosperity and its domestic political stability were linked inextricably to an open Western Europe and that, by fostering peace, an open international economic system would contribute to U.S. security. U.S. policymakers believed that economic openness could not take root in Western Europe if the Continent reverted to multipolar power politics. In this respect, America's postwar Western European grand strategy was neither cold war–driven nor counterhegemonic. The aims of that strategy had been decided on even before World War II had ended, and they required the United States to establish its own hegemony on the Continent. As the cold war unfolded, it was superimposed on this preexisting grand strategic foundation. Even if there had been no Soviet threat, the United States would have maintained a permanent military presence in Western Europe, because the attainment of its economic Open Door aims compelled it to act as Western Europe's stabilizer (or "pacifier") to keep the Western Europeans—especially the French and Germans—from being at each other's throats.

The United States also wanted to make certain that Western Europe did not emerge as an independent pole of power—a "third force"—in the international system. Thus the United States had to keep the Western Europeans together economically but apart strategically to prevent them from coalescing and contesting U.S. hegemony. Hence, the United States promoted Western European integration to "de-nationalize" the foreign and security policies of the Western European states, and it established its hegemony on the Continent to subordinate the Western Europeans to American leadership in the realms of "high politics." The most important piece of evidence supporting this explanation is the fact that although the cold war ended some fifteen years ago, the United States has not given up its hegemonic role on the Continent and has opposed the European Union's emergence as an independent strategic pole of power in the international system.

In recent years, a small group of historians led by Marc Trachtenberg have advanced the revisionist "exit strategy" thesis that, far from *deliberately* seeking to establish hegemony over Western Europe, the United States wanted to foster the emergence of a politically (as well as economically) integrated Western Europe as a "third force" in international politics capable of lifting the crushing burdens of containment from America's shoulders by assuming responsibility for its own defense.[1] As a description of America's postwar Western European grand strategy, the exit strategy school's argument is not compelling. Because it is a cold war–centric argument, it ignores the question of whether the cold war was the dominant, or a distinctly secondary, factor driving America's postwar Western European grand strategy.

The historical record does not support Trachtenberg's claim that postwar Western Europe came together only because of the Soviet threat.[2] Exit strategy historians overlook the fact that the foundations of that strategy were put in place during World War II, when Washington determined that western Germany would have to be resuscitated economically and reintegrated into the larger European economy; that America's prosperity was tied to an economically open and integrated Western Europe; that economic nationalism and multipolar power politics could not be allowed to revive in postwar Europe because these were inimical to U.S. Open Door economic interests on the Continent; and that the communists had to be kept out of power in Western Europe because they would adopt autarkic economic policies and close the Continent to the United States economically. Indeed, as Michael Hogan has pointed out, the origins of America's post–World War II economic Open Door objectives in Western Europe had their roots in Washington's post–World War I European policy.[3] For Open Door—not cold war—reasons, the United States, not the Soviet Union, was postwar Western Europe's federator (as well as its pacifier).

Did U.S. officials in the late 1940s and early 1950s favor a "united" Western Europe as the exit strategy historians contend? Certainly in *public,* U.S. officials often said they did. Even the Kennedy administration—which worked assiduously to make certain that a truly independent "European Europe" was strangled in the crib—professed to support a united Western Europe linked with the United States in a "partnership" anchored in the "Atlantic Community." Drawing on the experience of two world wars, postwar U.S. officials believed there could be no stability on the Continent—the sine qua non for the United States to realize its economic Open Door goals—if the Europeans reverted to their bad old ways of nationalism and power politics. Washington therefore promoted integration and supranational institutions in Western Europe precisely to de-nationalize interstate relations among the Western Europeans.[4] But the United States had zero intention of allowing Western Europe to become a truly autonomous pole of power in the international system.

Rhetorically, U.S. officials supported the idea of a united Western Europe acting as an "equal partner," because they feared that prolonged Western European dependence on the United States would have a corrosive impact on transatlantic relations. However, as Geir Lundestad says:

> One should not necessarily take all these statements about the undesirability of European dependence on the United States at face value. It is easy to go against dependence as such; *it is more difficult to do so when independence actually leads to opposition.* We also have to keep in mind that virtually all American policymakers definitely wanted even a united Europe to cooperate closely with

the United States within an Atlantic framework. Most policymakers probably assumed that Europe would come to do so. *Somehow Europe was to be independent and dependent on the United States at the same time.*[5]

U.S. declarations favoring Western European unity must not be conflated with a desire to see a united Western Europe emerge as an *independent* geopolitical "third force." Leaving Eisenhower aside for the moment, every other post-1945 administration right down to the Bush II administration has been determined to ensure that Western Europe does *not* emerge as an autonomous pole of power in the international system.[6] During the Truman administration, Secretary of State Dean Acheson adamantly opposed the concept of an independent Western European third force. It is true, however, that some other administration officials did endorse the idea of a united Western Europe emerging as a third force. However, those who held this view did so because "they had assumed Europe would unite and enter into a mutually beneficial partnership with the United States, with which it would share similar interests."[7] By the time the Kennedy administration came to power, the United States discerned clearly that if integration produced a true third-force Western Europe, America's hegemony on the Continent would be endangered. Hence, the United States sought to "hold [Western European integration] in check or mitigate it through strong Atlantic institutions."[8] From the end of World War II to the present day, what the United States has wanted is "America's Europe": an economically integrated, peaceful, and stable (Western) Europe, but not one capable of acting apart from, or in opposition to, the United States on strategic and diplomatic issues of importance to Washington.[9]

Finally, there is the Eisenhower issue. It is plausible that, for generational and cultural reasons, Eisenhower did not believe that there should be a permanent U.S. military presence in postwar Western Europe. But the evidence is not nearly as conclusive as the exit strategy school historians claim. Eisenhower may have had offshore balancing instincts, but his views about the U.S. military role in Western Europe were complex and seem to have rested more on his approach to nuclear strategy, and his fiscal conservatism, than on a specific grand strategic preference for offshore balancing.

Concerned about the economic implications of U.S. overseas commitments, Eisenhower certainly wanted the Western Europeans to take up more of the burden of providing conventional forces for NATO so that the United States could bring most of its troops home from the Continent.[10] He believed that the decision to deploy six U.S. divisions to Europe in 1951 had been a temporary expedient to defend Western Europe until it had built up its own capacity for self-defense, at which point *most* of the American troops would go home.[11] He also believed that the increasing role of nuclear weapons in NATO strategy lessened the need for a large U.S. ground presence in Western Europe.[12] At the same time, however, the historical record shows clearly that Eisenhower never contemplated leaving the Western Europeans on their own militarily. In November 1959 he stated that "never in our lifetime will all our troops be withdrawn from Europe because it is important to carry the flag."[13] Even if most U.S. troops were withdrawn, Eisenhower intended that a residual force would remain in Europe as a trip wire, and planned to leave in place the most dangerous aspect (for the United States) of the U.S. commitment to Western Europe—the U.S. strategic nuclear umbrella.[14] Eisenhower's personal preference may have been to reduce the U.S. commitment to Western Europe, but he seems to have realized that, in the real world of American grand strategy, there was no chance that such a retraction of American power was going to take place.[15] Whatever Eisenhower may have hoped to do in terms of withdrawing U.S. forces from the Continent, the U.S. military commitment to Western Europe was *not* reduced during his administration.[16] Indeed, as Trachtenberg acknowledges, Eisenhower's views on devolving defense responsibilities from the United States to the Western Europeans through nuclear sharing, a Western European conventional force buildup, and the withdrawal of U.S. ground forces from the Continent were rejected by the administration's top foreign policy officials (including Dulles).[17] The fact that Eisenhower was the odd man out on these issues takes us to the nub of the matter.

Whether officials in the Truman and Eisenhower administrations consciously thought in terms of establishing U.S. hegemony on the Continent— and had a plan for doing so—is irrelevant. What *is* relevant is that (with the possible exception of Eisenhower) U.S. officials deliberately embraced a set of postwar grand strategic objectives—molded by the economic and political Open Doors—that *required* the United States to impose its hegemony on Western Europe. Eisenhower may not have understood the *logic* of America's postwar Open Door ambitions, but Dulles and other administration officials did. If the United States had left the Continent, Western Europe would have sunk back into its old habits of nationalism and multipolar politics, which would have been bad for the Open Door. In terms of fundamental postwar U.S. grand strategic objectives, protecting the Western Europeans from one another was more important than defending them against the Soviets, and it is something the United States would have been called on to do even if the Kremlin had been perceived as a benign factor in international politics. Ironically, however, it may be that although the cold war was a secondary factor in determining U.S. policy, without the glue provided by the Soviet threat it may prove impossible for the United States to maintain its hegemony on the Continent.

Policy Prescriptions

Doubtless, there are some who say—not without some justification—that America's post-1945 grand strategy was extraordinarily successful. After all, the United States contained—and ultimately defeated—the Soviet Union and transformed Western Europe and East Asia into zones of peace and prosperity. Given this track record, it fairly can be asked, Why should the United States discard what has proved to be a winning grand strategy? The answer is simple: the times and conditions are changing. Following World War II, America's overwhelming power, combined with the Soviet threat, ultimately caused Western Europe to accept—albeit unhappily—U.S. hegemony. Now, however, with the Soviet threat gone, the Europeans no longer need to submit to American dominance and increasingly are less willing to do so. Moreover, today other new great powers are emerging, and some of them will counter-balance American power. China is rising especially rapidly and closing the gap with the United States. A creeping multipolarization already is well underway in East Asia, because U.S. allies have well-founded doubts about the future credibility of America's security guarantees. At home, fundamental weaknesses in the U.S. economy raise doubts about America's long-term ability to sustain its hegemony. In other words, America's hegemonic position is being assailed by a combination of factors, and the costs and dangers of the present U.S. grand strategy are rising.

Conditions have changed in another way as well: the United States is not threatened by a rising Eurasian hegemon. During the last century, there have been three periods when the United States had to worry—or thought that it did—about the potential threat to its security posed by a rising Eurasian hegemon: World War I, World War II, and the cold war. However, the United States did not enter World War I to prevent Germany from gaining hegemony over Europe and threatening the security of the American homeland. This was an ex post facto rationale propounded well after World War I ended. Woodrow Wilson took the United States into the war to impose his vision of a new world order both on Germany and the Allies; however, from a grand strategic standpoint the United States could have—and should have—remained out of World War I. In 1940–41, on the other hand, it was reasonable for U.S. officials to believe that U.S. security *might* have been endangered if Germany had defeated Britain and the Soviet Union. After the fall of France, the United States appropriately acted as an offshore balancer by supplying the British and the Soviets with war matériel through Lend-Lease, fighting an undeclared naval war in the Atlantic against German U-boats to ensure that American supplies reached Britain and the Soviet Union, and preparing to enter the war in the event British or Soviet resistance appeared to be on the verge of collapsing.[18]

Finally, there is the cold war, which breaks down into two distinct periods: the immediate years following World War II (from 1945 to 1955), and the balance of the cold war. In hindsight, by rendering traditional calculations about the balance of power obsolete, the nuclear revolution may have rendered irrelevant historic U.S. concerns about a Eurasian hegemon. But U.S. strategists in the late 1940s could not know this. Given what they did know at the time, it made sense for the United States to help the Western Europeans get back on their feet, and, by containing the Soviet Union, to buy time for them to recover from the political and economic dislocations caused by World War II. Whether it was wise for the United States to remain on the Continent militarily *after* Western Europe had gotten back on its own two feet is a different question, however.

By many measures, America's grand strategy from 1945 to 1991 indeed was successful—but not without a price. Not only did U.S. postwar grand strategy impose great costs—and serious risks—on the United States, but the cold war obscured from view America's underlying hegemonic ambitions and the costs of pursuing them.[19] Some of these costs were tangible, measured in the opportunity cost of trillions of dollars diverted from other—arguably more economically productive and socially beneficial—uses to pursuing U.S. global ambitions. It was, after all, Dwight Eisenhower who said that "every gun that is made . . . signifies, in the final sense, a theft from those who hunger and are not fed, and from those who are cold but not clothed."[20] Other costs were more subtle: the expansion of state power, the accretion of power in the imperial presidency (and the concomitant diminution of congressional authority in the realm of foreign affairs), the decay of traditional social institutions, and a general coarsening of public discourse. Ironically, U.S. officials claimed that America's post–World War II grand strategy would prevent the United States from becoming a garrison state. Instead, the United States became, as Daniel Yergin described it, a national security state, and the consequences of that were not so clearly distinguishable from those of the garrison state—a point again made by Eisenhower when he warned of the dangers of the "military-industrial complex."[21] And, of course, there was the human cost, including the more than 54,000 Americans killed in Korea and 58,000 who lost their lives in Vietnam and are honored by name on a wall in the Washington Mall.

Inevitably, the United States would have paid some price for the policies it rightly pursued in the late 1940s. But this still leaves open the question posed by Michael Hogan: By abandoning hegemony in favor of offshore balancing, could the United States have maintained its security at a lower price?[22] If the United States, at an earlier stage, could have extricated itself from the hegemonic dimension of its cold war strategy, and its concomitant burdens, it would have been in its interest to do so. This, of course, raises another important question: Why has the United States stuck so long with its hegemonic strategy? Were U.S. policymakers foolish, or were they willfully indifferent to the burdens placed on the United States by its grand strategy?

The answer is both complex (a topic worthy of a book in its own right) and yet simple. In his book *Myths of Empire,* Jack Snyder talks about elites "hijacking" the state. This fails to make the point quite strongly enough. Dominant elites do not hijack the state; they *are* the state. The United States has pursued hegemony because that grand strategy has served the interests of the dominant elites that have formed the core of the U.S. foreign policy establishment since at least the late 1930s, when the New Deal resulted in the domestic political triumph of what Thomas Ferguson calls "multinational liberalism."[23] At the core of the multinational liberal coalition were large capital-intensive corporations that looked to overseas markets and outward-looking investment banks. This coalition displaced the so-called system of 1896, which was organized around labor-intensive industries that favored economic nationalism and opposed strategic internationalism.

The multinational liberal coalition that cemented its hold on power during the New Deal had its roots deep in the Eastern establishment; it also included the national media, important foundations, the big Wall Street law firms, and organizations such as the Council on Foreign Relations.[24] This coalition favored economic and political Open Doors and the strategic internationalism that accompanied them.[25] Although the bipartisan consensus among the U.S. foreign policy establishment favoring strategic internationalism and U.S. hegemony that was forged some six decades ago has occasionally been tested—notably during the Vietnam War—it has proved remarkably durable. Unless it undergoes a Damascene-like intellectual conversion, as long as the present foreign policy elite remains in power the United States will remain wedded to a hegemonic grand strategy. It probably will take a major domestic political realignment—perhaps triggered by setbacks abroad or a severe economic crisis at home—to bring about a change in American grand strategy.

Nevertheless, there is a powerful case to be made that the United States would be far better off if it had abandoned its hegemonic grand strategy and adopted an offshore balancing strategy decades ago. Here, the views ascribed to Eisenhower by the exit strategy school are instructive, because they show that offshore balancing—to which Eisenhower is said to have been inclined—was a viable alternative to U.S. hegemony in Western Europe (and elsewhere). Eisenhower's instincts were correct: the United States would have been better off if it had devolved to the Western Europeans—or to a revived Germany—the full responsibility for deterring a Soviet attack and for defending Western Europe if deterrence failed. Arguably, even in the late 1940s and early 1950s there were opportunities—in the form of German reunification or of mutual U.S.-Soviet disengagement from Central Europe—that the United States could have seized to withdraw from the Continent and adopt an offshore balancing strategy. And, from the 1960s onward, Western Europe clearly could have defended itself, which means that from the early 1950s counterhegemony does not explain American grand strategy.

The United States did not withdraw from Western Europe and adopt an offshore balancing strategy—Eisenhower's supposed preference—because America's Open Door objectives on the Continent were more important than containing the Soviet Union. If the United States had devolved the responsibility for checking the Soviets to a renascent Germany, Western Europeans would have felt threatened. If the United States had devolved the responsibility for containing the Soviet Union to a united Western European third force, its own hegemony would have been imperiled. Either way, America's Open Door strategy on the Continent would have unraveled.

One of the fundamental paradoxes of America's world position that profoundly influences its grand strategy stems from its unique position in the international system. Because of its enormous hard power capabilities, for nearly a century U.S. policymakers have been conscious of the fact that the United States potentially can, if it chooses, significantly influence its external environment. And possession of this power often has given rise to the desire to use it. At the same time, the very magnitude of U.S. power cuts against an active international role, because it means that when it comes to security, the United States has been pretty much self-sufficient. In Kenneth Waltz's words, it is precisely because the United States enjoys "the luxury of choice that vast power provides, [that] the question of the criteria of commitment, far from being academic, becomes vital."[26] America's power and geographical location has meant that it has been all too easy for the United States to make bad choices grand strategically—such as pursuing extraregional hegemony. Precisely because they understand that the United States is not immune to the hegemon's temptation—of becoming overcommitted abroad—realists have tended to define the requirements of U.S. security narrowly, not expansively.

Realists have generally been associated with one of the two main contending visions of America's proper place in the world that have shaped the periodic "great debates" about national purpose and the objectives of U.S. grand strategy—an ongoing debate between what H. W. Brands calls "exemplars" and "vindicators."[27] As Michael Hunt notes, the vindicators hold "that the American pursuit of lofty ambitions abroad, far from imperiling liberty, would serve to invigorate it at home, while creating conditions favorable to its spread in foreign lands."[28] This viewpoint underlies U.S. hegemony. There is, however, a very different, opposing vision—that of the exemplars—that holds that America's political institutions, prosperity, and social cohesion are best safeguarded by grand strategic restraint. Proponents of this vision have "argued that the pursuit of greatness diverted attention and resources from real problems at home and might under some circumstances even aggravate or compound those problems. Foreign crusades unavoidably diminished national ideals and well being."[29] Whereas hegemony's advocates believe that the United States can—indeed, *must*—transform the world, traditional realists have always feared that in attempting to transform the world, the United States itself will be transformed—and not for the better.

Robert Osgood observed that the "great debates" between the advocates of American strategic internationalism and realist proponents of restraint are really contests for control of the "symbolic spigots of popular idealism."

Realists have not fared well in these debates because they are trained to discuss grand strategy in terms of national interests and power only, rather than in terms of values. Realists must shed their reticence to explicate the values underlying their policy preferences, because this reluctance allows their opponents to portray them—unfairly—as amoral (or even immoral).

Realists have a moral, as well as prudential, case against American hegemony, and they should not shrink from making it, because—unlike U.S. hegemonists—they have identified clearly the price the United States pays in trying to realize its hegemonic ambitions. This is why realists have warned that overconcentrated power, even an imbalance in America's favor, can have dangerous consequences; insisted that U.S. strategy distinguish vital from secondary interests; and argued against U.S. involvement in peripheral conflicts. Most of all, they have been aware that hegemonic power has both a seductive, and corrupting, effect on those who wield it—even the United States. In Waltz's words: "The possession of great power has often tempted nations to the unnecessary and foolish employment of force, vices from which we are not immune."[30]

Leading realists—George F. Kennan, Walter Lippmann, Hans Morgenthau, Robert W. Tucker, and Kenneth Waltz—have always feared that a hegemonic grand strategy would lead to excessive interventionism and cause the United States to adopt both a crusading mentality and a spirit of intolerance. They also have been rightly concerned that a *too* powerful United States would instill feelings of fear and insecurity in other states in the international system. And realists have understood that the United States would pay a price at home for overreaching abroad. For realists, foreign policy restraint, not the pursuit of hegemony, has been the *real* key to defending America's core values. For all of these reasons Kennan, Lippmann, Morgenthau, Tucker, and Waltz opposed America's Vietnam policy, just as the current generation of realists took the lead in opposing the Iraq War.

Great powers cannot escape from power politics, which is why grand strategy must be grounded in a conception of the national interest. Realists have always known, however, that the very term "national interest" invariably has a moral—or normative—dimension. This is because there is no single, objectively "true" national interest.[31] Rather, the concept of "national interest describes a starting point, an approach to formulating policy."[32] Thinking in terms of national interest improves the quality of statecraft by forcing decision makers to ask the right questions—about the relations of ends to means, about what is necessary versus what merely is desirable—when they formulate grand strategy. Applied to grand strategy, the concept of national interest reminds policymakers that they must be guided by what the sociologist Max Weber called the "ethic of responsibility"—which, in layman's terms, restates the familiar injunction that the road to hell is paved with good intentions, and, hence, that they must "be calculators instead of crusaders."[33]

Structural realism never has been disconnected from these normative concerns. Kenneth Waltz has stressed the dangers that ensue whenever power becomes too tightly concentrated (whether internationally or domestically). As he has put it, "I distrust hegemonic power, whoever may wield it, because it is so easily misused."[34] Here, Waltz echoed Edmund Burke's famous—and very timely—injunction about the boomerang effects that follow when overwhelming power is married to overweening ambition:

> Among precautions against ambition, it may not be amiss to take one precaution against our *own*. I must fairly say, I dread *our* own power and our *own* ambition; I dread our being too much dreaded. . . . It is ridiculous to say we are not men, and that, as men we shall never wish to aggrandize ourselves in some way or other . . . we may say that we shall not abuse this astonishing and hitherto unheard of power. But every other nation will think we shall abuse it. It is impossible but that, sooner or later, this state of things must produce a combination against us which may end in our ruin.[35]

Burke's warning resonates today, because, as Walter LaFeber observes, "In the post–September 11 world, exceptionalism, combined with the immensity of American power, hinted at the dangers of a nation so strong that others could not check it, and so self-righteous that it could not check itself."[36] Realists understand that notions of American exceptionalism can warp U.S. grand strategy. Waltz—echoing Morgenthau's injunction that the task of realism is to prevent statesmen from "moral excess and political folly"—has recognized that a hegemonic United States would be tempted to equate its own preferences with justice, and be just as likely as other powerful states to use its power unwisely: "One cannot assume that the leaders of a nation superior in power will always define policies with wisdom, devise tactics with finite calculation, and apply force with forbearance."[37] It is for this reason that realists like Lippmann, Kennan, Morgenthau, and Waltz have highlighted the dangers that await if the United States gives in to the temptations of hegemonic power, and have counseled that the United States should pursue a grand strategy based on prudence and self-restraint.

There are two mechanisms that can prevent the United States from succumbing to the hegemon's temptation. First is a roughly equal distribution of power in the international system, because confronted by countervailing power the United States would be forced to forego hegemony in favor of a more cautious strategy.[38] The other possible restraining mechanism is that America's own domestic political system will restrain "national leaders from dangerous and unnecessary adventures."[39] For the present, at least, there is no counterbalancing power that can compel the United States to forsake its pursuit of hegemony. Thus, the United States must follow a policy of self-restraint if it is to avoid hegemony's adverse geopolitical and domestic consequences. Since World War II, such self-restraint seldom has been abundant— and it has become even scarcer during the Bush II administration. Grand strategic self-restraint can be developed only—if at all—by engaging a vigorous intellectual debate about hegemony's consequences and about America's grand strategic options—and only if that debate carries over into the public policy arena. Here, the torch has been passed to a new generation of realists to make the case against American hegemony and its accompanying perils. Both because of its analytical power and its moral sensibilities, realism, far from being dead, remains as compelling and relevant as ever.

Notes

Introduction

1. Notable examples of this argument are Jim Mann, *Rise of the Vulcans: The History of Bush's War Cabinet* (New York: Viking, 2004); Ivo H. Daalder and James M. Lindsay, *America Unbound: The Bush Revolution in Foreign Policy* (Washington, D.C.: Brookings Institution, 2003). For an excellent rebuttal, see Melvyn P. Leffler, "Bush's Foreign Policy," *Foreign Policy* 144 (September–October 2004): 22–28.
2. *The National Security Strategy of the United States* (Washington, D.C.: The White House, September 2002), 30 (emphasis added).
3. Walter LaFeber, *America, Russia, and the Cold War, 1945–1996*, 8th ed. (New York: McGraw-Hill, 1997), 354–55.
4. For a similar argument, see John Lewis Gaddis, *Surprise, Security, and the American Experience* (Cambridge: Harvard University Press, 2004).
5. Barry R. Posen, "Command of the Commons: The Military Foundations of American Hegemony," *International Security* 28, no. 1 (Summer 2003): 19.
6. John J. Mearsheimer, *The Tragedy of Great Power Politics* (New York: W. W. Norton, 2001).
7. Mary Ann Heiss, "The Evolution of the Imperial Idea and U.S. National Identity," *Diplomatic History* 26, no. 4 (Fall 2002): 528.
8. Mearsheimer, *Tragedy of Great Power Politics*, 40.
9. Andrew Gamble, "Hegemony and Decline: Britain and the United States," in *Two Hegemonies: Britain 1846–1914 and the United States 1941–2001*, ed. Patrick Karl O'Brien and Armand Clesse (Aldershot, Eng.: Ashgate, 2002), 130; Robert O. Keohane, *After Hegemony: Cooperation and Discord in the World Political Economy* (Princeton: Princeton University Press, 1984), 32.
10. Robert Gilpin, *War and Change in World Politics* (Cambridge: Cambridge University Press, 1981), 29–30, 144. International political economists claim that one of the attributes of hegemony is the provision of "public," or "collective," goods to the international system. See Charles P. Kindleberger, *The World in Depression, 1929–1939* (Berkeley: University of California Press, 1973). Although not a necessary attribute of hegemony, by supplying collective goods hegemons give "other states an interest in following their lead." Gilpin, *War and Change*, 30.
11. Mearsheimer, *Tragedy of Great Power Politics*, 40.
12. According to Keohane and Nye, hegemony prevails in the international system when "one state is powerful enough to maintain the essential rules governing interstate relations, *and willing to do so*" (emphasis added). Robert O. Keohane and Joseph S. Nye Jr., *Power and Interdependence: World Politics in Transition* (Boston: Little, Brown, 1977), 44.
13. Mearsheimer, *Tragedy of Great Power Politics*, 415 n. 13.
14. Gilpin, *War and Change*, 28.
15. Kenneth N. Waltz, *Theory of International Politics* (Reading, Mass.: Addison-Wesley, 1979), 191–92.
16. Robert J. Art, *A Grand Strategy for America* (Ithaca: Cornell University Press, 2003), 2.

17. For representative arguments in favor of American hegemony, see Zbigniew Brzezinski, *The Grand Chessboard: American Primacy and Its Geostrategic Imperatives* (New York: Basic Books, 1997); Stephen G. Brooks and William C. Wohlforth, "American Primacy in Perspective," *Foreign Affairs* 81, no. 4 (July–August 2002): 20–33; Robert Kagan and William Kristol, "The Present Danger," *National Interest* 59 (Spring 2000): 57–69; Zalmay Khalilzad, "Losing the Moment? The United States and the World after the Cold War," *Washington Quarterly* 18, no. 2 (Spring 1995): 87–107. For critiques of America's hegemonic grand strategy, see Samuel P. Huntington, "The Lonely Superpower," *Foreign Affairs* 78, no. 2 (March–April 1999): 35–49; Christopher Layne, "Rethinking American Grand Strategy," *World Policy Journal* 15, no. 2 (Summer 1998): 8–28; Charles William Maynes, "The Perils of (and for) an Imperial America," *Foreign Policy* 111 (Summer 1998): 36–49.

18. William C. Wohlforth, "The Stability of a Unipolar World," *International Security* 24, no. 1 (Summer 1999): 4–41. See also Brooks and Wohlforth, "American Primacy in Perspective."

19. For arguments based on the "balance-of-threat" theory that the United States can escape the fate of hegemons because of its benevolence, see Stephen M. Walt, *Taming American Power: The Global Response to U.S. Primacy* (New York: W.W. Norton, 2005); Michael Mastanduno, "Preserving the Unipolar Moment: Realist Theories and U.S. Grand Strategy after the Cold War," *International Security* 21, no. 4 (Spring 1997): 44–98. The seminal work on "balance-of-threat" theory is Stephen M. Walt, *The Origins of Alliances* (Ithaca: Cornell University Press, 1987).

20. See Joseph S. Nye Jr., *The Paradox of American Power: Why the World's Only Superpower Can't Go It Alone* (New York: Oxford University Press, 2002), esp. chaps. 1 and 5; Nye, *Bound to Lead: The Changing Nature of American Power* (New York: Basic Books, 1990); Nye, *Soft Power: The Means to Success in World Politics* (New York: Public Affairs, 2004); G. John Ikenberry, "Democracy, Institutions, and American Restraint," in *America Unrivaled: The Future of the Balance of Power*, ed. G. John Ikenberry (Ithaca: Cornell University Press, 2002), 213–38; G. John Ikenberry, "Institutions, Strategic Restraint, and the Persistence of Postwar Order," *International Security* 23, no. 3 (Winter 1998–1999): 43–78.

21. Nye, *Paradox of American Power*; Stephen M. Walt, "Beyond Bin Laden: Reshaping U.S. Foreign Policy," *International Security* 26, no. 3 (Winter 2001–2002): 56–78.

22. As Stephen Van Evera observes, "All evaluation of public policy requires the framing, and evaluation of theory, hence it is fundamentally theoretical." Stephen Van Evera, *Guide to Methods for Students of Political Science* (Ithaca: Cornell University Press, 1997), 91.

23. Barry R. Posen, *The Sources of Military Doctrine: France, Britain, and Germany between the World Wars* (Ithaca: Cornell University Press, 1984), 13.

24. Walt, *Origins of Alliances*, 2.

25. Posen, "Command of the Commons," 44.

26. See Gideon Rose, "Neoclassical Realism and Theories of Foreign Policy," *World Politics* 51, no. 1 (October 1998): 144–72. See also the discussion of neoclassical realism in Colin Elman, "Horses for Courses: Why *Not* Neorealist Theories of Foreign Policy?" *Security Studies* 6, no. 1 (Autumn 1996): 26–30.

27. Thomas G. Paterson, "Defining and Doing the History of American Foreign Relations: A Primer," in *Explaining the History of American Foreign Relations*, ed. Michael Hogan and Thomas G. Paterson (Cambridge: Cambridge University Press, 1991), 40. For a similar argument, see Melvyn P. Leffler, *A Preponderance of Power: National Security, the Truman Administration, and the Cold War* (Stanford: Stanford University Press, 1992), x.

28. For similar approaches utilizing structural realism as a first cut before looking at unit-level approaches, see Stephen M. Walt, *Revolution and War* (Ithaca: Cornell University Press, 1996), 4; Fareed Zakaria, *From Wealth to Power: The Unusual Origins of America's World Role* (Princeton: Princeton University Press, 1998), 16–17.

29. The seminal work on the Open Door is William Appleman Williams, *The Tragedy of American Diplomacy* (New York: Delta, 1962).

30. Leffler, *Preponderance of Power*, 13. See also Melvyn P. Leffler, "National Security," in Hogan and Paterson, *Explaining the History of American Foreign Relations*, 204.

31. See Robert J. Art, "Geopolitics Updated: The Strategy of Selective Engagement," *International Security* 23, no. 3 (Winter 1998–1999): 80.

32. U.S. grand strategy is, as former Secretary of State James A. Baker III has put it, "a complex mixture of political idealism and realism." James A. Baker III, *The Politics of Diplomacy: Revolution, War, and Peace, 1989–1992* (New York: G. P. Putnam's Sons, 1995), 654. Or, as the Bush II administration's *2002 National Security Strategy of the United States* puts it, U.S. grand strategy is "based on a distinctly American internationalism that reflects the union of our values and our national interests."

33. These terms are used, respectively, by David Stiegerwald, *Wilsonian Idealism in America* (Ithaca: Cornell University Press, 1994); Tony Smith, "Making the World Safe for Democracy," *Diplomatic History* 23, no. 2 (Spring 1999): 183; Charles Krauthammer, "Democratic Realism: An American Foreign Policy for a Unipolar World," 2004 Irving Kristol Lecture, American Enterprise Institute, February 10, 2004, http://www.aei.org/include/news_print.asp?news ID=19912.

34. Walt, *Revolution and War*, 4. See also Waltz, *Theory of International Politics*, 71.

35. As Kenneth Waltz observes, "In the absence of counterweights, a country's internal impulses prevail, whether fueled by liberal or by other urges." Kenneth N. Waltz, "Structural Realism after the Cold War," in G. John Ikenberry, ed., *America Unrivaled*, 48.

36. I am not the first realist to offer a theory that incorporates several explanatory variables. Important contributions to structural realism such as balance-of-threat theory and "fine-grained" realism reject single variable explanations, and, to that extent, are precedents for my extraregional hegemony theory. On balance-of-threat theory, see Walt, *Origins of Alliance* and *Revolution and War*. On fine-grained defensive realism, see Stephen Van Evera, *Causes of War: Power and the Roots of Conflict* (Ithaca: Cornell University Press, 1999).

37. Stephen Walt set the precedent, subsequently adopted in many neoclassical realist works (including this one), of writing "detailed narrative history." As he rightly observes, "Valid empirical tests require a sophisticated understanding of the historical record." Walt, *Revolution and War*, viii.

38. Rose, "Neoclassical Realism," 167.

39. The dilemma neoclassical realists face "is their appreciation of the degree to which their central, parsimonious independent variable needs to be studied *in conjunction with* a variety of messy contextual factors in order to say much of interest about their subject matter. For neoclassical realism, to paraphrase Clausewitz, explaining foreign policy is usually very simple, but even the simplest explanation is difficult." Rose, "Neoclassical Realism," 166 (emphasis in original).

40. John Lewis Gaddis, "Expanding the Data Base: Historians, Political Scientists, and the Enrichment of Security Studies," *International Security* 12, no. 1 (Summer 1987): 15. The conventional wisdom among political scientists is that good theories should be "parsimonious"; that is, have one, or very few, independent, or intervening, variables. However, parsimony should not be invested with totemic significance, and some leading political scientists say it is overrated: parsimony is "only occasionally appropriate," and, hence, "we should never insist on parsimony as a general principle of designing theories." Gary King, Robert O. Keohane, and Sidney Verba, *Designing Social Scientific Inquiry: Scientific Inference in Qualitative Research* (Princeton: Princeton University Press, 1994), 20.

41. On this point, see Gordon Craig, "The Historian and the Study of International Relations," *American Historical Review* 88, no. 1 (June 1983): 9; Edward Ingram, "The Wonderland of the Political Scientist," *International Security* 22, no. 1 (Fall 1997): 52; Melvyn P. Leffler, "Presidential Address: New Approaches, Old Interpretations, and Prospective Reconfigurations," *Diplomatic History* 19, no. 2 (Spring 1995): 179.

42. Leffler, "New Approaches, Old Interpretations," 179.

43. Stephen Van Evera, "What Are Case Studies? How Should They Be Performed?" unpublished memo, September 1993, Department of Political Science, MIT. See also Alexander L. George and Andrew Bennett, *Case Studies and Theory Development in the Social Sciences* (Cambridge: MIT Press, 2005); Van Evera, *Guide to Methods*, 64–67; Walt, *Revolution and War*, 15–16.

44. When World War II ended, "American policymakers believed that Western Europe was the most critical region in the world in shaping the postwar balance of power between the United States and the Soviet Union." Melvyn P. Leffler, "The United States and the Strategic Dimensions of the Marshall Plan," *Diplomatic History* 12, no. 3 (Summer 1998): 278.
45. Edward Meade Earle, introduction to *Makers of Modern Strategy* (Princeton: Princeton University Press, 1971), viii.
46. Geoffrey Parker, *The Grand Strategy of Philip II* (New Haven: Yale University Press, 1998), 1.
47. Paul Kennedy, ed., *Grand Strategies in War and Peace* (New Haven: Yale University Press, 1991), 5 (emphasis in original).

1. Theory, History, and U.S. Grand Strategy

1. Core realist works include E. H. Carr, *The Twenty Years' Crisis, 1919–1939: An Introduction to the Study of International Relations* (New York: Harper Torchbooks, 1964); John J. Mearsheimer, *The Tragedy of Great Power Politics* (New York: W. W. Norton, 2001); Hans J. Morgenthau, *Politics among Nations: The Struggle for Power and Peace*, rev. Kenneth W. Thompson, 6th ed. (New York: Alfred A. Knopf, 1986); Kenneth N. Waltz, *Theory of International Politics* (Reading, Mass.: Addison-Wesley, 1979). For helpful overviews of realism, see Robert G. Gilpin, "No One Loves a Realist," *Security Studies* 5, no. 3 (Spring 1996): 3–26; Gilpin, "The Richness of the Tradition of Political Realism," in *Neorealism and Its Critics*, ed. Robert O. Keohane (New York: Columbia University Press, 1986), 301–21.
2. David L. Anderson, "Paradigm Lost," *Diplomatic History* 25, no. 4 (Fall 2001): 700.
3. International politics is state-centric because politics is about relations between organized social groups, and states are the primary organized social groups. Realists recognize the existence of so-called nonstate actors (for example, terrorist groups) but believe that great powers are the primary actors in international politics. "Anarchy" in international politics refers to the absence of a central authority—world government—capable of making and enforcing rules of behavior on states. Anarchy makes international politics a self-help system. When threatened, states must take care of themselves, because there is no international 911 that they can dial to get protection.
4. As Hans Morgenthau observed: "When we refer to the power of a nation by saying that this nation is very powerful and that nation is weak, we always imply a comparison. . . . It is one of the most elemental and frequent errors in international politics to neglect this relative character of power and to deal instead with the power of a nation as though it were an absolute." Morgenthau, *Politics among Nations*, 174.
5. In an anarchic, self-help system, great powers' defensive searches for security can boomerang and cause greater insecurity. When a state increases its military capabilities, prudence constrains others to respond in kind, leading to an open-ended cycle of move and countermove. Yet there is no real way for great powers to avoid this, because fear and insecurity are the facts of life in international politics. The security dilemma is more accurately conceived as the "insecurity condition," because as long as there are rivals out there, great powers never can take security for granted. See John Herz, *Political Realism and Political Idealism* (Chicago: University of Chicago Press, 1951), 24. See also Robert Jervis, "Cooperation under the Security Dilemma," *World Politics* 30, no. 2 (January 1978): 167–214.
6. Waltz, *Theory of International Politics*, 91–92. For similar views, see Gilpin, "Richness of Political Realism," 305; Mearsheimer, *Tragedy of Great Power Politics*, xi, 13–14, 31, 35.
7. On the key issues dividing offensive from defensive realists, see William Curti Wohlforth, *The Elusive Balance: Power and Perceptions during the Cold War* (Ithaca: Cornell University Press, 1993), 11–14; Fareed Zakaria, *From Wealth to Power: The Unusual Origins of America's World Role* (Princeton: Princeton University Press, 1998), 13; Eric J. Labs, "Offensive Realism and Why States Expand Their Security Aims," *Security Studies* 6, no. 4 (Summer 1997): 7–8; Gideon Rose, "Neoclassical Realism and Theories of Foreign Policy," *World Politics* 51, no. 1 (October 1998): 149.
8. For analysis of competing defensive realist and offensive realist hypotheses about how the distribution of power affects international political outcomes and the grand strategies of states, see Jack S. Levy, "The Causes of War: A Review of Theories and Evidence," in *Be-*

havior, Society, and Nuclear War, vol. 1, ed. Philip E. Tetlock, Jo L. Husbands, Robert Jervis, Paul C. Stern, and Charles Tilly (New York: Oxford University Press, 1989), 228–35, 256–58. See also Benjamin Miller, "Competing Realist Perspectives on Great Power Crisis Behavior," *Security Studies* 5, no. 3 (Spring 1996): 309–57. Because of its destabilizing power configuration—the constant temptation for two to gang up on one—tripolarity has been seen as a discrete form of polarity that should be distinguished from multipolarity (seen as a system of four or more great powers). See Randall L. Schweller, *Deadly Imbalances: Tripolarity and Hitler's Strategy of World Conquest* (New York: Columbia University Press, 1998); Waltz, *Theory of International Politics,* 163. John Mearsheimer further distinguishes between "balanced" multipolar systems (where power is more or less equally distributed among the great powers) and "unbalanced" systems (where there is an asymmetric distribution of power in favor of one of the great powers, which, by definition, is a *potential* hegemon). Mearsheimer, *Tragedy of Great Power Politics,* 44–45.

9. Barry R. Posen, *The Sources of Military Doctrine: France, Britain, and Germany between the World Wars* (Ithaca: Cornell University Press, 1984), 16–19; Walt, *War and Revolution,* 4, 18–19; Charles Glaser, "Realists as Optimists: Cooperation as Self-Help," *International Security* 19, no. 3 (Winter 1994–1995): 71–72. Offensive realists believe bipolar systems are more stable than multipolar systems, but defensive realists split on this issue. Mearsheimer, Posen, and Waltz claim that bipolarity is more stable. Mearsheimer, *Tragedy of Great Power Politics,* 338–44; Posen, *Sources of Military Doctrine,* 63–65; Waltz, *Theory of International Politics,* 161–76; Kenneth N. Waltz, "The Stability of a Bipolar World," *Daedalus* 93, no. 3 (Summer 1964): 881–909. For the argument that multipolar systems are more stable than bipolar ones, see Dale C. Copeland, "Neorealism and the Myth of Bipolar Stability," *Security Studies* 5, no. 3 (Spring 1996): 30–89. See also Stephen Van Evera, "Primed for Peace: Europe after the Cold War," *International Security* 15, no. 3 (Winter 1990–1991): 33–40.

10. Stephen Van Evera, *Causes of War: Power and the Roots of Conflict* (Ithaca: Cornell University Press, 1999), 6, 9. Similarly, Fareed Zakaria says that defensive realists believe that "the international system provides incentives only for moderate, reasonable behavior." Zakaria, "Realism and Domestic Politics: A Review Essay," *International Security* 17, no. 1 (Summer 1992): 190.

11. Jeffrey W. Taliaferro, "Security Seeking under Anarchy: Defensive Realism Revisited," *International Security* 25, no. 3 (Winter 2000–2001): 131, 136–41. Another reason defensive realists believe the international political system tends to discourage great power expansion is that conquest does not pay economically. Van Evera, "Primed for Peace," 14–16. This argument builds on Richard Rosecrance, *The Rise of the Trading State* (New York: Basic Books, 1986). For the counterargument, see Peter Lieberman, *Does Conquest Pay? Exploitation of Occupied Industrial Societies* (Princeton: Princeton University Press, 1996).

12. Van Evera, *Causes of War,* esp. chap. 6. Van Evera argues (123) that "when conquest is hard, states are deterred from aggression by fear that victory will prove costly or unattainable." He claims (190–91) "real offense dominance is rare in modern times" and concludes (192) that "the prime threat to the security of modern great powers is . . . themselves," because they tend to overestimate the efficacy of the offense. See also Jack Snyder, *Myths of Empire: Domestic Politics and International Ambition* (Ithaca: Cornell University Press, 1991), 22–23.

13. "When conquest is hard, states are blessed with neighbors made benign by their own security and by the high cost of attacking others. Hence states have less reason to expect attack. This leaves all states even more secure and therefore willing to pursue pacific policies." Van Evera, *Causes of War,* 125; Glaser, "Realists as Optimists," 51–52, 58–60, 64, 67; Sean M. Lynn-Jones, "Offense-Defense Theory and Its Critics," *Security Studies* 4, no. 4 (Summer 1995): 670. Defensive realists also believe that nuclear weapons have shifted the balance decisively toward defense, at least among nuclear-armed rivals. While conceding that the offense-defense balance may operate at the nuclear level, offensive realists like Mearsheimer believe it is irrelevant at the conventional level. John J. Mearsheimer, "Back to the Future: Instability in Europe after the Cold War," *International Security* 15, no. 1 (Summer 1990): 13 n. 14.

14. Glaser, "Realists as Optimists," 70–72.

15. Paul Kennedy, *The Rise and Fall of the Great Powers: Economic Change and Military Conflict from 1500 to 2000* (New York: Random House, 1987); Snyder, *Myths of Empire*, 6; Lynn-Jones, "Offence-Defense Theory," 664 n. 10.

16. Posen, *Sources of Military Doctrine*, 68–69 (emphasis in original). Similarly, Van Evera claims: "Aggressors are more often punished than rewarded. . . . Aggression seldom succeeds. Aggressor states are usually contained or destroyed." Van Evera, *Causes of War*, 9. See also Stephen M. Walt, *The Origins of Alliances* (Ithaca: Cornell University Press, 1987), 17–18, 27.

17. Militarism, hypernationalism, social imperialism, and social stratification are among the domestic factors that purportedly cause such greedy strategies and lead ruling elites to believe that expansion can be a winning strategy. See Jack Snyder, *The Ideology of the Offensive: Military Decision Making and the Disasters of 1914* (Ithaca: Cornell University Press, 1984); Snyder, *Myths of Empire*; Van Evera, *Causes of War*, 256–57; Van Evera, "Primed for Peace," 18–29. See also Glaser, "Realists as Optimists," 391–94; Schweller, "Realism's Status-Quo Bias: What Security Dilemma?" *Security Studies* 5, no. 3 (Spring 1996): 90–121; Schweller, "Bandwagoning for Profit: Bringing the Revisionist State Back In," *International Security* 19, no. 1 (Summer 1994): 72–107.

18. For an excellent critique of defensive realism on this and other points, see Zakaria, *From Wealth to Power*, 11, 28, 34; Zakaria, "Realism and Domestic Politics," 177–98.

19. Mearsheimer, *Tragedy of Great Power Politics*, xi, 13–14, 35; Zakaria, *From Wealth to Power*, 13; Labs, "Offensive Realism and War Aims," 1, 7–8.

20. In the competitive arena of international politics, "a strategy that seeks to maximize security through a maximum of relative power is the rational response to anarchy." Labs, "Offensive Realism and War Aims," 12, 15. See also Zakaria, *From Wealth to Power*, 19, 30.

21. The claim that expansion causes the security dilemma is implicit in Posen's observations that defensive, and deterrent, military postures have benign effects and that offensive doctrines have the opposite effect. Posen, *Sources of Military Doctrine*, 16, 19. Snyder goes a step farther, contending that international systemic constraints can never be "by themselves an adequate reason for overexpansion or for the conflictual character of great power relations." Snyder, *Myths of Empire*, 13.

22. Mearsheimer, *Tragedy of Great Power Politics*, 33.

23. As Tellis says, because "no state can be certain that its competitors will not use their military capabilities to threaten its existence and autonomy, every state is constrained to attempt eliminating or subjugating its competitors before it suffers a similar fate." Ashley J. Tellis, "The Drive to Domination: Towards a Pure Realist Theory of Politics" (PhD diss., Department of Political Science, University of Chicago, 1984), 381.

24. Mearsheimer, *Tragedy of Great Power Politics*, 34, 35. See also Tellis, "Drive to Domination," 381.

25. As Mearsheimer says, "weaker states will be reluctant to pick fights with more powerful states because the weaker states are likely to suffer military defeat." Mearsheimer, *Tragedy of Great Power Politics*, 33.

26. Ibid., 5–6. On the uncertainties states face in assessing near- and long-term power relationships with rivals, see Tellis, "Drive to Domination," 372 n. 4. Morgenthau says that a great power "must try to have at least a margin of safety that will allow it to make erroneous calculations and still maintain the balance of power. To that effect, all nations actively engaged in the struggle for power must actually aim not at a balance—that is, equality—of power, but at superiority of power in their own behalf." Morgenthau, *Politics among Nations*, 227–28. See also Mearsheimer, *Tragedy of Great Power Politics*, 34–35.

27. Ibid., 40.

28. As Mearsheimer puts it, "Every great power would like to dominate the world, but none has ever had or is likely to have the military capability to become a global hegemon." Ibid., 236.

29. Ibid., 41.

30. Ibid, 40–42.

31. Ibid., 41, 140–41.

32. Ibid., 168.

33. Offensive and defensive realists agree on this. See Mearsheimer, *Tragedy of Great Power Pol-*

itics, 44; Walt, *Origins of Alliances,* 23–25; Robert Jervis, "Cooperation under the Security Dilemma," *World Politics,* 30, no. 2 (January 1978): 194–95. Writing in the early 1940s, Spykman observed that for the United States, security from powerful Eurasian states was a function of the interactive effects of geography (distance) and military capabilities (air and naval power). Nicholas J. Spykman, *America's Strategy in World Politics: The United States and the Balance of Power* (New York: Harcourt, Brace and World, 1942), 441.

34. Mearsheimer, *Tragedy of Great Power Politics,* 135–36.

35. Jervis somewhat understates it when he observes that "in the crowded continent of Europe, security requirements were hard to mesh." Jervis, "Cooperation under the Security Dilemma," 183.

36. Mearsheimer, *Tragedy of Great Power Politics,* 126, 135–36; Jervis, "Cooperation under the Security Dilemma," 194–95.

37. Mearsheimer, "Back to the Future," 13 n. 15.

38. Ibid.

39. Mearsheimer, *Tragedy of Great Power Politics,* 143.

40. Ibid., 212–13.

41. For example, he says (212–13) that "even though Napoleon, Kaiser Wilhelm, and Hitler all lost their bids to dominate Europe, each won major battlefield victories, conquered huge tracts of Europe, and came close to achieving their goals." Far from demonstrating that hegemony can be a winning strategy, these examples show that close counts in horseshoes, not in grand strategy. Napoleonic France, Wilhelmine Germany, and Nazi Germany all paid a fearful price pursuing their failed bids for hegemony. All three were bled white by their exertions, and each experienced regime change as a result of its defeat. To support his argument that conquest can indeed be a paying proposition, Mearsheimer (39–40) also invokes Germany's victories over Poland (1939) and France (1940) and observes "if Hitler had restrained himself after the fall of France and had not invaded the Soviet Union, conquest probably would have paid handsomely for the Nazis." The suggestion that Germany should have "restrained" itself after defeating France directly contradicts Mearsheimer's key offensive realist axiom: that great powers can attain security *only* be defeating their rivals and gaining regional hegemony. Mearsheimer's theory predicts that Germany would do just what it did in 1941: seek to remove the last obstacle blocking its attainment of hegemony in Europe, the Soviet Union.

42. Mearsheimer observes that while "one out of five is not an impressive success rate," nevertheless "the American case demonstrates that it is possible to achieve regional hegemony." In fact, the success rate is not one out of five but one out of *eight.* States that have tried for regional hegemony include not only the United States, imperial Japan, Napoleonic France, Wilhelmine Germany, and Nazi Germany but also the Hapsburg Empire (Charles V), Spain (Philip II), and France under Louis XIV (the latter three made Mearsheimer's 1991 list of failed hegemons but are omitted from his 2002 list).

43. For a similar argument with respect to U.S. attainment of regional hegemony, see Colin Elman, "Extending Offensive Realism: The Louisiana Purchase and America's Rise to Regional Hegemony," *American Political Science Review* 98, no. 4 (November 2004): 563–76.

44. John J. Mearsheimer, "The Future of the American Pacifier," *Foreign Affairs* 80, no. 5 (2001): 49.

45. Mearsheimer sets out "to show that offensive realism can be used to explain both the foreign policy of individual states and international outcomes." *Tragedy of Great Power Politics,* 422 n. 60. Instead of offering both a structural theory and a theory of grand strategy, what Mearsheimer really sets out is not a structural theory at all but rather two distinct theories of grand strategy: an offensive one for Eurasian continental great powers, and a defensive realist one for insular great powers.

46. Mearsheimer acknowledges that the concept of a status quo great power—one that seeks "to maintain the existing balance of power"—is a defensive realist concept. Ibid., p. 21. He also states that "the United States . . . is the most powerful state on the planet today. But it does not dominate Europe and Northeast Asia the way it does the Western Hemisphere, and it has no intention of trying to conquer and control these regions, mainly because of the stopping power of water." Ibid., 41. See also 140–41, 170, 235–36.

47. Ibid., 236–37. For regional hegemons, water apparently stops in one direction only: it prevents them from imposing their hegemony on distant regions, but it does not protect them from being threatened should a hegemon—what Mearsheimer terms a "peer competitor"—emerge in a distant region. Consequently, he says (41, 42, 236–37) that "states that achieve regional hegemony" also "seek to prevent great powers in other regions from duplicating their feat," because these peer competitors could make trouble for them in their own backyard.

48. Ibid., 42, 141, 236–37, 252.

49. In Mearsheimer's words, "Offensive realism predicts that the United States will send its army across the Atlantic when there is a potential hegemon in Europe that the local powers cannot contain by themselves." Ibid., 252; see also 237.

50. "If anything," Mearsheimer states, "the United States has been anxious to avoid sending troops to Europe and East Asia, and when it has been forced to do so, it usually has been anxious to bring them home as soon as possible." Ibid., 235.

51. Ibid., 239. Also, ibid., 265–66.

52. Patrick E. Tyler, "U.S. Strategy Plan Calls for Insuring No Rivals Develop," *New York Times* (March 8, 1992), A1.

53. *A National Security Strategy of Engagement and Enlargement* (Washington, D.C.: The White House, 1995), 1; "Remarks by Samuel R. Berger," June 18, 1996, http://clinton6.nara .gov/1996/06/1996-06-18-remarks-by-samuel-berger-at-the-wilson-center.html.

54. President Bill Clinton, "Remarks to the People of Detroit," October 22, 1996, http:// clinton6.nara.gov/1996/10/1996-10-22-president-speech-on-foreign-policy-in-detroit-mi .html.

55. *Report of the Quadrennial Defense Review* (Washington, D.C.: Department of Defense, May 1997), v, 5.

56. Ronald Preussen has suggested that historians and political scientists should reexamine American grand strategy during the late 1940s and the 1950s to see whether it reflected a "*latent* unipolarity." Ronald W. Preussen, "Book Review: James McAllister, *No Exit: America and the German Problem, 1943–1954*," *Journal of Cold War Studies* 6, no. 3 (Summer 2004): 151. There was nothing "latent" about America's unipolar aspirations during the 1940s and 1950s.

57. "Remarks by Dr. Condoleeza Rice to the International Institute of Strategic Studies," London, June 26, 2003, www.whitehouse.gov/news/releases/2003/06/print/20030626.html.

58. Patrick E. Tyler, "Pentagon Drops Goal of Blocking New Superpowers," *New York Times*, 24 May 1992. Similarly, President George W. Bush decried the "series of destructive national rivalries" that have characterized great power relations. By maintaining its military strength "beyond challenge," he said, the United States would make "the destabilizing arms races of other eras pointless, and [limit] rivalries to trade and other pursuits of peace." President George W. Bush, Graduation Speech at United States Military Academy, June 1, 2002. http://www.whitehouse.gov/news/releases/2002/06/print/20020601-3.html.

59. *National Security Strategy of the United States.*

60. Zalmay Khalilzad, "Losing the Moment? The United States and the World after the Cold War," *Washington Quarterly* 18, no. 2 (Spring 1995): 94.

61. Fred Charles Ikle, "The Ghost in the Pentagon," *National Interest* 19 (Spring 1990): 14.

62. *1997 Quadrennial Defense Review*, 12.

63. "Remarks by Secretary of Defense William J. Perry to the Japan Society," New York City, September 12, 1995, *Defense Issues* 10, no. 87. http://www.defenselink.mil/speches/1995/ s19950912-perry.html.

64. Secretary of Defense William S. Cohen, "Remarks Prepared for Delivery at Microsoft Corporation," Redmond, Wash., February 18, 1999, http://www.defenselink.mil/speeches/ 1999/s19990218-secdef.html. Emphasis added.

65. *Quadrennial Defense Review Report* (Washington, D.C.: Department of Defense, September 2001), 15.

66. Mearsheimer, *Tragedy of Great Power Politics*, 79.

67. Ibid., 528 n. 63 (emphasis added). Similarly, in 1991 Mearsheimer wrote that "*America's hegemonic position* in NATO, the military counterpart to the EC [now the EU], mitigated

the effects of anarchy on the Western democracies and facilitated cooperation among them." Mearsheimer, "Back to the Future," 47. Emphasis added.

68. "If one state achieves hegemony, the system ceases to be anarchic and becomes hierarchic." Mearsheimer, *Tragedy of Great Power Politics*, 415 n. 13.

69. Ibid., 265–66.

70. Kenneth Waltz, "Evaluating Theories," in *Realism and the Balancing of Power: A New Debate*, ed. John A. Vasquez and Colin Elman (Upper Saddle River, N.J.: Prentice-Hall, 2003), 91.

71. In Zakaria's words, rising powers "will not expand anywhere, anytime" but rather "will expand at advantageous moments against weaker neighbors." Zakaria, *From Wealth to Power*, 20.

72. As Nicholas Spykman observes: "The growth and expansion of the Untied States has been challenged by every great power in Europe except Italy. We achieved our position of hegemony only because the states of that continent were never able to combine against us and because preoccupation with the balance of power at home prevented them from ever detaching more than a small part of their strength for action across the Atlantic." Spykman, *America's Strategy in World Politics*, 448–49. For a similar argument, see Karen A. Rasler and William R. Thompson, *The Great Powers and Global Struggle, 1490–1990* (Lexington: University Press of Kentucky, 1994), 18.

73. In addition to Open Door "revisionism," the other two main schools are cold war orthodoxy (which has given rise to a post–cold war "neo-orthodoxy") and postrevisionism. For overviews of the main debates and schools of thought, see Jerald A. Combs, *American Diplomatic History: Two Centuries of Changing Interpretations* (Berkeley: University of California Press, 1983), and Michael Hogan, ed., *America in the World: The Historiography of American Foreign Relations since 1941* (Cambridge: Cambridge University Press, 1995). Also useful is Michael Kort, *The Columbia Guide to the Cold War* (New York: Columbia University Press). For a survey of the historiography up to 1941—which provides an indispensable context for studying U.S. postwar grand strategy—see Michael Hogan, ed., *Paths to Power: The Historiography of American Foreign Relations to 1941* (Cambridge: Cambridge University Press, 2000).

74. Joseph A. Fry, "From Open Door to World Systems: Economic Interpretations of Late Nineteenth Century American Foreign Relations," *Pacific Historical Review* 65, no. 2 (May 1996): 27.

75. David Healy, *U.S. Expansionism: The Imperialist Urge in the 1890s* (Madison: University of Wisconsin Press, 1970), 255.

76. Robert Gilpin, *War and Change in World Politics* (Cambridge: Cambridge University Press, 1981), 95, 24.

77. The seminal work of the Open Door school is William Appleman Williams, *Tragedy of American Diplomacy* (New York: Delta, 1962). For a balanced assessment of how it influenced the historical debate about U.S. grand strategy, see Bradford Perkins, "*The Tragedy of American Diplomacy*: Twenty-Five Years After," in Lloyd C. Gardner, *Redefining the Past: Essays in Diplomatic History* (Corvallis: Oregon State University Press, 1986), 21–34. As Perkins suggests, Williams's interpretation is a "stimulus, not a blueprint" for explaining U.S. grand strategy.

78. Vietnam-era critics claimed that the Open Door school was outside the bounds of legitimate historical inquiry and failed to conform to accepted norms of scholarship. For example, see Robert James Maddox, *The New Left and the Origins of the Cold War* (Princeton: Princeton University Press, 1973). For a more reasoned critique, see Robert W. Tucker, *The Radical Left and American Foreign Policy* (Baltimore: Johns Hopkins University Press, 1971).

79. Michael Hogan, "The 'Next Big Thing': The Future of Diplomatic History in a Global Age," *Diplomatic History* 28, no. 1 (January 2004): 13.

80. The political and economic Open Doors reflect the influence of Wilsonian, or liberal, ideology. Wilsonianism's bottom line is "that only a world that respects the right of democratic self-determination, fosters nondiscriminatory markets, and has institutional mechanisms to ensure the peace can be an international order ensuring the national security and so permitting liberty at home." Tony Smith, *America's Mission: The United States and the*

Worldwide Struggle for Democracy in the Twentieth Century (Princeton: Princeton University Press, 1994), 327.

81. On the concept of "core values," see Melvyn P. Leffler, *A Preponderance of Power: National Security, the Truman Administration, and the Cold War* (Stanford: Stanford University Press, 1992), 13; Leffler, "National Security," in *Explaining the History of American Foreign Relations*, ed. Michael Hogan and Thomas G. Paterson (Cambridge: Cambridge University Press, 1991), 202–13.

82. Frank Ninkovich, *Modernity and Power: A History of the Domino Theory in the Twentieth Century* (Chicago: University of Chicago Press, 1994), 53.

83. Williams, *Tragedy of American Diplomacy*, 11, 21–30, 79, 82, 200, 210. Explaining the origins of the Open Door Williams says (30), U.S. policymakers believed that economic depression threatened their domestic goals of "democracy and social peace," and they "concluded that overseas economic expansion provided a primary means of ending that danger." He also stresses (186–87, 206) that the Open Door was based on the *belief*—not the objective condition of U.S. dependency on overseas markets—that economic expansion was necessary for America's economic well-being and its domestic political stability. In fact, from 1789 until the 1970s, imports and exports combined constituted only between 6–10% of U.S. GDP. Only beginning in the 1980s did imports and exports reach their current combined share of GDP (16–22%), among the lowest of the major advanced industrial countries.

84. Ibid., 116.

85. Ibid., 43. Williams (229) argues that over time the different themes underpinning the Open Door (including American exceptionalism and Frederick Jackson Turner's "frontier thesis") were "synthesized into an ideology." Odd Arne Westad stresses that the ideology of the U.S. foreign policy elite is a "meaningful concept" because of "the remarkable consistency with which the U.S. foreign policy elite has defined the nation's international purpose the past three to four generations." As he views it, that ideology stresses "U.S. responsibility for the global expansion of freedom"—essentially in the form of the political and economic Open Doors (though he does not use these terms). Odd Arne Westad, "The New Cold War International History: Three (Possible) Paradigms," *Diplomatic History* 24, no. 4 (Fall 2000): 554.

86. Responding to J. A. Thompson's criticism that Williams's argument ultimately rested not on economic or political factors but on ideas, Joseph Fry says "that is precisely the point." Williams emphasized that U.S. policymakers and key economic actors shared a worldview that equated economic expansion with America's national security, economic welfare, and the health of its domestic political institutions. Fry says that "the most enduring feature of *The Tragedy of American Diplomacy*" is precisely Williams's argument about the role of ideas in shaping perceptions of the national interest and the policies the United States followed in pursuit of the national interest. Fry, "Open Door to World System," 300.

87. Ross A. Kennedy, "Woodrow Wilson, World War I, and an American Conception of National Security," *Diplomatic History* 25, no. 1 (Winter 2001): 1.

88. Ibid., 3.

89. Frank Ninkovich, *The Wilsonian Century: U.S. Foreign Policy since 1900* (Chicago: University of Chicago Press, 1999), 124.

90. Rather than "threats of physical conquest," Wilsonian ideology is concerned with the possibility of a "poisoning of the world political environment by powers hostile to liberal democracy." Ibid., 13.

91. Ibid., 125.

92. Williams, *Tragedy of American Diplomacy*, 43, 49.

93. Healy, *U.S. Expansionism*, 39.

94. Williams, *Tragedy of American Diplomacy*, 155.

95. For example, see Wayne S. Cole, *An Interpretive History of American Foreign Relations* (Homewood, Ill.: Dorsey Press, 1968); Healy, *U.S. Expansionism*; Walter LaFeber, *The Cambridge History of American Foreign Relations*, vol. 2: *The American Search for Opportunity, 1865–1913* (Cambridge: Cambridge University Press, 1993).

96. John Gallagher and Ronald Robinson, "The Imperialism of Free Trade," in *The Decline, Re-*

vival, and Fall of the British Empire: The Ford Lectures and Other Essays by John Gallagher, ed. Anil Seal (Cambridge: Cambridge University Press, 1982).

97. Williams, *Tragedy of American Diplomacy*, 37–38.

98. Ibid., 88–89; 124.

99. Ibid., 59–64.

100. Ibid., 196–98.

101. Ibid., 172.

102. Ibid., 98–101; 111–113; 183–200. On American perceptions that German and Japanese policies of closure threatened U.S. Open Door interests, see Thomas McCormick, " 'Every System Needs a Center Sometimes': An Essay on Hegemony and Modern American Foreign Policy," in Gardner, *Redefining the Past*, 202–3. On the Bolshevik threat to America's core values, see N. Gordon Levin, *Woodrow Wilson and World Politics: America's Response to War and Revolution* (New York: Oxford University Press, 1970).

103. For a good discussion of commercial liberalism, see Arthur A. Stein, "Governments, Economic Interdependence, and Cooperation," in Tetlock et al., eds., *Behavior, Society, and International Conflict*, 241–324.

104. Rosecrance, *Rise of the Trading State*.

105. Williams, *Tragedy of American Diplomacy*, 123–27, 166. Although the Open Door requires order and stability, U.S. economic and political penetration abroad often has caused a destabilizing backlash in the form of revolution and nationalism. The Open Door, therefore, often creates the very conditions that prompt U.S. intervention. See LaFeber, *American Search for Opportunity*.

106. Williams, *Tragedy of American Diplomacy*, 125.

107. Kenneth Waltz, *Man, the State, and War: A Theoretical Analysis* (New York: Columbia University Press, 1959), 118.

108. In a seminal 1983 article, Michael Doyle put a scholarly gloss on these Wilsonian legacies by setting forth what has come to be known as the "democratic peace theory." Michael Doyle, "Kant, Liberal Legacies, and Foreign Affairs: Part I," *Philosophy and Public Affairs* 12, no. 3 (Summer 1983): 205–35.

109. Williams, *Tragedy of American Diplomacy*, 210.

110. Ibid.

111. On hegemonic stability theory, see Robert Gilpin, *U.S. Power and the Multinational Corporation: The Political Economy of Foreign Direct Investment* (New York: Basic Books, 1975); Gilpin, *War and Change*; Charles P. Kindleberger, *The World in Depression, 1929–1939* (Berkeley: University of California Press, 1975).

112. McCormick, "Every System Needs a Center," 199.

113. McCormick uses the terms umpire and cop to describe the hegemon's military role. Ibid.

114. The two leading statements of first-wave offensive realism are Zakaria, *From Wealth to Power*, and Eric J. Labs, "Offensive Realism and War Aims." First-wave offensive realism builds on a foundation laid by Gilpin in *War and Change*.

115. Zakaria, *From Wealth to Power*, 9–10, 18–22.

116. As Zakaria says, a state's "definition of security, of the interests that require protection, usually expands in tandem with a nation's material resources." Ibid., 184–85.

117. Zakaria, *From Wealth to Power*, 5, 18–20. Similarly, Robert Gilpin: "As the power of a state increases, it seeks to extend its territorial control, its political influence, and/or its domination of the international economy." Gilpin, *War and Change*, 106.

118. As Zakaria notes, great power expansion can take different forms: "States that have experienced significant growth in their material resources have relatively soon redefined and expanded their political interests abroad, measured by their increases in military spending, initiation of wars, acquisition of territory, posting of soldiers and diplomats, and participation in great power decision-making." Zakaria, *From Wealth to Power*, 3.

2. World War II and the Foundations of American Global Hegemony

1. For example, see Michael Hogan, *Informal Entente: The Private Structure of Cooperation in Anglo-American Economic Diplomacy* (Columbia: University of Missouri Press, 1977); Akira

Iriye, *The Cambridge History of American Foreign Relations*, vol. 3, *The Globalizing of America, 1913–1945* (Cambridge: Cambridge University Press, 1993); Melvyn P. Leffler, *The Elusive Quest: America's Pursuit of European Stability and French Security, 1919–1933* (Chapel Hill: University of North Carolina Press, 1979). For an excellent survey of the historiography of U.S. foreign policy during the interwar years, see Brian McKercher, "Reaching for the Brass Ring: The Recent Historiography of Interwar American Foreign Relations," in *Paths to Power: The Historiography of American Foreign Relations to 1941*, ed. Michael Hogan (Cambridge: Cambridge University Press, 2000).

2. Frank Costigliola, *Awkward Dominion: American Political, Economic, and Cultural Relations with Europe, 1919–1933* (Ithaca: Cornell University Press, 1984). Costigliola shows (263–65) that during the 1920s and early 1930s the Europeans understood both that the United States already was the world's preeminent power and that they were constrained by America's *latent* hegemony.

3. See Costigliola, *Awkward Dominion*; Michael Hogan, *The Marshall Plan: America, Britain, and the Reconstruction of Western Europe, 1947–1952* (Cambridge: Cambridge University Press, 1987), 4–18. See also Michael Hogan, "Revival and Reform: America's Twentieth Century Search for a New Economic Order Abroad," *Diplomatic History* 8, no. 4 (Fall 1984): 287–310. As Hogan observes (289), "European integration and German reintegration" were the major U.S. objectives on the Continent after both world wars.

4. President Calvin Coolidge stated that "our interests all over the earth are such that a conflict anywhere would be enormously to our disadvantage." Quoted in Costigliola, *Awkward Dominion*, 264, 269.

5. For an excellent account of how the groundwork for America's post-1945 extraregional hegemony was laid during the interwar years—and of London's fears that a rising United States would displace Britain from its position of global preeminence—see B. J. C. McKercher, *Transition of Power: Britain's Loss of Global Preeminence to the United States, 1930–1945* (Cambridge: Cambridge University Press, 1999).

6. McKercher argues that notwithstanding America's gains in relative economic power at Britain's expense during World War I, during the interwar years it was not inevitable that the United States would assume Britain's mantle as global hegemon. Britain, he argues, retained a number of diplomatic, military, and financial strengths and was determined to resist U.S. encroachment and maintain its dominant role in the international system. Brian McKercher, "Wealth, Power, and the New International Order: Britain and the American Challenge in the 1920s," *Diplomatic History* 12, no. 4 (Fall 1988): 411–42.

7. Hajo Holborn, *The Political Collapse of Europe* (Westport, Conn.: Greenwood Press, 1982 [1951]).

8. The United States was able to overcome the stopping power of water during World War II, because it caught a couple of huge breaks. First, the United States was able to use Britain as a jumping-off point to invade Europe and as an airbase from which it gained control over Europe's skies, which was the precondition of a successful invasion. Second, throughout the war, some 80% of Germany's ground forces were tied down fighting the Soviet Union and, hence, were unavailable to oppose the Anglo-American invasion.

9. Paul Kennedy, *The Rise and Fall of the Great Powers: Economic Change and Military Conflict from 1500 to 2000* (New York: Random House, 1987), 357–61. See also Melvyn P. Leffler, *A Preponderance of Power: National Security, the Truman Administration, and the Cold War* (Stanford: Stanford University Press, 1992), 2–3.

10. Kennedy, *Rise and Fall of the Great Powers*, 357.

11. In 1943, Edward Meade Earle and Harold Sprout prepared a report for the Intelligence Section of the Army's General Staff, "The Changing Power Position of Great Britain as a Factor in the Defense Problem of the United States," which assessed Britain's relative power decline. See Mark A. Stoler, *Allies and Adversaries: The Joint Chiefs of Staff, the Grand Alliance, and U.S. Strategy in World War II* (Chapel Hill: University of North Carolina Press, 2000), 128.

12. Quoted in Robert Dallek, *Franklin D. Roosevelt and American Foreign Policy, 1932–1945* (New York: Oxford University Press, 1979), 479.

13. Quoted in Gabriel Kolko, *The Politics of War: The World and United States Foreign Policy, 1943–1945* (New York: Random House, 1968), 400.
14. Quoted in Michael S. Sherry, *Preparing for the Next War: American Plans for Postwar Defense, 1941–1945* (New Haven: Yale University Press, 1977), 202 (emphasis added).
15. Cordell Hull, *The Memoirs of Cordell Hull*, vol. 1 (New York: Macmillan, 1948), 731–32.
16. On U.S. planning during World War II for the postwar world, see Patrick J. Hearden, *Architects of Globalism: Building a New World Order during World War II* (Fayetteville: University of Arkansas Press, 2002).
17. Harley Notter, *Postwar Foreign Policy Preparation, 1939–1945* (Washington, D.C.: U.S. Government Printing Office, 1949), 20.
18. The United States built the postwar international economic order "because American leaders enjoyed both the means and the will to exercise leadership of the global economy." Robert A. Pollard, *Economic Security and the Origins of the Cold War, 1945–1950* (New York: Columbia University Press, 1985), 2.
19. For an overview of these efforts, see Georg Schild, *Bretton Woods and Dumbarton Oaks: American Economic and Political Postwar Planning in the Summer of 1944* (New York: St. Martin's, 1995); Hearden, *Architects of Globalism*, 175–85.
20. Pollard, *Economic Security*, 10.
21. See the statements of U.S. officials quoted in Kolko, *Politics of War*, 252–54. On the role of the Open Door in U.S. planning for the postwar world, see Hearden, *Architects of Globalism*, 39–64.
22. Pollard, *Economic Security*, 16.
23. Hearden, *Architects of Globalism*, 17–18, 73–76; Pascaline Winand, *Eisenhower, Kennedy, and the United States of Europe* (New York: St. Martin's Press, 1993), 1–8. U.S. planners wanted postwar Europe to be a prosperous and efficient market for U.S. exports, but they feared that an integrated Europe might become a geopolitical rival or adopt autarkic postwar policies that would lock out the United States. Writing on the cusp of the U.S. entry into the war, Nicholas Spykman warned that the emergence of a politically federated Europe would be inimical to America's postwar geopolitical interests. Nicholas J. Spykman, *America's Strategy in World Politics: The United States and the Balance of Power* (New York: Harcourt, Brace and World, 1942), 465–66.
24. Hearden, *Architects of Globalism*, 12–15, 30–31, 66.
25. See ibid., 65–92. As Hearden says (65), "Postwar planners in Washington intended to provide European countries with funds required for economic reconstruction so that they could resume the production and exportation of goods and thereby earn dollars needed to purchase American products."
26. Ibid., 77–78, 229–56. Germany's postwar treatment was a contentious issue in Washington, where some officials—notably Treasury Secretary Henry Morgenthau—rejected the idea that Germany needed economic rehabilitation and advocated a draconian policy. On the contending approaches to postwar Germany, see Michael R. Beschloss, *The Conquerors: Roosevelt, Truman, and the Destruction of Hitler's Germany, 1941–1945* (New York: Simon and Schuster, 2002); Carolyn Woods Eisenberg, *Drawing the Line: The American Decision to Divide Germany, 1944–1949* (Cambridge: Cambridge University Press, 1996).
27. Hearden, *Architects of Globalism*, 39.
28. Hull, *Memoirs*, 1:84, 75.
29. Ibid., 1:81, 84.
30. Quoted in Pollard, *Economic Security*, 13.
31. Hull, *Memoirs*, 1:364.
32. Ibid., 1:84, 235, 363–65.
33. Quoted in Warren Kimball, *The Juggler: Franklin Roosevelt as Wartime Statesman* (Princeton: Princeton University Press, 1991), 44–45.
34. Stoler, *Allies and Adversaries*, ix.
35. Ibid.
36. Preemptive strikes, and preventive war, against the Soviet Union were serious options during the Eisenhower and early Kennedy administrations. See Marc Trachtenberg, *A Con-*

structed Peace: The Making of the European Settlement, 1945–1963 (Princeton: Princeton University Press, 1999), 160–66, 292–94; Russell D. Buhite and William Christopher Hamel, "War for Peace: The Question of American Preventive War against the Soviet Union, 1945–1955," *Diplomatic History* 14, no. 3 (Summer 1990): 367–85. In the early 1960s, the Kennedy administration also very seriously considered a preemptive strike on China's nuclear weapons development complex. See William Burr and Jeffrey T. Richelson, "Whether to 'Strangle the Baby in the Cradle'," *International Security* 25, no. 3 (Winter 2000–2001): 54–99.

37. On the U.S. need for postwar bases, with particular emphasis on the Pacific, see William Roger Louis, *Imperialism at Bay: The United States and the Decolonization of the British Empire, 1941–1945* (New York: Oxford University Press, 1978), 259–73. See also Sherry, *Preparing for the Next War*, 42–47; Leffler, *Preponderance of Power*, 56–59; Stoler, *Allies and Adversaries*, 137–40, 158–60, 218–19; Lester J. Foltos, "The New Pacific Barrier: America's Search for Security in the Pacific, 1945–1947," *Diplomatic History* 13, no. 3 (Summer 1989): 317–42; Melvyn P. Leffler, "The American Conception of National Security and the Beginnings of the Cold War, 1945–1948," *American Historical Review* 89, no. 2 (April 1984): 346–81.

38. Leffler, "American Conception of National Security," 350–51, 353–54.

39. During World War II, officials concluded that the United States would need to retain formidable postwar military capabilities "not only to repel an attack against its own shores but also to protect its overseas commercial and financial interests." Hearden, *Architects of Globalism*, 201. When U.S. military officers defined what America's important postwar interests would be, Open Door economic interests were always at, or near, the top of the list. For example, see Stoler, *Allies and Adversaries*, 139, 217–18. Roosevelt envisaged ground troops being quickly brought home, because U.S. interests on the Continent could be protected adequately by air and naval power. Hearden, *Architects of Globalism*, 205; Sherry, *Preparing for the Next War*, 46.

40. On the U.S. role in France, see Irwin M. Wall, *The United States and the Making of Postwar France, 1945–1954* (Cambridge: Cambridge University Press, 1991). On the U.S. role in Italy see John Lamberton Harper, *America and the Reconstruction of Italy, 1945–48* (Cambridge: Cambridge University Press, 1986); James E. Miller, *The United States and Italy, 1940–1950: The Politics and Diplomacy of Stabilization* (Chapel Hill: University of North Carolina Press, 1986).

41. Hearden, *Architects of Globalism*, 13–14.

42. Prior to World War II's outbreak, the United States "had possessed no military or political position in the region." But once the United States entered the war, its presence in the region increased "dramatically." Robert M. Hathaway, *Ambiguous Partnership: Britain and America, 1944–1947* (New York: Columbia University Press, 1981), 48.

43. For accounts of how U.S. interests in the Middle East/Persian Gulf expanded during and after World War II, see David A. Miller, *Search for Security: Saudi Arabian Oil and American Foreign Policy, 1939–1949* (Chapel Hill: University of North Carolina Press, 1980); Michael B. Stoff, *Oil, War, and American Security: The Search for a National Policy on Foreign Oil, 1941–1947* (New Haven: Yale University Press, 1980); Daniel Yergin, *The Prize: The Epic Quest for Oil, Power, and Money* (New York: Simon and Schuster, 1991), 391–410.

44. Quoted in Kolko, *Politics of War*, 313.

45. See Stoler, *Allies and Adversaries*, 214–15, 254.

46. In August 1946, the State Department concluded that if Turkey fell into Moscow's orbit it would "in the natural course of events, [result] in Greece and the whole Near and Middle East, including the Eastern Mediterranean, falling under Soviet control and in those areas being cut off from the Western world." *FRUS 1946*, 7:841. These regions could not be allowed to come under Soviet control because it would entail the loss of the region's oil and disruption of the lines of communication to India and China. On the decision to maintain a U.S. naval presence in the Mediterranean, see Walter Millis, ed., *The Forrestal Diaries* (New York: Viking Press, 1951), 11; Bruce R. Kuniholm, *The Origins of the Cold War in the Near East: Great Power Conflict and Diplomacy in Iran, Turkey, and Greece* (Princeton: Princeton University Press, 1980), 373–74. On the Middle East's increasing importance as a base for U.S. airpower, see Leffler, *Preponderance of Power*, 112–13, 238–39.

47. Kuniholm, *Origins of the Cold War in the Near East*, 301–2.
48. One of Kuniholm's major themes is that traditional Anglo-Russian competition for influence in the Near East revived during World War II and the United States, as the eager heir to Britain's imperial responsibilities, became progressively more engaged in the region. Kuniholm, *Origins of the Cold in the Near East*, 121–213.
49. John Lewis Gaddis, "The Tragedy of Cold War History," *Diplomatic History* 17, no. 1 (Winter 1993): 3–4.
50. These aspirations existed independently from the cold war. While focusing on the *immediate* challenges to America's East Asia interests posed by the Soviet Union and the Communist victory in China's civil war, NSC 48/1—a key statement of U.S. cold war Asia strategy—said that in the longer term other challenges to the United States's regional dominance could emerge: "It is conceivable that in the course of time a threat of domination may come from such nations as Japan, China, or India or from an Asiatic bloc." NSC 48/1 (December 23, 1949), "The Position of the United States with Respect to Asia," NA, RG 273, 2520, Box 6, p. 3.
51. Sherry, *Preparing for the Next War*, 159–60, 167–68.
52. PPS 4, "Certain Aspects of the European Recovery Problem from the United States Standpoint," July 23, 1947, in Anna Kasten Nelson, ed., *The State Department Policy Planning Staff Papers*, vol. 1 (New York: Garland, 1983), 56 (hereinafter *PPSP*)
53. Paper Prepared by Kennan, February 7, 1949, *FRUS 1949*, 3:93.
54. NSC 5416 (April 10, 1954), "U.S. Strategy for Developing a Position of Military Strength in the Far East," NA, RG 273, 2520, Box 31, p. 8.
55. During the war, Assistant Secretary of State Dean Acheson, an Anglophile, accused the Treasury Department of "envisaging a victory where both enemies and allies were prostrate—enemies by military action, allies by bankruptcy." Quoted in Robert Skidelsky, *John Maynard Keynes: Fighting for Freedom, 1937–1946* (New York: Viking, 2000), 127.
56. Ibid., 99, 126, 133. Describing the views of Treasury Secretary Henry Morgenthau (and his key advisers), Skidelsky writes (99): "He would support Britain in the war against Germany, but not to preserve Britain's world position. The United States, not Britain, would be the leader of the postwar free world, the dollar would replace the pound as the world's leading currency. He would do all he could to help Britain, but as a satellite, not as an ally."
57. See Kolko, *Politics of War*, 298–300, 307–11.
58. Roosevelt told Churchill, "I am having the oil question studied by the Department of State and my oil experts, but please do accept my assurances that we are not making sheep's eyes at your oil fields in Iraq or Iran." Churchill replied, "Let me reciprocate by giving you the fullest assurance that we have no thought of trying to horn in upon your interests or property in Saudi Arabia." Roosevelt to Churchill, March 3, 1944 [R-485]; Churchill to Roosevelt, March 4, 1944 [C-601] in *Churchill and Roosevelt: The Complete Correspondence*, ed. Warren F. Kimball, vol. 3, *Alliance Declining, February 1944–April 1945* (Princeton: Princeton University Press, 1984), 14–17.
59. Hathaway, *Ambiguous Partnership*, 48.
60. Quoted in Richard J. Aldrich, *Intelligence and the War against Japan: Britain, America, and the Politics of Secret Service* (Cambridge: Cambridge University Press, 2000), 308 (emphasis added).
61. Aldrich, *Intelligence and the War against Japan*, 122–23.
62. On this aspect of U.S. policy, see Aldrich, *Intelligence and the War against Japan*; Hearden, *Architects of Globalism*, 92–118; Louis, *Imperialism at Bay*; Christopher Thorne, *Allies of a Kind: The United States, Britain, and the War against Japan, 1941–1945* (London: Hamish Hamilton, 1978).
63. On U.S. efforts to gain the upper hand over Britain in Thailand and use that as a wedge for Open Door expansion in the region, see Aldrich, *Intelligence and the War against Japan*, 197, 320–21.
64. Skidelsky, *Keynes: Fighting for Freedom*, 92.
65. On Anglo-American economic relations during World War II, including Lend-Lease, Bretton Woods, and the postwar U.S. loan to Britain, see Hathaway, *Ambiguous Partnership*, 16–

35, 71–86, 182–201; Kimball, *The Juggler*, 43–61; Pollard, *Economic Security*, 66–74; David Reynolds, *The Creation of the Anglo-American Alliance, 1937–1941: A Study in Competitive Cooperation* (Chapel Hill: University of North Carolina Press, 1981), 145–68, 269–80; Skidelsky, *Keynes: Fighting for Freedom*, 96–133, 335–72, 403–53.

66. Hathaway, *Ambiguous Partnership*. This is the title of chapter 5.

67. Skidelsky, *Keynes: Fighting for Freedom*, 133.

68. Reynolds, *Creation of the Anglo-American Alliance*, 167.

69. Pursuant to Lend-Lease's terms, London could not export goods containing materials obtained through Lend-Lease or containing materials *similar* to those obtained through Lend-Lease. Skidelsky, *Keynes: Fighting for Freedom*, 132; Reynolds, *Creation of the Anglo-American Alliance*, 273–74.

70. Skidelsky, *Keynes: Fighting for Freedom*, 112.

71. See Reynolds, *Creation of the Anglo-American Alliance*, 271–72; Skidelsky, *Keynes: Fighting for Freedom*, 321–22.

72. Hathaway, *Ambiguous Partnership*, argues (198) that the postwar loan was an example of Anglo-American partnership. This is a minority view. Robin Edmonds says Anglo-American relations hit "rock bottom" during the loan negotiations, which were "the nadir of Anglo-American relations in the 1940s." Robin Edmonds, *Setting the Mould: The United States and Great Britain, 1945–1950* (Oxford: Clarendon Press, 1986), 94, 103. Other historians emphasize that London accepted Washington's terms because of Britain's security dependence on the United States. See Fraser Harbutt, *The Iron Curtain: Churchill, America, and the Origins of the Cold War* (New York: Oxford University Press, 1986), 149; Elizabeth Barker, *The British between the Superpowers, 1945–1950* (Toronto: University of Toronto Press, 1983), 25–26; John Kent, *British Imperial Strategy and the Origins of the Cold War, 1944–1949* (London: Leicester University Press, 1993), 118.

73. See Aldrich, *Intelligence and the War against Japan*, 102–3, 122, 138, 304.

74. Quoted in Skidelsky, *Keynes: Fighting for Freedom*, 98.

75. Quoted in ibid., 103.

76. David Dimbleby and David Reynolds, *An Ocean Apart: The Relationship between Britain and America in the Twentieth Century* (New York: Random House, 1988), xiv.

77. Correlli Barnett, *The Collapse of British Power* (London: Eyre Methuen, 1972). See note 11, above.

78. Kolko, *Politics of War*, 488.

79. Kimball, *The Juggler*, 59–60.

80. Ibid., 100.

3. U.S. Grand Strategy and the Soviet Union, 1945–1953

1. For a concise statement of the cold war orthodoxy, see Arthur Schlesinger Jr., "Origins of the Cold War," *Foreign Affairs* 46, no. 1 (October 1967): 32–52. The leading example of post–cold war neo-orthodoxy is John Lewis Gaddis, *We Now Know: Rethinking Cold War History* (New York: Oxford University Press, 1997).

2. As Daniel Yergin observes, Soviet ideology was not alone in contributing to the cold war. "There was also the American ideology—the ideas and outlook that U.S. leaders brought to international affairs, their *world set*." Daniel Yergin, *Shattered Peace: The Origins of the Cold War and the National Security State* (Boston: Houghton Mifflin, 1978), 8. Emphasis in original.

3. For early works by (traditional) realist scholars ascribing the cold war to clashing great power interests, see Louis J. Halle, *The Cold War as History* (New York: Harper and Row, 1967); William H. McNeill, *America, Britain, and Russia: Their Cooperation and Conflict, 1941–1946* (New York: Oxford University Press, 1953); Walter Lippmann, *The Cold War: A Study in U.S. Foreign Policy* (New York: Harper and Row, 1947); Hans J. Morgenthau, *In Defense of the National Interest: A Critical Examination of American Foreign Policy* (New York: Knopf, 1951).

4. Deborah Welch Larson, *The Origins of Containment: A Psychological Explanation* (Princeton: Princeton University Press, 1985), 19.

5. Robert L. Messer, "Paths Not Taken: The United States Department of State and Alternatives to Containment, 1945–46," *Diplomatic History* 1, no. 4 (Fall 1977): 297–319; Lippmann, *Cold War.*

6. Odd Arne Westad makes a similar point, arguing that "it was to a great extent American ideas and their influence that made the Soviet-American conflict into a *Cold War*." He argues that the Kremlin was aware of the Soviet Union's weakness in relation to a hegemonic America, and hence, unlike the United States, was constrained in the extent to which ideology could determine its grand strategy. Odd Arne Westad, "The New International History of the Cold War: Three (Possible) Paradigms," *Diplomatic History* 24, no. 4 (Fall 2000): 554 (emphasis in original).

7. Gaddis, *We Now Know,* 292. Gaddis argues that Stalin's brutality combined with Communist ideology explains the cold war and that his foreign and domestic policies cannot be separated. Ibid., 293–94, 289–91. The Russian historians Vladislav Zubok and Constantine Pleshakov offer a more subtle analysis, pointing out that during 1945–47 Stalin's personality and diplomatic methods were at cross-purposes with his hope of avoiding confrontation with the United States. Vladislav Zubok and Constantine Pleshakov, *Inside the Kremlin's Cold War: From Stalin to Khrushchev* (Cambridge: Harvard University Press, 1996), 24, 47, 74. As Yergin points out, there was no invariable correlation between Stalin's bloody domestic rule and Soviet foreign policy: "The USSR behaved as a traditional great power, intent upon aggrandizing itself along the lines of historic Russian goals, favoring spheres of influence, secret treaties, Great Power consortiums, and other methods and mores from the 'old diplomacy'." Yergin, *Shattered Peace,* 12.

8. Walter LaFeber, *America, Russia, and the Cold War, 1945–1996,* 8th ed. (New York: McGraw-Hill, 1997), 19–20.

9. Contrary to the claims of neo-orthodox historians, the evidence to date from the Soviet archives falls far short of validating their arguments. See Melvyn P. Leffler, "The Cold War: What Do We Now Know?" *American Historical Review* 104, no. 2 (April 1999): 501–24; Melvyn P. Leffler, "Inside Enemy Archives: The Cold War Reopened," *Foreign Affairs* 75, no. 4 (July–August 1996): 120–35.

10. Writing without access to the Soviet archives, this is the conclusion reached by LaFeber, *America, Russia, and the Cold War;* Melvyn P. Leffler, *A Preponderance of Power: National Security, the Truman Administration, and the Cold War* (Stanford: Stanford University Press, 1992); Yergin, *Shattered Peace.* Scholars who have had access to the Soviet archives have reached a similar conclusion. For example, see Caroline Kennedy-Pipe, *Stalin's Cold War: Soviet Strategies in Europe, 1943–1956* (Manchester: Manchester University Press, 1995); Zubok and Pleshakov, *Inside the Kremlin's Cold War,* 7; Vladimir O. Pechantnov, "The Big Three after World War II: New Documents on Soviet Thinking about Postwar Relations with the United States and Great Britain," Cold War International History Project Working Paper No. 13 (Washington, D.C.: Woodrow Wilson International Center for Scholars, May 1995).

11. Leffler, *Preponderance of Power,* 512.

12. Yergin, *Shattered Peace,* 11.

13. Ibid.

14. Melvyn P. Leffler, "The American Conception of National Security and the Beginnings of the Cold War," *American Historical Review* 89, no. 2 (April 1984): 365.

15. The leading account of the Moscow foreign ministers conference and the ensuing rift between Truman and Byrnes is Robert L. Messer, *The End of an Alliance: James F. Byrnes, Roosevelt, Truman, and the Origins of the Cold War* (Chapel Hill: University of North Carolina Press, 1982), 137–79. See also Yergin, *Shattered Peace,* 147–51.

16. In the "Long Telegram," Kennan said of the Soviet Union: "We have here a political force committed to the belief that with the US there can be no permanent *modus vivendi,* that it is desirable and necessary that the internal harmony of our society be disrupted, our traditional way of life destroyed, the international authority of our state be broken, if Soviet power is to be secure." "The Long Telegram," in *Containment: Documents on American Policy and Strategy, 1945–1950,* ed. Thomas H. Etzold and John Lewis Gaddis (New York: Columbia University Press, 1978), 61. On the Iron Curtain speech and the collaboration between

Churchill and Truman that preceded it, see Fraser Harbutt, *Iron Curtain: Churchill, America, and the Origins of the Cold War* (New York: Oxford University Press), 151–52.

17. "American Relations with the Soviet Union: A Report to the President by the Special Counsel to the President," in Etzold and Gaddis, *Containment*, 66. For a critique of the Clifford/Elsey report, see Leffler, *Preponderance of Power*, 130–37.

18. Ibid., 69 (emphasis added).

19. See Patrick J. Hearden, *Architects of Globalism: Building a New World Order during World War II* (Fayetteville: University of Arkansas Press, 2002), 12–15, 24–27. For discussion of how the "lessons" of 1940 influenced postwar U.S. policymakers (many of whom served in the Roosevelt administration during 1940–1941), see Leffler, *Preponderance of Power*, 21–24.

20. See Leffler, "American Conception of National Security," 357, 365, 374, 377. This "strong-point" view of U.S. grand strategy was articulated by Kennan, who said that America's grand strategic goal was to prevent the Soviet Union from controlling any of the three major centers of industrial power: the United Kingdom, western Germany (the Ruhr), and Japan. See John Lewis Gaddis, *Strategies of Containment: A Critical Appraisal of Postwar American National Security Policy* (New York: Oxford University Press, 1982), 30–31.

21. Leffler, "American Conception of National Security," 365; for official U.S. policy statements reflecting this view, see 374, 377.

22. On this point, I disagree with John Lewis Gaddis, who argues that the U.S. aim "was not so much control as denial: the American interest was not to dominate other power centers itself, but to see to it that no one else did so either." Gaddis, *Strategies of Containment*, 64.

23. Leffler, *Preponderance of Power*, 498. As Leffler observes (17), the goal of postwar U.S. grand strategy "was to align Western Europe, West Germany, and Japan permanently with the United States."

24. Ibid., 255 (Japan); 277 (Western Europe/West Germany), 283–84 (Germany), 392–93 (Japan), 409 (Germany), 428 (Japan), 453 (Western Europe), 460 (Germany), 464 (Japan), 468–69 (Japan and Germany).

25. Leffler, "American Conception of National Security," 365.

26. Leffler, *Preponderance of Power*, 261–62; Leffler, "American Conception of National Security," 369.

27. Because of U.S. atomic and strategic airpower superiority, the Soviet Union's economic and technological inferiority, and Soviet concern about maintaining a grip on Eastern Europe, U.S. policymakers were confident that the Soviets would not initiate a war of conquest against Western Europe. For discussion, see Leffler, *Preponderance of Power*, 6, 163, 205, 209–10, 216–62; Leffler, "American Conception of National Security," 359–62. For the argument that Leffler underestimates the Soviet threat, see Marc Trachtenberg, "Melvyn Leffler and the Origins of the Cold War," *Orbis* 39, no. 3 (Summer 1995): 439–55.

28. Zubok and Pleshakov, *Inside the Kremlin's Cold War*, 6, 74.

29. Leffler, "American Conception of National Security," 365. On Washington's fears of postwar turmoil, see Leffler, *Preponderance of Power*, 6–7, 9, 161–64, 190–92.

30. This is one of Leffler's central conclusions in both *A Preponderance of Power* and, more forcefully, "The American Conception of National Security." Similarly, Yergin demonstrates that postwar U.S. policymakers came to view the Soviet threat through the prism of "the new doctrine of national security," which was based on "an expansive interpretation of American security needs" and thus "represented a major redefinition of America's relation to the rest of the world." Yergin, *Shattered Peace*, 12–13.

31. Yergin, *Shattered Peace*, 196.

32. Leffler, "American Conception of National Security," 367.

33. Ibid., 378.

34. Leffler, *Preponderance of Power*, 182, 504. As Yergin puts it, "The extension of American power around the Soviet rim could only increase the Soviet sense of danger, leading the Russians to respond in such a way as to increase, rather than decrease, the very range of dangers that United States had sought to forestall." Yergin, *Shattered Peace*, 270.

35. Leffler, *Preponderance of Power*, 186, 204. See also George F. Kennan, *Memoirs, 1925–1950* (Boston: Little, Brown, 1967), 378–79.

36. Zubok and Pleshakov, *Inside the Kremlin's Cold War*, 50.

37. Scott D. Parrish, "The Turn toward Confrontation: The Soviet Reaction to the Marshall Plan," in Scott D. Parrish and Mikhail M. Narinsky, "New Evidence on the Soviet Rejection of the Marshall Plan, 1947: Two Reports," Cold War International History Project Working Paper No. 9 (Washington, D.C.: Woodrow Wilson International Center for Scholars, March 1994), 4.

38. The Kremlin viewed the Marshall Plan as a U.S. move to create a powerful, encircling, anti-Soviet alliance and it stimulated Moscow's fear of revived German power—the depth of which Washington seems not to have understood. See Zubok and Pleshakov, *Inside the Kremlin's Cold War,* 4–53, 105; Kennedy-Pipe, *Stalin's Cold War,* 109, 120–21, 125–32; Parrish, "Turn toward Confrontation," 19–22, 32. On the Marshall Plan's impact on U.S.-Soviet relations, see LaFeber, *America, Russia, and the Cold War,* 69–72; Leffler, *Preponderance of Power,* 184–86; Yergin, *Shattered Peace,* 324–26. That Washington viewed the Marshall Plan as an instrument to pry Eastern Europe loose from Soviet control is argued in Michael Cox and Caroline Kennedy-Pipe, "The Tragedy of American Diplomacy: Rethinking the Marshall Plan," *Journal of Cold War Studies* 7, no. 1 (Winter 2005): 97–134. As Cox and Kennedy-Pipe point out, U.S. strategy backfired because, instead of drawing Eastern Europe into the Western orbit, it caused the Soviets to tighten their grip.

39. Washington's offer to join the Marshall Plan was structured deliberately to be an offer Moscow would refuse. See Michael Hogan, *The Marshall Plan: America, Britain, and the Reconstruction of Western Europe, 1947–1952* (Cambridge: Cambridge University Press, 1987), 44–45, 51–53; Kennedy-Pipe, *Stalin's Cold War,* 108; LaFeber, *America, Russia, and the Cold War,* 59; James McAllister, *No Exit: America and the German Problem, 1943–1954* (Ithaca: Cornell University Press, 2002), 130–32; Yergin, *Shattered Peace,* 314–15. Soviet intelligence apparently warned the Kremlin that the Marshall Plan was intended to consolidate American dominance in Western Europe and challenge the Soviet position in Germany and Eastern Europe. Zubok and Pleshakov, *Inside the Kremlin's Cold War,* 105.

40. Melvyn P. Leffler, "The Struggle for Germany and the Origins of the Cold War," *Occasional Paper* No. 16 (Washington, D.C.: German Historical Institute, 1996), 49. On Moscow's fears that the Marshall Plan was an offensive U.S. strategy aimed at weakening Soviet influence in Eastern Europe, and the Soviet response, see Kennedy-Pipe, *Stalin's Cold War,* 120–24; Yergin, *Shattered Peace,* 315–17; Zubok and Pleshakov, *Inside the Kremlin's Cold War,* 120, 129–33; Parrish, "Turn toward Confrontation," 4, 19–20, 25–32.

41. Leffler, *Preponderance of Power,* 204. On the Kremlin's reaction to currency reform and the preliminary steps to create a West German state, see Kennedy-Pipe, *Stalin's Cold War,* 124–38; Zubok and Pleshakov, *Inside the Kremlin's Cold War,* 50–54; Leffler, "Struggle for Germany," 53–54, 57–60.

42. Leffler, *Preponderance of Power,* 218–19.

43. Leffler, "American Conception of National Security," 379.

44. Ibid.

45. Yergin, *Shattered Peace,* 197. Similarly, Leffler says that American policymakers

> realized that their security interests stretched across the globe and required a favorable configuration of power on the Eurasian land mass. They wanted to resist Soviet expansion in Western Europe, the Middle East, and Northeast Asia. They wanted control over western Germany and all of Japan. They wanted to contain the communist left in France, Italy, Greece, Korea, and China. They wanted to modify traditional imperial practices, co-opt the forces of revolutionary nationalism, and ensure Western control of the underdeveloped world. (Leffler, *Preponderance of Power,* 97)

46. On FDR, see Warren Kimball, *The Juggler: Franklin Roosevelt as Wartime Statesman* (Princeton: Princeton University Press, 1991), 169, 182–83, and also chapter 6. On the factors driving—and limiting—U.S. attempts to keep open the Soviet sphere in Eastern Europe, see Geir Lundestad, *The American Non-Policy towards Eastern Europe, 1943–1947: Universalism in an Area Not of Essential Interest to the United States* (Tromso, Norway: Universitetsforlaget, 1978), esp. 39–80. Also see Eduard Mark, "Charles E. Bohlen and the Acceptable Limits of Soviet Hegemony in Eastern Europe: A Memorandum of 18 October 1945," *Diplomatic History* 3, no. 2 (Spring 1979): 201–13; Eduard Mark, "American Policy toward Eastern Europe and the Origins of the Cold War, 1941–1946: An Alternative Interpreta-

tion," *Journal of American History* 68, no. 2 (September 1981): 313–16; Messer, "Paths Not Taken."

47. In 1943, the Joint Strategic Survey Committee told the Joint Chiefs of Staff that, when War II ended, "Russia will be in a military position to impose whatever territorial settlements it desires in Central Europe and the Balkans." Quoted in Mark A. Stoler, *Allies and Adversaries: The Joint Chiefs of Staff, the Grand Alliance, and U.S. Strategy in World War II* (Chapel Hill: University of North Carolina Press, 2000), 127. During the war, FDR acknowledged that there would be little the United States could do to prevent the Soviets from imposing their grip in regions occupied by the Red Army. See Stoler, *Allies and Adversaries*, 126, 189. See also Lundestad, *American Non-Policy towards Eastern Europe*, 188; Yergin, *Shattered Peace*, 58. Truman, too, was aware that "he could not eliminate Soviet predominance in countries that were occupied by the Soviet army." Leffler, *Preponderance of Power*, 34.

48. U.S.-Soviet differences over Eastern Europe were exacerbated by the ambiguity in U.S. policy bequeathed to the Truman administration by FDR. FDR's policy toward the Kremlin was fundamentally based on realpolitik, but it was sold to the American public (and Congress) in Wilsonian terms that rejected "spheres of influence" diplomacy. See Yergin, *Shattered Peace*, 45–46, 48, 57–58, 66, 68. Fraser Harbut argues that the Yalta Declaration on Liberated Europe was FDR's way of warning Stalin that if Moscow violated its principles, U.S. domestic reaction would compel Washington to adopt a more confrontational policy. Harbutt, *Iron Curtain*, 58, 71, 87–92. In December 1945 the State Department reaffirmed that the United States "should continue to maintain that events" in Soviet-occupied Eastern Europe "are the responsibility of the three nations signatory to the Yalta Declaration on Liberated Europe." The State Department also decried the Soviet-imposed "economic blackout" of Eastern Europe. In conformity with its Open Door policies of "favoring access to all raw materials by all nations and of equal economic opportunity in all areas," the United States should use its "full influence to break down the firm hold which the Soviet Government is endeavoring to fasten on Eastern and Central Europe." Memorandum Prepared in the Department of State, "Foreign Policy of the United States—Fundamentals," December 1, 1945, *FRUS 1946*, 1:1137.

49. In "American Policy toward Eastern Europe," Eduard Mark argues that the United States was unwilling to allow Moscow a free hand to engage in political repression but was willing to accept the Soviet Union's geopolitical primacy in Eastern Europe. Even those U.S. policymakers who acknowledged the legitimacy of Soviet security interests in Eastern Europe, and who remained hopeful that postwar U.S.-Soviet relations would be harmonious, were unwilling to allow Moscow to impose a closed sphere of influence in the region. See Mark, "Bohlen and the Acceptable Limits of Soviet Hegemony"; Messer, "Paths Not Taken."

50. In 1945–47, Moscow's policy in the region allowed for considerable domestic pluralism in Czechoslovakia, Hungary, Austria, and Finland. Evidence suggests that the Kremlin hoped to avoid the need to "Sovietize" Eastern Europe—and thereby avoid a rupture with the United States—by following a "popular front" strategy. This policy was abandoned both because it failed to bring "friendly" governments to power democratically and as a response to the Marshall Plan and American policies with respect to Germany. See Eduard Mark, "Revolution by Degrees: Stalin's National-Front Strategy for Europe, 1941–1947," Cold War International History Project Working Paper No. 31 (Washington, D.C.: Woodrow Wilson International Center for Scholars, February 2001). On the Kremlin's view of its Eastern European security requirements, see Kennedy-Pipe, *Stalin's Cold War*, especially chaps. 2–3.

51. See Leffler, *Preponderance of Power*, 34–35.

52. William Appleman Williams argues that Washington decided to extend the Open Door into Eastern Europe before policymakers knew the atomic bomb would work. They assumed that when the war ended U.S. economic power would compel Moscow to agree to Washington's demands. William Appleman Williams, *The Tragedy of American Diplomacy* (New York: Delta, 1962), 244. Whether Truman ordered the use of atomic weapons believing this was the only way to avoid an invasion of Japan and compel Tokyo to end the war quickly or whether he was engaged in "atomic diplomacy" to set the tone for postwar U.S.-Soviet relations remains a contested issue. For the current "state of the art" on this

debate, see J. Samuel Walker, "Recent Literature on Truman's Atomic Bomb Decision: A Search for Middle Ground," *Diplomatic History* 29, no. 2 (April 2005): 311–34.

53. So did Stalin. See Zubok and Pleshakov, *Inside the Kremlin's Cold War,* 39–46.

54. For discussion of atomic weapons and economic power as potential instruments that the United States could use to influence events in Eastern Europe, see Lundestad, *American Non-Policy towards Eastern Europe,* 359–408. "The proponents of toughness," Leffler observes, "believed that the United States possessed the power to set the terms for a harmonious relationship with the Russians." Leffler, *Preponderance of Power,* 31. Similarly, Yergin notes that the U.S. ambassador to the Soviet Union, Averell Harriman, believed that "Soviet cooperation was possible, although he defined cooperation to include Russian subservience to the American system or, as he put it, 'our concept.' " Yergin, *Shattered Peace,* 76.

55. Yergin suggests that from the Kremlin's perspective, the U.S. policy of insisting on openness in Eastern Europe while simultaneously excluding the Soviets from Japan and Italy must have seemed "ominous and perverse, as well as an insult to their status as a Great Power." Yergin, *Shattered Peace,* 132.

56. As Walter LaFeber puts it: "Thus at the outset of the Cold War, Truman's problem was certainly not the threat of Soviet invasion of Asia or Europe. Nor was it American public opinion. The problem lay in East Europe, where Stalin militarily roped off the region—and thus directly challenged the Atlantic Charter principles and the growing belief in Washington that the American system could only work globally." LaFeber, *America, Russia, and the Cold War,* 28–29.

57. Leffler, *Preponderance of Power,* 35.

58. For Washington, Soviet actions in Eastern Europe seemed to exceed what was needed to ensure its geopolitical interests. Thus, "It was but a small step to the conclusion that the objective of Soviet foreign policy was something other than security." Mark, "Bohlen and the Acceptable Limits of Soviet Hegemony," 213. On the litmus test issue, see Leffler, *Preponderance of Power,* 34–36, 49–54; Lundestad, *American Non-Policy towards Eastern Europe,* 110–12; Yergin, *Shattered Peace,* 84–86.

59. Yergin argues that Eastern Europe—especially Poland—became a litmus test because Truman administration policymakers equated U.S. national security with the establishment of an Open Door world, "a world safe for liberal democracy and liberal capitalism." Thus, Poland became "a test of Russian intentions: Would the Soviets subscribe to the universal system (which really was an American system) or would they pursue a distinct strategy of their own?" But, "the Americans had structured the test in such a way as to ensure negative results; they had chosen a poor question. For Russia, Stalin had emphasized at Yalta, Poland was 'not only a question of honor but of security.' This was practical arithmetic; not merely Stalinist Russia, but any great power, its armies in the field, would seek to assure itself of the orientation of its neighbors." Yergin, *Shattered Peace,* 84–85.

60. Illustrative is a spring 1946 memorandum written by H. Freeman ("Doc") Matthews, chief of the State Department's West European Division:

> As long as present Soviet policies and attitude in regard to other countries remain unchanged, the U.S. must accept the fact that it is confronted with the threat of an expanding totalitarian state which continues to believe and act on the belief that the world is divided into two irreconcilably hostile camps, i.e., Soviet and non-Soviet. . . . [Soviet expansion will be] continuous and unlimited . . . [not] motivated primarily by a legitimate desire to obtain security for the Soviet Union. (Memorandum by the Acting Department of State Member [Matthews] to the State-War-Navy Coordinating Committee, April 1, 1946, *FRUS 1946,* 1:1167.)

61. Lundestad, *American Non-Policy towards Eastern Europe,* 41.

62. Ibid., 415.

63. Yergin, *Shattered Peace,* 84. Yergin also observes that during World War II "American leaders no longer simply found dictatorship abhorrent; they felt *responsible* for what happened all over the world. They were gripped again by messianic liberalism, the powerful urge to reform the world that has been called Wilsonianism" (emphasis in original).

64. Gabriel Kolko argues that, in spring 1945, U.S. policymakers "did not rely on 'trust,' and

to the extent they considered postwar cooperation with the USSR it was with the explicit assumption Russia would cease to be Bolshevik, which inferred expansionism, and adopt American canons of behavior and beliefs." Gabriel Kolko, *Politics of War: The World and United States Foreign Policy, 1943–45* (New York: Random House, 1968), 399.

65. Yergin, *Shattered Peace*, 244.

66. Williams, *Tragedy of American Diplomacy*, 258. During his ambassadorship in Moscow, Harriman said, "I am afraid Stalin does not and never will fully understand our interest in a free Poland as a matter of principle. He is a realist in his actions, and it's hard for him to appreciate our faith in abstract principles." Quoted in Yergin, *Shattered Peace*, 52. Harriman either missed the point or was being disingenuous. Doubtless, Stalin knew very well that the U.S. interest in Poland was not based on "abstract principle" but rather reflected America's view of its security interests—a view shaped by Open Door ideology.

67. "In many ways," Geir Lundestad notes, "the distrust instilled in Soviet-American diplomacy by divergences over Eastern Europe determined the climate for the treatment of other disputes." Lundestad, *American Non-Policy towards Eastern Europe*, 107–8. For the argument that events in the Middle East (Iran, Turkey) and Germany—*not* Eastern Europe—were the catalyst for the cold war, see Marc Trachtenberg, *A Constructed Peace: The Making of the European Settlement, 1945–1963* (Princeton: Princeton University Press, 1999), 34–41.

68. Commenting on the hard line that Truman took on Poland during his April 23, 1945, meeting with Soviet foreign minister V. M. Molotov, presidential chief of staff Adm. William D. Leahy commented that "it will have a beneficial effect on the Soviet attitude toward the rest of the world. They have always known *we have the power*, and now they should know *we have the determination to insist* upon the declared right of all people to choose their own form of government." Quoted in Yergin, *Shattered Peace*, 83 (emphasis added).

69. See Kimball, *The Juggler*, 88, 195, 198–99.

70. N. Gordon Levin Jr., *Woodrow Wilson and World Politics: America's Response to War and Revolution* (New York: Oxford University Press, 1968); Ronald E. Powaski, *The Cold War: The United States and the Soviet Union, 1917–1991* (New York: Oxford University Press, 1998). Charles Bohlen, Loy Henderson, and George F. Kennan were groomed as Soviet experts by Robert Kelley, who, from 1925 to 1937, headed the State Department's East European Division. For a brief discussion of Kelley's influence, see H. W. Brands, *Inside the Cold War: Loy Henderson and the Rise of the American Empire, 1918–1961* (New York: Oxford University Press, 1991), 24–27. As Brands notes (25), Kelley believed "that the Soviet Union could not make a fit partner for diplomatic intercourse with the United States." See also Bruce R. Kuniholm, *The Origins of the Cold War in the Near East: Great Power Conflict and Diplomacy in Iran, Turkey, and Greece* (Princeton: Princeton University Press, 1980), 238; Yergin, *Shattered Peace*, 18–21, 26–29.

71. The two leading works by diplomatic historians that illustrate the offensive nature of U.S. grand strategy toward the Soviet Union in the late 1940s and early 1950s are Leffler, *Preponderance of Power*, and Gregory F. Mitrovich, *Undermining the Kremlin: America's Strategy to Subvert the Soviet Bloc, 1947–1956* (Ithaca: Cornell University Press, 2000). Mitrovich (179–80) describes U.S. policy as an offensive strategy and also says that Leffler, too, demonstrates "that American objectives were not only offensive in nature, but were much more aggressive" than historians like John Lewis Gaddis are prepared to admit.

72. In his Long Telegram, Kennan argued that the "internal soundness and permanence of [the Communist] movement [in the Soviet Union] need not yet be regarded as assured." Quoted in Etzold and Gaddis, *Documents on American Policy and Strategy*, 62.

73. NSC 20/4, "U.S. Objectives with Respect to the USSR to Counter Soviet Threats to U.S. Security," in Etzold and Gaddis, *Documents on American Policy and Strategy*, 209.

74. Ibid., 211.

75. Mitrovich, *Undermining the Kremlin*. See also Peter Grose, *Operation Rollback: America's Secret War behind the Iron Curtain* (Boston: Houghton Mifflin, 2000); Leffler, *Preponderance of Power*, 235–37.

76. Mitrovich, *Undermining the Kremlin*, 36.

77. "Kennan's paramount contribution to American policy was his determination that con-
certed U.S. action could dramatically transform Soviet international behavior. Kennan
was one of the first analysts to recognize and believe that its collapse was possible with positive assistance from the United States." Mitrovich, *Undermining the Kremlin*, 28.

78. Far from being new, the muscular grand strategic objectives outlined in NSC 68 simply
reaffirmed the goals set forth in NSC 20/4 and other planning documents. Leffler, *Preponderance of Power*, 356, 359. On NSC 68, see Gaddis, *Strategies of Containment*, 90–109; Leffler,
Preponderance of Power, 355–60; Samuel F. Wells Jr., "Sounding the Tocsin: NSC 68 and the
Soviet Threat," *International Security* 4, no. 2 (Fall 1979): 116–68.

79. NSC 68, "United States Objectives and Programs for National Security," *FRUS 1950*,
1:235–92. The phrase "preponderant power" does not appear in NSC 68 itself. However, it
was a term frequently used by Nitze. See Memorandum from Nitze to the Deputy Undersecretary of State, July 14, 1952, *FRUS 1952–54*, 2:59. Similarly, an unsigned 1952 State Department Policy Planning Staff memo (which, from its language, may have been written by
Nitze, who was the director), stated: "Given the polarization of power around the U.S. and
the U.S.S.R. to seek less than preponderant power would be to opt for defeat. Preponderant power must be the objective of U.S. policy." Paper Drafted by the Policy Planning Staff,
"Basic Issues Raised by Draft NSC 'Reappraisal of U.S. Objectives and Strategy for National Security'," undated, *FRUS 1952–54*, 2:64. Referring to the effects of the two world
wars, NSC 68 observed (237):

> During the span of one generation, the international distribution of power has been fun-
> damentally altered. For several centuries *it had proved impossible for any one nation to gain
> such preponderant strength that a coalition of other nations could not in time face it with greater
> strength*. The international scene was marked by recurring periods of violence and war,
> but a system of sovereign and independent states was maintained, over which *no state was
> able to achieve hegemony*. (Emphasis added.)

80. LaFeber, *America, Russia, and the Cold War*, 97.

81. The word "containment" is placed in quotation marks throughout NSC 68. According to
NSC 68 the goals of the "containment" strategy were to: "(1) block further expansion of
Soviet power, (2) expose the falsities of Soviet pretensions, (3) induce a retraction of the
Kremlin's control and influence, and (4) in general, so foster the seeds of destruction
within the Soviet system that the Kremlin is brought at least to the point of modifying its
behavior to conform to generally accepted international standards." NSC 68, *FRUS 1950*,
1:252.

82. Ibid., 253.

83. Ibid., 284 (emphasis added). NSC 68 reflected Washington's belief that "the very existence of the Soviet Union constituted a nightmare." Leffler, *Preponderance of Power*, 359. As
LaFeber puts it, NSC 68 signaled that Truman and Acheson "were no longer satisfied with
containment. They wanted Soviet withdrawal and an absolute victory." LaFeber, *America,
Russia, and the Cold War*, 97.

84. NSC 68, *FRUS 1950*, 1:252–253, 272, 274, 284. Similarly, a 1952 State Department Policy
Planning Paper stated that U.S. grand strategic objectives encompassed "the retraction of
Soviet power and a change in the Soviet system." Paper Drafted by the Policy Planning
Staff, "Basic Issues Raised by Draft NSC 'Reappraisal of U.S. Objectives and Strategy for
National Security,'" undated, *FRUS 1952–54*, 2:65.

85. Ibid., 241–42.

86. NSC 68 stated that "aggregate superior military strength" was the "indispensable backdrop" to the offensive form of "containment" that it advocated. Ibid., 253.

87. Ibid., 244. Leffler, *Preponderance of Power*, 372.

88. NSC 68 called for the United States to "take dynamic steps to reduce the power and influence of the Kremlin inside the Soviet Union and other areas under its control. The objective would be the establishment of friendly regimes not under Kremlin domination" (284).
To implement this strategy, the Joint Chiefs of Staff recommended that the United States
adopt a plan of "affirmative measures of economic, clandestine, subversive, and psychological character to foment and support unrest and revolution in selected strategic satel-

lite countries and Russian political divisions. The objective would be the establishment of friendly regimes not under Kremlin domination." Memorandum by the Joint Chiefs of Staff to Secretary of Defense Marshall, January 15, 1951, *FRUS 1951,* 1:62.

89. NSC 68, 272–76, 291. As Acheson explained:

> [By building up] situations of strength [the United States would] show the Soviet leaders by successful containment that they could not hope to expand their influence throughout the world and must modify their policies. Then, and only then, could meaningful negotiation be possible on the larger issues that divided us. In the meantime, the search for miracle cures for the earth's ills was a dangerous form of self-delusion, which only diverted us from the hard duties of our times. (Dean Acheson, *Present at the Creation: My Years in the State Department* [New York: W. W. Norton, 1969], 380)

90. Memorandum of a Conversation by Acheson, March 24. 1950, *FRUS 1950,* 1:208. In a similar vein, George Perkins, the assistant secretary of state for European Affairs, told Acheson that even if the United States achieved the situation of strength contemplated by the proposed NSC 68 buildup, it still would be futile to negotiate with the Soviet Union "until such time as the Kremlin has changed its philosophy," and that he "could not conceive of any settlement with the Kremlin which would be satisfactory which did not involve the lifting of the Iron Curtain." Memorandum by Perkins to Acheson, April 3, 1950, *FRUS 1950,* 1:215–16. As Mitrovich observes, instead of practicing normal great power diplomacy with the Kremlin, Washington's goal was "to employ psychological warfare and covert action to undermine the Soviet government and either compel it to abandon its expansionistic ambitions or cause the collapse of the communist bloc altogether." Mitrovich, *Undermining the Kremlin,* 178.

91. NSC 68, 279. Here, NSC 68 implicitly reflects the antipathy of U.S. policymakers toward multipolarity. Why officials like Nitze assumed a "neutral" Germany or Japan would bandwagon with the Soviet Union is unclear. What is clear is that as independent poles of power in the international system, a "neutral" Germany or Japan no longer would be under *Washington's* control.

92. Ibid., 290. As NSC 68 stated (284), U.S. grand strategy would "engage the Kremlin's attention, keep it off balance and force an increased expenditure of Soviet resources in counteraction." As Leffler puts it:

> Acheson, Nitze, and Lovett constantly reiterated that the administration's objectives were no different than they had been in 1948 when NSC 20/4 was first approved. They wanted to redraw Russia's borders to its pre-1939 status, destroy the Cominform, retract the influence of the Soviet Union, and eventually cause the Soviet system to weaken and decay. If the free world gathered enough strength, Nitze emphasized that the contradictions in the Communist system would be exposed, the satellites would be drawn to the west, and the Kremlin's control would falter. Successful containment would evolve into roll back. (Leffler, *Preponderance of Power,* 491)

Using archival sources not available to Leffler, Mitrovich shows that instead of waiting sequentially for "containment" to succeed and then attempting to roll back Soviet power, the Truman administration pursued these policies simultaneously. Mitrovich, *Undermining the Kremlin,* 180.

93. Mitrovich rejects the notion that the United States was seeking "global *economic* hegemony" but acknowledges that postwar U.S. policy *did* reflect "the prevailing belief that the presence of competing autarkic economic systems inevitably leads to economic and political instability." Mitrovich does recognize that the *logic* of NSC 20/4 and NSC 68 inexorably led to U.S. geopolitical global hegemony. Mitrovich, *Undermining the Kremlin,* 180–81.

94. The classic exposition of this argument is A. W. DePorte, *Europe between the Superpowers: The Enduring Balance* (New Haven: Yale University Press, 1979).

95. See Carolyn Woods Eisenberg, *Drawing the Line: The American Decision to Divide Germany, 1944–1949* (Cambridge: Cambridge University Press, 1996); Bruce Kuklick, *American Policy and the Division of Germany: The Clash with Russia over Reparations* (Ithaca: Cornell University Press, 1972); Leffler, *Preponderance of Power;* Leffler, "The Struggle for Germany." See also Yergin, *Shattered Peace,* 366–67, and McAllister, *No Exit,* 116–20. McAllister admits that the Soviet Union had a much greater interest in preserving a unified Germany in

1945–46 than did the United States, and there may have been a "missed opportunity" to preserve German unity. Nonetheless, arguing that Stalin would have never accepted a Western-style democratic all-German government, he remains reluctant to put the blame for Germany's division on Washington.

96. Marc Trachtenberg argues that the U.S. aim—or at least that of Secretary of State James F. Byrnes—was to reach a friendly agreement on Germany's division that would allow the western Allies and the Soviet Union to administer their respective parts of Germany as they saw fit. Trachtenberg, *Constructed Peace,* chap. 1. Similarly, McAllister argues that it was Byrnes "more than anyone else who consistently took the lead in dividing Germany both during and after Potsdam." Although Byrnes may not have intended Germany's division to become a source of diplomatic conflict, "he preferred division on any terms to a united Germany that would allow the Soviets any real influence in the western zones." McAllister, *No Exit,* 78.

97. In framing their postwar German policy, U.S. policymakers were guided by two "lessons of the past" drawn from the Versailles Treaty and its aftermath: (1) that the imposition of massive reparations on Germany had been both an economic and political disaster; (2) that through the Dawes and Young plans of 1924 and 1929 U.S. taxpayers had subsidized Germany's reparations payments. For an analysis refuting the latter claim, see John Backer, *The Decision to Divide Germany: American Foreign Policy in Transition* (Durham: Duke University Press, 1978), 46–58.

98. As Carolyn Woods Eisenberg observes, "By making the costs of needed imports into Germany a 'first charge' on German exports, the Western powers were reducing the supply of goods available for reparations." Eisenberg, *Drawing the Line,* 83–84. Yergin describes the first-charge principle's effect on the Soviet Union: "Germany was to be integrated into a multilateral, but American-dominated, world economic order before reparations (in effect, aid) went to the Soviet ally." Yergin, *Shattered Peace,* 96. On the reparations/first charge issue, also see McAllister, *No Exit,* 79–84.

99. Leffler, "Struggle for Germany," 18–22.

100. Leffler, *Preponderance of Power,* 64–65. To revive coal production, large quantities of food, clothing, timber, and machinery first had to be imported into Germany. On the eve of the Potsdam summit, senior Truman administration officials "concluded that the sums necessary to pay for these imports should be a first charge on all German exports from current production and from stocks on hand. In other words, money received from German sales abroad should be used to pay for imports rather than for anything else." See also Eisenberg, *Drawing the Line,* 82–86. On the Potsdam negotiations and agreement on German reparations, see Eisenberg, *Drawing the Line,* 98–113.

101. The American preoccupation with coal production had profound implications for U.S.-Soviet relations. Not only would the amount of reparations going to Soviet Russia have to be scaled down from the figure of $10 billion tentatively agreed on at Yalta as a basis for discussion, but in addition the Kremlin might have to defer reparations until the coal industry was revived and until the imports necessary for the coal industry's rehabilitation were paid for with German exports. (Leffler, *Preponderance of Power,* 65)

See also Eisenberg, *Drawing the Line,* 85–86.

102. For Washington "there was never any serious contest between German requirements and Russian ones. If both could be met that was desirable. But if forced to pick between two desperate parties, *America's economic interests* dictated Germany." Eisenberg, *Drawing the Line,* 84 (emphasis added).

103. On the creation of the Bizone, see Eisenberg, *Drawing the Line,* 233–43, and Leffler, *Preponderance of Power,* 118–20. Although the U.S. military government (OMGUS) hoped that the Bizone would lead to Allied agreement on treating Germany economically as a unified entity, the State Department viewed the Bizone "as the first step in a deliberate strategy of dividing the country." Eisenberg, *Drawing the Line,* 233.

104. Well into 1946, an influential minority of U.S. officials—including Undersecretary of State Dean Acheson, Assistant Secretary of State for Economic Affairs Will Clayton, and Gen. Lucius D. Clay, the military governor of the U.S. occupation zone—favored treat-

ing Germany as a single economic entity. They believed this would afford the United States the opportunity to extend *its* political influence throughout Germany. However, the prevailing view in Washington was shaped by apprehension that the Communists would exploit the widespread economic impoverishment and social dislocation in the western occupation zones to gain indirect control over the Ruhr.

105. Moscow's interest was to have Germany treated as a single economic unit, and Soviet foreign minister Molotov responded to the Bizone by playing the "German card"—including a call for German reunification—at the July 1946 foreign ministers conference in Paris. From then on, the United States believed itself to be in a competition with Moscow to control Germany. See Eisenberg, *Drawing the Line*, 237–40; Leffler, *Preponderance of Power*, 235.

106. On the Moscow conference, see Backer, *Decision to Divide Germany*, 166–70; Eisenberg, *Drawing the Line*, 278–308, 314–17; Leffler, *Preponderance of Power*, 151–55; Yergin, *Shattered Peace*, 296–301; Leffler, "Struggle for Germany," 38–40. Eisenberg points out (315) that, combined with the first-charge principle, Washington's determination to use West Germany as a locomotive for Western European economic recovery "meant in practice that it would be years before the Soviet Union could receive *any* more current production reparations from its own zone or western Germany" (emphasis in original).

107. Creation of the Bizone was a portent for U.S.-Soviet relations: "Reconstructing Western Europe and integrating western Germany were more important than catering to Soviet demands for reparations or allaying its concerns about its security." Leffler, *Preponderance of Power*, 121.

108. Eisenberg, *Drawing the Line*, 319.

109. Ibid., 224.

110. The German question came up again at the November/December 1947 Council of Foreign Ministers meeting in London. The United States rebuffed Soviet overtures for an accord on Germany because "an agreement with the Soviets was not nearly as desirable as implementing the ERP [Marshall Plan] and integrating western Germany into a Western bloc." Leffler, *Preponderance of Power*, 199. Washington wanted the London conference to fail so that the United States could proceed with its plans to set up a separate West German state. Eisenberg, *Drawing the Line*, 353–61; Yergin, *Shattered Peace*, 330–35.

111. Quoted in Eisenberg, *Drawing the Line*, 488. From the end of World War II until the end of the Berlin blockade, Moscow had not reached a firm decision on whether it preferred a reunified Germany or a divided one. Leffler, "Struggle for Germany," 25–26; Kennedy-Pipe, *Stalin's Cold War*. Kennedy-Pipe stresses that from 1946 until 1953 Moscow was open to German reunification and a joint U.S.-Soviet policy to prevent a resurgent German threat.

112. PPS 37, "Policy Questions concerning a Possible German Settlement," August 12, 1948, *FRUS 1948*, 2:1288–96. PPS 37 also is reprinted in Etzold and Gaddis, *Documents on American Policy and Strategy*, 135–43. For discussion of Kennan's PPS 37 German strategy and the debate within the State Department triggered by PPS 37 and Kennan's follow-up proposals in November 1948 and spring 1949, see Eisenberg, *Drawing the Line*, 439–40, 478–79, 481–82; McAllister, *No Exit*, 156–59; Anders Stephanson, *Kennan and the Art of American Foreign Policy* (Cambridge: Harvard University Press, 1989), 144–50; Leffler, "Struggle for Germany," 60–62.

113. PPS 37, 1290.

114. Ibid.

115. Ibid.

116. Although Kennan's view was clearly in the minority in the State Department, it did attract some support from senior State Department officials Philip Jessup and Charles W. Yost. See Jessup to Acheson, April 19, 1949, *FRUS 1949*, 3:861; Yost to Jessup, May 21, 1949, *FRUS 1949*, 3:891–92.

117. Paper Prepared in the Department of State, "United States Interests, Positions, and Tactics at Paris," November 5, 1949, *FRUS 1949*, 3:299.

118. Even as late as 1953, the Eisenhower administration fretted that in West Germany "the institutions of democracy have yet to undergo a real test." It still might succumb to "extremist nationalism," which would make it a "difficult and not entirely reliable partner."

NSC 160/1, "United States Position with Respect to Germany," August 17, 1953, *FRUS 1952–54*, 7:511–12.

119. On U.S. fears that West Germany either would balance between the United States and the Soviet Union or ally with the Kremlin, see Memorandum of a Conversation by Fisher, November 30, 1953, *FRUS 1952–54*, 5:857; McCloy to Acheson, August 3, 1950; *FRUS 1950*, 3:181; Riddleberger to Acheson, April 2, 1949, *FRUS 1949*, 3:235. Paper Prepared in the Department of State, "United States Interests, Positions, and Tactics at Paris," November 5, 1949, *FRUS 1949*, 3:299.

120. Summary of a Record of a Meeting of United States Ambassadors at Paris, October 21–22, 1949, *FRUS 1949*, 4:485–86. See also Memorandum by Fuller to Bowie, July 7, 1953, *FRUS 1952–54*, 7:482.

121. Summary of a Record of a Meeting of United States Ambassadors at Paris, October 21–22, 1949, *FRUS 1949*, 4:485. For other expressions of concern about German nationalism, see NSC 160/1, "United States Position with Respect to Germany," August 17, 1953, *FRUS 1952–54*, 8:511–12; Paper Prepared in the Department of State, "United States Interests, Positions, and Tactics at Paris," November 5, 1949, *FRUS 1949*, 3:299.

122. Paper Prepared by Kennan, March 8, 1949, *FRUS 1949*, 3:98. See also PPS 37.

123. For example, see Dulles to Macmillan, December 10, 1955, *FRUS 1955–57*, 4:363; Policy Directive for the United States High Commissioner in Germany, November 17, 1949, *FRUS 1949*, 3:319–20; Summary of a Record of a Meeting of United States Ambassadors at Paris, October 21–22, 1949, *FRUS 1949*, 4:485–86; Acheson to the Embassy in the United Kingdom, May 11, 1949, *FRUS 1949*, 3:872–74.

124. Summary Record of a Meeting of United States Ambassadors at Paris, October 22, 1949, *FRUS 1949*, 3:289. Robert Murphy, who had served as General Clay's political adviser, thought Western European opposition to incorporating a West German state into Western European economic and political institutions "is in fact *likely to be less in the case of a manageable portion of Germany rather than with a united Germany* of preponderant magnitude and uncertain orientation." Paper Prepared by Murphy, March, 23 1949, *FRUS 1949*, 3:125 (emphasis added).

125. U.S. officials always saw Germany's containment as the key to the United States's European grand strategy. Leon Fuller, a member of the State Department Policy Planning Staff, stated that "U.S. policy should envisage an integrated Europe in which German participation is so hedged by safeguards that it cannot develop into hegemony." He also said that reconstituted German military power "must be subject to supra-national organs of control and not be permitted to develop as a national army under national control. Germany's containment would be facilitated by its close association with and *dependence upon the broader Atlantic community*." Memorandum by Leon Fuller (PPS) to Nitze, September 4, 1952, *FRUS 1952–54*, 7:359–60 (emphasis added).

126. In 1949 the diplomat Foy Kohler warned the Soviets would seek "peace settlements" with Germany and Austria that would go far toward removing U.S. military power from Europe, which "would shake Western foreign policy to very bottom." Kohler to Acheson, May 6, 1949, *FRUS 1949*, 3:864–67. Acheson said in 1949 that "the withdrawal of American and British troops from Germany would be too high a price" to pay for German reunification. Acheson to the Embassy in the United Kingdom, May 11, 1949, *FRUS 1949*, 3:872–74. The Eisenhower administration also responded coolly to the prospect of mutual U.S.-Soviet disengagement from Europe. See Western European Chiefs of Mission Conference: Summary Conclusions and Recommendations, May 8, 1957, *FRUS 1955–57*, 4:600; Verbatim Minutes of Western European Chiefs of Mission Conference, May 6, 1957, *FRUS 1955–57*, 4:586.

127. Barbour to Acheson, January 14, 1951, *FRUS 1951*, 3:1064–65.

128. Responding to Stalin's 1952 proposal to create a reunified, neutral Germany with an independent military capability, Acheson said that the

US Govt considers that such provision wld be a step backwards and might jeopardize the emergence in Eur of a new era in which internantl relations wld be based on cooperation and not on rivalry and distrust. Being convinced of the need of a policy of Eur unity, the US Govt is giving its full support to plans designed to secure the participation of Ger in a purely defensive Eur community which will preserve freedom, prevent aggression, and preclude the revival of natl militarism. US Govt believes that the proposal of the Sov. Govt for formation of Ger natl fores is inconsistent with the achievement of this objective. (Acheson to McCloy, May 22, 1952, *FRUS 1952–54,* 7:190)

129. Acheson stated: "Our major premise is that our concern is with the future of Europe and not with Germany as a problem by itself. We are concerned with the integration of Germany into a free and democratic Europe. We have made and are making progress to this end with the part of Germany which we control and we shall not jeopardize this progress by seeking a unified Germany as in itself good." Acheson to the Embassy in the United Kingdom, May 11, 1949, *FRUS 1949,* 3:872–73.
130. Leffler, "Struggle for Germany," 36–37.
131. Ibid., 69.
132. Acheson to the Embassy in the United Kingdom, May 11, 1949, *FRUS 1949,* 3:873.
133. Acheson to McCloy, April 12 1952, *FRUS 1952–54,* 7:203–6; Memorandum by Louis Pollak, "Departmental Views on Germany," April 2, 1952, *FRUS 1952–54,* 7:194–98; U.S. Minutes of Second Meeting between President Truman and Prime Minister Pleven, January 30, 1951, *FRUS 1951,* 4:325–26; McCloy to Acheson, January 29, 1951, *FRUS 1951,* 3:1068. The Eisenhower administration's policy on German reunification was similar to the Truman administration's. See NSC 160/1, "United States Position with Respect to Germany," August 17, 1953, *FRUS 1952–54,* 7:514–15.
134. U.S. Minutes of Second Meeting between President Truman and Prime Minister Pleven, January 30, 1951, *FRUS 1951,* 4:325–26.
135. U.S. Minutes of Third Meeting between President Truman and Prime Minister Pleven, January 30, 1951, *FRUS 1951,* 4:337. McCloy understood that Moscow would not accept reunification on U.S. terms. McCloy to Acheson, January 29, 1951, *FRUS 1951,* 3:1068.
136. As Robert Murphy argued, "It may be expected that the establishment of a stable and orderly democratic political organization in Western Germany with a reasonably prosperous economy, will exert an inevitable magnetic force on Eastern Germany and make even more difficult Soviet control of that area." Paper Prepared by Murphy, March 23, 1949, *FRUS 1949,* 3:125. Once West Germany was militarily and economically integrated into the Euro-Atlantic community, Secretary of State John Foster Dulles contended that

> [The] Soviets will eventually be forced to reanalyze their policy toward the satellite states and give them some form of semi-autonomous character. . . . [They] will not be able to maintain their total control of the satellite states by their present methods but will probably have to transform them into buffer states, perhaps they will evolve into a status similar to Finland. It is after there is evolution in this direction that East Germany may be able to join West Germany. (Memorandum of Conversation [Dulles/Adenauer] by Mac-Arthur, February 20, 1954, *FRUS 1952–54,* 7:1210)

For the Eisenhower administration, German reunification on American terms "would represent *a major step in rolling back the iron curtain* and enlarging the basis for an enduring peace in Europe." See also NSC 160/1, "United States Position with Respect to Germany," August 17, 1953, *FRUS 1952–54,* 7:514–15 (emphasis added).
137. Although Washington's official policy line held that West German integration would strengthen "the West" and thereby lead to reunification—and the concomitant rollback of Soviet power in Eastern Europe—it is clear from the relevant documents that U.S. officials *knew* that the opposite was true, that it would make reunification impossible for a *very* long time. As John Lewis Gaddis put it, "Reunification would remain the declared goal, but neither the United States nor its allies would risk security or prosperity to achieve it." Gaddis, *We Now Know,* 123. For arguments that German reunification was possible during the late 1940s and early 1950s, see Eisenberg, *Drawing the Line,* 237–40, 312–17, 356–61, 487–88; Stephanson, *Kennan and the Art of Foreign Policy,* 154–56. Leffler argues that German reunification would have resulted in tighter—not looser—Soviet control over Eastern Europe and that the U.S. decision to divide Germany was, on balance, a prudent one. Leffler, "Struggle for Germany," 74–75.
138. See Ruud Van Dijk, "The 1952 Stalin Note Debate: Myth or Missed Opportunity for German Unification?" Cold War International History Project, Working Paper No. 14 (May

1996). While concluding that the 1952 Soviet overture was a public relations gambit to sidetrack the processes leading to West German sovereignty and accession to the European Defense Community, Van Dijk admits that the United States was only interested in German reunification based on Soviet acceptance of Washington's maximalist terms. John Lewis Gaddis takes a similar position. Gaddis, *We Now Know,* 127–29. Zubok and Pleshakov suggest that although Stalin feared West Germany's rearmament and military and economic integration into the Euro-Atlantic community, he was not prepared to sacrifice a communized, Soviet-dominated East Germany in 1952. Zubok and Pleshakov, *Inside the Kremlin's Cold War,* 159. For arguments that the 1952 Soviet demarche really was a missed opportunity for a German settlement, see Kennedy-Pipe, *Stalin's Cold War,* 161–63; Wilfried Loth, "The Origins of Stalin's Note of 10 March 1952," *Cold War History* 4, no. 2 (January 2004): 66–88; Adam B. Ulam, "A Few Unresolved Mysteries about Stalin and the Cold War in Europe: A Modest Agenda for Research," *Journal of Cold War Studies* 1, no. 1 (Winter 1999): 110–16. On the 1953 Soviet proposal—and the post-Stalin Politburo infighting that was its backdrop—see Zubok and Pleshakov, *Inside the Kremlin's Cold War,* 159–63.

139. William C. Wohlforth, "New Evidence on Moscow's Cold War: Ambiguity in Search of Theory," *Diplomatic History* 21, no. 2 (Spring 1997): 235.

140. As Adam Ulam comments: "Washington still 'feared to negotiate,' and the State Department wasted little effort in flatly rejecting Moscow's initiative. The reasons given for the rejection, however, were embarrassingly unconvincing." Ulam, "A Few Unresolved Mysteries about Stalin and the Cold War," 114–15. As James McAllister says, debate about the March 1952 Soviet overture "should not obscure a rather obvious point. No matter how serious Stalin might or might not have been about negotiating a united Germany in 1952, it is hard to see how even a 'reasonable' Soviet proposal would have been acceptable to the Western powers." McAllister, *No Exit,* 221.

141. As Eisenberg puts it, "The curtailment of Soviet power had never been the exclusive preoccupation of the [Truman] administration. Since the end of the war, policy makers had wished to use German resources to promote an integrated, free market economy in Western Europe." Eisenberg, *Drawing the Line,* 482. Similarly, Leffler comments that "in the context of the late 1940s, a united Germany was not likely to have harmonized with the goals of establishing a peaceful, integrated, productive, and democratic Europe." Leffler, "Struggle for Germany," 76.

4. The Open Door and American Hegemony in Western Europe

1. See Robert A. Pollard, *Economic Security and the Origins of the Cold War, 1945–1950* (New York: Columbia University Press, 1985), 103; Carolyn Woods Eisenberg, *Drawing the Line: The American Decision to Divide Germany, 1944–1949* (Cambridge: Cambridge University Press, 1996), 323; Michael Hogan, *The Marshall Plan: America, Britain, and the Reconstruction of Western Europe, 1947–1952* (Cambridge: Cambridge University Press, 1987), 36.

2. Eisenberg, *Drawing the Line,* 322–23. Similarly, Pollard, who dissociates himself from revisionism, says that "American interests in West European recovery would have required a revision of policies in Germany even if the Truman administration had not realized the value of mobilizing a West German state in the service of the United States in the Cold War." Pollard, *Economic Security,* 105.

3. Alan S. Milward, *The Reconstruction of Western Europe, 1945–1951* (Berkeley: University of California Press, 1984), 59–60.

4. U.S. policymakers believed that "closed economic blocs not only hurt trade but easily developed into political blocs. Friction between such blocs caused world wars." Walter LaFeber, *America, Russia, and the Cold War, 1945–1996,* 8th ed. (New York: McGraw-Hill, 1997), 9.

5. Walter LaFeber shows how "the Ghosts of Depression Past and Depression Future" shaped postwar U.S. grand strategy: "Washington officials believed another terrible economic depression could be averted only if global markets and raw materials were fully open to all peoples on the basis of equal opportunity." LaFeber, *America, Russia, and the*

Cold War, 8–9. See also Pollard, *Economic Security,* 7–8, 23–24. Early 1946 Senate testimony by Leo T. Crowley of the Export-Import Bank highlighted these concerns and anticipated the coming of a postwar "dollar gap" that would crimp American exports: "There has been during the war an enormous expansion in manufacturing capacities in the United States, and this expansion has been concentrated very largely in heavy industry. *Unless foreign markets for the products of American heavy industry are found* during the period which immediately lies ahead, *many war-expanded industries will be obliged to curtail their operations and, accordingly to reduce their employment of labor.*" Statement of Honorable Leo T. Crowley, Chairman, Board of Trustees, Export-Import Bank of Washington before Senate Banking and Currency Committee, July 17, 1945, *FRUS 1946,* 1:1397 (emphasis added).

6. Quoted in Charles L. Mee Jr., *The Marshall Plan: The Launching of the Pax Americana* (New York: Simon and Schuster, 1984), 79. Clayton, a Southerner whose fortune was made in cotton exports, had a special interest in having overseas markets open to American exports.

7. See Statement of Leo Crowley, July 17, 1945, *FRUS 1946,* 1:1397–98; Memorandum Prepared by the Staff Committee of the National Advisory Council, February 8, 1946, *FRUS 1946,* 1:1415. On the role of Western Europe's dollar gap as a catalyst for the Marshall Plan, see Milward, *Reconstruction of Western Europe,* 3–4, 5–55; Pollard, *Economic Security,* 60–61.

8. See Pollard, *Economic Security,* 63–64.

9. In *The Reconstruction of Europe,* Alan Milward makes a powerful counterargument to the generally accepted view that Western Europe was in dire straits economically in spring 1947. He claims that Western Europe was not facing a fundamental economic crisis but only a short-term foreign exchange–balance of payments problem. See Alan S. Milward, "Was the Marshall Plan Really Necessary?" *Diplomatic History* 13, no. 2 (Spring 1989): 231–53.

10. Quoted in Imanuel Wexler, *The Marshall Plan Revisited: The European Recovery Program in Economic Perspective* (Westport, Conn.: Greenwood, 1983), 14.

11. Report of the Special "Ad Hoc" Committee of the State-War-Navy Coordinating Committee, April 21, 1947, *FRUS 1947,* 3:210–11.

12. Ibid., 211.

13. Ibid., 210.

14. Ibid., 214–15. See also Memorandum by Kennan, May 16, 1947, *FRUS 1947,* 3:221.

15. Historians are split on the extent to which the Marshall Plan was conceived as a part of America's containment strategy vis-à-vis the Soviet Union. John Gimbel argues that "the Marshall Plan originated as a crash program to dovetail German economic recovery with a general European recovery program in order to make German economic recovery politically acceptable in Europe and the United States. It was not a plan conceived of by long-range planners as a response to the Soviet Union or as an element of the Cold War." John Gimbel, *The Origins of the Marshall Plan* (Stanford: Stanford University Press, 1976), 5. Daniel Yergin says: "The Marshall Plan had two basic aims, which commingled and cannot really be separated—to halt the communist advance into Western Europe, and to stabilize an international economic environment favorable to capitalism." Daniel Yergin, *Shattered Peace: The Origins of the Cold War and the National Security State* (Boston: Houghton Mifflin, 1978), 309. Michael Hogan and Melvyn Leffler both acknowledge that cold war concerns played in big role in the Marshall Plan. Hogan also stresses that America's post–World War II European policy had the same objectives as its post–World I policy (and that its origins obviously predated the cold war). Leffler concedes that U.S. Open Door economic interests were important in driving U.S. policy after World War II, reinforcing Washington's cold war strategic goals. Hence, "U.S. officials could usually pursue economic and strategic interests in tandem" (14). Hogan, *Marshall Plan;* Hogan, "Revival and Reform: America's Twentieth Century Search for a New International Economic Order," *Diplomatic History* 8, no. 4 (Fall 1984): 287–310; Melvyn P. Leffler, *A Preponderance of Power: National Security, the Truman Administration, and the Cold War* (Stanford: Stanford University Press, 1992).

16. PPS/1, "Policy with Respect to American Aid to Western Europe," May 23, 1947, in Anna Kasten Nelson, ed., *The State Department Policy Planning Staff Papers*, vol. 1 (New York: Garland, 1983), 5 (hereinafter *PPSP*).
17. Ibid.
18. Ibid., 11. The Truman Doctrine was announced in President Truman's March 12, 1947 speech to Congress seeking support for the administration's package of military and economic assistance to Greece and Turkey.
19. PPS/4, "Certain Aspects of the European Recovery Problem from the United States' Standpoint," July 23, 1947, *PPSP*, 1:31. In notes prepared for Secretary of State Marshall, Kennan argued that the Marshall Plan was necessary for two reasons: "so that they can buy from us" and "so that they will have enough self-confidence to withstand outside pressures." Memorandum Prepared by the Policy Planning Staff, July 21, 1947, *FRUS 1947*, 3:335.
20. PPS/4, *PPSP* 1:63.
21. Ibid.
22. Memorandum by Clayton for Acheson, May 27, 1947, *FRUS 1947*, 3:231.
23. By providing "public goods" for the international economic system after World War II, the United States conformed to the policy prescriptions of the international political economy version of "hegemonic stability theory." See Robert Gilpin, *War and Change in World Politics* (Cambridge: Cambridge University Press, 1981); Gilpin, *U.S. Power and the Multinational Corporation: The Political Economy of Foreign Direct Investment* (New York: Basic Books, 1975); Charles P. Kindleberger, *The World in Depression, 1929–1939* (Berkeley: University of California Press, 1973). As the State Department's Theodore Draper argued, unless the United States offset the termination of Marshall Plan aid by importing more goods from Western Europe, America's export industries would suffer. Draper to Eisenhower, June 5 1953, *FRUS 1952–54*, 5:404–5. See also Memorandum for the President, July 8, 1953, *FRUS 1952–54*, 5:434.
24. The Marshall Plan's long-term goal was to "encourage the rapid creation of a free trade area and realistic exchange relationships in Western Europe, as steps toward raising productivity and putting Europe on a better competitive position in the world." NSC 52/3, "Government Programs in National Security and International Affairs for the Fiscal Year 1951," September 29, 1949, *FRUS 1949*, 1:388.
25. Attachment to Memorandum to the President, "The Problem of the Future Balance of Payments of the United States," February 16, 1950, *FRUS 1950*, 1:839.
26. Ibid., 841.
27. Caffery to Secretary of State, March 28, 1948, *FRUS 1948*, 3:407. Also see Wood to Porter, August 25, 1951, *FRUS 1951*, 4:51. As Hogan points out, the preference of U.S. officials for Western European economic integration was strongly influenced by their belief that the United States's own large, integrated market was an appropriate economic model for Western Europe. Hogan, *Marshall Plan*, 27, 39, 427–28. See also Michael J. Hogan, "The Search for a 'Creative Peace': The United States, European Unity, and the Origins of the Marshall Plan," *Diplomatic History* 6, no. 3 (Summer 1982): 267–88; Hogan, "Revival and Reform"; Milward, *Reconstruction of Western Europe*, 216–17; Wexler, *Marshall Plan Revisited*, 155–57, 205–8, 218.
28. In launching the Marshall Plan and promoting European integration, the United States "would erase the traditional territorial constraints on European enterprise, abolish old habits of bilateralism and restrictionism, and eliminate archaic concerns with national self-sufficiency and autonomy." Hogan, *Marshall Plan*, 54.
29. Memorandum of Conversation, Prepared in the Department of State, September 15, 1949, *FRUS 1949*, 4:657.
30. Summary of Discussion on Problems of Relief, Rehabilitation and Reconstruction of Europe, May 29, 1947, *FRUS 1947*, 3:234.
31. Aide Memoire by the British Foreign Office for Bevin, n.d., *FRUS 1947*, 3:285.
32. Caffery to Marshall, July 10, 1947, *FRUS 1947*, 3:317. Numerous U.S. policymakers took up the argument about the adverse implications of Western Europe's division into separate national economies. John Foster Dulles, for example, in 1947 said that "a Europe divided

into small compartments" could not be "a healthy Europe." Quoted in Hogan, *Marshall Plan,* 37.

33. As Eisenberg notes, Washington viewed the global depression of the 1930s "as the product of autarky." Consequently, "in fashioning their remedies for war, the planners took economic integration as a prime ingredient to which other elements would be added. If nations, especially those troubled lands of Europe, would eliminate artificial barriers against foreign currencies and products, permitting free market forces to direct the flow of economic activity, each would become more prosperous and less belligerent." Eisenberg, *Drawing the Line,* 17–18. See also Pollard, *Economic Security,* 7–13.

34. Quoted in Hogan, *Marshall Plan,* 91. Hogan also notes (192) that U.S. officials continually stressed "that Western Europe must . . . replace old habits of political conflict and economic rivalry" with new habits of political and economic collaboration, including integration and supranationality.

35. Ibid., 26, 293–94.

36. If Communists came to power in Western Europe, the Continent "might pursue protectionist, beggar-thy-neighbor policies, in turn reducing American exports, weakening the already fragile structure of world trade and finance, and undermining the economic foundations of the peace." Pollard, *Economic Security,* 133. For postwar U.S. policymakers, "multilateral trade was a mechanism to stymie trade alliances that not only could erode American prosperity but could also foster configurations of power that endangered American security." Leffler, *Preponderance of Power,* 20.

37. Leffler, *Preponderance of Power,* 20.

38. Summary of a Record of a Meeting of United States Ambassadors in Paris, October 21–22, 1949, *FRUS 1949,* 4:492.

39. As an NSC paper put it, the United States had to "prevent the development of a France which might eventually become the bastion of an inherently hostile 'continental system' dominated by the U.S.S.R." "France," January 9, 1948, NA, RG273, Mill Papers, Mill 15, Box 1. Also see Leffler, *Preponderance of Power,* 160. The "continental system" was Napoleonic France's unsuccessful attempt to organize a continental European embargo on trade with Britain, and thereby bring London to its knees.

40. Quoted in Mee, *Marshall Plan,* 238.

41. Memorandum, September 29, 1947, *FRUS 1947,* 3:476. See also Leffler, *Preponderance of Power,* 13, 161–63. Leffler says (162) that U.S. policymakers "were convinced that regimented trade abroad would eventually jeopardize economic and political freedom at home," because America's domestic political and economic systems "could not remain insulated from patterns of international commerce."

42. U.S. policymakers feared that "the existence of a large economic bloc under Soviet tutelage would reshape world commercial patterns, impel the United States to turn in on itself, and require the U.S. government to impose controls over production and trade and infringe on personal freedoms." Leffler, *Preponderance of Power,* 191. LaFeber observes that U.S. policymakers dreaded the domestic consequences if the world slid back into 1930s-style autarky: "If that recurred, Americans could survive only through massive governmental intervention into their society. If the government dominated the economy, however, it would also regulate individual choice and perhaps severely limit personal freedom." LaFeber, *Russia, America, and the Cold War,* 8.

43. Leffler, *Preponderance of Power,* 162 (emphasis added).

44. In December 1947, the CIA stated that "France is of greater strategic importance to the US than any other continental European country." "The Current Situation in France," December 15, 1947, NA, RG 273, Mill Papers, Mill 15, Box 1. Similarly, a January 1948 National Security Council paper stated that the U.S. position in all of Western Europe—including Germany, Austria, Italy, and the Mediterranean—would become untenable if the Communists came to power in France. "France," January 9, 1948, NA, RG 273, Mill Papers, Mill 15, Box 1. France was described as "the keystone of Continental Western Europe." Acting Secretary of State to Harriman, December 3, 1948, *FRUS 1948,* 3:306. See also Caffery to Marshall, May 12, 1947, *FRUS 1947,* 3:710–11; Caffery to Marshall, September 30, 1947, *FRUS 1947,* 3:761–62; Lovett to Truman, October 2, 1947, *FRUS 1947,*

3:763. The U.S. ambassador to Paris, Jefferson Caffery, had told the State Department as early as October 1944 that the United States had an interest in keeping the French Communist Party out of power, because as "France goes, the Continent of Europe probably will go." Quoted in John W. Young, *France, the Cold War and the Western Alliance, 1944–1949: French Foreign Policy and Post-War Europe* (Leicester: Leicester University Press, 1990), 38.

45. On the May 1946 aid package and the negotiations leading up to it, see William I. Hitchcock, *France Restored: Cold War Diplomacy and the Quest for Leadership in Europe, 1944–1954* (Chapel Hill: University of North Carolina Press, 1998), 35–36, 59–60; Pollard, *Economic Security*, 74–77.

46. Discussing U.S. aid to France (and Italy) in 1946, Robert A. Pollard says the United States intervened "blatantly, but effectively" in the French and Italian elections in 1946 by providing emergency loans to the non-Communist governments in Paris and Rome. Pollard, *Economic Security*, 73.

47. Secretary of State to Harriman, December 3, 1948, *FRUS 1948*, 3:307.

48. For example, see Caffery to Marshall, October 2, 1948, *FRUS 1948*, 3:661; Leffler, *Preponderance of Power*, 158–59.

49. Melvyn P. Leffler, "The United States and the Strategic Dimensions of the Marshall Plan," *Diplomatic History* 12, no. 3 (Summer 1998): 281.

50. As a draft Policy Planning Staff paper put it, the United States should "make full use of its political, economic and, if necessary, military power in such a manner as may be found most effective to prevent France from falling under the domination of the USSR, either through external armed attack or through Soviet dominated communist movements within France." "Draft—Position of the Untied States with Respect to France," April 1, 1948, NA, RG 273, Mill Papers, Mill 15, Box 1. Leffler, *Preponderance of Power*, 195–97. LaFeber states that in May 1946, because of concerns that the French Communist Party was on the verge of coming to power in France, President Truman ordered U.S. Army occupation forces in Western Germany to be prepared to intervene in France. LaFeber, *America, Russia, and the Cold War*, 44.

51. Hogan, *Marshall Plan*, 335, 27, 87, 136, 424. As Milward says, "The growth of national income would still those bitter quarrels over its distribution which had been part of the fabric of European political life and unite large areas of political opinion in one common political and economic goal, an increase in national income *per capita*." Milward, *Reconstruction of Western Europe*, 60. The Communists were viewed by Washington as a major cause of these political battles over income redistribution and as a threat to Western Europe's economic revival. Leffler, *Preponderance of Power*, 157.

52. Milward, *Reconstruction of Western Europe*, 59–60.

53. Ibid., 60.

54. Ibid.

55. Memorandum of the Fourth Meeting of the Working Group Participating in the Washington Exploratory Talks on Security, July 20, 1948, *FRUS 1948*, 3:193.

56. Kennan, *Memoirs, 1925–1950* (Boston: Little, Brown, 1967), 318–19. See also Leffler, *Preponderance of Power*, 359.

57. Milward, *Reconstruction of Western Europe*, 123.

58. Ibid., 60, 123.

59. Mee, *Marshall Plan*, 230. Also see LaFeber, *America, Russia, and the Cold War*, 57.

60. Michael J. Hogan, "Paths to Plenty: Marshall Planners and the Debate over European Integration," *Pacific Historical Review* 53, no. 3 (August 1984): 338.

61. Secretary Marshall stated: "Aside from the demoralizing effect on the world at large and the possibilities for disturbances arising as a result of the desperation of the people concerned, the consequences to the economy of the United States should be apparent to all." Press Release Issued by the Department of State, June 4, 1947, "Remarks of Secretary of State George C. Marshall at Harvard University on June 5, 1947," *FRUS 1947*, 3:238. Clayton said that Western Europe's political, economic, and social disintegration would have "awful" consequences for the "peace and security of the world" *and* would have a "disastrous" effect on America's domestic economy. Memorandum by Clayton for Acheson, May 27, 1947, *FRUS 1947*, 3:231.

62. Paper Prepared in the Department of State, "The Economic Situation," April 30, 1950, *FRUS 1950*, 3:848.
63. LaFeber points out that the Truman administration's main objective in 1947 was "to prevent a collapse of the European and American economies." He then makes the key point that "the Western economies would have been in grave difficulties whether or not communism existed." LaFeber, *Russia, America, and the Cold War*, 57.
64. As the State Department Policy Planning Staff observed in 1950, "Whether or not there was a Soviet threat the West would face serious problems adapting itself to postwar conditions in such a way as to assure the stability of free institutions. The urgency of such adaptation has been *intensified* by the Soviet threat (and the willingness to adapt increased)." Paper Prepared by the Policy Planning Staff, "The Current Position in the Cold War," April 14, 1950, *FRUS 1950*, 3:859 (emphasis added).
65. Hogan, *Marshall Plan*, 8.
66. Both Hogan and Milward make the important point that U.S. policy aimed at finishing the business that remained after World War I: creating an enduring political and economic settlement that would bring peace and stability to the Continent. Ibid., 18–19; Milward, *Reconstruction of Western Europe*, 52, 56–57, 462. On the continuity in U.S. aims in Europe during the two postwar periods, also see Hogan, "Revival and Reform."
67. Minutes of the First Meeting of the Washington Exploratory Talks on Security, July 6, 1948, *FRUS 1948*, 3:151; Minutes of the Fourth Meeting of the Washington Exploratory Talks on Security, July 8, 1948, *FRUS 1948*, 3:167–68.
68. Statement by Dulles to the North Atlantic Council, December 14, 1953, *FRUS 1952–54*, 5:461. As Dulles further said, "The people of the US and Congress believed firmly that the division of Europe was the cause of wars in the past. The Europeans have an obligation to tie themselves together and to attain strength in that way so that if will not be necessary to call upon the US again. Any weakening in the move towards unification would be disillusioning here." Memorandum of a Conversation, June 7, 1955, *FRUS 1955–57*, 4:292. On the reasons U.S. policymakers favored Western European "unity" following World War II, see Hogan, "Search for a 'Creative Peace.'"
69. Minutes of the First Meeting of the Washington Exploratory Talks on Security, July 6, 1948, *FRUS 1948*, 3:151.
70. Wolfram Hanreider, *Germany, Europe, and America* (New Haven: Yale University Press, 1989).
71. Hogan, *Marshall Plan*, 128.
72. Acheson knew that "even if there were no Soviet threat the United States still would have an interest in preventing a renewal of hostilities between France and Germany." Timothy P. Ireland, *Creating the Entangling Alliance: The Origins of the North Atlantic Treaty Organization* (Westport, Conn.: Greenwood, 1981), 109. As James McAllister says, "The ascendancy of the Soviet Union in 1945 made solving the problem of German power in Europe much more complicated, but the latter problem would have existed even without the former." James McAllister, *No Exit: America and the German Problem, 1943–1954* (Ithaca: Cornell University Press, 2002), 75.
73. My argument differs from that of John Lewis Gaddis, who claims that each of the key U.S. decisions about Germany between 1946 and 1952 were the result of "improvisations" and that "Washington had no 'grand design.'" John Lewis Gaddis, *We Now Know: Rethinking Cold War History* (New York: Oxford University Press, 1997), 125. Whether one calls it a "grand design" or not, my argument is that the *logic* of America's political and economic Open Door goals inexorably resulted in the imposition of American hegemony on Western Europe.
74. John J. McCloy, U.S. High Commissioner to the newly created Federal Republic of Germany, observed: "German nationalism should not and need not be allowed to get out of hand. We have the power and we should have the determination to crack down immediately on the Germans if they get out of line." Summary of a Record of a Meeting of United States Ambassadors at Paris, October 21–22, 1949, *FRUS 1949*, 4:488.
75. Paper Prepared in the Department of State, "United States Interests, Positions, and Tactics at Paris," November 5, 1949, *FRUS 1949*, 3:299.

76. Ibid., 295–96.
77. PPS 4, *PPSP* 1:56–57.
78. Milward, *Reconstruction of Western Europe*, 126.
79. PPS 4, *PPSP* 1:55.
80. Eisenberg, *Drawing the Line*, 15.
81. Quoted in Melvyn P. Leffler, "American Grand Strategy from World War to Cold War, 1940–1950," in *From War to Peace: Altered Strategic Landscapes in the Twentieth Century*, ed. Paul Kennedy and William I. Hitchcock (New Haven: Yale University Press, 2000), 70.
82. Gimbel, *Origins of the Marshall Plan*, 4–5.
83. An important subtext of U.S. strategy in the 1945–1948 period is the split between the War Department and Army, on the one hand, and the State Department, on the other. For bureaucratic and policy reasons, the Army and War Departments favored Germany's economic rehabilitation. Because it regarded France as the key to U.S. strategy in Western Europe, the State Department wanted to "disarm" Germany economically and use its resources to rebuild Western Europe, especially France. See Gimbel, *Origins of the Marshall Plan*, 25–35, 39–49, 83–90, 117–22; Hogan, *Marshall Plan*, 29–35, 57–60. The differences on German policy between the State Department, and the Army and OMGUS is a central theme in Eisenberg, *Drawing the Line.*
84. William Hitchcock comments that the French believed they had a unique opportunity to employ German resources for French and western European recovery and use them to help overcome their long-standing economic inferiority. Under French political tutelage, German industrial power could be employed to the benefit of all of Europe, but "Germany itself would remain so shackled by administrative controls as to be rendered incapable of threatening the political equilibrium of the continent." Hitchcock, *France Restored*, 16.
85. See Eisenberg, *Drawing the Line*, 167–76, 206–12.
86. With respect to postwar French fears of German resurgence, see Policy Statement of the Department of State: France, September 20, 1948, *FRUS 1948*, 3:657–58; Bruce to Acheson, September 23, 1949, *FRUS 1949*, 4:665; Memorandum of a Conversation by Harriman [with French President Auriol], March 31, 1951, *FRUS 1951*, 4:378–79.
87. On post–World I French policy toward Germany, see Walter A. McDougall, *France's Rhineland Diplomacy, 1914–1924: The Last Bid for a Balance of Power in Europe* (Princeton: Princeton University Press, 1978); Stephen A. Schuker, *The End of French Predominance in Europe: The Financial Crisis of 1924 and the Adoption of the Dawes Plan* (Chapel Hill: University of North Carolina Press, 1976); Marc Trachtenberg, *Reparation in World Politics: France and European Economic Diplomacy, 1916–1923* (New York: Columbia University Press, 1980).
88. Milward, *Reconstruction of Western Europe*, 127.
89. William I. Hitchcock, "Reversal of Fortune: Britain, France, and the Making of Europe, 1945–1956," in Kennedy and Hitchcock, *From War to Peace*, 90. For an extended discussion of French policy toward Germany from mid-1945 to mid-1947, see Hitchcock, *France Restored*, 46–62, 67–71.
90. Hogan, *Marshall Plan*, 177. On the strategic objectives underlying the Monnet Plan, see Gimbel, *Origins of the Marshall Plan*, 116–17, 157, 196–98; Hogan, *Marshall Plan*, 32, 61, 65, 177, 195; Milward, *Reconstruction of Western Europe*, 126–67. For discussion of how U.S. Marshall Plan goals conflicted with France's Monnet Plan objectives, see Leffler, *Preponderance of Power*, 186–88.
91. Gimbel, *Origins of the Marshall Plan*, 157; Milward, *Reconstruction of Western Europe*, 129.
92. Preferential access to German coal was crucial to the Monnet Plan's goals of modernizing French industry and increasing French exports. Also, by taking the lion's share of German coal for its own industries, France would choke off Germany's economic revival. Hitchcock, *France Restored*, 67.
93. Milward, *Reconstruction of Western Europe*, 137.
94. Gimbel, *Origins of the Marshall Plan*, 116–17.
95. State Department officials implicitly decided that U.S. interests would be served best by a divided Germany during the first half of 1946. On the other hand, up until the March 1947 Moscow foreign ministers conference, Clay still hoped that the United States and the

Soviet Union could agree on administering Germany as a single entity. See Eisenberg, *Drawing the Line*, 255–57, 277–80, 287–89, 312–17.

96. Policy Statement of the Department of State: France, September 20, 1948, *FRUS 1948*, 3:655

97. Eisenberg, *Drawing the Line*, 324.

98. From the end of World War II until the early 1960s, fear of Germany remained a "constant preoccupation" of French foreign policy. Georges-Henri Soutou, "France and the Cold War, 1944–63," *Diplomacy and Statecraft* 12, no. 4 (December 2001): 35–52. For the counterargument that Paris regarded the Soviet Union, not Germany, as the main threat to its postwar security, see Michael Cresswell and Marc Trachtenberg, "France and the German Question, 1945–1955," *Journal of Cold War Studies* 5, no. 3 (Summer 2003): 5–28.

99. Hitchcock, "Reversal of Fortune," 91. For an extended discussion of how Paris revised its German policy in light of the Marshall Plan, see Hitchcock, *France Restored*, 74–82, 87–132.

100. U.S. officials understood that "until we can make progress in getting certain of Germany's neighbors, above all France, to take a constructive and healthy attitude toward Germany's future role in European affairs [U.S. plans for European integration] are unlikely to be realized." Acting Secretary of State to Harriman, December 3, 1948, *FRUS 1948*, 3:303.

101. Ibid., 309.

102. Ibid.

103. Paper Prepared by Murphy, March 23, 1949, *FRUS 1949*, 3:121.

104. Douglas to Marshall, March 2, 1948, *FRUS 1948*, 2:111.

105. Memorandum from Kennan to Marshall, January 20, 1948, *FRUS 1948*, 3:7.

106. The Secretary of State to the Embassy in the United Kingdom, February 28, 1948, *FRUS 1948*, 2:101.

107. Quoted in Arnold A. Offner, *Another Such Victory: President Truman and the Cold War, 1945–1953* (Stanford: Stanford University Press, 2002), 247.

108. Summary of Record of a Meeting of United States Ambassadors at Paris, October 21–22, 1949, *FRUS 1949*, 4:490 (comments of Averell Harriman). See also Acting Secretary of State to Harriman, December 3, 1948, *FRUS 1948*, 3:309. On Washington's recognition that its West European integration strategy depended on U.S. military guarantees that France would not be menaced by Germany, see Leffler, *Preponderance of Power*, 198, 203, 207, 219. Similarly, Timothy Ireland argues that the key U.S. aim of the Atlantic Alliance was to guarantee the security of France and the rest of Western Europe against any potential menace from a revived West Germany. As Ireland points out, this policy—and the centrality of Germany in determining the U.S. military role on the Continent—were not cold war driven. Timothy P. Ireland, *Creating the Entangling Alliance*, 4–8.

109. For Bruce's comments, see Summary of Record of a Meeting of United States Ambassadors at Paris, October 21–22, 1949, *FRUS 1949*, 4:492 (comments of David K. Bruce). See also Memorandum of a Conversation by Acheson, January 15, 1952, *FRUS 1952–54*, 5:41–42. In this conversation, French foreign minister Robert Schuman stressed that the U.S. military presence in Western Europe was vital to Western European integration, and he asked Acheson to keep U.S. forces in Germany for "as long as necessary." For Acheson's view, see Memorandum of a Conversation by Acheson with Senators Connally and Vandenberg, February 14, 1949, *FRUS 1949*, 4:109. U.S. policymakers understood that Paris regarded the North Atlantic Treaty "as a defense against Germany as well as Russia." Dulles to Acheson, April 21, 1950, *FRUS 1950*, 3:60.

110. Paris and Washington shared these concerns. The French also worried that if Germany became too powerful, it might pursue its irredentist claims and drag Western Europe into a war with the Soviet Union. On French fears, see Policy Statement of Department of State: France, September 20, 1949, *FRUS 1949*, 3:657–58; U.S. Minutes of a Meeting between Presidents Truman and Auriol, *FRUS 1951*, 4:366. On U.S. fears, including concerns that a neutral Germany would play off the West against the Soviet Union, see, for example, Riddleberger to Acheson, April 2, 1949, *FRUS 1949*, 3:233–35; Summary of a Record of a Meeting of United States Ambassadors at Paris [Remarks of High Commis-

sioner John J. McCloy], October 21–22, 1949, *FRUS 1949*, 4:485–86; Paper Prepared in the Department of State, "United States Interests, Positions, and Tactics at Paris," November 5, 1949, *FRUS 1949*, 3:299; Acheson to U.S. Delegation at Tripartite Preparatory Meetings, May 2, 1950, *FRUS 1950*, 3:914. See also Soutou, "France and the Cold War," 43–44.

111. Klaus Schwabe, "The Cold War and European Integration, 1947–63," *Diplomacy and Statecraft* 12, no. 4 (December 2001): 24.

112. Ireland points out that U.S. involvement in Western European economic recovery led, step-by-step, to greater U.S. involvement in European political affairs. "Specifically," he says, "in order to help restore Europe, the United States would have to consider becoming involved in the European balance of power." Ireland, *Creating the Entangling Alliance*, 37.

113. Paper by Kennan, February 7, 1949, *FRUS 1949*, 3:93. See also Paper Prepared by Murphy, March 23, 1949, *FRUS 1949*, 3:122; Acheson to Truman, March 31, 1949 [Annex, Paper Prepared in the Department of State, "U.S. Policy Respecting Germany"], *FRUS 1949*, 3:146. In early 1948, Washington privately was assuring Paris that the United States would guarantee French security against a renewed German threat. See Ireland, *Creating the Entangling Alliance*, 69–72, 91–92. The French and other Western Europeans pressed for a more formal military commitment because the mere presence of U.S. occupation forces in Germany—which Washington unilaterally could withdraw at any time—was deemed an insufficient security guarantee.

114. Paper Prepared in the Department of State, "United States Interests, Positions, and Tactics at Paris," November 5, 1949, *FRUS 1949*, 3:295–96 (emphasis added).

115. During the 1949 Senate hearings on the North Atlantic Treaty's ratification, Truman administration officials made it clear that the treaty was not a response to a perceived Soviet military threat to Western Europe—which Washington believed was deterred by U.S. atomic weapons—or to threats from internal subversion. Rather, it was an instrument for the United States to "strengthen its political ties with, and influence over, Europe through the creation of common military institutions." LaFeber, *America, Russia, and the Cold War*, 83.

116. For arguments that underscore the centrality of the German problem as the driving force behind U.S. and French support of West European integration in the late 1940s and the 1950s, see Geir Lundestad, *"Empire" by Integration* (New York: Oxford University Press, 1998); Schwabe, "Cold War and European Integration."

117. Paper Prepared by Murphy, March 23, 1949, *FRUS 1949*, 3:120.

118. Paper Prepared by Kennan, March 8, 1949, *FRUS 1949*, 3:96 (emphasis added).

119. Acheson believed that Germany would make a "dangerous nationalist turn" unless its "resources and energies can be harnessed to the security and welfare of Western Europe as a whole." Acheson to Bruce, October 19, 1949, *FRUS 1949*, 4:469–70. As Robert Murphy said, a separate, powerful Germany was a danger, and the best approach would be "to try so to integrate the economic and strategic interests of Germany with those of its Western neighbors as to diminish the incentives and opportunities for separate disruptive action." Paper Prepared by Murphy, March 23, 1949, [Annex, Paper Prepared in Department of State n.d.] *FRUS 1949*, 3:132. On the relation between the German problem and Washington's (and Paris's) support for Western European integration, see Schwabe, "Cold War and European Integration."

120. Paper Prepared by Kennan, February 7, 1949, *FRUS 1949*, 3:90–91; Paper Prepared by Murphy, March 23, 1949, *FRUS 1949*, 3:119–20. The Murphy paper is virtually identical to Kennan's.

121. Alan Milward stresses Acheson's role in pushing Paris to take the lead in integrating West Germany into Western Europe economically. Milward, *Reconstruction of Western Europe*, 391–92. See also Hogan, *Marshall Plan*, 378; Leffler, *Preponderance of Power*, 319; Lundestad, *"Empire" by Integration*, 33–35.

122. Draft of Tripartite Declaration, Dunn to Department of State, May 16, 1952, *FRUS 1952–54*, 5:661.

123. Paper Prepared by Kennan, February 7, 1949, *FRUS 1949*, 3:90–91 (emphasis added);

Paper Prepared by Murphy, March 23, 1949, *FRUS 1949*, 3:119–20. As another State Department paper stated, "Without the creation of institutional machinery to ensure that separate national interests are subordinated to the best interests of the community, an adequate means for incorporating Germany will not exist and the objectives with respect to Germany outlined above cannot be attained." Paper Prepared in the Department of State, n.d., *FRUS 1949*, 3:133. Similarly, Leffler says that Washington believed that economic interdependence and supranational institutions were important not only for economic reasons "but also for co-opting German power, establishing the preconditions for German rearmament, and thwarting Soviet preponderance." Leffler, *Preponderance of Power*, 411.

124. Memorandum of a Conversation, June 7, 1955, *FRUS 1955–57*, 4:292. See also Statement by Dulles to the North Atlantic Council, December 14, 1953, *FRUS 1952–54*, 5:461.

125. Minutes of the Seventh Meeting of the Policy Planning Staff, January 24, 1950, *FRUS 1950*, 3:622.

126. Lunestad, *"Empire" by Integration*, 16.

127. As Secretary of State Marshall said, the United States urged Western Europe to take "steps which before the war would have seemed beyond the realm of practical politics." He went on to say, "We intend to encourage publicly and privately the progressively closer integration first of free Europe and eventually of as much of Europe as possible." While paying lip service to the notion that integration should result from the voluntary actions of the Western Europeans rather than being imposed by Washington, U.S. officials acknowledged that "the European governments are unlikely to take the bold and difficult measures essential to accomplish effective integration in the absence of continuing pressure, and assistance, from us." Acting Secretary of State to Harriman, December 3, 1948, *FRUS 1948*, 3:301–2. The United States, the State Department argued, "must . . . constantly seek new ways of guiding France and the other countries of western Europe toward greater economic and political integration." Policy Statement of the Department of State: France, September 20, 1948, 3:659. See also Mee, *Marshall Plan*, 170–73, 186–203; Milward, *Reconstruction of Western Europe*, 81–89.

128. Thus, to solve the Franco-German problem, the European Coal and Steel Community sought to "fuse the two countries in such a way that each would lose its independent power to do harm to the other. They then could cooperate without fearing that what benefited one invariably threatened the other." David Calleo, *Europe's Future: The Grand Alternatives* (New York: Norton, 1967), 48.

129. Acheson to Bruce, October 19, 1949, *FRUS 1949*, 4:471.

130. For representative warnings about European "disunity," see Minutes of the Seventh Meeting of the Policy Planning Staff, January 24, 1950, *FRUS 1950*, 3:620; Luce to Department of State, May 4, 1954, *FRUS 1952–54*, 5:954. In 1948, John Foster Dulles argued that the Marshall Plan should be directed to "the end of ultimate union or fusion among the West European countries. He emphasized that *any attempt to freeze the West European countries in their old habits of thought, association, and economy would be futile and, in his opinion, against our national interests.*" Memorandum of a Conversation by Lovett, April 27, 1948, *FRUS 1948*, 3:106 (emphasis added).

131. Dulles Remarks at Press Conference, December 14, 1953, *FRUS 1952–1954*, 5:468.

132. Paper Prepared by Kennan, February 7, 1949, *FRUS 1949*, 3:92. De-nationalizing the Western European states' defense policies was a clear goal of the Truman administration's 1949 Mutual Defense Assistance bill, which provided the Western Europeans with military aid. The administration acknowledged that the program's key goals were to get the West Europeans to pool "their industrial and manpower resources" and to subordinate their "nationalistic tendencies." Quoted in LaFeber, *America, Russia, and the Cold War*, 84.

133. Paper Prepared by Kennan, *FRUS* 1949, 3:92.(emphasis added)

134. Referring to NATO and the ECSC, Secretary of State John Foster Dulles observed, "These represent important unifying efforts, but it cannot be confidently affirmed that these organizations are clearly adequate to ensure against a tragic repetition of the past where the Atlantic community, and particularly Western Europe, has been torn apart by in-

ternecine struggles." U.S. Delegation at North Atlantic Council Ministerial Meeting to Department of State, May 5, 1956, *FRUS 1955–57*, 4:68–69.

135. Policy Statement of the Department of State, September 20, 1948, *FRUS 1948*, 3:652–53. Secretary of State Acheson stated that the aim of integration was to bring about a "radical change" in the political and economic relations of the Western European states. Acheson to Bruce, October 19, 1949, *FRUS 1949*, 4:471.

136. Paper Prepared in the Department of State, n.d., *FRUS 1949*, 3:133; Matthews to Burns, August 16, 1950 [Enclosure, "Establishment of a European Defense Force—Estimate of the Situation] *FRUS 1950*, 3:213. Washington believed that the EDC offered a "unique opportunity" to attain the "ancient Eur[opean] dream of unity." Taking advantage of this opportunity held the "promise of a new era of peace, strength, and prosperity for opening up for Eur[ope]" and the prospect that the "jealousies and rivalries which have caused so many wars can be controlled at long last." Acheson to McCloy, April 12, 1952, *FRUS 1952–54*, 3:205.

137. Acheson to Bruce, June 28, 1951, *FRUS 1951*, 3:802; Bruce to Acheson, July 3, 1951, *FRUS 1951:* 3:805–6.

138. Lundestad claims that "the need to integrate Germany with Western Europe in general and with France in particular" was the single most important motive underlying post–World War II U.S. support for Western European integration. Lundestad, *"Empire" by Integration*, 22.

139. The office of the U.S. High Commissioner in Germany noted that because of Germany's rapid economic recovery, there was an "ever greater imbalance in the power relationship between Ger[many] and France"—an imbalance that endangered American plans for Western European integration. Donnelly to Department of State, August 28, 1952, *FRUS 1952–54*, 7:355–56.

140. McBride Minutes [of US-UK-FR foreign ministers meeting in Washington, D.C.], July 11, 1953, *FRUS 1952–54*, 5:1622–23 (emphasis added).

141. Dulles Remarks at Press Conference, December 14, 1953, *FRUS 1952–54*, 5:468 (emphasis added). On another occasion, Dulles said, "The problem in Europe has been the recurrent conflicts between France and Germany leading to recurrent wars. Unless these conflicts are buried, difficulties between them are apt to reappear." Memorandum of Discussion of State—MSA—JCS Meeting, January 28, 1953, *FRUS 1952–54*, 5:712.

142. Although Eisenhower often pointed to the Soviet threat as a reason to push forward with the EDC, Western European integration, and NATO as means of reconciling France and Germany, Dulles noted that there "were other powerful reasons that impelled us in the same direction." Memorandum of Conversation by Vernon Walters, Eisenhower-Laniel Meeting, December 5, 1953, *FRUS 1952–54*, 5:1771. On another occasion, Dulles stressed that Western European integration—including the EDC—promoted long-term U.S. interests that existed independently of the cold war. See Trulock Minutes, Third Tripartite Foreign Ministers Meeting, July 15, 1954, *FRUS 1952–54*, 5:1661–62.

143. Memorandum by Fuller to Nitze, September 4, 1952, *FRUS 1952–54*, 7:357–61.

144. Report by the North Atlantic Military Committee, D/MC-D/2, December 12, 1950, *FRUS 1950*, 3:542–43. As the North Atlantic Military Committee stated, the three bulwarks against German aggression were the Ruhr's vulnerability to air attack, NATO's maintenance of military forces greater than Germany's, and Allied forces in Germany.

145. The French defense minister, Jules Moch, categorically declared that France would not accept German rearmament if it led to the establishment of a German army on "a national basis." Bruce to Acheson, August 1, 1950. *FRUS 3*:172.

146. Memorandum by Acheson on a Meeting with the President, July 31, 1950, *FRUS 1950*, 3:167–68.

147. Memorandum of Conversation, September 12, 1950, *FRUS 1950*, 3:287.

148. Matthews to Burns, August 16, 1950, *FRUS 1950*, 3:214–16; Memorandum of Conversation, September 12, 1950, *FRUS 1950*, 3:287; Acheson to Bruce, October 17, 1950, *FRUS 1950*, 3:385.

149. U.S. Delegation at North Atlantic Council Meeting to Department of State, April 24, 1953, *FRUS 1952–54*, 5:375. McCloy endorsed the EDC because "at one step it would fully

integrate Germany into Western Europe and be the best possible insurance against German aggression." McCloy to Acheson, August 3, 1950, *FRUS 1950*, 3:181.

150. Dulles was an especially ardent champion of a federal approach to European integration. He believed the United States could "only make Europe a permanently secure place by merging significant government functions, including French and German, into supranational institutions." Quoted in Kevin Ruane, "Agonizing Reappraisals: Anthony Eden, John Foster Dulles and the Crisis of European Defence, 1953–54," *Diplomacy and Statecraft* 13, no. 4 (December 2002): 167.

151. Ibid., 155. According to Klaus Schwabe, "Of all the projects for European integration there was none with which the United States under Truman and his successor Eisenhower identified more closely than the EDC." It was seen as the only way to develop a Western deterrent in Europe while keeping Germany down and the Soviet Union out. "In the long run it promised the founding of a European Federal Union closely allied with the United States." Schwabe, "Cold War and European Integration," 26.

152. Memorandum by Fuller to Nitze, September 4, 1952, *FRUS 1952–54*, 7:360–61.

153. For the Anglo-American diplomacy over the EDC that climaxed with adoption of the Eden proposals, see Ruane, "Agonizing Reappraisals." Under the terms of the agreement, West Germany simultaneously was admitted to full membership in the Brussels treaty (renamed the Western European Union) and in NATO. Bonn voluntarily agreed to limit its army to a maximum of twelve divisions, and to forgo the production of strategic bombers, guided missiles, warships of over three thousand tons, and weapons of mass destruction (nuclear, chemical, biological). To secure French assent to the Eden proposals, Britain also pledged to maintain four divisions on the Continent and not to withdraw them without the consent of a majority of the Brussels treaty's membership.

154. Memorandum by Fuller to Nitze, September 4, 1952, *FRUS 1952–54*, 7:360 (emphasis added).

155. Matthews to Burns, August 8, 1950, *FRUS 1950*, 3:213.

156. For example, Acheson said that he would not want international forces in Europe to be replaced by national ones, especially German. Acheson to Bruce, June 28, 1951, *FRUS 1951*, 3:802. Dulles noted that a strong SACEUR "will minimize the possibility of individual nations exercising an independent military initiative in Europe." Dulles to Eisenhower, November 12, 1954, *FRUS 1952–54*, 5:1475. The SACEUR, Gen. Alfred Gruenther, told Dulles that it was "impossible for any single member nation to use its armed forces in Europe for nationalistic adventures. This effectively abolishes the danger, for example, of a revived German General Staff going off on its own." Memorandum of Discussion at 216th Meeting of the NSC, October 6, 1954, *FRUS 1952–54*, 5:1381; Dulles to Eisenhower, September 28, 1954, *FRUS 1952–54*, 5:1293.

157. See Bruce to Acheson, July 3, 1951, *FRUS 1951*, 3:805–6; Acheson to Bruce, June 28, 1951, *FRUS 1951*, 3:802.

158. Statement by Dulles to North Atlantic Council, December 14, 1953, *FRUS 1952–54*, 5:463.

159. For the argument that Dulles was bluffing, see Ruane, "Agonizing Reappraisals." Although the Eisenhower administration hoped that *eventually* some U.S. troops could be brought back from Western Europe, there was no chance the United States would follow through on Dulles's threat, because, as Ruane puts it (177), "the American government had no intention of wholesale withdrawal, still less of leaving a vacuum at the heart of European defence." The question of whether Eisenhower really intended to withdraw U.S. forces from Western Europe is treated in more detail in the conclusion of this book.

160. During the Truman administration, Acheson acknowledged that even if the EDC plan was successful, the United States would need to stay in Western Europe as a hedge against any Western European state seceding from the EDC. Acheson understood, however, that Washington had to spin its policy in this regard—which was intended primarily to reassure the French—so it would not *appear* to be directed solely at Germany. See Memorandum of Conversation by Penfield, February 17, 1952, *FRUS 1952–54*, 5:53–54; Acheson to Truman, February 16, 1952, *FRUS*, 5:78–79. In 1953–54, the Eisenhower administration also rejected the idea of bringing U.S. troops home from Europe, because doing so

would cause the French to reject the EDC, and also because the Western Europeans would fear they would be "left either to the mercy of the Soviets or to *internecine strife.*" Bonbright to Murphy, February 1, 1954, *FRUS 1952–54,* 5:482 (emphasis added). See also Murphy to Bonbright, February 10, 1954, *FRUS 1952–54,* 5:484; Memorandum of a Discussion of the 174th Meeting of the National Security Council, December 10, 1953, *FRUS* 1952–54, 5:450–51 [Comments of President Eisenhower].

161. Publicly, however, the United States needed to take the position that "our troops are not in Europe to police the obligations of our friends but to prevent aggression from without," because, Acheson said, "any suggestion to the contrary would be most disadvantageous." Acheson to Truman, February 16, 1952, *FRUS 1952–54, 5*:78–79.

162. Acheson to Bruce, September 19, 1952, *FRUS 1952–54,* 5:324.

163. As one senior U.S. official insightfully observed, "astute Soviet moves toward relaxation of East-West tension might at some time create very strong pressures at home for withdrawal of US participation in collective defense effort." Spofford to Acheson, January 8, 1951, *FRUS 1951,* 3:821–22.

164. Hughes to Department of State, June 29, 1953, *FRUS 1952–54,* 5:420.

165. Ibid.

5. The Containment of Europe

1. My definition of balancing is based on Robert Art's. See Robert J. Art, "Europe Hedges Its Security Bets," in *Balance of Power: Theory and Practice in the Twenty-first Century,* ed. T. V. Paul, James J. Wirtz, and Michel Fortmann (Stanford: Stanford University Press, 2004), 179–80. For discussion of how to define counterhegemonic balancing, see chapter 7.

2. For example, see D. C. Watt, "Perceptions of the United States in Europe, 1945–1983," in *The Troubled Alliance: Atlantic Relations in the 1980s,* ed. Lawrence Freedman (New York: St. Martin's, 1983), 28–43. Watt points out that since 1945 the Western Europeans have viewed the United States as an adversary as well as an ally.

3. Arthur A. Stein, "The Hegemon's Dilemma: Great Britain, the United States, and the International Economic Order," *International Organization* 38, no. 2 (Spring 1984): 355–86.

4. Stein defines the hegemon's dilemma:

> A hegemonic power's decision to enrich itself is also a decision to enrich others more than itself. Over time, such policies will come at the expense of the hegemon's relative standing and will bring forth challengers. Yet choosing to sustain its relative standing . . . is a choice to keep others impoverished at the cost of increasing its own wealth. Maintaining its relative position has obvious costs not only to others but to itself. Alternatively, maximizing its absolute wealth has obvious benefits but brings even greater ones to others. (Arthur A. Stein, *Why Nations Cooperate: Circumstance and Choice in International Relations* [Ithaca: Cornell University Press, 1990], 139)

5. Frank Costigliola, "The Pursuit of Atlantic Community: Nuclear Arms, Dollars, and Berlin," in *Kennedy's Quest for Victory: American Foreign Policy, 1961–1963,* ed. Thomas G. Paterson (New York: Oxford University Press, 1989), 25.

6. Francois Duchene points out that in the early postwar years, when American statesmen spoke of Western European integration or "unity" they "mostly meant free trade throughout western Europe." Francois Duchene, *Jean Monnet: The First Statesman of Interdependence* (New York: W. W. Norton), 185.

7. Thus, for example, although Secretary of State Dean Acheson was a strong supporter of Western European economic integration, he was, as Douglas Brinkley understatedly comments, "somewhat more reticent on the issue of political unification." Douglas Brinkley, "Dean Acheson and European Unity," in *NATO: The Founding of the Atlantic Alliance and the Integration of Europe,* ed. Francis H. Heller and John R. Gillingham (New York: St. Martin's, 1992), 130.

8. Asked to explain U.S. support for Western European unity, McGeorge Bundy, national security advisor during the Kennedy administration, acknowledged that "great states do not usually rejoice in the emergence of other great powers." However, he pointed to "the current contest with the Soviet Union" as the reason the United States could encourage

with equanimity the emergence of a united Western Europe. Quoted in Geir Lundestad, *"Empire" by Integration: The United States and European Integration* (New York: Oxford University Press, 1998), 22.

9. As Lundestad observes, U.S. policymakers use the term "Atlantic Community" as "a code phrase for overall American leadership." Ibid., 40.

10. Quoted in Walter LaFeber, *America, Russia, and the Cold War, 1945–1996*, 8th ed. (New York: McGraw-Hill, 1997), 83.

11. Paper Prepared by the Policy Planning Staff, "The Current Position in the Cold War," April 14, 1950, *FRUS 1950*, 3:859.

12. Acheson to Certain Diplomatic Offices, January 29, 1951, *FRUS 1951*, 3:761. Acheson believed that "unity in Europe requires the continuing association and support of the United States." Without U.S. involvement on the Continent, Acheson said, Western Europe would "split apart" and presumably slide into its bad old habits of realpolitik. Quoted in Brinkley, "Acheson and European Unity," 140.

13. David Calleo, *Europe's Future: The Grand Alternatives* (New York: W. W. Norton, 1967), 139.

14. Acheson and Lovett to Truman, July 30, 1951, *FRUS 1951*, 3:850 (emphasis added). Similarly, Lewis Douglas, the influential U.S ambassador to London, reacted to the Schuman Plan by stating that "it is important that the plan not be used as a vehicle: To underwrite the economic base of a 'third force'. . . . The greatest safeguard we have against the perversion of the plan in a 'third force' direction rests in the existence of NAT itself." Douglas to Acheson, June 6, 1950, *FRUS 1950*, 3:722.

15. Acheson to Bruce, September 19, 1952, *FRUS 1952–54*, 5:324 (emphasis added).

16. William I. Hitchcock, "Reversal of Fortune: Britain, France, and the Making of Europe, 1945–1956," in *From War to Peace: Altered Strategic Landscapes in the Twentieth Century*, ed. Paul Kennedy and William I. Hitchcock (New Haven: Yale University Press, 2000), 100–101. Similarly, Lundestad argues that "particularly in France, the Suez humiliation magnified support for European integration, in part to make it easier for France and Europe to stand up even to the U.S." Lundestad, *"Empire" by Integration*, 135.

17. Lundestad, *"Empire" by Integration*, 135.

18. Duchene, *Jean Monnet*, 186–87. LaFeber points out that the creation of the Common Market on 1 January 1959 (pursuant to the 1957 Treaty of Rome) had *political* as well as economic consequences for the transatlantic relationship. The Common Market, he says, was Western Europe's first step toward achieving political unification and toward creating a "middle bloc between the United States and the Soviet Union." LaFeber, *America, Russia, and the Cold War*, 201.

19. Frederic Bozo, *Two Strategies for Europe: De Gaulle, the United States, and the Atlantic Alliance*, trans. Susan Emanuel (Lanham, Md.: Rowman and Littlefield, 2001), xiv, 59. For discussion of the clashing grand designs for Europe of de Gaulle and Kennedy, also see Pascaline Winand, *Eisenhower, Kennedy, and the United States of Europe* (New York: St. Martin's, 1993), 245–64.

20. Bozo, *Two Strategies for Europe*, 60.

21. De Gaulle expressed his doubts about the U.S. nuclear guarantee during President Kennedy's June 1961 visit to Paris. Memorandum of Conversation, June 1, 1961, *FRUS 1961–63*, 13:310–12, 315. Briefing members of Congress about the Paris talks, Kennedy cut to the heart of the Alliance's strategic crisis: "The whole position in Europe has changed since NATO was founded. Then there was a nuclear monopoly, now there is a nuclear balance. The United States could say that it was prepared to act by trading New York for Paris, but would we really do so?" Memorandum of Conversation with the President and the Congressional Leadership, June 6, 1961, *FRUS 1961–63*, 13:668. The literature on nuclear strategy, including the problem of extended deterrence in NATO, is voluminous. An excellent overview is Lawrence Freedman, *The Evolution of Nuclear Strategy* (London: Macmillan, 1989). See also David N. Schwartz, *NATO's Nuclear Dilemmas* (Washington, D.C.: Brookings Institution, 1983); Jane E. Stromseth, *The Origins of Flexible Response: NATO's Debate over Strategy in the 1960s* (London: Macmillan, 1988). For contemporaneous views of French nuclear strategists, see Andre Beaufre, *Deterrence and Strategy*, trans. R. H.

Barry (New York: Praeger, 1966); Pierre Gallois, *The Balance of Terror: Strategy for the Nuclear Age*, trans. Richard Howard (Boston: Houghton Mifflin, 1961).

22. Quoted in Edward A. Kolodziej, *French International Policy under De Gaulle and Pompidou: The Politics of Grandeur* (Ithaca: Cornell University Press, 1974), 91.
23. Ibid., 90–91. Similarly, LaFeber observes that de Gaulle "feared unchecked American military and economic power, believing that, because the United States would use the power unilaterally and irresponsibly, the French could suffer annihilation without representation." LaFeber, *America, Russia, and the Cold War*, 227.
24. Bozo, *Two Strategies for Europe*, 80.
25. The Fouchet Plan was a clear break with the supranationalist approach to integration that had underlain both the European Coal and Steel Community and the EEC. The EEC's smaller members rejected it, because they feared it was a vehicle for establishing French (or Franco-German) hegemony over Western Europe. See Bozo, *Two Strategies for Europe*, 78–79; Desmond Dinan, *Ever Closer Union: An Introduction to European Integration*, 2nd ed. (Boulder, Colo.: Lynne Rienner, 1999), 43; Jeffrey Glen Giauque, *Grand Designs and Visions of Unity: The Atlantic Powers and the Reorganization of Western Europe, 1955–1963* (Chapel Hill: University of North Carolina Press, 2002), 126–57.
26. On the American Grand Design, see Bozo, *Two Strategies for Europe*, 60–62; David DiLeo, "George Ball and the Europeanists in the State Department, 1961–1963," in *John F. Kennedy and Europe*, ed. Douglas Brinkley and Richard T. Griffiths (Baton Rouge: Louisiana University Press, 1999), 263–80; Giauque, *Grand Designs and Visions of Unity*, 98–125.
27. Bozo, *Two Strategies for Europe*, 61.
28. Costigliola, "Pursuit of Atlantic Community," 25.
29. Bozo, *Two Strategies for Europe*, 78.
30. As Pascaline Winand observes:

> Since World II, one of the main reasons for United States support for European integration had been the desire to prevent the specter of nationalism from reemerging on the Continent. Very much a part of the tradition that had evolved since the war, the Europeanists in the Kennedy administration hailed the obsolescence of the nation-state as a positive development on the European scene. Some among them hoped it would facilitate the benevolent leadership of the United States in Europe, which would be made easier by the absence of contenders for European hegemony. (*United States of Europe*, 246)

31. Embassy in Germany to Dept. of State, April 17, 1966, *FRUS 1964–68*, 13:367.
32. Embassy in France to Department of State, February 3, 1963, *FRUS 1961–63*, 13:171.
33. Memorandum from Ball to President Kennedy, June 20, 1963, *FRUS 1961–63*, 13:205.
34. Ibid., 205–13. The U.S. ambassador to Bonn made clear the kind of Western Europe Washington supported was one under its aegis: "The US had consistently supported European unity efforts which will enable Europe to play its true role in an Atlantic partnership, contribute to an effective NATO, be open to other eligible countries and not diminish the progress made in the Community." Embassy in Germany to the Department of State, January 15, 1965, *FRUS 1964–68*, 13:176
35. Bozo, *Two Strategies for Europe*, 61.
36. Remarks of President Kennedy to the National Security Council, January 22, 1963, *FRUS 1961–63*, 13:486.
37. Bozo, *Two Strategies for Europe*, 81.
38. Department of State to Embassy in United Kingdom, March 14, 1963, *FRUS 1961–63*, 13:527–28.
39. Memorandum of Conversation, May 28, 1962, *FRUS 1961–63*, 13:709.
40. Memorandum of Meeting, May 11, 1962, *FRUS 1961–63*, 13:697.
41. Embassy in France to Department of State, February 3, 1963, *FRUS 1961–63*, 13:171. As Bozo explains, U.S. officials favored Monnet's supranational approach to European unity rather than the Gaullist Fouchet Plan, because they "hoped that by attenuating the unfavorable effects of European 'nationalisms,' it would reduce the capacity of the Six to be an obstacle to U.S. influence." Bozo, *Two Strategies for Europe*, 81.

42. Department of State to the Embassy in Germany, February 2, 1966, *FRUS 1964–68*, 13:308–9.
43. On the background to the Franco-German treaty, see Bozo, *Two Strategies for Europe*, 83–84; Giauque, *Grand Designs and Visions of Unity*, 77–97, 196–223.
44. During their November 14, 1962 meeting, when Kennedy urged West Germany to provide more troops for NATO's conventional defense, Adenauer countered with the need to equip the Bundeswehr with its own tactical nuclear weapons. Memorandum of Conversation, November 14, 1962, *FRUS 1961–63*, 13:452–53. See also Lawrence Freedman, *Kennedy's Wars: Berlin, Cuba, Laos, and Vietnam* (New York: Oxford University Press, 2000), 92–111; Stromseth, *Origins of Flexible Response*, chap. 7.
45. On this aspect of the Berlin Crisis, see Freedman, *Kennedy's Wars*, 75–89; Marc Trachtenberg, *A Constructed Peace: The Making of the European Settlement, 1945–1963* (Princeton: Princeton University Press, 1999), 324–30, 339–51; Thomas Alan Schwartz, "Victories and Defeats in the Long Twilight Struggle: The United States and Western Europe in the 1960s," in *The Diplomacy of the Crucial Decade: American Foreign Relations during the 1960s*, ed. Diane B. Kunz (New York: Columbia University Press, 1994), 124–27; Costigliola, "Pursuit of Atlantic Community," 40–43.
46. Summary Record of NSC Executive Committee Meeting No. 39, January 31, 1963, *FRUS 1961–63*, 13:62–63.
47. Bozo describes these U.S. efforts against the Franco-German treaty as "orchestrating a vast maneuver aiming to annul its effects." Bozo, *Two Strategies for Europe*, 105.
48. Ibid. The United States made clear to Bonn and Paris that it would "take a very serious view" of any secret understandings pursuant to the treaty about Franco-German collaboration in the development of nuclear weapons. Memorandum from Rusk to Kennedy, February 26, 1963, JFKL, POF 117a, German Security (January 1963 to March 1963).
49. Summary Record of NSC Executive Committee Meeting No. 40, February 5, 1963, *FRUS 1961–63*, 13:175.
50. Trachtenberg, *Constructed Peace*, 375–76.
51. Ibid., 376.
52. Rusk to the Embassy in France, May 18, 1963, *FRUS 1961–63*, 13:704; Memorandum of Conversation, March 22, 1963, *FRUS 1961–63*, 13:191; Memorandum of Conversation, February 5, 1963, *FRUS 1961–63*, 13:182–87. U.S. talking points for German foreign minister von Brentano's March 1963 visit to Washington stressed that "we . . . should leave von Bretano with no illusions about our views on a bilateral Franco-German relationship which might be divisive in NATO and form the basis for a closed, autarchic Continental system." Talking Points, n.d., JFKL, POF 117a, German Security (January 1963 to March 1963).
53. Trachtenberg, *Constructed Peace*, 377. See also Roger Morgan, "Kennedy and Adenauer," in Brinklet and Griffiths, *John F. Kennedy and Europe*, 27.
54. On the MLF, see Bozo, *Two Strategies for Europe*, 110–13, 117–21; Lundestad, *"Empire" by Integration*, 73–78; Trachtenberg, *Constructed Peace*, 312–15, 365–68; Lawrence F. Kaplan, "The MLF Debate," in Brinkley and Griffiths, *John F. Kennedy and Europe*, 51–65; Schwartz, "United States and Western Europe," 129–36.
55. Memorandum from McGeorge Bundy to Kennedy, "The United States and De Gaulle—The Past and the Future," January 30, 1963, JFKL, NSF 216a, MLF Gen. (July 1962 to December 1962), 8.
56. Memorandum from Ball to Kennedy, "Answer to Eight Questions," June 17, 1962, JFKL, NSF 226, Answer to Question 7. *After* noting the adverse impact a nuclear Germany would have on European integration and the Atlantic Community, Ball also said that it would undermine Washington's efforts to stabilize East-West relations. On U.S. fears that the French and British nuclear forces would serve to catalyze West Germany's emergence as a nuclear power, see Bozo, *Two Strategies for Europe*, 62–63. See also Trachtenberg, *Constructed Peace*, 336–42, 344–45, 356–77.
57. Dean Acheson's March 1961 report on U.S. policy toward NATO set the tone with respect to the Washington's views on European national nuclear forces. He labeled (44) such forces "a wasteful, divisive, and dangerous proliferation of national nuclear capabilities."

He further warned that if Germany acquired a national nuclear force "it would strain NATO cohesion—possibly to the breaking point." "A Review of North Atlantic Problems for the Future" ("Acheson report"), March 1961, JFKL, NSF 220.

58. After the French nuclear force had become a reality, and de Gaulle had passed from the scene, the United States did lend assistance to the French nuclear program. See Richard H. Ullman, "The Covert French Connection," *Foreign Policy* 75 (Summer 1989): 3–33.

59. Winand, *United States of Europe*, 227.

60. On both points discussed in this paragraph, see Memorandum, "Nuclear Sharing and MRBMs", February 9, 1962, JFKL, NSF 216a, MLF-General (January 1961 to June 1962), 12.

61. Ball to Kennedy, "Answer to 8 Questions," Answer to Question 1, 4.

62. Record of the 508th Meeting of the NSC, January 22, 1963, *FRUS 1961–63*, 8:458–60. This quote was attributed to Kennedy in a memorandum for the record written by General Maxwell D. Taylor, who was present at the meeting. Ibid, 459 n. 4.

63. Winand, *United States of Europe*, 243.

64. Memorandum from McGeorge Bundy to Kennedy, "Action on Nuclear Assistance to France," May 7, 1962, JFKL, PDF 116a, France-Security 1962, 8.

65. Memorandum of Conversation, November 12, 1965, *FRUS 1964–68*, 13:266.

66. Memorandum of Conversation, April 20, 1965, *FRUS 1964–68*, 13:199.

67. Memorandum of Conversation, February 6, 1961, *FRUS 1961–63*, 13:1–2. Rusk underscored that even if cold war tensions abated, NATO would still need to stay in business, hence it was important not to think of NATO simply as an instrument of containment: "We must, of course, be careful to combat the impression that NATO is merely a military alliance, that its hour of need has passed, and that the defense of NATO is simply a defense of the status quo." Department of State to Embassy in Germany, May 23, 1966, *FRUS 1964–68*, 13:399.

68. Talking Paper Prepared in the Department of Defense, undated, *FRUS 1964–68*, 13:728.

69. Ibid.

70. Letter from Rusk to Senator Mansfield, April 21, 1967, *FRUS 1964–68*, 13:562.

71. Memorandum by the Acheson Group, undated, *FRUS 1964–68*, 13:406–7.

72. For neorealist predictions, see John J. Mearsheimer, *The Tragedy of Great Power Politics* (New York: W. W. Norton, 2001), 384–92; Mearsheimer, "The Future of America's Continental Commitment," in *No End to Alliance: The United States and Western Europe: Past, Present, and Future*, ed. Geir Lundestad (New York: St. Martin's, 1998), 221–42; Stephen M. Walt, "The Ties That Fray: Why Europe and America Are Drifting Apart," *National Interest*, no. 54 (Winter 1998–99): 3–11. On the other hand, neoliberal institutionalists profess not to be the least bit surprised that NATO has outlived the cold war. See Celeste A. Wallender, "NATO after the Cold War," *International Organization* 54, no. 4 (Autumn 2000): 705–36.

73. John J. Mearsheimer, *The Tragedy of Great Power Politics* (New York: W. W. Norton, 2001), 390.

74. Ibid., 390–92. Mearsheimer claims that the United States intervenes militarily in Europe (and East Asia) *only* for counterhegemonic reasons. John Mearsheimer, "The Future of America's Continental Commitment," in *No End to Alliance—The United States and Western Europe: Past, Present, and Future*, ed. Geir Lundestad (New York: St. Martin's, 1998), 221–24. Therefore, barring the unlikely emergence of Germany or Russia as contenders for regional hegemony, "the United States will probably bring its troops home" from Europe "in the first decade of so of the new century." Mearsheimer, *Tragedy of Great Power Politics*, 387.

75. In making his case that the United States is an offshore balancer, Mearsheimer contends that before 1990 there is "hardly any evidence" that the Untied States has been willing to commit troops to Europe to maintain regional stability. "American armies," he says, "were sent there to prevent the rise of peer competitors, not to maintain peace." Mearsheimer, *Tragedy of Great Power Politics*, 389.

76. For example, see Robert E. Hunter, "Starting at Zero: U.S. Foreign Policy for the 1990s," *Washington Quarterly* 15, no. 1 (Winter 1992): 27–42; William G. Hyland, "The Case for Pragmatism," *Foreign Affairs: America and the World 1991/92* 71, no. 2 (1991–92): 38–52; Michael Mandelbaum, "The Bush Foreign Policy," *Foreign Affairs: America and the World*

1990/91 70, no. 1 (1990–91): 4–22; Charles William Maynes, "America without the Cold War," *Foreign Policy* 78 (Spring 1990): 3–25.

77. For example, see James Chace, *The Consequences of the Peace: The New Internationalism and American Foreign Policy* (New York: Oxford University Press, 1992); John Lewis Gaddis, "Toward the Post–Cold War World," *Foreign Affairs* 70, no. 2 (Spring 1991): 102–22; Joseph S. Nye Jr., "What New World Order?" *Foreign Affairs* 71, no. 2 (Spring 1992): 95; Gregory F. Treverton, "The New Europe," *Foreign Affairs: America and the World 1991/92* 71, no. 2 (1991–92): 94–112.

78. Ostpolitik's architects were Willy Brandt—during his term as foreign minister in the Christian Democratic/Social Democratic "Grand Coalition" (1966–69) and during his ensuing chancellorship—and his adviser Egon Bahr. Ostpolitik involved four sequential steps that ultimately would culminate in the withdrawal of both superpowers from Central Europe and the dissolution of their respective alliance systems. This would clear the path for German reunification by prying Germany free from the viselike grip of *both* superpowers. See Walter F. Hahn, "West Germany's Ostpolitik: The Grand Design of Egon Bahr," *Orbis* 16, no. 1 (Winter 1973): 859–80. On West Germany's geopolitical options and their fundamental continuity with those of Germany from 1871 to 1939, see David Calleo, *The German Problem Reconsidered: Germany and the World Order, 1870 to the Present* (Cambridge: Cambridge University Press, 1978). For contemporary analyses of Ostpolitik, see William Griffiths, *The Ostpolitik of the Federal Republic of Germany* (Cambridge: Cambridge University Press, 1978), and Lawrence L. Whetten, *Germany's Ostpolitik: Relations between the Federal Republic and the Warsaw Pact* (New York: Oxford University Press, 1974).

79. See A. W. DePorte, *Europe between the Superpowers: The Enduring Balance* (New Haven: Yale University Press, 1979).

80. "Current Issues of European Security," August 12, 1970, NA, RG 273, NSSM-83. The copy of this document in the archives is not paginated. The remaining quotations in this paragraph are from this document.

81. Ibid.

82. "U.S. Strategies and Forces for NATO (U)," NSSM-84, n.d., NA, RG 273, NSSM 84.

83. Ibid., 22.

84. Ibid. (emphasis added).

85. Ibid., 23.

86. Karsten Voigt, "The Function of Defense Alliances in the Future," address to the "NATO at 40" conference, Cato Institute, Washington, D.C., April 4, 1989.

87. In U.S. foreign policy circles, George F. Kennan was the leading advocate of this view. See PPS 43, "Considerations Affecting the Conclusion of a North Atlantic Security Pact," November 23, 1948, in Thomas H. Etzold and John Lewis Gaddis, eds., *Containment: Documents on American Policy and Strategy, 1945–1950* (New York: Columbia University Press, 1978), 157. Out of office, Kennan revived this idea in 1958. George F. Kennan, "A Chance to Withdraw Our Troops in Europe," *Harper's* 216, no. 1293 (February 1958): 34–41.

88. As Defense Secretary Dick Cheney said, "America should continue to anchor its strategy to the still-valid doctrines of deterrence, flexible response, forward defense, security alliances. . . . Even the extraordinary events of 1989 do not mean that America should abandon this strategic foundation." "Statement of Secretary of Defense Dick Cheney," Senate Budget Committee, February 5, 1990, 3.

89. The American foreign policy community came to believe that U.S. interests in Europe were best furthered by the Yalta system of a divided Continent and a divided Germany. See DePorte, *Europe between the Superpowers.*

90. Quoted in LaFeber, *America, Russia, and the Cold War,* 338.

91. Philip Zelikow and Condoleezza Rice, *Germany Unified and Europe Transformed: A Study in Statecraft* (Cambridge: Harvard University Press, 1995), 169–70 (emphasis added).

92. George Bush and Brent Scowcroft, *A World Transformed: The Collapse of The Soviet Empire, the Unification of Germany, Tiananmen Square, the Gulf War* (New York: Knopf, 1998), 230–31 (emphasis added).

93. As Ronald Asmus comments, the Clinton administration "wanted to update and modernize NATO to assume new roles that the American public could relate to and support,

thereby ensuring its future relevance." Ronald D. Asmus, *Opening NATO's Door: How the Alliance Remade Itself for a New Era* (New York: Columbia University Press, 2002), 25. Throughout his book, Asmus reiterates (118–19, 124–25, 132, 178–79, 260–61, 290–91) that Clinton administration officials were deeply concerned with keeping NATO "relevant" in order to preserve America's position as the major player in European security. See also Richard Holbrooke, "America, a European Power," *Foreign Affairs* 74, no. 2 (March–April 1995): 38–51.

94. Asmus, *Opening NATO's Door,* 178. As Albright said, the United States had a window of opportunity to "recast the foundation of the Alliance. . . . If we get it right, NATO will last for another fifty years. . . . If we don't, the U.S. and Europe are likely to slowly drift apart and the Alliance will atrophy." Quoted in ibid., 178–79.

95. Ibid., 261.

96. Ibid., 290.

97. Bush and Scowcroft, *World Transformed,* 188. Former President Bush, who, before November 1989 was probably the senior U.S. policymaker most willing to entertain the possibility of German reunification, has made clear that his support for that outcome was rather tepid. Ibid., 187–88.

98. Zelikow and Rice make clear that the Bush I administration was determined to use NATO to contain a reunified Germany: "Germany would continue to rely on NATO for protection. . . . The Germans would thus forego pursuit of a purely national defense, including the development of their own nuclear weapons." Zelikow and Rice, *Germany Unified and Europe Transformed,* 169–70.

99. U.S. fears that Bonn and Moscow would cut a separate reunification deal were fanned by Chancellor Helmut Kohl's December 1989 "ten point" reunification plan and by Foreign Minister Dietrich Genscher's January 1990 speech at Tautzig on "German Unity in a European Framework." Commenting on Kohl's silence about a reunified Germany's ties to NATO, Scowcroft said that a Germany outside NATO would "gut the Alliance." Bush and Scowcroft, *World Transformed,* 196–97. In December 1989, Washington made Germany's full membership in NATO the prerequisite of reunification. Bush communicated this to Kohl during their February 1990 Camp David meeting. Ibid., 113, 133, 147, 172–73, 211. With respect to the role of the Two Plus Four talks in ensuring U.S. interests, Baker observes that "without such a process, the odds of the Germans and the Soviets going it alone and cutting a private deal disadvantageous to Western interests (as they had with the agreements of Brest-Litovsk in 1918, Rapallo in 1922, and the Molotov-Ribbentrop accord in 1939) would increase." James A. Baker III, *The Politics of Diplomacy: Revolution, War, and Peace, 1989–1992* (New York: G. P. Putnam's Sons, 1995), 198–99.

100. As Baker told Gorbachev in May 1990, "if Germany was not anchored to the existing security institution [NATO], then we would have a powerful new entity in Europe concerned about developing its [own] security measures." Baker, *Politics of Diplomacy,* 273.

101. Bush and Scowcroft, *World Transformed,* 205; Zelikow and Rice, *Germany Unified and Europe Transformed,* 197. Gorbachev understood fully the nature of U.S. objectives. As he told Baker in May 1990, "Sometimes I have the sense that you want an edge, you may seek an advantage [on Germany and NATO] . . . that's going to mean a very serious development in the strategic balance." Baker, *Politics of Diplomacy,* 248–49.

102. Zelikow and Rice, *Germany Unified and Europe Transformed,* 252.

103. Ibid., 197.

104. The Bush I administration recognized that Moscow needed "cover" to accept Washington's terms. As Baker says, "That meant we had to work with our European partners to adapt NATO and CSCE to make them *appear* less threatening to the Soviet people." Baker, *Politics of Diplomacy,* 231–32 (emphasis added).

105. U.S. officials told their Soviet counterparts that unless attached to NATO, a reunified, neutral Germany would become a nuclear-armed loose cannon. Bush and Scowcroft, *World Transformed,* 239, 273; Zelikow and Rice, *Germany Unified and Europe Transformed,* 181–82.

106. Gorbachev noted the inconsistency in Washington's simultaneous claims that a democratic, unified Germany could be trusted to behave responsibly but that a reunified Ger-

many could be a troublemaker unless embedded in NATO. Bush and Scowcroft, *World Transformed*, 257, 272.

107. Bush and Scowcroft, *World Transformed*, 253; Zelikow and Rice, *Germany Unified and Europe Transformed*, 215.

108. Baker told Gorbachev in May 1990 that the United States was not forcing Germany to remain in NATO. Bush and Scowcroft, *World Transformed*, 273.

109. Zelikow and Rice, *Germany Unified and Europe Transformed*, 274.

110. Baker, *Politics of Diplomacy*, 257.

111. See Zelikow and Rice, *Germany Unified and Europe Transformed*, 175, 180; Bush and Scowcroft, *World Transformed*, 239.

112. As President Clinton said: "I know that some in Russia still look at NATO through a Cold War prism and, therefore, look at our proposals to expand it in a negative light. . . . By reducing rivalry and fear, by strengthening peace and cooperation, NATO will promote greater stability in Europe and Russia will be among the beneficiaries." President Bill Clinton, "Remarks to the People of Detroit," October 22, 1996, http://clinton6.nara .gov/1996/10/1996-10-22-president-speech-on-foreign-policy-in-detroit. Similarly, a senior Pentagon official said, "NATO is not an alliance against Russia." Undersecretary of Defense for Policy Walter Slocombe, "Partnership for Peace and NATO-Russian Relations," (Washington, D.C.: CSIS, March 2, 1995) www.defenselink.mil/cgi-bin/dlprint .cgi?http. See also Strobe Talbott, "Why NATO Should Grow," *New York Review of Books* 42, no. 13 (August 10, 1995).

113. On Russia's reaction to NATO expansion, see J. L. Black, *Russia Faces NATO Expansion: Bearing Gifts or Bearing Arms?* (Lanham, Md.: Rowman and Littlefield, 2000).

114. Ronald D. Asmus, "Double Enlargement: Redefining the Atlantic Partnership after the Cold War," in *America and Europe: A Partnership for a New Era*, ed. David C. Gompert and F. Stephen Larrabee (Cambridge: Cambridge University Press, 1997), 19–50.

115. As President Clinton stated, the United States was "building a NATO capable not only of deterring aggression against its own territory, but of meeting challenges to our security beyond its territory." President Clinton, "Remarks on Foreign Policy," San Francisco, February 26, 1999, http://clinton4.nara.gov/textonly/WH/New/html/19990227-9743 .html. Similarly, Undersecretary of Defense Walter Slocombe said: "Real, immediate challenges to NATO allies have been mounting to the south. Flash points have emerged in the Mediterranean, in Southwest Asia, in the Balkans and in North Africa. The potential spread of instability across the Mediterranean would not only threaten friendly regimes of North Africa and the prospects for peace in the Middle East, it would also threaten Europe with new social and security problems." Slocombe, "Partnership for Peace and NATO-Russian Relations." See also Zbigniew Brzezinski, *The Grand Chessboard: American Primacy and Its Geostrategic Imperatives* (New York: Basic Books, 1997). Brzezinski calls for transforming NATO into a trans-Eurasian security system that would encompass all of Europe, Central Asia and the Caucasus, and East Asia.

116. On the need for a post–cold war U.S. commitment to prevent Europe from relapsing into security competitions, see Robert J. Art, "Why Western Europe Needs the United States and NATO," *Political Science Quarterly* 111, no. 1 (Spring 1996): 1–39; Stephen Van Evera, "Why Europe Matters, Why the Third World Doesn't," *Journal of Strategic Studies* 13, no. 2 (June 1990): 1–51.

117. As Secretary of State Albright put it, "Instability that is dangerous and contagious is best stopped before it reaches NATO's borders." Secretary of State Madeleine K. Albright, "Press Conference at NATO Headquarters," Washington, D.C.: United States Department of State, Office of the Spokesman, December 8, 1998.

118. As Senator Richard Lugar stated during the April 27, 1998, Senate Foreign Relations Committee hearings on NATO expansion: "If history teaches us anything, it is that the United States is always drawn into such European conflicts because our vital interests are ultimately, albeit somewhat belatedly, engaged."

119. President Clinton, "Remarks on Foreign Policy," San Francisco, February 26, 1999.

120. Slocombe, "Partnership for Peace and NATO-Russian Relations."

121. As President Clinton said, "I came to office convinced that NATO can do for Europe's East what it did for Europe's West: prevent a return to local rivalries, strengthen democracy against future threats, and create the conditions for prosperity to flourish." President Clinton, "Remarks to the People of Detroit."
122. Although the Bush II administration wanted to keep NATO out of the invasions of Afghanistan and Iraq, it has sought NATO assistance in the postwar occupation of those countries. The administration has had some success in getting NATO to participate in Afghanistan, and less so with respect to Iraq.
123. Jolyon Howorth and John T. S. Keeler, "The EU, NATO, and the Quest for European Autonomy," in *Defending Europe: The EU, NATO, and the Quest for European Autonomy*, ed. Jolyon Howorth and John T. S. Keeler (New York: Palgrave Macmillan, 2002), 7.
124. For background on how ESDP evolved from the European Security and Defense Initiative—which was a classic transatlantic burden-sharing exercise designed to strengthen the Alliance's "European pillar"—see Stuart Croft, Jolyon Howorth, Terry Teriff, and Mark Webber, "NATO's Triple Challenge," *International Affairs* 76, no. 3, (July 2000): 496–518; Howorth and Keeler, "The EU, NATO, and the Quest for European Autonomy"; and Frederic Bozo, "The Effects of Kosovo and the Danger of Decoupling," in Howorth and Keeler, *Defending Europe*, 61–77.
125. Joseph Fitchett, "EU Force Takes Shape with Pledges of Troops," *International Herald Tribune*, November 20, 2000; "EU to Shape Reaction Force," *International Herald Tribune*, November 18, 2000.
126. Philip Webster, Richard Beeston, and Martin Fletcher, "French Trigger NATO Furore," *Times* (London), December 8, 2000; Michael Evans, "Chirac Blows Cover of New European Army," *Times* (London), December 8, 2000; Anton La Guardia, Michael Smith, "France Snubs America over European Army," *Daily Telegraph*, December 7, 2000.
127. Quoted in Douglas Hamilton and Charles Aldinger, "EU Force Could Spell NATO's End, Cohen Says," *Washington Post*, December 6, 2000.
128. Robert Fox, "US to Pull Out of NATO if EU Force Goes Ahead," *Sunday Telegraph*, October 29, 2000.
129. Quoted in Matthew Campbell and Stephen Grey, "Bush Aides Launch Assault on Euro Army," *Sunday Times* (London), December 17, 2000.
130. "NATO Reaction Force Proposal Speaks to U.S. Dual Priorities," Stratfor.com, November 20, 2002, http://www.stratfor.info/Story.neo?storyId=207681.
131. The literature on this is voluminous. Good starting points are Michael P. Hogan, *The Marshall Plan: America, Britain, and the Reconstruction of Western Europe, 1947–1952* (Cambridge: Cambridge University Press, 1987); Lawrence S. Kaplan, *The United States and NATO: The Formative Years* (Lexington: University Press of Kentucky, 1984); Melvyn P. Leffler, *A Preponderance of Power: National Security, the Truman Administration, and the Cold War* (Stanford: Stanford University Press, 1992).
132. Lundestad, *"Empire" by Integration*, 40. As Undersecretary of State Thomas R. Pickering put it, "Our vision is a simple one: we want a Europe whole and free *in partnership with the United States as part of a new Atlantic Community* which is a force for progress in the world." Pickering, "Remarks at French-American Chamber of Commerce, Washington, D.C.," November 3, 2000, http://state.gov/www/policy_remarks/2000/001103_pickering_transatl.html. (emphasis added).
133. Washington's calls for an equal partnership between a strong Europe and the United States "ring a little hollow . . . it is highly doubtful that the United States has ever wanted a Europe really equal to the U.S." Lundestad, *"Empire" by Integration*, 166.
134. As Cohen stated in October 2000, "NATO will continue to be the indispensable anchor of American engagement in European security matters and the foundation for assuring the collective defense of Alliance members." Secretary of Defense William S. Cohen, "Informal NATO Defense Ministerial Meeting—Remarks as Prepared for Delivery," October 10, 2000, http://defenslink.mil/speeches/2000/s20001010-secdef.html.
135. See Joseph Fitchett, "EU Takes Steps to Create a Military Force, without Treading on NATO," *International Herald Tribune*, March 1, 2000; James Kitfield, "European Dough-

boys," *National Journal* 32, no. 9 (February 26, 2000): 610; Carol J. Williams, "Conference Highlights Flaws of NATO's Kosovo Campaign," *Los Angeles Times*, February 6, 2000.

136. Albright, "Press Conference at NATO Headquarters," (emphasis added).

137. Slocombe, "Partnership for Peace and NATO-Russian Relations." As Deputy Secretary of State Strobe Talbott said, the key question about ESDP was "will it help keep the alliance together?" "Remarks at a Conference on the Future of NATO," Royal Institute of International Affairs, London, October 7, 1999, http://www.state.gov/www/policy_remarks/1999/991997_talbott_london.html.

138. Bozo, "Effects of Kosovo," 68, 75.

139. Albright, "Press Conference at NATO Headquarters."

140. Judy Dempsey, "EU Leaders Unveil Plan for Central Military HQ," *Financial Times*, April 30, 2003, 5.

141. Quoted in ibid.

142. Quoted in Judy Dempsey, "U.S. Seeks Showdown with EU over NATO," *Financial Times*, October 17, 2003.

143. Judy Dempsey, "Italians in Vanguard of Push for EU Arms Industry, Despite US Misgivings," *Financial Times*, July 11, 2003, 4.

144. See Philip Stephens, "A Divided Europe Will Be Easy for America to Rule," *Financial Times*, May 23, 2003, 13; Gerard Baker, "America's Divided View of European Unity," *Financial Times*, May 8, 2003, 13; "Divide and Rule?" *The Economist*, April 26, 2003, 47.

145. Leffler, *Preponderance of Power*, 17.

6. Liberal Ideology and U.S. Grand Strategy

1. David Stiegerwald, "The Reclamation of Woodrow Wilson," *Diplomatic History* 23, no. 1 (Winter 1999): 79–99.

2. John Lewis Gaddis, *The United States and the End of the Cold War: Implications, Reconsiderations, Provocations* (New York: Oxford University Press, 1992), 215.

3. On this point, see John A. Thompson, "Another Look at the Downfall of 'Fortress America,'" *Journal of American Studies* 26, no. 3 (December 1992): 393–408; John A. Thompson, "The Exaggeration of American Vulnerability: The Anatomy of a Tradition," *Diplomatic History* 16, no. 1 (Winter 1992): 23–27.

4. William Appleman Williams, *Empire as a Way of Life: An Essay on the Causes and Character of America's Present Predicament along with a Few Thoughts about an Alternative* (New York: Oxford University Press, 1980), 53.

5. "For over two centuries the aspiration toward an eventual condition of absolute security has been viewed as central to an effective American foreign policy." James Chace and Caleb Carr, *America Invulnerable: The Quest for Absolute Security from 1812 to Star Wars* (New York: Summit Books, 1988), 12.

6. For a similar argument, see Robert W. Tucker, "The American Outlook," in *America and the World: From the Truman Doctrine to Vietnam*, ed. Robert E. Osgood et al. (Baltimore: Johns Hopkins University Press, 1970), 50–51. For arguments that its post-1990 hegemony was an opportunity for U.S. geopolitical *and* ideological expansion, see Zalmay Khalilzad, "Losing the Moment? The United States and the World after the Cold War," *Washington Quarterly* 18, no. 2 (Spring 1995): 87–107; Charles Krauthammer, "The Unipolar Moment," *Foreign Affairs* 70, no. 1 (1990–91): 23–33; William Kristol and Robert Kagan, "Toward a Neo-Reaganite Foreign Policy," *Foreign Affairs* 75, no. 4 (July–August 1996): 18–32.

7. Robert H. Johnson, *Improbable Dangers: U.S. Conceptions of Threat in the Cold War and After* (New York: St. Martin's, 1994), 12.

8. On milieu goals, see Arnold Wolfers, *Discord and Collaboration: Essays in International Politics* (Baltimore: Johns Hopkins University Press, 1962), 73–77. Even some realists incorporate Wilsonian goals into their preferred visions of U.S. grand strategy. For example, Robert Art counts the export of democracy and maintenance of an open international

economy among the six objectives of his "selective engagement" strategy. Robert J. Art, *A Grand Strategy for America* (Ithaca: Cornell University Press, 2003), 7–8, 123.

9. Walter LaFeber, *America, Russia, and the Cold War, 1945–1996*, 8th ed. (New York: McGraw-Hill, 1997), 235.

10. Frank A. Ninkovich, *Modernity and Power: A History of the Domino Theory in the Twentieth Century* (Chicago: University of Chicago Press, 1994), 113. See also Ross A. Kennedy, "Woodrow Wilson, World War I, and an American Conception of National Security," *Diplomatic History* 25, no. 1 (Winter 2001): 1–32.

11. Louis Hartz, *The Liberal Tradition in America* (San Diego: Harcourt Brace, 1991).

12. Liberal absolutism has had an inhibiting effect on the study of political science in the United States. Unlike other academic disciplines, political science "was not really asked, directly or otherwise, to follow the dictates of science wherever they might lead, to dissect political reality as dispassionately as other disciplines were called upon to analyze things in their realms of concern. Instead, because America was so overwhelmingly devoted to the principles and practices of democratic liberalism, the end for political science was virtually laid down in advance." David Ricci, *The Tragedy of Political Science: Politics, Scholarship, and Democracy* (New Haven: Yale University Press, 1984), 70.

13. Lloyd C. Gardner, *A Covenant with Power: America and World Order from Wilson to Reagan* (New York: Oxford University Press, 1984), 27.

14. Quoted in Michael S. Sherry, *In the Shadow of War: The United States since the 1930s* (New Haven: Yale University Press, 1995), 3.

15. Quoted in Tucker, "American Outlook," 52. Similarly, Secretary of State Dean Acheson argued that in the cold war the United States was "faced with a threat not only to our country, but to the civilization in which we live and to the whole physical environment in which that civilization can exist." Quoted in Frank Ninkovich, *The Wilsonian Century: U.S. Foreign Policy since 1900* (Chicago: University of Chicago Press, 1999), 174.

16. Quoted in Ninkovich, *Wilsonian Century*, 125.

17. Quoted in Lloyd C. Gardner, *Pay Any Price: Lyndon Johnson and the Wars for Vietnam* (Chicago: Ivan R. Dee, 1995), 28. During the Vietnam War, Walt Rostow justified U.S. policy in Southeast Asia by stating that "we cannot build order and progress at home in a world where U.S. withdrawal from its responsibilities results in an international environment of chaos and violence." Quoted in ibid., 370.

18. Art asserts that "all great powers have sought to externalize their form of governance," and they only refrain from proselytizing when they are too weak to do so. As a general proposition of great power behavior, this is far too sweeping a statement. As a description of *American* behavior, however, it is right on target. Art, *Grand Strategy for America*, 29.

19. Robert E. Osgood, *Ideals and Self-Interest in America's Foreign Relations: The Great Transformation of the Twentieth Century* (Chicago: University of Chicago Press, 1953), 93.

20. For good overviews of the scholarly debate, see Michael E. Brown, Sean M. Lynn-Jones, and Steven E. Miller, eds., *Debating the Democratic Peace* (Cambridge: MIT Press, 1996), and Miriam Fendius Elman, ed., *Paths to Peace: Is Democracy the Answer?* (Cambridge: MIT Press, 1997). For the argument that liberalism causes peace, see John M. Owen, *Liberal Peace, Liberal War: American Politics and International Security* (Ithaca: Cornell University Press, 1997).

21. See Henry S. Farber and Joanne Gowa, "Polities and Peace," *International Security* 20, no. 2 (Fall 1995): 123–46; David E. Spiro, "The Insignificance of the Liberal Peace," *International Security* 19, no. 2 (Fall 1994): 50–86.

22. There have been at least four major crises where two democracies have been on the brink of war: the 1861 "*Trent* Affair" crisis (U.S./Britain); the 1895 Venezuela Boundary crisis (U.S./Britain); the 1898 Fashoda crisis (Britain/France); and the 1923–24 Ruhr Occupation crisis (France/Germany). In each of these crises, geopolitical factors—not democratic peace theory—explain why war was avoided. For extended discussion, see Christopher Layne, "Kant or Cant? The Myth of the Democratic Peace," *International Security* 19, no. 2 (Fall 1994): 5–49. Similarly, liberal France and liberal Britain went to the brink of war several times between 1830 and 1848. Again, war was avoided because of realpolitik, not because of the "liberal peace." See Christopher Layne, "Lord Palmerston and the Tri-

umph of Realism: Anglo-French Relations, 1830–1848," in Elman, *Paths to Peace.* The most notable case of a major war among democracies was World War I on the western front, which pitted Britain and France against Wilhelmine Germany. For a detailed discussion, see Christopher Layne, "Shell Games, Shallow Gains, and the Democratic Peace," *International History Review* 13, no. 4 (December 2001): 799–813.

23. Walter McDougall, *Promised Land, Crusader State: The American Encounter with the World since 1776* (New York: Houghton Mifflin, 1997).

24. As the statesman Elihu Root put it during World War I: "To be safe democracy must kill its enemy when it can and where it can. The world can not be half democratic and half autocratic." Quoted in Bruce Russett, *Grasping the Democratic Peace* (Princeton: Princeton University Press, 1993), 3.

25. For example, Deputy Defense Secretary Paul Wolfowitz has stated that regardless of whether Iraq possessed weapons of mass destruction the invasion was justified, because "we have an important job to do in Iraq, an absolutely critical job to do, and that is to help the Iraqi people to build a free and democratic country." Quoted in Thom Shanker, "Wolfowitz Defends War, Illicit Iraqi Arms or Not," *New York Times*, February 1, 2004, A8.

26. "Remarks by the President at the 20th Anniversary of the National Endowment for Democracy," November 6, 2003, http://www.whitehouse.gov/news/releases/2003/11/print/20031106–3.html, p. 5.

27. As President Bush put it, "The failure of Iraqi democracy would embolden terrorists around the world, increase dangers to the American people, and extinguish the hopes of millions in the region. Iraqi democracy will succeed—and that success will send forth the news, from Damascus to Teheran—that freedom can be the future of every nation. The establishment of a free Iraq at the heart of the Middle East will be watershed event in the global democratic revolution." Ibid. Rice contends that a "free, democratic, and successful Iraq can serve as a beacon, and a catalyst" in the effort to transform the Middle East. "Remarks by Condoleeza Rice, Assistant to the President for National Security Affairs, to the Chicago Council on Foreign Relations," October 8, 2003, http://www.whitehouse.gov/news/releases/2003/10/print/20031008–4.html, p. 3.

28. In President Bush's words, "As long as the Middle East remains a place where freedom does not flourish, it will remain a place of stagnation, resentment, and violence ready for export. And with the spread of weapons that can bring catastrophic harm to our country and to our friends, it would be reckless to accept the status quo." "Remarks by the President at the 20th Anniversary of the National Endowment for Democracy." Rice has argued that the Middle East suffers from a "freedom deficit." In his January 2004 State of the Union speech, President Bush reaffirmed the administration's dedication to achieving a democratic transformation in the Middle East, and, again, linked this policy to U.S. national security.

29. As Kenneth Waltz observes: "Crusades are frightening because crusaders go to war for righteous causes, which they define for themselves and try to impose on others." Kenneth Waltz, "Structural Realism after the Cold War," *International Security* 25, no. 1 (Summer 2000): 12.

30. In an Orwellian sense, these denials are valid. If American values are—as advertised—universal, then the United States is not imposing *American* values on others. Rather, it is just helping others resolve something of a "false consciousness" problem by getting them to jettison their particularist, wrong values and adopt "universal" ones in their stead.

31. Michael Hunt observes that American liberal ideology denigrates other cultures and stereotypes them as backward. These stereotypes "raise in Americans false expectations that it is an easy enterprise to induce and direct political change and economic development." When these expectations are frustrated—as invariably is the case—the United States tends to "resort to forms of coercion or violence otherwise unthinkable." Michael H. Hunt, *Ideology and U.S. Foreign Policy* (New Haven: Yale University Press, 1987), 176. Ninkovich points out that "American internationalism has always been anti-cultural in its bias." Ninkovich, *Modernity and Power,* 23.

32. Hans J. Morgenthau, *In Defense of the National Interest: A Critical Examination of American Foreign Policy* (Washington, D.C.: University Press of America, 1982), 37, 93.

33. In Hans Morgenthau's words, when states claim their ideals are universally applicable,

    compromise, the virtue of the old diplomacy, becomes the treason of the new; for the mutual accommodation of conflicting claims, possible or legitimate within a common framework of moral standards, amounts to surrender when the moral standards are themselves the stakes of the conflict. Thus the stage is set for a contest among nations whose stakes are no longer their relative positions within a political and moral system accepted by all, but the ability to impose upon other contestants a new universal political and moral system recreated in the image of the victorious nation's political and moral convictions. (Hans J. Morgenthau [revised, Kenneth A. Thompson], *Politics among Nations: The Struggle for Power and Peace*, 6th ed. [New York: Alfred A. Knopf, 1985], 271)

    Commenting on the Bush II administration's push to export democracy globally, former National Security Advisor Brent Scowcroft noted that the problem with such an absolutist worldview is that it can make U.S. policy inflexible, because "if you believe you are pursuing absolute good, then it is a sin to depart from it." Quoted in David J. Rothkopf, "Inside the Committee That Runs the World," *Foreign Policy* 147 (March–April 2005): 33.

34. See Condoleeza Rice, interview with the Washington Post editorial board, March 25, 2005, http://www.state.gov/secretary/rm/2005/43863.htm.

35. "Remarks by the President at the 20th Anniversary of the National Endowment for Democracy," 5.

36. Roula Khalaf, "U.S. Democracy Drive Heartens the Islamists," *Financial Times*, May 20, 2005, 5.

37. On illiberal democracies, see Fareed Zakaria, *The Future of Freedom: Illiberal Democracy at Home and Abroad* (New York: W. W. Norton, 2003); Zakaria, "The Rise of Illiberal Democracy," *Foreign Affairs* 76, no. 6 (November–December 1997): 22–43. For rebuttals to Zakaria, see John Shattuck and J. Brian Atwood, "Why Democrats Trump Autocrats," *Foreign Affairs* 77, no. 2 (March–April 1998): 167–70; Marc F. Plattner, "Liberalism and Democracy: Can't Have One without the Other," *Foreign Affairs* 77, no. 2 (March–April 1998): 171–80. On the war proneness of newly democratizing states, which, in contrast to "mature" democracies, usually are illiberal, see Jack Snyder and Edward Mansfield, "Democratization and the Danger of War," *International Security* 20, no. 1 (Summer 1995): 5–38.

38. Lawrence Freedman, "A Legacy of Failure in the Arab World," *Financial Times*, January 26, 2004, 13.

39. Quoted in Craig S. Smith, "Chirac Says War in Iraq Spreads Terrorism," *New York Times* (online ed.), November 18, 2004. In February 2005, CIA Director Porter J. Goss stated: "Islamic extremists are exploiting the Iraqi conflict to recruit new anti-U.S. jihadists. These jihadists who survive will leave Iraq experienced and focused on acts of urban terrorism. They represent a potential pool of contacts to build transnational terrorist cells, groups and networks in Saudi Arabia, Jordan, and other countries." Quoted in Dana Priest and Josh White, "War Helps Recruit Terrorists, Hill Told: Intelligence Officials Talk of Growing Insurgency," *Washington Post*, February 17, 2005, A1.

40. Tucker, "American Outlook," 52.

41. President Bill Clinton, "Remarks to the American Society of Newspaper Editors," April 1, 1993. Similarly, Deputy Secretary of State Strobe Talbott declared that "the way a government treats its own people is not just an 'internal matter'," because there are "issues of both universal values and regional peace at stake." Deputy Secretary of State Strobe Talbott, "Robert C. Frasure Memorial Lecture," Tallinn, Estonia, January 24, 2000, www.state.gov/www/policy_remarks/2000/000124_talbott_tallinn.html. The Bush II administration took this approach with respect to Iraq. For Deputy Secretary of Defense Wolfowitz's views linking U.S. security to democratization of Iraq and the Middle East, see Bill Keller, "The Sunshine Warrior," *New York Times Magazine*, September 22, 2002, 50–51.

42. Tucker, "American Outlook," 48.

43. As Robert Gilpin observes: "An economic system . . . does not arise spontaneously owing to the operation of an invisible hand and in the absence of an exercise of power. Rather, every economic system rests on a particular political order, and its nature cannot be understood aside from politics." Robert Gilpin, *U.S. Power and the Multinational Corporation: The Political Economy of Foreign Direct Investment* (New York: Basic Books, 1975), 41. Gilpin

also comments (85) that economic interdependence is "not self-sustaining, but is maintained only through the actions . . . of the dominant powers."

44. Firms are "highly sensitive to the nature of interstate relations. As international instability and tensions rise, so too does the possibility that serious ruptures in interstate relations could harm the interests of merchants trading between those markets." David M. Rowe, "Trade and Security in International Politics," paper presented to the annual meeting of the International Studies Association, Chicago, February 22–25, 1995, 31–32. Similarly, Robert Art argues that the United States must prevent either major wars or security competitions "that heighten tension and are not good for trade" because otherwise these will be "disruptive to America's considerable economic stakes" in Eurasia. Art, *Grand Strategy for America*, 57, 140.

45. John Gallagher and Ronald Robinson, "The Imperialism of Free Trade," in *The Decline, Revival, and Fall of the British Empire: The Ford Lectures and Other Essays by John Gallagher*, ed. Anil Seal (Cambridge: Cambridge University Press, 1982), 7.

46. Quoted in Gardner, *Covenant with Power*, 41.

47. Brent Scowcroft, "Who Can Harness History? Only the U.S.," *New York Times*, July 2, 1993, A15.

48. Dick Cheney, "The Military We Need in the Future," *Vital Speeches of the Day* 59, no. 1 (October 15, 1992): 13. Cheney also stated that "we are a trading nation, and our prosperity is directly linked to peace and stability in the world."

49. Secretary of Defense William S. Cohen, "Remarks Prepared for Delivery at the Microsoft Corporation," Redmond, Wash., February 18, 1999, http://www.defenselink.mil/speches/1999/s19990218-secef.html (emphasis added).

50. As Robert Art says, quite apart from counterhegemonic concerns, selective engagement advocates "also worry about the destructive effects of great-power wars and intense security competitions even if no hegemon emerges from either," because "such wars and competitions could disrupt America's Eurasian trade and investment." Art, *Grand Strategy for America*, 205.

51. With respect to Europe see Deputy Secretary of State Strobe Talbott, "Address at the Royal United Services Institute, London, U.K.," March 10, 1999, http://www.state.gov/www/policy_remarks/1999/991997_talbott_london.html. With respect to East Asia, the Pentagon's 1995 *Security Strategy for East Asia–Pacific* states that "the stability and prosperity of the Asia-Pacific region is a matter of vital national interest affecting the well-being of all Americans." *United States Security Strategy for the East Asia–Pacific Region* (Washington, D.C.: Department of Defense, Office of International Security Affairs, 1995), 7.

52. Samuel R. Berger, "Remarks to the Bilderberg Steering Committee," November 4, 1999, http://clinton6.nara.gov/1999/11/1999-11-04-remarks-by-samuel-berger-to-bilderberg-steering-committee.html. Berger went on to say that U.S. interests invariably would be threatened by conflicts in the Middle East, Korea, South Asia, and the Balkans.

53. Assistant to the President Samuel R. Berger, "The Price of American Leadership," The White House, Office of the Press Secretary, May 1, 1998. *The United States Security Strategy for the East Asia–Pacific Region 1998* makes the same point (10): "U.S. force presence mitigates the impact of historical regional tensions and allows the United States to anticipate problems, manage potential threats and encourage peaceful resolution of disputes."

54. Secretary of Defense Dick Cheney, *Defense Strategy for the 1990s: The Regional Defense Strategy* (Washington, D.C.: Department of Defense, January 1993), 6, 7. The Clinton administration's *National Security Strategy of Engagement and Enlargement* stated (10) that forward deployment of U.S. military forces "allows the United States to use its position of trust to prevent the development of power vacuums and dangerous arms races, thereby underwriting regional stability by precluding threats to regional security."

55. Alberto R. Coll, "Power, Principles, and Prospects for a Cooperative International Order," *Washington Quarterly* 16, no. 1 (Winter 1993): 8. Coll served as a deputy assistant secretary of defense in the Bush I administration. In the same vein, in his June 2002 West Point commencement address, President George W. Bush decried the "series of destructive national rivalries" that have characterized great power relations. By maintaining its military strength "beyond challenge," he said, the United States would make "the destabilizing

arms races of other eras pointless, and [limit] rivalries to trade and other pursuits of peace."

56. *2001 Quadrennial Defense Review*, http://www.defenselink.mil/pubs/qdr2001.pdf, 1, 15.

57. As the Pentagon put it, "It is not to our interest or those of the other democracies to return to earlier periods in which multiple military powers balanced one against another in what passed for security structures, while regional or even global peace hung in the balance." *Defense Strategy for the 1990s*, 7. This point was well expressed by Secretary of Defense William J. Perry:

> Some critics argue that our military presence and security alliances are relics of the Cold War. The most extreme among them say that we should pull back our forces from the region, terminate our agreements that provide security for our allies and allow normal balance-of-power politics to fill the security vacuum. This is a seductive line of thought, but it has dangerous consequences. For years, the U.S. provided a secure environment which allowed the Asian Pacific nations to build their economies rather than their national defense structures. . . . If we were to withdraw our military forces from the region, *this would all change.* Countries would be forced to rethink their needs, with building up defense structures at or near the top of the list. Rapid growth of military structures, plus historic animosities, would be a volatile mix that could quickly destabilize the region . . . dramatically increasing the risk of regional conflict.

"Remarks by Secretary of Defense William J. Perry to the Japan Society," New York City, September 12, 1995, http://www.defenselink.mil/speeches/1995/s19990912-perry.html (emphasis added).

58. As Stephen Rosen puts it, U.S. policy is one of "extending security guarantees to others in order to remove their need for independent military capabilities. . . . American military forces stationed abroad help fulfill this function, even after the collapse of the Soviet Union." Stephen Peter Rosen, "An Empire, If You Can Keep It," *National Interest* no. 71 (Spring 2003): 57.

59. Quoted in Alvin H. Bernstein, "The Strategy of a Warrior State: Rome and the Wars against Carthage, 264–201 B.C." in *The Making of Strategy: Rulers, States, and War*, ed. Williamson Murray, MacGregor Knox, and Alvin Bernstein (Cambridge: Cambridge University Press, 1994), 65.

60. Zalmay Khalilzad, a senior national security official in both Bush administrations, states:

> The credibility of U.S. alliances can be undermined if key allies, such as Germany and Japan, believe that the current arrangements do not deal adequately with threats to *their* security. It could also be undermined if, over an extended period, the United States is perceived as lacking the will or capability to lead in protecting *their* interests. (emphasis added)

Zalmay Khalilzad, "U.S. Grand Strategies: Implications for the World," in Khalilzad, ed., *Strategic Appraisal 1996* (Santa Monica, Calif.: RAND Corporation, 1996), 24.

61. *1997 Quadrennial Defense Review*, 12. See also *2001 QDR*, 11.

62. Maintaining U.S. credibility is "among the most critical of all foreign policy objectives." Robert J. McMahon, "Credibility and World Power: Exploring the Psychological Dimension in Postwar American Diplomacy," *Diplomatic History* 15, no. 4 (Fall 1991): 455. Similarly, Ninkovich argues that "at the heart of America's complex cold-war foreign policy was an abiding obsession with credibility"—which required not just the threat to use U.S. military power but "the continual use of force . . . lest confidence in American leadership unravel." Ninkovich, *Wilsonian Century*, 182.

63. As McMahon observes, U.S. officials must be concerned that "if a signal of irresolution is conveyed, or an image of weakness projected, even in an area of peripheral strategic and economic value, American credibility could be severely damaged, possibly leading other allies or adversaries to take actions detrimental to the United States in vital areas." McMahon, "Credibility and World Power," 457.

64. Ibid., 459.

65. In Thomas Schelling's classic formulation, "Few parts of the world are intrinsically worth the risk of serious war by themselves . . . but defending them or running risks to protect

them may preserve one's commitments to action in other parts of the world at later times."
Thomas C. Schelling, *Arms and Influence* (New Haven: Yale University Press, 1966), 124.
Similarly, Art argues that the forward deployment of U.S. forces in Eurasia usually will
deter war, but when deterrence fails the United States must respond militarily: "otherwise
America's forward presence would lose credibility and its beneficial effects would evapo-
rate." Art, *Grand Strategy for America*, 147.

66. Thompson, "Exaggeration of American Vulnerability." On the domino theory see Robert
Jervis, "Domino Beliefs and Strategic Behavior," in *Dominoes and Bandwagons: Strategic Be-
liefs and Great Power Competition in the Eurasian Rimland*, by Robert Jervis and Jack Snyder
(New York: Oxford University Press, 1991), 20–50. Douglas McDonald shows how U.S. policymakers have used domino imagery to mobilize congressional and public support for
U.S. interventions during the cold war. Douglas J. Macdonald, "The Truman Administration and Global Responsibilities: The Birth of the Falling Domino Principle," in Jervis and
Snyder, *Dominoes and Bandwagons*, 112–44. Macdonald (136) makes a candid—albeit cynical—case for the utility of the domino theory as a instrument of threat exaggeration:

> The use of the domino principle as a strategic calculus and policy justification may exag-
> gerate the actual threat to a worst-case potential threat, but it is arguable that it is neces-
> sary in a democracy to provide the resources and political will to meet a real, though
> lesser, crisis situation. Oversell may in fact be a rational policy choice. Clearly decision
> makers in the United States have seen and used it this way.

If the threats to American security were real, policymakers would not need to engage in
threat exaggeration and "oversell." That raises the key question: If the threats are over-
sold, what are the *real* reasons that U.S. policymakers favor strategic internationalism?

67. Jerome Slater, "The Domino Theory and International Politics: The Case of Vietnam," *Security Studies* 3, no. 2 (Winter 1993–94): 186–224.

68. John Galbraith used the turbulent frontier thesis to explain why, although officials in London favored nonexpansionist policies in India, Malaya, and South Africa during the nineteenth century, the British governors of those colonies followed expansionist strategies to
gain security: "The 'turbulent frontier' contributed to the paradox of the nineteenth century empire that 'grew in spite of itself.'" John S. Galbraith, "The 'Turbulent Frontier' as
a Factor in British Expansion," *Comparative Studies in Society and History* 2, no. 2 (January
1960): 168.

69. Robert Jervis, "Cooperation under the Security Dilemma," *World Politics* 30, no. 2 (January
1978): 169.

70. There is widespread agreement about this dynamic. For example, Johnson says the process
of never-ending expansion occurs because "uncertainty"—fear of what might happen if
the United States does not intervene—"leads to self-extension, which leads in turn to new
uncertainty and further self-extension." Johnson, *Improbable Dangers*, 296. See also Wolfers,
Discord and Collaboration, 154, and Chace and Carr, *America Invulnerable*, 319.

71. This term is borrowed from Ronald Robinson and John Gallagher, with Alice Denny,
Africa and the Victorians: The Official Mind of Imperialism, rev. ed. (London: Macmillan,
1981). Robinson and Gallagher describe how the need to defend Britain's economic interdependence with India was the driving force behind London's nineteenth-century
grand strategy. To defend India and the lines of communication to it, Britain established
one defensive position after another—the second to protect the first, the third to safeguard the second, and so on. Britain's defensive perimeters pushed outward, but never established security for India and the sea routes connecting it with England. Since 1945, Europe, East Asia, and the Persian Gulf have been "America's India" in grand strategy.

72. In addition to the sources cited in notes 69–76, this discussion is based on several sources,
including David L. Anderson, *Trapped by Success: The Eisenhower Administration and Vietnam,
1953–1961* (New York: Columbia University Press, 1991); William S. Borden, *The Pacific Alliance: United States Foreign Economic Policy and Japanese Trade Recovery, 1947–1955* (Madison:
University of Wisconsin Press, 1984); Steven Hugh Lee, *Outposts of Empire: Korea, Vietnam,
and the Origins of the Cold War in Asia, 1949–1954* (Montreal: McGill-Queen's University
Press, 1995); Ronald L. McGlothen, *Controlling the Waves: Dean Acheson and U.S. Foreign Pol-*

icy (New York: W. W. Norton, 1993); Michael Schaller, "Securing the Great Crescent: Occupied Japan and the Origins of Containment in Southeast Asia," *Journal of American History* 69, no. 2 (Summer 1982): 392–414.

73. Southeast Asia was important for Western Europe, because exports from their colonies in the region to the United States were a means of earning dollars. Also, they could import raw materials like rubber and petroleum from these colonies instead of the United States and conserve their dollar reserves. On how U.S. involvement in Southeast Asia was driven by the region's importance to the Western Europeans as well as to Japan, see Andrew J. Rotter, *The Path to Vietnam: Origins of the American Commitment to Southeast Asia* (Ithaca: Cornell University Press, 1987), 49–69.

74. "The origins of U.S. involvement in the Indochinese quagmire lay less in direct American economic interests in the region than in political obligations to allied countries." Robert A. Pollard and Samuel F. Wells Jr., "1945–1960: The Era of American Economic Hegemony," in *Economics and World Power*, ed. William Becker and Samuel F. Wells (New York: Columbia University Press, 1984), 350.

75. PPS 51, "United States Policy toward Southeast Asia," May 19, 1949, in *The State Department Policy Planning Staff Papers*, vol. 3, ed. Anna Kasten Nelson (New York: Garland, 1983), 33–35. In this document (54), the Policy Planning Staff argued that the United States "should seek vigorously to develop the economic interdependence between SEA [Southeast Asia], as a supplier of raw materials, and Japan" and Western Europe (and India).

76. Ibid., 35.

77. Ibid., 38.

78. According to Leffler, "core and periphery were interdependent. If Indochina fell and if it had a domino effect on its neighbors, Japan's industrial heartland might be co-opted," and Western industrialized nations would be weakened as well. Melvyn P. Leffler, *A Preponderance of Power: National Security, the Truman Administration, and the Cold War* (Stanford: Stanford University Press, 1992), 479.

79. Quoted in Lloyd C. Gardner, *Approaching Vietnam: From World War II through Dienbienphu, 1941–1954* (New York: W. W. Norton, 1988), 197. This was the position of both the Truman and Eisenhower administrations. See Memorandum by the Central Intelligence Agency, SE-13, "Probable Developments in the World Situation through Mid-1953," September 24, 1951, *FRUS 1951*, 1:204; Estimate Prepared by the Board of National Estimates, "Estimate of the World Situation through 1954," November 21, 1952, *FRUS 1952–54*, 2:194; National Intelligence Estimate, NIE-99, "Estimate of the World Situation through 1955," October 23, 1953, *FRUS 1952–54*, 2:560.

80. LaFeber points out that the Kennedy administration "gulped down" the Eisenhower-Dulles vision of falling dominoes in Southeast Asia to ensure that Japan would not turn toward China for raw materials and markets. LaFeber, *America, Russia, and the Cold War*, 230.

81. "Letter from President Clinton to Speaker of the House Newt Gingrich," White House Press Office, November 13, 1995, p. 1 (emphasis added).

82. Secretary of Defense William S. Cohen, "Remarks to the Boston Chamber of Commerce," http://defenselink.mil/speeches/1998/s19980917-secdef.html.

83. Talbott, "Address at the Royal United Services Institute."

84. *MacNeil/Lehrer Newshour*, May 6, 1993, Transcript No. 4622.

85. William E. Odom, "Yugoslavia: Quagmire or Strategic Challenge?" *Hudson Briefing Paper* No. 146 (Indianapolis: Hudson Institute, November 1992), 2.

86. President Bill Clinton, "Remarks to AFSCME Biennial Convention," Washington, D.C., March 23, 1999, http://clinton4.nara.gov/textonly/WH/New/html/19990323-1110.html.

87. For example, Deputy National Security Advisor James Steinberg claimed that if the United States failed to exercise leadership in Bosnia, NATO's credibility would be undermined. See James Steinberg, "Foreign Policy Myopia," *Washington Post*, January 19, 1996, A19. As William Odom put it, "Only a strong NATO with the U.S. centrally involved can prevent Western Europe from drifting into national parochialism and eventual regression from its present level of economic and political cooperation." Odom, "Quagmire or Strategic Challenge?" 2.

88. Art, *Grand Strategy for America*, 154–57.
89. Robert J. Art, "A Defensible Defense: America's Grand Strategy after the Cold War," *International Security* 15, no. 4 (Spring 1991): 45.
90. Robert J. Art, "Why Western Europe Needs the United States and NATO," *Political Science Quarterly* 111, no. 1 (Spring 1996): 1–39.
91. Art, *Grand Strategy for America*, 154–57.
92. Secretary of Defense William Cohen, "Remarks at Microsoft Corporation."
93. As the Pentagon has put it:

> The presence of severe international tensions or immediate national security threats enable authoritarian regimes to argue that democracy is a luxury and that strong and assertive central control is required to meet challenges. Conversely, a secure regional environment enables nations to focus on internal development, both economic and political, and provides the breathing space for invention, experimentation and development that a transition to democracy requires. (*The United States Security Strategy for the East-Asia Pacific Region 1998*)

> Secretary of Defense William Cohen stated that "America's engagement continues to be a stabilizing influence for both prosperity and democracy." Secretary of Defense William S. Cohen, "Prepared Remarks for the Inaugural of the William S. Cohen Lecture Series," University of Maine—Orono, March 20, 1998, http://defenselink.mil/speeches/1998/s19980320-secdef.html.

94. Robert Art recognized this more than a decade ago when he said that "it is not economic interdependence that has brought peace among great powers" but U.S. nuclear deterrence that has brought about economic interdependence. Robert J. Art, "A U.S. Military Strategy for the 1990s: Reassurance without Dominance," *Survival* 34, no. 4 (Winter 1992–93): 7–8. Art and I agree on this point, but disagree on the policy conclusions we draw from it.
95. *United States Security Strategy for the East-Asia Pacific Region, 1995*, 1. Joseph S. Nye Jr., who, as assistant secretary of defense was the principal author of this policy paper, has written:

> Political order is not sufficient to explain economic prosperity, but it is necessary. Analysts who ignore the importance of this political order are like people who forget the oxygen they breathe. Security is like oxygen—you tend not to notice it until you begin to lose it, but once that occurs there is nothing else that you will think about. (Joseph S. Nye Jr., "The Case for Deep Engagement," *Foreign Affairs* 74, no. 4 [July–August 1995]: 91)

7. The End of the Unipolar Era

1. For the argument that U.S. hegemony would be of relatively short (twenty years) duration because unipolarity would trigger balancing against U.S. hegemony, see Christopher Layne, "The Unipolar Illusion: Why New Great Powers Will Rise," *International Security* 17, no. 4 (Spring 1993): 5–51. See also Kenneth Waltz, "The Emerging Structure of International Politics," *International Security* 18, no.2 (Fall 1994): 44–79. The most cogent argument that American hegemony will be long lasting and contribute to international stability, is William C. Wohlforth, "The Stability of a Unipolar World," *International Security* 24, no. 1 (Summer 1999): 5–41. See also Michael Mastanduno, "Preserving the Unipolar Moment: Realist Theories and U.S. Grand Strategy after the Cold War," *International Security* 21, no. 4 (Spring 1997): 44–98.
2. William C. Wohlforth, "U.S. Strategy in a Unipolar World," in *America Unrivaled: The Future of the Balance of Power,* ed. G. John Ikenberry (Ithaca: Cornell University Press, 2002), 103–4. See also Wohlforth, "Stability of a Unipolar World," and Stephen G. Brooks and Wohlforth, "American Primacy in Perspective," *Foreign Affairs* 81, no. 4 (July–August 2002): 20–33.
3. For an explanation of the factors that can prevent timely and efficient counterhegemonic balancing, see John J. Mearsheimer, *The Tragedy of Great Power Politics* (New York: W. W. Norton, 2001), 341–44; Kenneth N. Waltz, *Theory of International Politics* (Reading, Mass.: Addison-Wesley, 1979), 164–70, 196–98; Mancur Olson and Richard Zeckhauser, "An Eco-

nomic Theory of Alliances," *Review of Economics and Statistics* 48, no. 3 (August 1966): 266–79.

4. This concept of a coalition magnet is suggested by the observation of Michel Fortmann, T. V. Paul, and James Wirtz that one of the conditions likely to trigger a hard-balancing coalition against the United States in the future is "when one or more of the major powers gains sufficient capabilities to challenge U.S. power." Fortmann, Paul, and Wirtz, "Conclusions: Balance of Power at the Turn of the New Century," in *Balance of Power: Theory and Practice in the 21st Century*, ed. T. V. Paul, James J. Wirtz, and Michel Fortmann (Stanford: Stanford University Press, 2004), 372.

5. Robert Gilpin, *War and Change in International Politics* (Cambridge: Cambridge University Press, 1981), 191. Gilpin focuses on the logic of preventive war strategies for a declining hegemon seeking to preserve its preponderant position in the international system, but the same logic applies to a hegemon still at the top of its game geopolitically. Preventive war ensures that potential challengers never become strong enough to threaten the hegemon's dominance.

6. *National Security Strategy of the United States* (Washington, D.C.: The White House, September 2002) (emphasis added).

7. Ibid., 12–13, 15.

8. David Frum and Richard Perle—two prominent neoconservatives with ties to the Bush II administration—hint at this when they argue that the U.S. invasion of Iraq "gave other potential enemies a vivid and compelling demonstration of America's ability to win swift and total victory over significant enemy forces with minimal U.S. casualties." David Frum and Richard Perle, *An End to Evil: How to Win the War on Terror* (New York: Random House, 2003), 33.

9. For examples of unipolar agnosticism, see Joseph S. Nye Jr., *The Paradox of American Power: Why the World's Only Superpower Can't Go It Alone* (New York: Oxford University Press, 2002), esp. chaps. 1 and 5; G. John Ikenberry, "Democracy, Institutions, and American Restraint," in *America Unrivaled: The Future of the Balance of Power*, ed. G. John Ikenberry (Ithaca: Cornell University Press, 2002), 213–38; Ikenberry, "Institutions, Strategic Restraint, and the Persistence of the Postwar Order," *International Security* 23, no. 3 (Winter 1998–99), 43–78; Stephen M. Walt, "Keeping the World 'Off-Balance': Self-Restraint and U.S. Foreign Policy," in Ikenberry, *America Unrivaled*, 121–54; Walt, "Beyond Bin Laden: Reshaping U.S. Foreign Policy," *International Security* 26, no. 3 (Winter 1998–99), 59–62, 56.

10. On hegemonic stability theory, see Robert Gilpin, *War and Change in World Politics;* Gilpin, *U.S. Power and the Multinational Corporation: The Political Economy of U.S. Foreign Direct Investment* (New York: Basic Books, 1975); Charles P. Kindleberger, *The World in Depression, 1929–1939* (Berkeley: University of California Press, 1973).

11. Gilpin, *War and Change*, 144–45.

12. G. John Ikenberry, "Strategic Reactions to American Preeminence: Great Power Politics in the Age of Unipolarity," Report to the National Intelligence Council, July 28, 2003, p. 35; www.cia.gov/nic..confreports.

13. The discussion in the following paragraphs is based on the sources cited in note 9 and on Michael Mastanduno and Ethan B. Kapstein, "Realism and State Strategies after the Cold War," in *Unipolar Politics: Realism and State Strategies after the Cold War*, ed. Ethan B. Kapstein and Michael Mastanduno (New York: Columbia University Press, 1999, 1–27; Ethan B. Kapstein, "Does Unipolarity Have a Future?" in Mastanduno and Kapstein, *Unipolar Politics*, 464–90; T. V. Paul, "Introduction: The Enduring Axioms of Balance of Power Theory," in Paul, Wirtz, and Fortmann, *Balance of Power*, 1–25; Fortmann, Paul, and Wirtz, "Conclusions."

14. Ikenberry contends that most of the other potential counterbalancers to the United States are in a "security box" and need U.S. protection against actual or potential regional rivals. These states "have reason to remain tied to the United States" because "there are no good substitutes for military junior partnership." Ikenberry, "Strategic Reactions to American Preeminence," 10.

15. Barry R. Posen, "Command of the Commons: The Military Foundations of American Hegemony," *International Security* 28, no. 1 (Summer 2003): 5–46.

16. Other states may be happy to avail themselves of the collective goods provided by U.S. hegemony, but they are not indifferent to the relative distribution of power in the international system. They must be concerned, because today's ally (or purportedly benevolent hegemon) can always become tomorrow's rival. States "pay close attention to how cooperation might affect relative *capabilities* in the future." Joseph M. Grieco, "Anarchy and the Limits of Cooperation: A Realist Critique of the Newest Liberal Institutionalism," *International Organization* 42, no. 3 (Summer 1988): 500 (emphasis in original). See also Michael C. Webb and Stephen D. Krasner, "Hegemonic Stability Theory: An Empirical Assessment," *Review of International Studies* 15, no. 2 (April 1989): 184–85.

17. Stephen M. Walt, *The Origins of Alliances* (Ithaca: Cornell University Press, 1987), 21.

18. Ibid., 22–26.

19. As Walt puts it, "The United States is by far the world's most *powerful* state, but it does not pose a significant *threat* to the vital interests of the major powers." Walt, "Keeping the World 'Off-Balance,'" 139 (emphasis in original).

20. This claim parallels Mearsheimer's claim about the "stopping power of water."

21. Walt, "Keeping the World 'Off-Balance,'" 137. For a similar argument, see Wohlforth, "U.S. Strategy," 107.

22. Just as all politics are said to be local, Wohlforth argues that geopolitics are similarly local. States worry about nearby threats, not distant ones, and thus are "more concerned with their neighborhoods than with the global equilibrium." Wohlforth, "U.S. Strategy," 102.

23. Jack Levy argues that counterbalancing coalitions are unlikely to form against preponderant offshore powers, such as nineteenth-century Britain or the United States today, because these offshore powers "have fewer capabilities for imposing their will on major continental states, fewer incentives for doing so, and a greater range of strategies for increasing their influence by other means." Jack S. Levy, "What Do Great Powers Balance against and When?" in Paul, Wirtz, and Fortmann, *Balance of Power*, 42.

24. See T. V. Paul, "Balancing under Near-Unipolarity: America and the New Balance of Power Dynamics," *International Security* 30, no.1 (Summer 2005): 46–71.

25. Ibid.

26. Paul is clearly a unipolar agnostic who subscribes to balance-of-threat theory. He makes clear that although U.S. policies today are not sufficiently threatening to prompt others to respond with hard balancing, that could change:

> As long as the U.S. abstains from an active empire building strategy and thereby challenging the sovereignty and territorial integrity of a large number of states, a hard balancing coalition is unlikely to emerge in the foreseeable future, globally or regionally. However, an overt imperial strategy, as proposed by some Bush Administration officials, will propel hard balancing efforts as other great powers will fear that their sovereignty and power status will be compromised if American power is not actively counterbalanced. (Ibid.)

27. Keir Lieber and Gerard Alexander, "Waiting for Balancing: Why the World Is Not Pushing Back," *International Studies* 30, no. 1 (Summer 2005): 109–39.

28. Ikenberry, "Strategic Reactions," 28.

29. Walt, "Keeping the World 'Off-Balance'," 141–52.

30. Ikenberry, "Institutions, Strategic Restraint, and the Persistence of Postwar Order," 76–77.

31. G. John Ikenberrry, introduction to Ikenberry, *America Unrivaled*, 10.

32. G. John Ikenberry and Charles A. Kupchan, "The Legitimation of Hegemonic Power," in *World Leadership and Hegemony*, ed. David P. Rapkin (Boulder, Colo.: Lynne Rienner, 1990), 52.

33. Remarks by Samuel R. Berger, "American Power: Hegemony, Isolationism or Engagement," Council on Foreign Relations, October 21, 1990, http://clinton4.nara.gov/text only/WH/EOP/NSC/html/speeches/19991021.html.

34. "President's State of the Union Message to Congress and the Nation," *New York Times*, January 21, 2005, p. A14; *2002 National Security Strategy*, p. i.

35. Walt's distinction between power and threat is not as clear-cut as it first seems, even in a multipolar setting. For example, he admits that every post-1648 bid for European hegemony was repulsed by a balancing coalition (*Origins of Alliances*, 28–29). But is not clear

whether he believes counterbalancing occurred because would-be hegemons were powerful or because they were threatening. One suspects that his answer would be "both." Power is an important factor in inducing balancing behavior, he says, but it is not the *only* one (21). In Walt's analysis, power and threat blend almost imperceptibly, and two of his threat variables, geographic proximity and offensive capabilities, correlate closely with military *power.*

36. As Colin Elman suggests, "It is possible that, when states are approaching capabilities of hegemonic proportions, those resources alone are so threatening that they 'drown out' distance, offense-defense, and intentions as potential negative threat modifiers." Elman, introduction to *Realism and the Balancing of Power: A New Debate,* ed. John A. Vasquez and Colin Elman (Upper Saddle River, N.J: Prentice-Hall, 2003), 16.
37. Mearsheimer, *Tragedy of Great Power Politics,* 33.
38. Others cannot afford to trust in America's benevolence, because "even if a dominant power behaves with moderation, restraint, and forbearance, weaker states will worry about its future behavior." Kenneth N. Waltz, "Structural Realism after the Cold War," in Ikenberry, *America Unrivaled,* 53.
39. "Minds can be changed, new leaders can come to power, values can shift, new opportunities and dangers can arise." Robert Jervis, "Cooperation under the Security Dilemma," *World Politics* 30, no. 2 (January 1978): 105.
40. Paul Sharp, "Virtue Unrestrained: Herbert Butterfield and the Problem of American Power," *International Studies Perspectives* 5, no. 3 (August 2004): 300–315.
41. Although balancing is the most common strategy employed by great powers to deal with the rise of a too-powerful rival they can follow others, including bandwagoning, buckpassing, bait-and-bleed, bloodletting, and hiding. For discussions, see Mearsheimer, *Tragedy of Great Power Politics,* 153–62 ; Walt, *Origins of Alliances,* 18–31; Paul Schroeder, "Historical Reality vs. Neo-Realist Theory," *International Security* 19, no. 1 (Summer 1994): 108–48; Randall L. Schweller, "Unanswered Threats: A Neoclassical Realist Theory of Underbalancing," *International Security* 29, no. 2 (Fall 2004): 167–68.
42. Schweller, "Unanswered Threats," 166.
43. Jack S. Levy, "Balances and Balancing: Concepts, Propositions, and Research Design," in Vasquez and Elman, *Realism and the Balancing of Power,* 129–30.
44. Colin Elman, introduction to Vasquez and Elman, *Realism and the Balancing of Power,* 8.
45. "Balancing means the creation or aggregation of military power through internal mobilization or the forging of alliances to prevent or deter the territorial occupation or political and military domination of the state by a foreign power or coalition." Schweller, "Unanswered Threats," 166. For similar definitions, see Mearsheimer, *Tragedy of Great Power Politics,* 139; Elman, introduction to Vasquez and Elman, *Realism and the Balancing of Power,* 8. See also Paul, introduction to *Balance of Power.*
46. Waltz, *Theory of International Politics,* 118, 168; Mearsheimer, *Tragedy of Great Power Politics,* 156–57; Levy, "What Do Great Powers Balance against and When?" 35.
47. As they try to catch up to the United States—and are vulnerable to preventive U.S. military action—potential great powers also will employ asymmetric strategies to offset superior U.S. military capabilities. See Christopher Layne, "The War on Terrorism and the Balance of Power: The Paradoxes of American Hegemony," in Paul, Wirtz, Fortmann, *Balance of Power,* 115–18.
48. This section is based on Robert A. Pape, "Soft Balancing against the United States," *International Security,* 30, no. 1 (Summer 2005): 7–45; Paul, "Balancing under Near-Unipolarity"; Paul, introduction to Paul, Wirtz, and Fortmann, *Balance of Power;* Stephen M. Walt, "Can the United States Be Balanced? If So, How?"—paper presented at the annual meeting of the American Political Science Association, Chicago, September 2004. For a very skeptical view of the efficacy of soft balancing, see Lieber and Alexander, "Waiting for Balancing." According to Paul:

> The conditions under which soft balancing behavior occurs are: (1) The hegemonic state's power position and military behavior are of growing concern but do not yet pose a serious challenge to the sovereign existence of other great powers; (2) The dominant state is a major source of public goods in both the economic and security areas which can-

not easily be replaced; and (3) The dominant state cannot easily retaliate as the balancing efforts by others are not overt or directly challenging its power with military means. (Paul, "Balancing under Near-Unipolarity")

49. For example, see the comments of Russian foreign minister Igor S. Ivanov quoted in Richard C. Paddock, "Summit Aims at Halting Militants," *Los Angeles Times*, August 26, 1999, p. A4; the comments of French foreign minister Hubert Vedrine quoted in Craig R. Whitney, "France Presses for a Power Independent of the U.S.," *New York Times*, November 7, 1999, p. A5; Tyler Marshall, "Anti-NATO Axis Poses Threat, Experts Say," *Los Angeles Times*, September 27, 1999, p. A1.

50. Mark Brawley, "The Political Economy of Balance of Power Theory," in Paul, Wirtz, and Fortmann, *Balance of Power*, 83.

51. See Jim Yardley, "Russian Denies War Games with China Are a Signal to Taiwan," *New York Times*, March 19, 2005, http://www.nytimes.com/2005/03/19/international/asia/19china.html.

52. As Robert Art puts it, a state engaging in semi-hard balancing "does not fear an increased threat to its physical security from another rising state; rather it is concerned about the adverse effects of that state's rise on its general position, both political and economic, in the international arena." Robert J. Art, "Europe Hedges Its Security Bets," in Paul, Wirtz, and Fortmann, *Balance of Power*, 180.

53. This phrase is borrowed from the conclusion to Fortmann, Paul, and Wirtz, *Balance of Power*, 366. For a very critical analysis of neorealist predictions about the unipolar era (including those of Layne, Mearsheimer, and Waltz), see Christopher J. Fettweis, "Evaluating IR's Crystal Balls: How Predictions of the Future Have Withstood Fourteen Years of Unipolarity," *International Studies Review* 6, no. 1 (March 2004): 79–104.

54. Waltz, "Structural Realism after the Cold War," 51.

55. As Waltz says, "The explanation for sluggish balancing is a simple one. In the aftermath of earlier great wars, the materials for constructing a new balance were readily at hand. Previous wars left a sufficient number of great powers standing to permit a new balance to be rather easily constructed." Ibid., 54.

56. On collective action problems generally, see Mancur Olson, *The Logic of Collective Action: Public Goods and the Theory of Groups* (Cambridge: Harvard University Press, 1965). On the impediments to counterhegemonic balancing caused by collective action problems, see Mearsheimer and Waltz, cited in note 3, above.

57. On Moscow's hostility to NATO expansion, see J. L. Black, *Russia Faces NATO Expansion: Bearing Gifts or Bearing Arms?* (New York: Rowman and Littlefield, 1999).

58. *Mapping the Global Future: Report of the National Intelligence Council's 2020 Project* (Washington, D.C.: Government Printing Office, December 2004), 47.

59. Ibid., 49. The Strategic Assessment Group's analysis of current and projected world power shares was based on the International Futures Model developed by Barry Hughes. For a discussion of methodology and a summary of the Strategic Assessment Group's findings, see Gregory F. Treverton and Seth G. Jones, *Measuring National Power* (Santa Monica: RAND Corporation, 2005), iii, ix–x.

60. The remainder of this section is based on Layne, "The Unipolar Illusion."

61. For a similar view, see Wohlforth, "Stability of a Unipolar World," 9.

62. Gilpin, *War and Change*, 95.

63. Paul Kennedy, *The Rise and Fall of Great Powers: Economic Change and Military Conflict from 1500 to 2000* (New York: Random House, 1987), xxii.

64. Waltz, "Structural Realism after the Cold War," 52.

65. On this point, see William Curti Wohlforth, *The Elusive Balance: Power and Perceptions during the Cold War* (Ithaca: Cornell University Press, 1993).

66. The following diplomatic historians conclude that France was Europe's only great power in 1660: G. R. R. Treasure, *Seventeenth Century France* (London: Rivingtons, 1966), 257–58; Derek McKay and H. M. Scott, *The Rise of the Great Powers, 1648–1815* (London: Longman, 1983); John B. Wolf, *Toward a European Balance of Power, 1620–1715* (Chicago: Rand McNally, 1970), 1. However, some international relations scholars who measure the concentration of power in the international system quantitatively disagree with this

conclusion. For example, see William R. Thompson, *On Global War: Historical-Structural Approaches to World Politics* (Columbia: University of South Carolina Press, 1988), 212. The following historians and international relations scholars describe mid-nineteenth century Britain as *the* hegemonic power in a unipolar international system: Michael Doyle, *Empires* (Ithaca: Cornell University Press, 1986), 236; Kennedy, *Rise and Fall of the Great Powers*, 152; Fareed Zakaria, "Realism and Domestic Politics: A Review Essay," *International Security* 17, no. 1 (Summer 1992): 186–87. For quantitative research supporting this conclusion, see Thompson, *On Global War*, 213, and William B. Moul, "Measuring the Balance of Power: A Look at Some Numbers," *Review of International Studies* 15, no. 2 (April 1989): 120. On the other hand, some historians and international relations scholars using qualitative case study methodology have argued that mid-Victorian Britain was not hegemonic and that its role in international politics is not comparable at all with that of the United States since 1990. For example, see Patrick Karl O'Brien, "The Pax Britannica and American Hegemony: Precedent, Antecedent, or Just Another History?" and John M. Hobson, "Two Hegemonies or One? A Historical-Sociological Critique of Hegemonic Stability Theory," in *Two Hegemonies: Britain 1846–1914 and the United States 1941–2001*, ed. Patrick Karl O'Brien and Armand Cleese (Aldershot, Eng.: Ashgate, 2002), 3–66, 305–25.

67. Other states might question the reliability of U.S. security guarantees:

> The unipolar state may realize some gains from alliance cooperation with its junior partners but, ultimately, its security is guaranteed by its own power capabilities. Subordinate states must always worry if this security protection will be forthcoming. These security asymmetries, as a result, create incentives for weaker and secondary states to seek alternative ways to protect themselves—loosening their security ties to the unipolar state and fostering regional alternatives. (Ikenberry, conclusion to *America Unrivaled*, 301)

68. See Guy Dinmore, Anna Fifield, and Victor Mallet, "The Rivals: Washington's Sway in Asia Is Challenged by China," *Financial Times*, March 18, 2005, p. 11; Jane Perlez, "Across Asia, Beijing's Star Is in Ascendance," *New York Times*, August 28, 2004. For a more equivocal view of China's rise, and the extent to which it poses a threat to U.S. interests in China, see David Shambaugh, "China Engages Asia: Reshaping the Regional Order," *International Security* 29, no. 3 (Winter 2004–2005): 64–99.

69. Perlez, "Beijing's Star Is in Ascendance."

70. See *Mapping the Global Future*, 28, 30, 35, 47–50; James Kynge, "World Is Dancing to a Chinese Tune," *Financial Times: Special Report—FT China*, December 7, 2004, p. 1.

71. Gilpin, *War and Change*, 156–210.

72. Karen Adams's research inferentially supports the existence of the hegemon's temptation. See Karen Ruth Adams, "Attack and Conquer? International Anarchy and the Offense-Defense-Deterrence Balance," *International Security* 28, no. 3 (Winter 2003–2004): 68, 81–82.

73. Gilpin, *War and Change*, 33–34. As Gilpin says (33), prestige is closely related to credibility, and (34) it "is achieved primarily through successful use of power, and especially through victory in war."

74. Quoted in Ann Scott Tyson, "U.S. Gaining World's Respect from Wars, Rumsfeld Asserts," *Washington Post*, March 11, 2005, p. A4.

75. The classic studies are Gilpin, *War and Change*, and Kennedy, *Rise and Fall of the Great Powers*.

76. Thus, as Edward Luttwak has observed, for both the Roman Empire and the United States "the elusive goal of strategic statecraft was to provide security for the civilization without prejudicing the vitality of its economic base and without compromising the stability of an evolving political order." Edward Luttwak, *The Grand Strategy of the Roman Empire: From the First Century A.D. to the Third* (Cambridge: Harvard University Press, 1976), 1.

77. Robert Gilpin, *The Political Economy of International Relations* (Princeton: Princeton University Press, 1987), 332.

78. This term is Niall Ferguson's. Niall Ferguson, *Colossus: The Price of America's Empire* (New York: Penguin Press, 2004), 262.

79. As Ferguson says, "America's fiscal overstretch is far worse today than anything [Kennedy] envisaged sixteen years ago." Ibid.

80. U.S. budget and trade deficits have not been a serious problem so far, because creditors believed that the United States could repay its debts. If, for economic or, conceivably, *geopolitical* reasons, others are no longer willing to finance American indebtedness, however, Washington's choices will be stark: significant dollar devaluation to increase U.S. exports (which will cause inflation and lower living standards) or raising interest rates sharply to attract foreign capital inflows (which will shrink domestic investment and worsen America's long-term economic problems). Given the deindustrialization of the U.S. economy over the past three decades, it is questionable whether, even with a dramatically depreciated dollar, the United States could export enough to make a major dent in its foreign debt. For the argument that fears about the trade deficit are exaggerated, see Joseph Quinlan and Marc Chandler, "The U.S. Trade Deficit: A Dangerous Obsession," *Foreign Affairs* 80, no. 3 (May–June 2001): 87–97.

81. From the U.S. standpoint, the most frightening soft-balancing scenario is the prospect that—more for geopolitical than economic reasons—the EU, China, and other key players (like OPEC) will collaborate to have the euro supplant the dollar as the international economic system's reserve currency.

82. See Niall Ferguson and Laurence J. Kotlikoff, "Going Critical: American Power and the Consequences of Fiscal Overstretch," *National Interest* 73 (Fall 2003): 22–32. See also Laurence J. Kotlikoff and Scott Burns, *The Coming Generational Storm: What You Need to Know about America's Economic Future* (Cambridge: MIT Press, 2004).

83. Alternatively, the United States could raise taxes dramatically. This would have negative long-term consequences for the economy, however. More important, perhaps, it is not clear that if confronted with a stark choice between hegemony or domestic welfare, either Congress or the public would accept being taxed as very high rates in order to sustain American preponderance.

84. Gilpin, *Political Economy of International Relations,* 347–48. For a more recent iteration of this analysis of U.S economic prospects, see Peter G. Peterson, *Running on Empty: How the Democratic and Republican Parties Are Bankrupting Our Future and What Americans Can Do about It* (New York: Farrar, Strauss and Giroux, 2004).

85. See Mark Mazzetti, "Military at Risk, Pentagon Warned," *Los Angeles Times,* May 3, 2005, http://www.latimes.com/news/printedition/front/la-na-strategy3may03; Thom Shanker, "Pentagon Says Iraq Effort Limits Ability to Fight Other Conflicts," *New York Times,* May 3, 2005, http://nytimes.com/2005/05/03/politics/03military.html; Ann Scott Tyson, "Two Years Later, Iraq War Drains Military," *Washington Post,* March 19, 2005, p. A1. Facing troop shortages, the Defense Department apparently has concluded that it will need allied military support to undertake future military interventions and subsequent occupations. The terms of reference for the Pentagon's 2005 Quadrennial Defense Review state that current security challenges "are such that the United States cannot succeed by addressing them alone." Quoted in Thom Shanker, "Pentagon Invites Allies for First Time to Secret Talks Aimed at Sharing Burdens," *New York Times,* March 18, 2005, p. A10. See also Mark Mazzetti, "Iraq War Compels Pentagon to Rethink Big-Picture Strategy," *Los Angeles Times,* March 11, 2005, http://www.latimes.com/news/printedition/front/la-na-mil warllmar11. It is doubtful whether allied help will be forthcoming in the future, however. One of the clear lessons of Iraq is that if American allies disagree with U.S. policy, they will withhold military support.

86. As Gilpin observes, "The critical significance of the differential growth of power among states is that it alters the cost of changing the international system and therefore the incentives for changing the international system." Gilpin, *War and Change,* 95.

87. Brooks and Wohlforth, "American Primacy," 33.

88. Layne, "Unipolar Illusion," 7.

89. Wohlforth, "Stability of a Unipolar World," 8 (emphasis added).

90. For a powerful argument that the entente with France and the continental commitment were ill-advised—and that Britain could, and should, have avoided being dragged into World War I—see Neill Ferguson, *Pity of War* (New York: Basic Books, 1999). See also Daniel A. Baugh, "British Strategy during the First World War in the Context of Four Centuries: Blue-Water versus Continental Commitment," in *Naval History: The Sixth Symposium*

of the U.S. Naval Academy, ed. Daniel M. Masterson (Wilmington, Del.: Scholarly Resources, 1987), 105–6.

8. The Strategy of Offshore Balancing

1. Barry R. Posen, "Command of the Commons: The Military Foundation of American Hegemony," *International Security* 28, no. 1 (Summer 2003): 5–46. Posen (6–7) distinguishes between primacy and selective engagement as two approaches to hegemony. The definitive argument for "selective engagement" is Robert J. Art, *A Grand Strategy for America* (Ithaca: Cornell University Press, 2003).
2. For a good overview of U.S. grand strategic options, see Michael E. Brown, Owen R. Cote Jr., Sean Lynn-Jones, and Steven E. Miller, eds., *America's Strategic Choices,* rev. ed. (Cambridge: MIT Press, 2000).
3. The European Wars from 1792 to 1815 include the Wars of the First, Second, and Third Coalitions; the French wars with Austria (1809) and Russia (1812); the Peninsular War against Britain and Spain (1808–13); and the War of the Fourth Coalition (1813–15).
4. The United States also was involved in the so-called Quasi-War with Revolutionary France from 1798 to 1800. Although the war affected U.S. commerce, it was not primarily *about* commerce. In the Quasi-War, which in today's parlance was a low-intensity conflict, the United States and France employed privateers (not their respective national navies) to wage a limited naval war against each other's commerce. For details see Richard W. Van Alstyne, *American Diplomacy in Action,* rev. ed. (Gloucester, Mass.: Peter Smith, 1968), 485–96.
5. For a social scientific take on the use of counterfactuals, see Philip E. Tetlock and Aaron Belkin, eds., *Counterfactual Thought Experiments in World Politics: Logical, Methodological, and Psychological Perspectives* (Princeton: Princeton University Press, 1996); James D. Fearon, "Counterfactuals and Hypothesis Testing in Political Science," *World Politics* 43, no. 2 (January 1991): 169–95. For counterfactual case studies by historians, see Niall Ferguson, ed., *Virtual History* (New York: Basic Books, 1999).
6. On the Kuhlmann peace feeler and the role America's entry into the war played in London's decision not to pursue it despite Lloyd George's initial interest, see David Stevenson, *Cataclysm: The First World War as Political Tragedy* (New York: Basic Books, 2004), 291–92.
7. Ibid., 296 (emphasis in original).
8. Ibid., 261.
9. For example, see Frank Costigliola, *Awkward Dominion: American Political, Economic, and Cultural Relations with Europe, 1919–1933* (Ithaca: Cornell University Press, 1984); Michael J. Hogan, *Informal Entente: The Private Structure of Cooperation in Anglo-American Economic Diplomacy, 1918–1928* (Columbia: University of Missouri Press, 1977); Akira Iriye, *The Cambridge History of American Foreign Relations,* vol. 3, *The Globalizing of America, 1913–1945* (Cambridge: Cambridge University Press, 1993); Melvyn P. Leffler, *The Elusive Quest: America's Pursuit of European Stability and French Security, 1919–1933* (Chapel Hill: University of North Carolina Press, 1979).
10. Michael A. Barnhart, "The Origins of the Second World War in Asia and the Pacific: Synthesis Impossible?" in *Paths to Power: The Historiography of American Foreign Relations to 1941,* ed. Michael J. Hogan (Cambridge: Cambridge University Press, 2000), 281.
11. With respect to America's entry into World War II, Frank Ninkovich observes that it is "easy to imagine all kinds of scenarios in which the United States might well have stayed out of war if different leaders had been at the helm or if other accidents of history had occurred." Frank Ninkovich, *The Wilsonian Century: U.S. Foreign Policy since 1900* (Chicago: University of Chicago Press, 1999), 136.
12. Zalmay Khalilzad et al., *The United States and Asia: Toward a New U.S. Strategy and Force Posture* (Santa Monica, Calif.: RAND Corporation, 2001), 43. If the United States is determined to prevent a "concentration of resources" that spawns a new peer competitor—China—the current grand strategy is the wrong one. China is emerging as a great power because of its domestic economic growth, not because of conquest. Peace and stability in the region only facilitate China's growth, and erode American primacy. U.S. strategy can-

not attain its goals in East Asia. Preventing a Soviet-like concentration of resources would require seriously impeding China's economic growth, through preventive war or fomenting internal disorder. Voices openly recommending such a policy include Bradley A. Thayer: "Confronting China: An Evaluation of Options for the United States," *Comparative Strategy* 24, no. 1 (January–March 2005): 71–98. Offshore balancing is a more sensible policy than this dangerous and confrontational strategy. The United States should allow Japan, India, and Russia to contain China.

13. Ibid., xiii.

14. On the Korean Peninsula, see Ted Galen Carpenter and Doug Bandow, *The Korean Conundrum: America's Troubled Relations with North and South Korea* (New York: Palgrave/Macmillan, 2004).

15. Ibid., 30–31, 87–93.

16. Ibid., 146.

17. One of the best overviews of the development of deterrence as both a theory and a strategy remains Lawrence Freedman, *The Evolution of Nuclear Strategy* (New York: St. Martin's, 1983). Influential contributions to American strategic thinking about deterrence include Henry A. Kissinger, *Nuclear Weapons and Foreign Policy* (New York: Harper, 1957); Thomas C. Schelling, *Arms and Influence* (New Haven: Yale University Press, 1966); Schelling, *The Strategy of Conflict* (Cambridge: Harvard University Press 1960); and Glenn Snyder, *Deterrence and Defense: Toward a Theory of National Security* (Princeton: Princeton University Press, 1961).

18. Patrick Morgan, *Deterrence: A Conceptual Analysis* (Beverly Hills, Calif.: Sage, 1983), 86.

19. Thomas Schelling has explained why extended deterrence raises such important concerns about credibility: "To *fight* abroad is a military act, but to *persuade* enemies or allies that one would fight abroad, under circumstances of great cost and risk, requires more than a military capability. It requires projecting intentions. It requires *having* those intentions, even deliberately acquiring them, and communicating them persuasively to make other countries behave." Schelling, *Arms and Influence*, 36 (emphasis in original).

During the cold war, many U.S. strategists suggested that to solve the "credibility of commitment" problem, the United States needed to (1) acquire strategic damage limitation capabilities (a counterforce strategic nuclear arsenal, ballistic missile defenses), and (2) uphold its commitments, by defending intrinsically unimportant areas, deliberately circumscribing its ability to back away from commitments, and demonstrating that it could act "irrationally." See Colin S. Gray, "Nuclear Strategy: A Case for a Theory of Victory," *International Security* 4, no. 1 (Summer 1979); Colin S. Gray and Keith Payne, "Victory Is Possible," *Foreign Policy* 39 (Summer 1980); and Earl Ravenal, "Alliance and Counterforce," *International Security* 6, no. 4 (Spring 1982): 26–43. Unlike Gray and Payne, Ravenal concluded that United States could not attain the strategic prerequisites for credible extended deterrence. For the argument that extended deterrence is credible even under the condition of mutual assured destruction see Robert Jervis, *Illogic of American Nuclear Strategy* (Ithaca: Cornell University Press, 1984); Charles L. Glaser, *Analyzing Strategic Nuclear Policy* (Princeton: Princeton University Press, 1990). On the "rationality of the irrational" see Stephen Maxwell, *Rationality in Deterrence,* Adelphi Paper No. 50 (London: International Institute of Strategic Studies, 1968).

20. Circular Telegram from Department of State to Embassies in the North Atlantic Treaty Organization Countries, July 10, 1959, *FRUS 1958–60,* 7:466.

21. U.S. embassies in the capitals of the Western European NATO allies were instructed to tell their respective host governments (1) that Herter's remarks were taken out of context; (2) that the authoritative statement of U.S. policy was Eisenhower's statement at the December 1957 NATO Heads of Government meeting ("I assure you in the most solemn terms that the United States would come, at once and with all appropriate force, to the assistance of any NATO nation subjected to armed attack"); and (3) to point out the U.S. record in resisting the Soviets since the end of World War II (Truman Doctrine, Berlin Airlift, Korea, Taiwan Strait) "as well as to the physical presence of large numbers of US forces in the NATO area, as clear evidence of our determination to stand by allied countries subjected to armed aggression or threat of force." Ibid., 465–66.

22. Quoted in Paul Lewis, "U.S. Pledge to NATO to Use Nuclear Arms Criticized by Kissinger," *New York Times*, September 2, 1979, A7.
23. Robert Jervis, "What Do We Want to Deter and How Do We Deter It?" in *Turning Point: The Gulf War and U.S. Military Strategy*, ed. L. Benjamin Ederington and Michael J. Mazar (Boulder, Colo.: Westview Press, 1994), 130.
24. Paul Huth, *Extended Deterrence and the Prevention of War* (New Haven: Yale University Press, 1988), 43.
25. Nuclear deterrence is effective when the defender's own survival is at stake but much less so in other situations. In the case of "limited" or "specific" challenges, the outcome is "determined by the parties' relative determination regarding the issue in dispute." Shai Feldman, "Middle East Nuclear Stability: The State of the Region and the State of the Debate," *Journal of International Affairs* 49, no. 1 (Summer 1995): 215. Also see T. V. Paul, *Asymmetric Conflicts: War Initiation by Weaker Powers* (Cambridge: Cambridge University Press, 1994). Some scholars have employed "prospect theory" to explain why a state could be motivated to choose war even though victory is doubtful. See John Arquilla and Paul K. Davis, *Extended Deterrence, Compellence, and the "Old World Order"* (Santa Monica, Calif.: RAND, 1992), and Paul K. Davis and John Arquilla, *Thinking about Opponent Behavior in Crisis and Conflict: A Generic Model for Analysis and Group Discussion* (Santa Monica, Calif.: RAND, 1991); Barbara Farnham, ed., *Avoiding Losses/Taking Risks: Prospect Theory and International Conflict* (Ann Arbor: University of Michigan Press, 1995). For a balanced assessment of prospect theory as applied to international relations see Jack S. Levy, "Prospect Theory and International Relations: Theoretical Applications and Analytical Problems," *Political Psychology* 13, no. 2 (1992): 283–310. See also Robert Jervis, *The Meaning of the Nuclear Revolution: Statecraft and the Prospect of Peace* (Ithaca: Cornell University Press, 1989), 30–31, and Schelling, *Arms and Influence*, 44.
26. On Taiwan's role in Sino-American relations, see Ted Galen Carpenter, *America's Coming War with China: A Collision Course over Taiwan* (New York: Palgrave Macmillan, 2006).
27. On "chain-ganging," see Jack Snyder and Thomas J. Christensen, "Chain Gangs and Passed Bucks: Predicting Alliance Patterns in Multipolarity," *International Organization* 44, no. 2 (Spring 1990): 137–66. For the argument that bipolar systems are more stable than multipolar ones, see Kenneth Waltz, *Theory of International Politics* (Reading, Mass.: Addison-Wesley, 1979), 161–76; Kenneth Waltz, "The Stability of a Bipolar World," *Daedalus* 93, no. 3 (Summer 1964): 881–909; John J. Mearsheimer, "Back to the Future: Instability in Europe after the Cold War," *International Security* 15, no. 1 (Summer 1990): 5–56. For the counterargument see Stephen Van Evera, "Primed for Peace: Europe after the Cold War," *International Security* 15, no. 3 (Winter 1990–1991): 7–57. For the argument that the international system's stability during the cold war was attributable to nuclear deterrence and that bipolarity was an irrelevant factor see Ted Hopf, "Polarity, the Offense-Defense Balance, and War," *American Political Science Review* 81, no. 3 (June 1991): 475–94.
28. See Carpenter, *America's Coming War with China*.
29. Quoted in Patrick E. Tyler, "As China Threatens Taiwan, It Makes Sure U.S. Listens," *New York Times*, January 24, 1996, A3.
30. Art, *Grand Strategy for America*, 147. Art also acknowledges (154–57) that there may be times when the United States must fight in the less important Eurasian peripheries in order to maintain the credibility of its alliances.
31. Jonathan Mercer, *Reputation and International Politics* (Ithaca: Cornell University Press, 1996).
32. During the cold war, the Soviet Union did not conclude that American defeats in the periphery undermined the credibility of U.S. commitments to areas of high intrinsic strategic value. See Ted Hopf, *Peripheral Visions: Deterrence Theory and American Foreign Policy in the Third World, 1965–1990* (Ann Arbor: University of Michigan Press, 1994).
33. This formulation is borrowed from Robert H. Johnson, *Improbable Dangers: U.S. Conceptions of Threat in the Cold War and After* (New York: St. Martin's, 1994), 144.
34. This is why leading academic students of U.S. grand strategy insist that it is better for states like Germany and Japan to remain under America's extended deterrence "nuclear umbrella" rather than acquiring their own nuclear deterrents. As Robert Art argues, if Ger-

many and Japan went nuclear, "that might risk the end of America's major alliances and the stabilizing presence that America's military presence provides at each end of Eurasia, resulting in the increased prospect of more nuclear spread to other Eurasian states, leading in turn to the further weakening of the global norm against nuclear spread, and so on." Art, *Grand Strategy for America*, 54. Michael Mandelbaum argues similarly. See Michael Mandelbaum, "Lessons of the Next Nuclear War," *Foreign Affairs* 74, no. 2 (March–April 1995): 27–28.

35. According to Kennedy's account of his June 1961 conversation with de Gaulle, the French president stated: "The whole position in Europe has changed since NATO was founded. Then there was a nuclear monopoly, now there is a nuclear balance. The United States could say that it was prepared to act by trading New York for Paris, but would we really do so?" Memorandum of Conversation with the President and the Congressional Leadership, June 6, 1961, *FRUS 1961–63*, 8:668.

36. Khalilzad et al., *United States and Asia*, 13.

37. Japan apparently is thinking seriously about acquiring nuclear weapons. Howard W. French, "Nuclear Arms Taboo Is Challenged in Japan," *New York Times*, June 9, 2002, http://www.nytimes.com/2002/06/09/international/asia/09JAPA.html; Howard W. French, "Koizumi Aide Hints at Change to No-Nuclear Policy," *New York Times*, June 4, 2002, http://www.nytimes.com/2002/06/04/international/asia/04JAPA.html.

38. Jonathan D. Pollack, "The Changing Political-Military Environment: Northeast Asia," in Khalilzad et al., *United States and Asia*, appendix A, 114.

39. Ibid., 120.

40. Ibid., 133. As Pollack puts it, "Korea and Japan . . . increasingly believe that the uncertainties and risks to their national interests are too great to warrant relying on U.S. power alone." Khalilzad et al., *United States and Asia*, 94.

41. On this point, see Peter Lieberman, "Ties That Blind: Will Germany and Japan Rely Too Much on the United States?" *Security Studies* 10, no. 2 (Winter 2000–2001): 98–138. Noting that U.S. alliances in Europe and East Asia primarily are intended to preserve unipolarity and to prevent the kind of geopolitical avalanche that would be triggered by German and Japanese re-nationalization, Lieberman shows that in the post–cold war world the credibility of America's commitment to go to war to defend Germany and Japan has diminished. If Germany and Japan rely on Washington strategically and a future crisis exposes the hollowness of U.S. commitments, resulting crash military buildups by Germany and Japan could be destabilizing, because "power shifts," he observes (99), "are more dangerous in foul weather than in fair." Lieberman concludes that a devolution of security responsibilities by the United States to Germany and Japan is premature for the moment, but he also says Washington should be on the lookout for the early warning signs of a commitment crisis, so that it can implement a policy of gradual re-nationalization before that option is foreclosed by events. Lieberman's arguments about extended deterrence closely track those presented here, which I first laid out in Christopher Layne, "From Preponderance to Offshore Balancing: America's Future Grand Strategy," *International Security* 22, no. 1 (Summer 1997): 86–124.

42. In the coming decades, a blanket prohibition of proliferation is neither possible nor desirable. U.S. policymakers therefore need to focus on asking controversial but important questions: Which states are acceptable proliferators and which are not? What criteria should be used in making this decision? How can the United States channel proliferation to minimize its disruptive impact on the international system? For an excellent discussion about the pros and cons of proliferation, see Scott D. Sagan and Kenneth N. Waltz, *The Spread of Nuclear Weapons: A Debate* (New York: W. W. Norton, 1995). Other useful discussions of these issues include Peter D. Feaver, "Command and Control in Emerging Nuclear Nations," *International Security* 17, no. 4 (Winter 1992–1993): 160–87; David Garnham, "Extending Deterrence with German Nuclear Weapons," *International Security* 10, no. 1 (Summer 1985): 96–110; John J. Mearsheimer, "Back to the Future," 7–8, 54; Mearsheimer, "The Case for a Ukrainian Nuclear Deterrent," *Foreign Affairs* 72, no. 3 (Summer 1993): 50–66.

43. There is little risk this kind of managed proliferation would cause a nuclear stampede by a

large number of states. Most middle and small powers, with limited resources, probably will decide to forego nuclear weapons and conclude that their security best would be enhanced by strengthening their conventional forces. See Steven E. Miller, "Fateful Choices: Nuclear Weapons, Ukrainian Security, and International Stability," in *Civil-Military Relations and Nuclear Weapons,* ed. Scott D. Sagan (Stanford: Stanford University Press, 1994), 139–63.

44. Art, *Grand Strategy for America,* 205.
45. Eugene Gholz and Daryl G. Press, "The Effects of Wars on Neutral Countries: Why It Doesn't Pay to Preserve the Peace," *Security Studies* 10, no. 4 (Summer 2001): 1–57.
46. Ibid., 3.
47. See Waltz, *Theory of International Politics,* 145–46. On the dependence of small states on the international economy, see Peter J. Katzenstein, *Small States in World Markets: Industrial Policy in Europe* (Ithaca: Cornell University Press, 1985).
48. For discussion of the four important economic advantages enjoyed by nonbelligerents, see Gholz and Press, "Effects of Wars on Neutral Countries," 15–16.
49. See Kathleen Burk, *Britain, America, and the Sinews of War, 1914–1918* (Boston: Allen and Unwin, 1985); Gholz and Press, "Effects of Wars on Neutral Countries," 25–43.
50. Gholz and Press, "Effects of Wars on Neutral Countries," 53.
51. Ibid., 56.
52. Ibid. For a similar analysis, see Lieberman, "Ties That Blind," 109–11.
53. For example, see Art, *Grand Strategy for America,* 208–9. I am deeply grateful to Daryl Press and Eugene Gholz for discussing their reactions to Art's critique of their article and for sharing their thoughts on the oil issue (including the current draft of their article on the subject).
54. The classic work is Julius W. Pratt, *The Expansionists of 1812* (New York: Macmillan, 1925).
55. On U.S. policy toward Japan during 1940–41, see Waldo Heinrichs, *Threshold of War: Franklin D. Roosevelt and American Entry into World War II* (New York: Oxford University Press, 1988); Jonathan G. Utley, *Going to War with Japan, 1931–1941* (Knoxville: University of Tennessee Press, 1985). In July 1940, following Japan's occupation of northern French Indochina, Washington embargoed the sale to Japan of high-quality scrap metal and high-octane gasoline. In response to Japan's occupation of southern French Indochina in July 1941, Washington froze all Japanese assets in the United States, and in early August blocked all exports of petroleum products from the United States to Japan.
56. This discussion is based on Stevenson, *Cataclysm,* 255–61.
57. See Charles Callan Tansill, *America Goes to War* (Boston: Little, Brown, 1938); Charles A. Beard, *The Devil Theory of War: An Inquiry into the Nature of History and the Possibility of Keeping Out of War* (New York: Vanguard, 1936). Priscilla Roberts has advanced a far more subtle and interesting argument: because France and Britain depended heavily on war matériel purchased from the United States, and, of course, on loans from American banks that allowed them to buy these goods, had the United States cut off its loans to the Allies in 1916, Britain and France would not have been able to sustain their war effort into 1917. Consequently, Germany would not have needed to reinstate unrestricted submarine warfare, and thus could have minimized the risk that the United States would enter the war. Priscilla Roberts, "The Anglo-American Theme: American Visions of an Atlantic Alliance, 1914–1933," *Diplomatic History* 21, no. 3 (Summer 1997): 342.
58. Stevenson, *Cataclysm,* 260. Similarly, John Thompson argues that there is no evidence sustaining the claim that Wilson "was primarily concerned with the economic effects of the U-boat campaign. Not only did he give no indication that this was for him an important consideration but the magnitude of the interests involved was not large." Even if the United States failed to challenge Germany's submarine campaign, the Allies would have continued to buy food and war matériel from the United States and ship them in their own merchant vessels. Thus, "what was a stake was a diminution of exports rather than their complete cessation." See John A. Thompson, "Economics and International Politics: Why Did the United States Enter World War I?" unpublished manuscript, St. Catherine's College, University of Cambridge (2005).
59. Art, *Grand Strategy for America,* 208.

60. Even defeated great powers stage relatively rapid economic comebacks. Even if economically important great powers in Eurasia suffered serious economic dislocation, their economic activity would be back to prewar levels in a fairly short time. See A. F. K. Organski and Jacek Kugler, "The Costs of Major Wars: The Phoenix Factor," *American Political Science Review* 71, no. 4 (December 1977): 1347–1366.

61. Apparently, Joint Chiefs of Staff Chairman General Colin Powell opposed a U.S. attack on Kuwait and Iraq and favored sticking to a strategy of deterrence and containment. See Christopher Layne, "Why the Gulf War Was Not in the National Interest," *Atlantic Monthly* (July 1991), 55, 65.

62. John J. Mearsheimer and Stephen M. Walt, "An Unnecessary War," *Foreign Policy*, no. 134 (January 2003): 50–59.

63. Daryl Press and Eugene Gholz, "Protecting 'The Prize': Oil and the U.S. National Interest," paper presented at the Annual Meeting of the American Political Science Association, Chicago, Illinois, September 2004. Gholz and Press reached this conclusion based on their study of the internal unrest and oil strikes in Iran (1978–79) and the 2002 Venezuelan oil strike.

64. High oil prices are driving consuming nations to shift to alternative energy sources. See Fiona Harvey, "High Oil Price Drives Users to Other Fuels," *Financial Times*, March 16, 2005.

65. Asked by the *Washington Post* editorial board whether the Bush II administration's policy of promoting a democratic transformation in the Middle East would create more turmoil and open the door to power for radical Islamic groups, Rice responded in the negative, adding: "Can we be certain of that? No. But do I think there is a strong certainty that the Middle East was not going to be stable anyway? Yes. And when you know that the status quo is no longer defensible, then you have to be willing to move in a different direction." Condoleeza Rice, interview with the Washington Post editorial board, March 25, 2005, http://www.state.gov/secretary/rm/2005/43863.htm.

66. See Robert J. Samuelson, "A New Era for Oil?" *Washington Post*, March 30, 2005, A15; Samuelson, "Is the Global Economy Unstable?" *Washington Post*, March 16, 2005, A23; Kevin Morrison and Javier Blas, "IEA Says World Must Turn Away from Oil," *Financial Times*, March 11, 2005. Ian Rutledge argues that worries about U.S. dependence on imported—especially Gulf—oil were an important factor driving the U.S. invasion of Iraq. He claims that the United States wanted to establish a pliant Iraqi government that would open its oil industry to U.S. investment and counter Saudi market power in setting oil prices. According to Rutledge, Bush administration officials were concerned that Saudi Arabia would not make the massive capital investments needed to increase production enough to supply U.S. and global demand at a price American consumers would accept. Control of Iraqi oil would alleviate this problem. See Ian Rutledge, *Addicted to Oil: America's Relentless Drive for Energy Security* (London: I. B. Tauris, 2005).

67. For a decade-old but very prescient analysis of how East Asia's rising demand for energy could result in geopolitical competition, see Kent E. Calder, *Pacific Defense: Arms, Energy, and America's Future in Asia* (New York: William Morrow, 1996). For more recent discussion, see David Zweig and Bi Jianhai, "China's Global Hunt for Energy," *Foreign Affairs* 84, no. 5 (September/October 2005): 25–38.

68. For an excellent analysis of buck-passing as a grand strategy, see John J. Mearsheimer, *The Tragedy of Great Power Politics* (New York: W. W. Norton, 2001), 269–72.

69. On the relationship between geography and buck-passing in multipolar systems, see ibid., 271–72. See also Snyder and Christensen, "Chain Gangs and Passed Bucks."

70. The arguments in favor of an offshore strategy were clearly articulated in the eighteenth century by the Tory proponents of an English "blue water" grand strategy. See Richard Pares, "American versus Continental Warfare, 1739–63," *English Historical Review* 5l, no. 203 (July 1936): 436–37.

71. See Robert W. Tucker, *The New Isolationism: Threat or Promise?* (New York: Universe Books, 1972), 40–51.

72. The argument that the United States intervened in World War I because of fear that Ger-

many was on the verge of gaining hegemony is Europe was advanced *retrospectively* in Walter Lippmann, *U.S. Foreign Policy: Shield of the Republic* (Boston: Little, Brown, 1943).

73. Mearsheimer, *Tragedy of Great Power Politics*, 142–43 (emphasis added).

74. The relationship between fears of European—especially German—penetration into the Western Hemisphere and U.S. foreign and strategic policy prior to World War I is explored in Richard D. Challener, *Admirals, Generals, and Foreign Policy, 1898–1914* (Princeton: Princeton University Press, 1973), and J. A. S. Grenville and George B. Young, *Politics, Strategy, and American Diplomacy: Studies in American Foreign Policy, 1873–1917* (New Haven: Yale University Press, 1966).

75. Stevenson, *Cataclysm*, 260. As Priscilla Roberts points out, although most leading members of the Eastern establishment were strongly pro-British, they argued the case for American entry into the war primarily on moral, *not* strategic, grounds. Roberts, "Anglo-American Theme," 343–46.

76. See Jerald A. Combs, *American Diplomatic History: Two Centuries of Changing Interpretations* (Berkeley: University of California Press, 1983), 379.

77. As George Baer observes, the 1916 naval construction program was intended to ensure that the U.S. Navy, acting alone, would be powerful enough to defeat any power or coalition that might challenge U.S. primacy in the Western Hemisphere. See George W. Baer, *One Hundred Years of Sea Power: The U.S. Navy, 1890–1990* (Stanford: Stanford University Press, 1994), 60–61. As President Woodrow Wilson declared, the purpose of the 1916 naval construction program was to make the U.S. Navy "incomparably the greatest navy in the world." Quoted in Kenneth J. Hagan, *This People's Navy: The Making of American Sea Power* (New York: Free Press, 1991), 252.

78. My thinking on these issues has been influenced by the work of John A. Thompson. I am deeply grateful to Professor Thompson for allowing me to read drafts of his work in progress and for his extensive ongoing dialogue by correspondence with me. See John A. Thompson, "Another Look at the Downfall of 'Fortress America'," *Journal of American Studies* 26, no. 3 (December 1992): 393–408; Thompson, "The Exaggeration of American Vulnerability: The Anatomy of a Tradition," *Diplomatic History* 16, no. 1 (Winter 1991): 23–27; Thompson, "America's Entry into World War II and Conceptions of National Security," *Diplomacy and Statecraft* (forthcoming).

79. In fact, as Richard Aldrich describes, the "evidence" Roosevelt relied on to hype this alleged German threat to the Western Hemisphere was based on documents and maps forged by British intelligence to manipulate U.S. public opinion and discredit opponents of U.S. intervention in the European war. Richard J. Aldrich, *Intelligence and the War against Japan: Britain, America, and the Politics of Secret Service* (Cambridge: Cambridge University Press, 2000), 100.

80. Hanson W. Baldwin, *United We Stand! Defense of the Western Hemisphere* (New York: Whittlesey House, 1941), esp. 75–82; Nicholas John Spykman, *America's Strategy in World Politics: The United States and the Balance of Power* (New York: Harcourt, Brace and World, 1942), 391–93, 397, 441, 443–45. On noninterventionists' opposition to the Roosevelt administration's drift toward involvement in World War II, see Justus D. Doenecke, *Storm on the Horizon: The Challenge to American Intervention, 1939–1941* (Lanham, Md.: Rowman and Littlefield, 2000).

81. Spykman, *America's Strategy in World Politics*, 451–55.

82. Robert J. Art, "The United States, the Balance of Power, and World War II: Was Spykman Right?" *Security Studies* 14, no. 3 (Summer 2005): 1–42. Art's analysis is a persuasive rebuttal to Spykman's economic strangulation argument.

83. Tucker, *New Isolationism*.

84. Michael S. Sherry, *In the Shadow of War: The United States since the 1930s* (New Haven: Yale University Press, 1995), 33–34.

85. This description of offshore balancing builds on Benjamin Schwarz and Christopher Layne, "A New Grand Strategy," *Atlantic Monthly* (January 2002), 36–42.

86. Hoffman, *Inside Terrorism* (New York: Columbia University Press, 1998), 14–15. See also James D. Kiras, "Terrorism and Irregular Warfare," in *Strategy in the Contemporary World: An*

Introduction to Strategic Studies, ed. John Bayliss, James Wirtz, Eliot Cohen, and Colin S. Gray (New York: Oxford University Press, 2002), 228–29.

87. As the former head of the CIA team responsible for analyzing bin Laden and al Qaeda has put it:

> In the context of ideas bin Laden shares with his brethren, the military actions of al Qaeda and its allies are acts of war, not terrorism. . . . meant to advance bin Laden's clear, focused, limited, and widely popular foreign policy goals: the end of U.S. aid to Israel and the ultimate elimination of that state; the removal of U.S. and Western forces from the Arabian Peninsula; the removal of U.S. and Western military forces from Iraq, Afghanistan, and other Muslim lands; the end of U.S. support for oppression of Muslims by Russia, China, and India; the end of U.S. protection for repressive, apostate Muslim regimes in Saudi Arabia, Kuwait, Egypt, Jordan, et cetera; and the conservation of the Muslim world's energy resources and their sale at higher prices.

Anonymous [Michael Scheuer], *Imperial Hubris: Why the West Is Losing the War on Terror* (Washington, D.C.: Brassey's, 2004), xviii.

88. Karl von Clausewitz, *On War,* ed. and trans. Michael Howard and Peter Paret (Princeton: Princeton University Press, 1976), 92.

89. Richard K. Betts, "The New Threat of Mass Destruction," *Foreign Affairs* 77, no. 1 (January–February 1998): 41. Betts was referring to the first attack on the World Trade Center in 1993.

90. The term "blowback" is borrowed from Chalmers Johnson, *Blowback: The Costs and Consequences of the American Empire* (New York: Metropolitan Books, 2000).

91. Anonymous, *Imperial Hubris,* 8.

Conclusion

1. Important statements of the exit strategy thesis are Marc Trachtenberg, *A Constructed Peace: The Making of the European Settlement, 1945–1963* (Princeton: Princeton University Press, 1998); Michael Cresswell, " 'With a Little Help from Our Friends': How France Secured an Anglo-American Continental Commitment, 1945–54," *Cold War History* 3, no. 1 (October 2002): 1–28; Cresswell, "Between the Bear and the Phoenix: The United States and the European Defense Community, 1950–54," *Security Studies* 11, no. 4 (Summer 2002): 89–124; Mark S. Sheetz, "Exit Strategies: American Grand Designs for Postwar European Security," *Security Studies* 8, no. 4 (Summer 1999): 1–43.

2. Trachtenberg, *Constructed Peace,* 62–63.

3. Michael J. Hogan, *The Marshall Plan: America, Britain, and the Reconstruction of Western Europe, 1947–1952* (Cambridge: Cambridge University Press, 1987), 3–12.

4. Indeed, the story Trachtenberg tells illustrates this point nicely. The "constructed peace" that took root in Europe in the 1960s reflected Washington's determination to "keep the Germans down" and prevent the reemergence of a powerful Germany as an independent actor in the international system. Keeping Germany down was so important to the United States that Washington collaborated tacitly with the Soviet Union to achieve this result. Moreover, whatever Eisenhower's views on a revival of German power—including German acquisition of nuclear weapons—other senior members of his administration, including Dulles, wanted to make sure that Germany did not once again run amok in Europe.

5. Geir Lundestad, *"Empire" by Integration: The United States and European Integration, 1945–1997* (New York: Oxford University Press, 1998), 18 (emphasis added).

6. As a Harvard professor, Henry Kissinger famously warned: "A united Europe is likely to insist on a specifically European view of world affairs—which is another way of saying that it will challenge American hegemony in Atlantic policy. This may well be a price worth paying for European unity; but American policy has suffered from an unwillingness to recognize that there is a price to be paid." Henry A. Kissinger, *The Troubled Partnership: A Re-Appraisal of the Atlantic Alliance* (New York: McGraw-Hill, 1965), 40.

7. Pascaline Winand, *Eisenhower, Kennedy, and the United States of Europe* (New York: St. Martin's, 1993), 81.

8. Ibid., 200. As Winand points out (254, 337–38), even George Ball—a leading Kennedy ad-

ministration "Europeanist"—came to recognize that a truly independent Europe would be bad for the United States, and argued that the United States should fall back on its traditional post–World War II policy of controlling "the development of Europe by using 'Atlantic' instruments." The main "Atlantic instrument" was NATO, a prime function of which was "ensuring the development of a Western Europe compatible with American interests." J. L. Harper notes that since World War II U.S. policymakers have favored (Western) European integration for economic and burden-sharing reasons. At the same time, however,

> the Americans have feared economic exclusion and greater competition but, above all, *a loss of political control* . . . if the Europeans did succeed in organizing themselves into an effective and relatively autonomous third force, there is little reason to believe that it would see eye to eye on important questions with the United States. The North Atlantic Treaty framework has therefore served to promote a degree of European cohesion and unity . . . while acting as a ceiling beyond which it cannot go. (John Lamberton Harper, *American Visions of Europe: Franklin D. Roosevelt, George F. Kennan, and Dean G. Acheson* [Cambridge: Cambridge University Press, 1994], 338–39)

9. In the early 1950s, U.S. policymakers "warmly applauded" the Western Europeans for pursuing integration through initiatives like the ECSC and the EDC.

> At the same time they worried that, in the long run, these institutions might encourage West Europeans to become a third force or to pursue policies independent of the United States. Consequently U.S. officials focused more of their own attention on developing NATO as an institutional device to insure U.S. leadership and to preserve cohesion within an Atlantic community that periodically would be afflicted with its own centrifugal forces. (Melvyn P. Leffler, *A Preponderance of Power: National Security, the Truman Administration, and the Cold War* [Stanford: Stanford University Press, 1992], 501)

In a similar vein, the late Wolfram Hanreider noted that a "central feature" of America's postwar German policy "was the intention, only superficially a paradox, to make the West Germans free and at the same time not free: free with respect to the personal liberties and constitutional safeguards that are the essence of a democratic political order, *but not free to formulate and implement an independent foreign policy.*" Wolfram Hanreider, *Germany, America, Europe: Forty Years of German Foreign Policy* (New Haven: Yale University Press, 1989), 5 (emphasis added).

10. Reflecting his innate and admirable brand of conservatism, Eisenhower stated in 1953, "We are defending a way of life and must be respectful of it as we proceed in our problem of building up strength, not only so as not to violate its principles and precepts, but also not to destroy from within what we are trying to defend from without." U.S. Delegation at the North Atlantic Council Meeting to Department of State, April 24, 1953, *FRUS 1952–54*, 5:374. Eisenhower was deeply concerned that in defending its way of life from the Soviet Union, the United States would become a "garrison state" and lose the very political and economic freedoms it was trying to preserve. 163rd Meeting of the NSC, September 24, 1953, *FRUS 1952–54*, 2:469.

11. Memorandum of Discussion at 390th Meeting of NSC, December 11, 1958, *FRUS 1958–60*, 7:367–68; Memorandum of Conversation, December 12, 1958, *FRUS 1958–60*, 7:370–71.

12. Eisenhower believed that fighting in Europe would escalate swiftly to an all-out nuclear exchange, and therefore the United States did not need to maintain large numbers of troops there. See Memorandum of Conversation, October 24, 1959, *FRUS 1958–60*, 7:489; Memorandum of Conversation with President Eisenhower, August 16, 1960, *FRUS 1958–60*, 7:612.

13. Memorandum of Conversation, November 24, 1959, *FRUS 1958–60*, 7:520.

14. As Eisenhower said:

> We must strengthen NATO by making Western Europe more self-dependent, but throughout our lifetime, we shall have token forces over there. We will have some naval strength, some ground installations and missile bases. We will contribute to the infrastructure requirements. But we ought to say to Europe: You should be ashamed to have our troops over there. (Ibid., 521)

In 1960, Eisenhower told the National Security Council that the United States would provide NATO with "SAC [the Strategic Air Command], a navy, and nuclear capability." Memorandum of Discussion, 457th Meeting of the NSC, August 25, 1960, *FRUS 1958–60*, 7:619.

15. Indeed, Eisenhower reluctantly acknowledged that while it may have been conceived originally as a short-term expedient, the presence of large numbers of U.S. ground forces in Europe had, in fact, become a permanent feature of American grand strategy. Memorandum of Discussion at the 400th Meeting of the NSC, March 26, 1959, *FRUS 1958–60*, 7:444–45.

16. Eisenhower's views on U.S. troop withdrawals were contradictory—far more so than the exit strategy historians depict. Although "burden sharing" was a big issue for him, it is a lot less clear that he was searching for an "exit strategy." Instead, like many U.S. officials, both before and after him, threats to reduce U.S. troop presence were brandished to get the Western Europeans to do more—not because the United States truly wanted to leave Western Europe. Thus, at a 1959 meeting of the National Security Council, Eisenhower said:

> When we talk of U.S. troop redeployment, everyone misinterprets our meaning. . . . Nothing could be more fatal than to withdraw our troops from Europe or to say that we are about to withdraw them. . . . [But] it was high time that the population of Europe did its part with respect to ground forces. However, the U.S. could not initiate a definite scheme for the reduction of U.S. forces, and in the absence of agreement by Europe, say this and only this is what we are going to do. . . . We were not talking about reducing forces or withdrawing forces, but about getting the NATO governments to understand our problems. (Memorandum of Discussion at the 424th Meeting of the NSC, November 12, 1959, *FRUS 1958–60*, 7:508–9, 511)

On the Truman administration's burden-sharing frustrations with Western Europe, see U.S. Minutes of Meeting between Presidents Truman and Auriol, March 29, 1951, *FRUS 1951*, 4:367; Memorandum by Acheson, July 6, 1951, *FRUS 1951*, 3:813–19; Memorandum for the Secretary of Defense (Johnson) [from the Service Secretaries and JCS], July 13, 1950, *FRUS 1950*, 3:134. No one who has read through the U.S. primary sources can doubt for a minute that, as long as there is a NATO, U.S. policymakers will be complaining about burden-sharing inequalities.

17. Trachtenberg, *Constructed Peace*, 152–53. Near the end of his second term, Eisenhower acknowledged that his views on U.S. troop withdrawals were at odds with those of the Pentagon and State Department (including his two secretaries of state, Dulles and Herter). For example, see Memorandum of Discussion at the 467th Meeting of the NSC, November 17, 1960, *FRUS 1958–60*, 7:653–54.

18. A case can be made that Franklin D. Roosevelt was more of an offshore balancer than Eisenhower. He hoped that, with U.S. support short of belligerency, Britain and France could contain Germany in the late 1930s. After the fall of France, he seems to have hoped that a combination of economic support and *limited* military involvement by the United States would be sufficient to prevent Germany from establishing its hegemony on the Continent. See Harper, *American Visions of Europe*, chap. 2, esp. 63–73. As Harper comments (73), "It will never be known for sure when—or even if—before December 7, 1941, Roosevelt became convinced that America's formal participation in the war was necessary and inevitable."

19. On the tangible and other costs of the cold war, see Michael Hogan, *A Cross of Iron: Harry S. Truman and the Origins of the National Security State, 1945–1954* (Cambridge: Cambridge University Press, 1998); Edward Pessen, *Losing Our Souls: The American Experience in the Cold War* (Chicago: Ivan R. Dee, 1993). Other books that explore the intangible costs of the Cold War are Michael Hunt, *Ideology and U.S. Foreign Policy* (New Haven: Yale University Press, 1987), and Michael S. Sherry, *In the Shadow of War: The United States since the 1930s* (New Haven: Yale University Press, 1995).

20. Eisenhower was speaking in April 1953 to the American Society of Newspaper Editors. Quoted in Christopher Layne, "The Real Conservative Agenda," *Foreign Policy*, no. 61 (Winter 1985–1986): 81.

21. As Michael Hogan observes:

> The merits of [U.S.] postwar foreign policies and the degree to which they advanced the cause of freedom are still subjects of historical debate. But there is no doubt that new responsibilities and new perceived threats led to an unprecedented peacetime allocation of resources to the military arm of the state, and to the creation of powerful government agencies that had not existed before. Both developments amounted to major departures from American tradition, both added enormously to the size and power of the state, and both took the state in new directions. (Hogan, *Cross of Iron*, 464)

22. Ibid., 481–82.
23. Thomas Ferguson, "From Normalcy to New Deal," *International Organization* 38, no. 1 (Winter 1984): 41–94.
24. The terms "dominant elite" and "foreign policy establishment" as used here carry no ideological connotations. It is well recognized that a dominant elite and a foreign policy establishment do exist in the United States. In their fascinating—and very mainstream—portrait of Averell Harriman, Dean Acheson, Charles Bohlen, John McCloy, George Kennan, and Robert Lovett, Isaacson and Thomas explain that they selected these six because

> they represent a cross section of the postwar policy Establishment. The values they embodied were nurtured in prep schools, at college clubs, in the boardrooms of Wall Street, and at dinner parties in Washington. They shared a vision of public service as a lofty calling and an aversion to partisan politics. They had a pragmatic and businesslike preference for realpolitik over ideology. As internationalists who respected the manners and traditions of Europe, they waged a common struggle against the pervasive isolationism of their time. (Walter Isaacson and Evan Thomas, *The Wise Men: Six Friends and the World They Made* [New York: Simon and Schuster, 1986], 25)

25. In his scholarly, balanced history of the Council on Foreign Relations, Robert Schulzinger observes that for sixty years "the Council demonstrated perhaps the most consistency in its economic studies" and that it stressed the world's interdependence and the need for cooperation—and that economic interdependence served U.S. interests. Robert D. Schulzinger, *The Wise Men of Foreign Affairs: The History of the Council on Foreign Relations* (New York: Columbia University Press, 1984), 247.
26. Kenneth N. Waltz, "The Politics of Peace," *International Studies Quarterly* 11, no. 3 (September 1967): 207.
27. H. W. Brands, *What America Owes the World* (Cambridge: Cambridge University Press, 1998).
28. Michael H. Hunt, *Ideology and U.S. Foreign Policy* (New Haven: Yale University Press, 1987), 42.
29. Ibid., 44. Hogan shows that the two narratives described by Hunt competed for grand strategic supremacy in the years immediately following World War II. One camp believed in limited government at home and a limited role abroad: "These values and traditions included a strong antipathy toward entangling alliances, a large peacetime military establishment, and the centralization of authority in the national government. . . . The rise of the national security state necessarily entailed economic and political adaptations that could undermine the very traditions and institutions that had made America great." This traditional view was matched up against the new cultural discourse of the national security state, the advocates of which "borrowed from a cultural narrative that celebrated American exceptionalism and American destiny" and argued that "leadership of the free world was a sacred mission thrust upon the American people by divine Providence, and the laws of both history and nature." Hogan, *Cross of Iron*, 8, 10, 15.
30. Kenneth N. Waltz, *Theory of International Politics* (Reading, Mass.: Addison-Wesley, 1979), 201.
31. Greg Russell shows that Morgenthau "refused to consider the national interest as a static, self-evident principle of statecraft whose formulation is immune from the complex interaction of domestic and external influences on the decision-making process in foreign policy." Greg Russell, *Hans J. Morgenthau and the Ethics of American Statecraft* (Baton Rouge: Louisiana State University Press, 1990), 104.
32. Michael Joseph Smith, *Realist Thought from Weber to Kissinger* (Baton Rouge: Louisiana State University Press, 1987), 164.

33. W. David Clinton, *The Two Faces of National Interest* (Baton Rouge: Louisiana State University Press, 1994), 259.
34. Waltz, "Reply to My Critics," in Robert O. Keohane, ed., *Neorealism and Its Critics,* ed. Robert O. Keohane (New York: Columbia University Press, 1986), 341.
35. Edmund Burke, "Remarks on the Policy of the Allies with Respect to France," *The Works of Edmund Burke,* vol. 4 (Boston: Little, Brown, 1901), 457.
36. Walter LaFeber, "The Bush Doctrine," *Diplomatic History* 26, no. 4 (Fall 2002): 558.
37. Waltz, *Theory of International Politics,* 201.
38. Ibid., 206.
39. Ibid.

Index

Note: Italic page numbers refer to tables and figures.

Acheson, Dean: and cold war, 257 n15; and Germany, 69, 86, 90, 233 n126, 233–34 n128, 234 n129, 240 n72, 243 n119, 251 n57; and NATO, 92, 96, 105, 250–51 n57; and Soviet Union, 64, 230 n89; and Taiwan, 187; and Western Europe, 96, 99, 197, 245 n135, 246 nn156, 160, 247 nn7, 161, 248 n12; and World War II victory, 221 n55

Adenauer, Konrad, 97, 102–3, 250 n44

Afghanistan, 2, 113, 153, 156

Alexander, Gerard, 138, 148–149

American grand strategy: Bush II administration's continuity of, 1–3, 122; cold war domination of, 89, 99, 101, 105–6; and extraregional hegemony theory, 15, *18*, 28–36, 194–98; history of, 1, 7–10; and multipolarity, 126–27; national security, 6, 119, 256 n5; and offshore balancing theory, *18*, 23–28; paradox of, 118–19; and realism, 9, *18*, 19–22, 202–5, 209 n32, 256–57 n8; theoretical dimensions of, 6, 120–21; transcendence of cold war, 3, 8, 12, 38–39, 43, 46–47, 56, 79–81, 110, 188, 195–96, 198, 221 n50, 240 nn63–64; types of, 159; Western Europe, 3, 57

American hegemonic grand strategy: and cold war, 26, 51–52, 61–64, 68, 70, 86, 105–16, 117, 199–200, 252 n88; and credibility, 168; de Gaulle's challenge to, 94, 97–100, 104–5, 116, 147, 248 n21; and dominant elites, 200–201, 281 n24; ending of, 147–56, 158, 190; and extraregional hegemony, 3, 22, 28–36, 193; and Franco-German treaty, 101–3, 250 nn48, 52; and geopolitical backlash, 5, 217 n105; and Germany, 47, 64–65, 68–70, 87, 102, 107, 110–11, 116, 234 n137; and hegemon's dilemma, 95, 247 n4; and inter-

national economy, 172–74, 177, 178, 276 n60; interwar roots of, 39–41, 218 n2; and maintenance of hegemony, 134; and Marshall Plan, 75, 237 n23; motivation for, 8–9, 37, 194; and national security, 7, 13–15, 19, 22, 57–58, 119, 191, 193–94; and Open Door, 28–30, 35–36, 38, 41, 68, 70, 72–76, 92, 110, 133, 172, 194–98; and overextension, 152–55, 203; and peacetime regional stabilization, 27–28, 72, 170; and postwar period, 39, 41–46; pursuit of, 1–3, 25; self-defeating nature of, 6, 193; and Soviet Union, 50–51, 57, 61–64, 68–70, 195, 199, 201–2, 227–28 n64, 228 n71, 229 nn79, 84, 230 nn92–93; and unipolar international systems, 25, 28, 46–50, 194, 214 n56; and U.S. military interventions, 7, 23, 190; and Western Europe as independent pole of power, 13, 26, 55–56, 64, 93–105, 113, 115–16, 249 n30; and Western Europe's economic integration, 70–72, 75–76, 85, 86–92, 95, 198, 237 nn27–28, 237–38 n32, 238 nn33–34, 244 n127; and Western Europe's regional stability, 72, 78–79, 81–92, 93, 94–95, 100, 105, 110, 112, 113, 116, 126, 130, 239 n51, 240 nn66, 68, 254 nn117, 118; and Western Europe's subordination, 86–87, 96–97, 113–16, 255 n133

American offshore balancing grand strategy: advantages of, 6, 7, 13, 14, 158; and burden shifting, 169–72, 181–82; consequences of U.S. disengagement, 172–86; and counterhegemonic alliances, 23–24, 26–27, 116, 182, 266 n23; and defensive realist theory, 15; and de Gaulle's challenge, 94, 101, 116; and Eisenhower, 197, 201; and energy strategy, 189; and Germany, 69; hegemony versus, 160–72, 192; implementation of, 186–90; and international economy,